THE WRITINGS OF
WILL ROGERS
III-3

SPONSORED BY

The Will Rogers Memorial Commission
and Oklahoma State University

THE WRITINGS OF WILL ROGERS

SERIES I: *Books of Will Rogers*
    1 *Ether and Me, or "Just Relax"*
    2 *There's Not a Bathing Suit in Russia & Other Bare Facts*
    3 *The Illiterate Digest*
    4 *The Cowboy Philosopher on The Peace Conference*
    5 *The Cowboy Philosopher on Prohibition*
    6 *Letters of a Self-Made Diplomat to His President*

SERIES II: *Convention Articles of Will Rogers*
    (in one volume)

SERIES III: *Daily Telegrams of Will Rogers*
    1 *Coolidge Years 1926-1929*
    2 *Hoover Years 1929-1931*
    3 **Hoover Years 1931-1933**
    4 *Roosevelt Years 1933-1935*

SERIES IV: *Weekly Articles of Will Rogers*
    (in four volumes)

SERIES V: *The Worst Story I've Heard Today*
    (in one volume)

OTHER VOLUMES TO BE ANNOUNCED

WILL ROGERS MEMORIAL COMMISSION

James C. Leake, *Chairman* Harry Hoagland
Roy G. Cartwright David R. Milsten
Edward L. Byrd Will Rogers, Jr.
Irving Fisher
  Governor George Nigh, *ex-officio*

MEMORIAL STAFF

Reba Neighbors Collins, Delmar Collins,
  Curator Manager

SPECIAL CREDIT

The late Paula McSpadden Love
Curator, 1938-73

OSU ADVISORY COMMITTEE

George A. Gries, *Chairman* Edward P. Pharr
W. David Baird Roscoe Rouse
Howard R. Jarrell William A. Sibley
  President Lawrence L. Boger, *ex-officio*

EDITORIAL CONSULTANTS

Ray B. Browne, *Bowling Green State University*
LeRoy H. Fischer, *Oklahoma State University*
Wilbur R. Jacobs, *University of California,
  Santa Barbara*
Howard L. Lamar, *Yale University*
Russel B. Nye, *Michigan State University*

Will Rogers'
DAILY TELEGRAMS

JAMES M. SMALLWOOD, *EDITOR*

Steven K. Gragert, *Assistant Editor*

Volume 3
THE HOOVER YEARS: 1931-1933

OKLAHOMA STATE UNIVERSITY PRESS
Stillwater, Oklahoma
1979

© 1979 Oklahoma State University Press

Printed in the United States of America
Library of Congress Catalog Card Number 78-78290
International Standard Book Number 0-914956-12-4

CONTENTS

INTRODUCTION — xii

Daily Telegrams 1931 — 1

Daily Telegrams 1932 — 115

Daily Telegrams 1933 — 249

NOTES — 275

INDEX — 369

Illustrations courtesy
Will Rogers Memorial
Claremore, Oklahoma

INTRODUCTION

In this volume, the third in Series III of *The Writings of Will Rogers,* the Daily Telegrams of the famed humorist, cowboy-philosopher are continued. The first volume of Rogers' widely syndicated daily newspaper column, which appeared from 1926 until his death in 1935, spanned the latter years of the presidency of Calvin Coolidge. The second volume covered the first two years of the administration of Herbert C. Hoover. Herein are found the telegrams published during the last two years (March 5, 1931, through March 3, 1933) of the presidency of Hoover. A subsequent release will present the columns written during the administration of Franklin D. Roosevelt (Volume IV).

The origins of Rogers' columns and a discussion of his methods of preparing them are found in the introduction to the series in Volume I. Similarly, therein the editors described their general guidelines, objectives, and procedures for endnote annotations. There were few editorial innovations in the second volume and few in this, the third release. The editors once again have reproduced Rogers' telegrams as they appeared in original, syndicated form.

Rogers' telegrams were accepted by most newspaper editors with little revision of the original drafts. Yet, a selected textual analysis reveals that slight variations appeared. When some editors saw certain phrases of which they disapproved, they deleted them; others edited references to political personalities; still others "blue-penciled" lines simply for brevity. Because Rogers' work was in some cases slightly altered, our editorial task in Volume III remains difficult—few original copies of the telegrams survive. Consequently, in this release we have continued to follow the guidelines established in Volume I. We have chosen the best available source for presentation. In most cases we have followed the *New York Times,* the newspaper which ran most of the articles and which is the most convenient for the use of future researchers. Other newspapers were consulted, however. When textual differences appeared, we attempted to show at least one major variation, selected from among the *Los Angeles Times,* the *Boston Daily Globe,* and the *Kansas City Times,* other newspapers which carried most of the telegrams.

Much of Rogers' humor was of a topical nature, geared to the happenings of his day. He sometimes referred to events which are not common knowledge to the present generation. He also referred to individuals who need identification. Consequently, endnotes have been used to identify people or explain events which would no longer be widely known. The editors, together with the editorial board and advisory committee of the Will Rogers Project, have decided to delete footnote numbers in the text to avoid needless distractions to the reader. Endnotes to the volume are "keyed" to the number of the telegrams and to the dates of their appearance.

The publication of The Writings of Will Rogers continues to require considerable effort on the part of many people. As always, since the inception of the Will Rogers Research Project, Will Rogers, Jr., and Reba Neighbors Collins, Curator of the Will Rogers Memorial, read the manuscript carefully and offered valuable advice for the endnotes. Glenn D. Shirley's editorial advice and designs for the books are greatly appreciated. Oklahoma State University President Lawrence L. Boger and Dean George Gries have provided encouragement. Special appreciation also is expressed for the continued support of the Will Rogers Memorial Commission, the Regents, administration, and advisory committee of Oklahoma State University, the Oklahoma Historical Society, the Oklahoma State Regents for Higher Education, and the Oklahoma Legislature. Earlier in this project the Kerr-McGee Foundation, the Phillips Petroleum Corporation, Mr. and Mrs. Robert W. Love, Mrs. T. S. Loffland, and Mr. Sylvan N. Goldman provided assistance. A special note of thanks go to four graduate students in history at Oklahoma State University who devoted the summer of 1978 researching for the project and who thus made the editors' task easier: Mike Everman, John Barnhill, Ed Derrick, and Bill Corbett. The editors also wish to acknowledge the assistance provided by Cathy Kunkel and Patty Nelson, secretaries for the Will Rogers Project who typed the manuscript.

James M. Smallwood
Steven K. Gragert

DAILY TELEGRAMS
1931-1933

DAILY TELEGRAMS — 1931

1440   Mr. Rogers Says California
             Will Surely Miss Einstein

    BEVERLY HILLS, Cal., March 5.—We finally found how to keep from calling an extra session of Congress—appropriate all the money at the last one.

    That little fellow Einstein sailed away for Germany today, and we sure do miss him in California. The radios, the banquet tables and the weeklies will never seem the same.

    He came here for rest and seclusion. He ate with everybody, talked with everybody that had any film left, attended every luncheon, every dinner, every movie opening, every marriage and two-thirds of the divorces.

    In fact, he made himself such a good fellow that nobody had the nerve to ask him what his theory was.

                              Yours,
                              Will Rogers.

1441   Mr. Rogers Sees Liquor Issue
             As Our Best Political Cleaver

    BEVERLY HILLS, Cal., March 6.—The Republican papers are having a field day laughing at the Democrats on account of their split over prohibition. Well, they better get all the laughs in they can, for wait till they meet and see their split, for they got more to split. Both sides are going to do exactly the same thing, they are going to straddle the thing, if they have to split their carcass clear up to their neck to do it.

    Neither side has got the nerve to come out in the open, for they are not sure which side the most votes are on. The minute they find out, they will both be on that so quick that it won't be an issue.

                              Yours,
                              Will Rogers.

1442   MR. ROGERS REVEALS HIS AGE,
       BUT MAY BE POOR AT FIGURES

SANTA BARBARA, Cal., March 8.—I am like my good friend Arthur Brisbane. The town that you are writing from that day is the one that you should come and settle in.

Now, this is Santa Barbara, on the bank of the same ocean he has so glowingly depicted to you at various times, and I am here this afternoon for a charity relief polo game between youth and old youth.

The combined age of the four boys we are playing is ninety years, while our team is exactly two hundred. Mr. Max Fleischmann, the fine sportsman and big-game hunter; Mr. Jim Wigmore of Cleveland, and Snowy Baker, Australia's greatest all-time all-round athlete, each are exactly 54, and myself with 38 makes two hundred.

                                       Yours,
                                       Will Rogers.

1443   MR. ROGERS REPORTS THE ARRIVAL
        OF 'POISON JAKE' ON THE COAST

BEVERLY HILLS, Cal., March 9.—There is not much humor in this, but there is a whole lot of warning.

This "Jamaica ginger jag" has hit our coast. Here is what you get in a two-ounce bottle for 50 cents:

First, the fingers and toes become numb; then the legs and knees become permanently paralyzed. It seldom reaches above the knees.

Among yesterday's cases was a barber with a wife and two children, hands totally paralyzed; a laborer with wife and three children, will never walk again; at Old Soldier's Home thirty-two deaths.

And all a druggist has to plead is that he didn't know it was poisoned.

This is not to be construed as a prohibition lecture. It's really an ad for just old "corn." It only paralyzes you temporarily.

                                       Yours,
                                       Will Rogers.

1444   WILL ROGERS TAKES NOTICE
             OF DIVORCE MILL COMPETITION

    BEVERLY HILLS, Cal., March 10.—The biggest thing in legislation nowadays is the different States' race for the divorce business.

    Arkansaw guarantees a divorce in three months including room and board. Nevada heard about it and called a special session of their Legislature and says:

    "We will give you one in six weeks, and if any other State goes under that time, we will give you a divorce, marriage, and another divorce all for the same time, and price. In other words, that's our business. We have built it up to what it is today. If there had been no Reno, you would still have been living with the same old gal. So, remember, we are the State that will divorce you, even if we have to do it by telegraph."

                        Yours,
                        Will Rogers.

1445   MR. ROGERS CREDITS SENATOR
             WITH BIGGEST LAUGH OF WEEK

    BEVERLY HILLS, Cal., March 11. — The biggest laugh of the week was caused, naturally, by a Senator (and they wasn't even in session, not even trying to be funny).

    It was by Jim Watson of Indiana, the Republican leader. The "progressives" are holding a meeting in Washington and he asked them to please define exactly how they stood on the following problems.

    Asking the Progressives to answer something that a Republican wouldn't answer if he was on his death-bed!

                        Yours,
                        Will Rogers.

1446   MR. ROGERS TAKES UP COSMETICS,
             BACON AND BEANS AND BALDNFSS

    BEVERLY HILLS, Cal., March 12.—As there was more money spent on cold cream and cosmetics last year than on bacon and beans, why naturally there must be more people interested in beautifying themselves.

The international beauty congress met in New York yesterday and they figured out that this rubbing something on your head to prevent baldness is really what causes it. They claim that you got to take stuff internally for it.

So from now on if you see a bald-headed bird reach for his flask, don't ask him for a swig. It's only irrigation juice for his roof.

Yours,
Will Rogers.

1447 Mr. Rogers Advises Old Parties
To Look Out For Progressives

BEVERLY HILLS, Cal., March 13.—Good many papers are poking fun at these "Progressives" who are meeting in Washington. Well those are the fellows that are going to run next year's government. Neither Republicans or Democrats can even get excused to get a drink without the "Progressives" (the balance of power) sanctioning it.

Be a good joke on both parties if these fellows had been right all these years and get a chance to prove it.

You watch this young La Follette. You're going to have a lot of dealings with him in years to come.

One thing, these "Progressives" won't have to be very good to be the best.

Yours,
Will Rogers.

1448 Mr. Rogers Seems To Believe
This Is The Little Man's Day

BEVERLY HILLS, Cal., March 15.—When you read about thousands of people clamoring to see their hero, you don't know if it's Mahatma Gandhi or Charley Chaplin.

The day of the big man (physically) has passed. Here is these two little figures, the most popular two men in the world today, Mahatma in his breechclout and Charley in his derby. Both of 'em too smart to let the king knight 'em.

Gandhi is trying to save India and Charley will do what he can for Hollywood.

Mr Hoover has found out where there was no Senators going for their vacation and he is going there, Porto Rico.

Yours,
Will Rogers.

1449   Mr. Rogers Reports A Blue Day
In His Usually Sunny Life

BEVERLY HILLS, Cal., March 16.—This is income tax day, and I am in no shape to be funny.

Why don't they do it all like they do the gasoline tax? You pay it when you buy it and you are through with it. Or, make the man that pays it to us take it out, or something.

The way it is they let us handle it one year, then two and a half months after it's all made and spent then they ask you to pay it.

But no one that made enough to pay a tax this year should kick. In fact it's increased taxes on incomes of over one hundred thousand net where the money should come from to supply work during slack time.

Yours,
Will Rogers.

1450   Mr. 'Shamus' Rogers Makes
A Few Remarks On Ireland

BEVERLY HILLS, Cal., March 17.—Well, today is the seventeenth of Ireland. Of all the nationalities that have helped to root the Indians out over here, the Irish are the only ones that have made enough impression on everybody till they celebrate their birthday.

And say, did you know that during all this depression over the world, and all countries having revolutions and changing leaders, why, old Ireland has come through the best of all of 'em?

When you are laying out your European trip this Spring, don't overlook the old Emerald Isle. It's got 'em all beat for beauty, romance, humor and hospitality, and the best horses in the world.

Yours,
Will Rogers.

1451   Will Rogers Is Interested
In The Statistics On Co-Eds

BEVERLY HILLS, Cal., March 18.—Right in the midst of all this depression and starvation, why one old boy hasn't had it so bad. He has been measuring 6,000 college girls. He compared 'em with co-eds fifty years ago.

I didn't know any one ever thought of measuring one fifty years ago, and from what our elderly women led us to believe, we didn't think they would have allowed it.

Well, this fellow finds that the present ones are higher, wider and thicker (he don't say if it's head or body), and these, he says, have more lung capacity.

Well, we knew that. Maybe because of the strenuous life at a female college, the parents only pick out the big dumb ones.

Yours,
Will Rogers.

1452   Mr. Rogers Thinks It Wise
To Keep In Good With Borah

BEVERLY HILLS, Cal., March 19.—Just before Mr. Hoover left for Porto Rico he had a long private conference with Senator Borah, and Borah told him to go ahead and enjoy himself.

You can't afford to be on the outs with Borah, that is, if you want to get anything done in this country.

There is an awful lot of people that would like to see Bill Borah President, and I would too.

Course, I don't believe he would take it, for he would have to make too great a personal sacrifice of prestige and and authority. It would be sorter like Mussolini being only the King.

Yours,
Will Rogers.

1453   Will Rogers Would Tax
Crime Out Of Existence

BEVERLY HILLS, Cal., March 20.—Every State in the Union gambles as much as Nevada does, but they were smart enough to pass a law and get some tax money out of it. If Wall Street paid a tax on every "game" they run, we would get enough revenue to run the government on.

Another thing, we don't seem to be able to even check crime, so why not legalize it and put a heavy tax on it. Make the tax for robbery so high that a bandit couldn't afford to rob any one unless he knew they had a lot of dough. We have taxed other industries out of business; it might work here.

Yours,
Will Rogers.

1454   MR. ROGERS HAS AN OPPONENT
         FOR THE DREISER-LEWIS WINNER

HOLLYWOOD, Cal., March 22.—Ought to match the winner of the Theodore Dreiser-Sinclair Lewis bout against Bernard Shaw. These writers fight mostly with sarcasm, and I think Shaw could lick both of 'em.

Mr. Hoover approaches Porto Rico with confidence. He knows there can't possibly be as much wrong with it as there is with us.

Thousands of people went from all over Southern California today to see the big race in Mexico, the Agua Caliente Handcap, but there was an awful lot that didn't go on account of the crowds. They knew they wouldn't have a chance to get to the bar.

Yours,
Will Rogers.

1455   ROGERS SEES PLANE UNSUITED
         FOR ANY BACK-SEAT DRIVING

BEVERLY HILLS, Cal., March 23.—Two fatal plane crashes here yesterday, with a man and woman in each plane, and both accidents avoidable. But members of each couple thought they were pilots, and got in the air and tried to prove it to each other. One couple, a man and wife, were arguing who was the pilot when they took off.

That's one way the auto is ahead of the plane, a woman can sit in the back seat and do all the "crabbing and gabbing" she wants to, but she can't reach the wheel.

If you are going to do any arguing with your wife or lady friends, you better get it over before you get in the air. Two people just can't land a plane.

Yours,
Will Rogers.

1456   WILL ROGERS PAYS TRIBUTE
TO DOG KILLED BY RATTLER

BEVERLY HILLS, Cal., March 24.—I have often thought my friend O. O. McIntyre gave more space in his column to his little dog than I do to the U.S. Senate. But it just shows Odd knows human nature better than I do. He knows that everybody at heart loves a dog, while I have to try and make converts to the Senate.

In London five years ago old Lord Dewar, a great humorist and character and the biggest whisky maker in the world, gave the children a little white dog (Sealingham), saying "If this dog knew how well he was bred he wouldn't speak to any of us."

We have petted him, complained at him, called him a nuisance. But when we buried him yesterday we couldn't think of a wrong thing he had ever done.

His bravery was his undoing. He lost to a rattlesnake, but his face was towards him.

Yours,
Will Rogers.

1457   MR. ROGERS ANALYZES BRIEFLY
PORTO RICAN OVERPRODUCTION

BEVERLY HILLS, Cal., March 25. — Been reading President Hoover's speech yesterday to the Porto Ricans. The keynote of the speech was "the rapid increase in population of the islanders."

He was in a tough spot. He didn't know whether to compliment 'em on being a virile race or condemn 'em for making the usual American mistake of overproduction. You see, there is not enough jobs there to take care of this increase, so what he tactfully wanted to impart to them was to control themselves till industry was on a par with affection.

He finally left the whole thing to young Teddy and departed for the Virgin Islands, where he hoped conditions would be better regulated.

Yours,
Will Rogers.

1458   ROGERS SEES GANGSTER BURIAL
        NOW MATTER OF CIVIC PRIDE

BEVERLY HILLS, Cal., March 26. — Well, Chicago is having the last laugh. The rest of the country rose up in wrath with pictures and editorials of Chicago killings, and its elaborate gangsters' funerals. Now if your town hasn't buried a gangster with a rose festival it's rather plebeian.

Los Angeles, backed by the Chamber of Commerce and the florists, are out for that trade now. They put on a trial funeral last week that looked like a movie opening night. The flowers were only limited by the amount they could ship in. Our slogan is "Before you shoot each other don't overlook Los Angeles."

Racketeering is America's biggest industry, and their funerals is "big business."

Yours,
Will Rogers.

1459   ROGERS TAKES UP HEROES,
        TAMMANY AND BUSINESS

BEVERLY HILLS, Cal., March 27. — This hero business is pretty ticklish, they are throwing rocks at Gandhi in India already. Chaplin is the sole survivor.

See where the Republicans threatened to make an issue out of the carrying-on of Tammany Hall. Tammany says, "Ye-ah, well you just start, and when we open up on you!" Prominent men or organizations can't get back at some enemy like they would like to, for their own nose is not clean.

They claim business is getting better, because there is fewer apples being sold on the street. Lord, that only means it's getting worse.

Yours,
Will Rogers.

1460   ROGERS WOULD GIVE OUR ISLES
        GRATIS TO OUR WORST ENEMIES

BEVERLY HILLS, Cal., March 29. — Mr. Hoover just got back from Porto Rico after a call with our little dark-brown cousins. He told 'em he would see that they had the same opportunities we enjoy here, so I guess he is having Charley Otis & Co., stock brokers, put in a branch down there. That will give them a leisure class, and the rest of 'em employment working for 'em.

The President didn't think much of the Virgin Islands; he thought we were bunked on that deal. I think myself we was perhaps influenced by the title.

We are mighty good colonizers. We ought to sell (or give away to some enemy) our island holdings, and concentrate entirely on the old headquarters ranch here at home.

Yours,
Will Rogers.

1461   ROGERS URGES A BETTER DEAL FOR OUR INDIAN CHARGES

BEVERLY HILLS, Cal., March 30. — See by the paper this morning where the Department of Indian Affairs have promised that they will have their Indian agents do better this year, I mean do better for the Indians, for a change.

If you want to read an interesting document (and it may have had something to do with this shakeup), read a new book just out called "Massacre." It gives you the dope. Lots of people think 'cause the Osages have oil that all Indians are rich. Why the Pine Ridge Agency Siouxs have eat so much horse meat, that they are wearing bridles instead of hats.

Yours,
Will Rogers.

1462   ROGERS SAYS ROCKNE'S DEATH HAS SHOCKED WHOLE NATION

HOLLYWOOD, Cal., March 31. — We are becoming so hardened and used to about any misfortune and bad luck that comes along that it takes a mighty big calamity to shock all this country at once. But Knute, you did it. Just as you have come from behind all your life and fooled 'em where they thought you didn't have a chance, you did it again.

We thought it would take a President or a great public man's death to make a whole nation, regardless of age, race or creed, shake their heads in real sincere sorrow and say, "Ain't it a shame he is gone." Well, that's what this country did today, Knute, for you. Why, you old bald-headed rascal, you died one of our national heroes. Notre Dame was your address, but every gridiron in American was your home.

Yours,
Will Rogers.

1463   Mr. Rogers Discovers That War
         Was Not Total Loss, After All

BEVERLY HILLS, Cal., April 1. — It's very seldom you find any good that come out of the war, but was talking to one of California's sanest and most conservative business men, Mr. Robert C. Gillis. He remarked, "The only investment that has proven sound during all this mess is the Liberty bond."

So the old three-minute speaker was telling the truth and didn't know it.

But the tough part about it is, everybody lost theirs by having to put 'em up as margins on things that was supposed to be sound. During the Coolidge cuckoo days they were considered the lowest form of investment.

When you look back on things now you wonder why everyone in America escaped the insane asylum during that time.

Yours,
Will Rogers.

1464   Will Rogers Wants To Know
         Why Parachutes Are Not Used

BEVERLY HILLS, Cal., April 2. — I don't think I could be accused of saying anything detrimental to commercial aviation. For I think it is the safest, and only way to travel, but every mode of transportation should use every possible invention that might add the least bit to safety.

Now a parachute wasn't invented just for some nut to go up and jump out for fun. Your Lindbergh, your Hawkes, Doolittle, Williams, Ingalls, all wear 'em. That's why most of 'em are still here.

Now I have never understood why commercial planes didn't use them. The wing came off Rockne's plane mighty high up to light as far away from the plane as it did. I always had a doubt if I would have the nerve to jump, but there would have been none about Rockne. He would have stepped out of there, pulled that ring, and told a funny joke on the way down.

It at least gives you a chance that you haven't got otherwise. The army and navy demand it, and they can't be wrong all the time. At least have 'em there, and leave it optional with the passenger.

Yours,
Will Rogers.

1465   WILL ROGERS SEES SOME JOBS
HE THINKS SHOULD BE UNFILLED

BEVERLY HILLS, Cal., April 3. — Just when the country was doing all it could to economize in government why along comes a law and says, "Every time your State gets so many thousand new population, they must all throw in and hire another Representative in their State for Congress."

Well, California foolishly grew, and now they got to pay for it. A dozen unemployed must be sent to Congress by the taxpayers. Well, California is split wide in two, the north of the State claim these new ones shall come from the south, and the south claim they should come from the north, and the taxpayers are so sore about having to hire extra ones that they don't care where they come from, but are telling 'em where to go.

Yours,
Will Rogers.

1466   WILL ROGERS PREFERS PLANE
TO A TAXICAB IN OLD MEXICO

EL PASO, Tex., April 5. — Had a great trip in here today over the American Airways passenger line. Kelsey, the pilot, has flown 400,000 miles without a sign of a mishap.

Glad to hear in Los Angeles this morning from the different air lines that the late accident had not interfered with travel.

Why, my hair turned from gray to white just fifteen minutes ago, in a taxi going over to Juarez, Old Mexico, when a Mexican missed us by inches. Would have given my life to have been in a plane.

Was going to the bull fight. Got my tickets, then saw an old pony that they was going to use in the fight, and I couldn't make it.

Yours,
Will Rogers.

1467   MR. ROGERS HOPS TO MEXICO CITY
       AND FINDS ALL IS WELL THERE

MEXICO CITY, April 6. — Viva la Mexico City!

This is a great old city and no excuse for anyone not coming. It don't take long. Left El Paso this morning and made the 1,200 miles in nine hours on the regular passenger line. The fare is $75; American pilots and fast Lockheed ships.

Country is peaceful, working and happy. That last revolution kinder discouraged their gangsters. This fellow Clark that took Morrow's place is doing a fine job here.

Seems good to not hear a prohibition argument or a speech on "business is slightly on the upgrade."

Yours,
Will Rogers.

1468   MR. ROGERS SENDS A FEW NOTES
       FROM THE AIR AS HE FLIES SOUTH

ABOARD AIRPLANE OVER GUATEMALA, via Brownsville, Tex., April 7. — Brisbane ought to be here now and write about progress in a regular passenger plane on regular daily run. Big three-motored Fords with American pilots today over tropical Mexico.

Just stopped at Guatemala City. Beautiful old city. We are now flying over its big coffee plantations.

I hand this to the radio operator on board. He radios to the nearest telegraph office. They send it to New York and they, in turn, wire it out to your paper, and the whole thing will be done before we land in the little country of San Salvador, where we spend the night.

Left Los Angeles Sunday morning. This is Tuesday evening. Would have only been to Chicago by train.

These farmers seem to be looking for their own relief. They farm clear up to the top of these mountains.

Yours,
Will Rogers.

1469 WILL ROGERS FINDS GREAT NEED FOR OUR HELP IN CARING FOR QUAKE-STRICKEN NICARAGUANS

MANAGUA, Nicaragua, April 8. — Well, here we are at Managua, Nicaragua. They tell you pictures don't lie, but the ones you saw of this earthquake did, for they didn't tell that eight days after it happened there is from one to three hundred bodies still under those ruins.

Sitting here in a marine tent writing this and am going to sleep here. The doctor is coming around to shoot me for typhoid and then I am going to learn to cuss and will be a real Marine.

Naturally what they need is money. The government or the people haven't got a cent. The Red Cross combined with the relief organization here has done great work as usual and still is. They are feeding about 8000. We have a great Minister of American affairs here, Mr. Hanna, no rich guy just appointed for the lark, but a man who has given 25 years' service to us. Lost everything they had but the clothes on their backs.

He and the President and the Red Cross say if through the Red Cross and public donations from up home they could get $250,000, it would relieve the situation as to food and get some roofs to cover these people. Now what they are afraid of is the rainy season, which starts in just a few weeks. Lord help you if you have no cover when it starts.

Goodness knows, you generous folks have been asked till you are ragged, but honest, if you saw it, you would dig again. I have finally found somebody poorer than a southern cotton renter farmer. Our government can't make the loan for food, at least it wouldn't for our own, so it just falls where everything else does—on the generosity and goodness of the American people. If you saw, as I did this morning, 2,500 mothers with babies in their arms go by and get their ration of milk you would say there was some poor devil that needed it worse than you do.

Will Rogers visits Managua, Nicaragua, shortly after the earthquake of March 31, 1931.

We promised to get the Marines out of here by June 1, and if we could get this sum and get things straightened out we can keep our promise, but we can't leave 'em in this shape now. Whether you believe the marines should be here or not, they have been a godsend during the last week. They have done some heroic work, but personally I don't think it's worth leaving 'em down here just for the sake of another earthquake.

We may dig a canal here some day, but we don't have to guard the place we are going to dig it. Nobody is going to sneak in and dig it while we are away.

Send your donations to Managua, Nicaragua, to American Red Cross in care of American Minister Hanna. It's worth all that just to get our boys back home. Two were saved today by a parachute jump patrolling a terrible country.

Let's help put 'em on their feet, call it a day, and all go home and tend to our own business.

Yours,
Will Rogers.

1470 WILL ROGERS OBSERVES THE LIGHTER SIDE OF CONDITIONS IN STRICKEN CITY OF MANAGUA

MANAGUA, Nicaragua, April 9. — The President says to Minister Hanna: "I wonder what Rogers can find humorous in our pitiful plight?" Well, you know these little small shakes occur quite frequently. This morning just as reveille bugle was blowing one come, and everybody jumped out of bed, so now they are going to use a quake instead of reveille every morning.

Here is some divine spark of relief for the anti-prohibitionists: Everything in town was destroyed but the brewery—churches, schools, banks, stores. But it was an act of Providence at that, for the water works were destroyed and all they had to drink was beer. The commandant sent twenty marines to protect it and with the 100 that was already there why they were able to hold it.

Even a quake has its good points. The Senate and Cabinet run out of town and haven't shown up since. What Hoover would give for the recipe!

Flew today with Major Mitchell, head of the air forces of the marines. Went all over the bandit country they patrol. You have to see this terrible mountainous country to see what these aviators have been up against. I could tell you for a week some of the things these aviators have done in this country.

Now they need money here and they need help. The poor people just walk about dazed. But in addition to money to help feed 'em and restore some sort of roof over their heads what I think is needed worse down here is Chick Sales.

Yours,
Will Rogers.

1471   WILL ROGERS SAYS LONGWORTH
       WAS BOTH ABLE AND POPULAR

SAN JOSE, Costa Rica, April 10. — Flew in here by Pan-American today. We was wakened exactly at the same time this morning by another little shake in Managua, now I am a prophet among the marines as I said they would use them for reveille.

Tomorrow this beautiful little country celebrates a national victory over the United States. Now I know how an Englishman feels in our country on the Fourth of July.

Our calamities come in bunches. Now Nick is dead, Washington won't seem the same to me. I used to go straight for his office and make it my headquarters at the Capitol all day. We would get Jack Garner (who loved Nick) and then I would between the two get the real "low down" on what the government wasn't doing.

I have been told many times by many Democrats that he was the most able and most popular man in Congress. Why is it a bum politician never dies?

Yours,
Will Rogers.

1472   WILL ROGERS ARRIVES IN PANAMA
       TO SEE IF BROOKHART WAS RIGHT

PANAMA, April 12. — Senator Brookhart has just been down at Panama and he was shocked and said the people down here were "just wallowing in sin," and he was going to introduce a bill in Congress to remove the canal to go between Cedar Rapids and Des Moines. So the people here asked me to come down to offset Brookhart and I kinder wanted to see (and perhaps join the wallowing).

I will say this for the folks down here. They are not wallowing in the canal. I flew in here yesterday from Costa Rica and I haven't seen the canal yet and can't find anybody that knows where it is.

There is one great thing about the tropics—it gives you a great alibi.

Yours,
Will Rogers.

1473   ROGERS THINKS CANAL A TUNNEL,
         AS HE IS UNABLE TO LOCATE IT

PANAMA, April 13. — I still can't locate that canal. I am beginning to believe it's a tunnel. The Pennsylvania, a big boat, is here today, going from Beverly Hills to New York. I have met 500 people around town today and asked them if they had seen the canal, and they all had the same answer, "No, but have one with us."

Tomorrow, Tuesday, is Pan-American day. We are celebrating it by rushing two cruisers to Nicaragua. The best thing to do with these countries is to get out, let 'em alone and then sell things cheaper and better than any other nation. Then we don't have to worry about relations and goodwill.

Yours,
Will Rogers.

1474   RUNNING KINGDOM OR REPUBLIC
         IS NO CINCH, SAYS WILL ROGERS

PANAMA CITY, April 14. — Spanish paper on the street just now says the King of Spain is out. He has had a stormy career and his troubles are all over now. I bet Mr. Hoover says "The lucky guy." Well, if they think running a republic is a cinch, all they got to do is to look around a little. I have been in eight republics in the last ten days, including our own, and every one of 'em ought to be under Mussolini.

The paper says the Republicans took over Spain; now watch some poor Spanish farmer try and get relief.

Yours,
Will Rogers.

18

1475   MR. ROGERS RECALLS ALFONSO
        AS BEING REAL 'REGULAR GUY'

PANAMA CITY, April 15. — King of Spain, the poor fellow, I feel kinder sorry for him. I met him while in Spain and he seemed just about the most "regular guy" you would want to talk to, and everybody has had to admire his personal nerve.

You know us up home. We just can't understand this Latin politics. The only time they even get to cheer is when one side overthrows the other, then they got to cheer mighty fast. What they need in all these Latin countries is a party that compares with our Democrats, one who loses and don't do nothing about it but talk.

Yours,
Will Rogers.

1476   ROGERS SEES SAN BLAS COUNTRY
        AND GULPS THE TROPICAL BEER

ON BOARD PAN AMERICAN PLANE, April 16. — You have read of the San Blas Indians (not Sam Dash, but San Blas). Well all morning we flew low over their beautiful coral islands. You can leave and visit them but you must get away before night. The old chief won't let you stop after dark. Due to his foresight they are the only 100 per cent pure Indians.

Coast of Colombia is beautiful. Cartagena with its old Spanish ports. Nearing Venezuela, stop for the night at Maracaibo. That's where all the foreign oil is coming in from that put our independent companies out of business.

I was told to not drink water in these tropical countries. I had never tried their beer with ham and eggs in the morning, but I am managing to gulp it down. However, I have heard of worse hardships.

Yours,
Will Rogers.

1477   MR. ROGERS FINDS IN VENEZUELA
        LATIN-AMERICAN 'ALFALFA BILL'

ON BOARD PAN-AMERICAN AIRPLANE NC943M, April 17. — Say that Venezuela is quite a country. They have a fellow named Gomez that is the local Alfalfa Bill Murray and he really runs it.

They might call him a dictator, but they are the only ones that seem to get anything done in these times. I want to get back down there and see him some time. He is the real McCoy.

Just breezing into Trinidad, Port of Spain, an English island, to spend the night, and the language will be as foreign to me as the Spanish.

Tomorrow, Saturday night, with Colonel Theodore Roosevelt at San Juan, Porto Rico. Oh, yes, and the Virgin Islands, get them tomorrow, too.

Yours,
Will Rogers.

1478   ROGERS KNOWS HE IS BACK HOME
        WHEN HE CAN SEE NO MARINES

MIAMI BEACH, Fla., April 19. — Back home! Must be American territory; I don't see any marines. Miami, the only place to bathe in the ocean in the Winter and a great city. Flew right over the whole length of Cuba, Haiti, San Domingo and Porto Rico today. Roosevelt is doing a real human job in Porto Rico, and they like him. He is kinder like Morrow. He has brought sympathy into diplomacy. Only been gone from California two weeks today. Been in fifteen countries, 8,000 miles, all for $600 fare, and I took no "good will" to them. In fact, they are mighty wise. They are wise to us.

Yours,
Will Rogers.

1479   WILL ROGERS NOW PROPOSES
        REVOLUTION IN WASHINGTON

WASHINGTON, D. C., April 20. — Show you what habit will do. Been flying every day till we could come to a capitol of some republic, then we would stay all night.

Well, I was flying to New York from Florida today on the splendid new East Coast air line, a great route over beautiful country from Jacksonville, with stops at Savannah, Charleston, Florence, Raleigh (where Uncle Josephus Daniels met me) and Richmond. I saw many old friends all along.

Well, when I got to this town I saw a dome, so I figured it must be a capitol, so I got off just through force of habit, and sure enough it was a capitol, but you wouldn't think it from the ones I visited. This is the quietest night I have spent. Managua with earthquake has got it on this.

Maybe I can show 'em how to start a revolution tomorrow.

Yours,
Will Rogers.

1480   ROGERS REPORTS WILD NIGHT
       WITH D. A. R. IN WASHINGTON

NEW YORK, N.Y., April 21. — Just flew in from Washington. Say, aviation is getting somewhere. A plane every hour on the hour between Washington and New York.

I told you it looked like a dull night in Washington last night. Say, I run into a D. A. R. convention aand those old colonial dames gave me one of the wildest nights I have had in years. I got their minds off their ancestors and they are just as human as anybody.

Had a long chat with Borah and we fixed up a few loose ends. Mr. Hoover says Sandino will be caught soon. I would hate to run and have that as my issue.

Jimmy Walker met his opponents in the first game today. Score: Walker 10, opponents 0.

Yours,
Will Rogers.

1481   MR. ROGERS QUOTES THE BIBLE
       ANENT THE WALKER CHARGES

NEW YORK, N.Y., April 22. — The King and Queen of Siam are here. Now we will get a real test of our wise crackers' ability. See who can say something without referring to the Siamese twins. I am tickled already and withdraw.

Pat Hurley, Secretary of War, left Washington for Oklahoma in a navy plane. Was the one the army owns broke down?

Mayor Walker's opponents have wisely decided to withdraw any reference to his private life. They had to withdraw it on account of a biblical quotation, "Let him without sin cast the first stone." So they would have to import somebody into New York to make the accusation.

Yours,
Will Rogers.

1482   MR. ROGERS'S BRIEF ROUND-UP
        OF THE NEWS OF THE WORLD

NEW YORK, N.Y., April 23. — Newspaper Publishers' Association from all over are in convention here and tonight is their banquet. Mr. Schwab and I are the speakers. Charley will make 'em all feel rich by his eternal optimism and I will bring 'em back to earth and their second mortgages with facts.

See where the King of Spain has gone over to England to make arrangements to live with his wife's people. Royalty is human after all.

I sho' would like to be stowed away in that plane with my friend Hawks over yonder.

Say, that little Queen of Siam is plum pretty.

Nobody in the Astor barber shop just now. The proprietor told me the market must be off.

Yours,
Will Rogers.

1483   WILL ROGERS SEES NEW YORK
        ONE "JUMPY" SPOT IN NATION

NEW YORK, N.Y., April 24. — Big brokerage firm failed here today and that throws 'em into another scare. You know, it's a funny thing, but the rest of the country is all feeling pretty good, but there in New York they are doing more beefing than all the rest of the country put together. I don't believe New York has got the nerve to stand it like like lots of folks all over the country. They can be hurting and won't let out a squawk, but this place's nerves are more jumpy.

But it's a great old town and I never in my life saw as many new high buildings. But everything's the "market" with 'em here.

Yours,
Will Rogers.

1484   Mr. Rogers Is Taken For A Ride
And Reports He Learned A Lot

NEW YORK, N.Y., April 26. — Been down near Lakewood, N. J., to spend the day with Mr. Arthur Brisbane at his beautiful new home. Bill Donovan, the fellow we all thought was going to be Attorney General, was there. Nice fellow.

With Mr. Brisbane and his wife and some of his children took a long horseback ride through the pine forests of his 10,000-acre estate. He raises fine horses.

Never mind what he writes, he told me 1937 would be our first prosperous year (only six more years to hold out.) Says Russia is all working, and we can't compete with 'em by passing resolutions against 'em. Says Hoover will be elected by a bigger majority than before. Says fewer hours and less days per week is our only labor solution. Says Smith will be, or nominate, the next Democratic candidate. Oh, and a lot more stuff he told me, but I am going to use most of it as my own.

You don't suppose I went clear down there just for the horseback ride, do you? I got horses at home, but I can't learn anything riding 'em.

Yours,
Will Rogers.

1485   Mr. Rogers Fires A Few Shots
At Random From The Capital

WASHINGTON, D.C., April 27. — Tonight's Gridiron dinner here in Washington, where the President attends and sees the cleverest kidding and satires, was put on by the newspaper men who know these big birds backwards.

Say, do you know that I run onto those D. A. R.'s still here. They run their conventions till every member gets to speak. They have been here so long that their badges are beginning to tarnish.

Times are so hard that Fort Worth, Texas, is the only town that can afford lobbyists here. Carter and his gang are after some Federal plunder, and he knows what it is.

Had a long chat with Secretary Stimson today, and he knows things about Nicaragua that none of these critics of his do.

Yours,
Will Rogers.

1486   WILL ROGERS FINDS ATLANTA
                MISSES HER LEADING CITIZEN

ATLANTA, Ga., April 28. — Flew into Atlanta from Washington. This is a great old city, but it's shot now, with Bobby Jones in Hollywood. But they are going to open up the hotels and stores as soon as he gets back.

They have planted cotton in the golf courses and the chiselers on Stone Mountain have nothing to work on till Jones comes back to be the model (you know they have put Bobby on the horse instead of Robert E. Lee).

My two friends here, Major Cohen and Clark Howell, are just keeping their papers going just to print pictures of what he is eating and what he is wearing in Hollywood.

Crowds rushed up to me at the field and said "Have you seen him? Is he well? When is he coming home? Oh, it's terrible here without him."

                        Yours,
                        Will Rogers.

1487   MR. ROGERS FINDS THE SOUTH
                PLANTING THINGS IT CAN'T EAT

FORT WORTH Tex., April 29. — It's just getting so there is nowhere in this country you want to go between two real towns where they haven't got a good reliable air line.

This bird flying us into Fort Worth now from Atlanta, Herb Kindred, is older than Rockefeller and has had 12,000 hours and not an accident. A man couldn't walk that far without getting hurt.

I have seen more plowed ground from Washington to Texas. Too bad most of it was for cotton. They haven't sold last year's crop yet. I wish these people would raise something they could eat, when they couldn't sell it.

Flew right over that new Texas oil field that has made oil so cheap that it's cheaper to strike a dry hole.

                        Yours,
                        Will Rogers.

1488   MR. ROGERS IS BACK AT THE POINT
               WHERE HE STARTED LONG FLIGHT

EL PASO, Tex., April 30. — Back in El Paso, where I left the United States just three weeks ago.

Have traveled 13,000 miles, all by regular passenger lines (no special plane or trip). Fare less than a thousand dollars. Not a forced landing, not a plane even late. Radio on every ship. You are in touch with even Hollywood while flying over Nicaragua.

Visited sixteen foreign countries, including New York City. Saw everything I was looking for but Sandino. I do want to see him. I don't believe he is responsible for everything that happens down there.

      Yours,
       Will Rogers.

1489 With All 'Beefing,' Says Rogers, It Is Hard To Tell Real Reds

HOLLYWOOD, Cal., May 1. — All the casualties are not in yet, but it seems to have been a mighty quiet May Day. Heretofore the Reds have battled with the police, but this year everybody is "beefing" so that you can't tell Red from a taxpayer. So everybody had an even break.

Old Hollywood has reconciled itself to conditions of the depression better than anywhere. They have just charged off 50 per cent of their husbands as a total loss, voluntarily cut alimony, reorganizing with less overhead and going back to pre-war mates and conditions.

      Yours,
       Will Rogers.

1490 Mr. Rogers Warns Persons Who Happen To Stop In Reno

SANTA MONICA, Cal., May 3. — It's good news to know that there is one industry that is flourishing.

Reno yesterday just divorced everybody that had been there six weeks. They just took the hotel registers of six weeks ago that day and issued a divorce to everybody whose names were on there. Some of them were people who had no intention of getting one, but they are so rushed they haven't time to go over the lists and see who wants one and who don't. They figure it's easier to let the few that didn't want one get married again.

So be careful if you don't want one. Don't register, or even be seen in Reno, or six weeks later you will receive word you have been divorced, whether you are married or not.

Yours,
Will Rogers.

1491   MR. ROGERS SEES SOME TRUTH
       IN AN ADVERSE REPORT ON US

BEVERLY HILLS, Cal., May 4. — Well, we got a dose of our own medicine this morning in the paper.

We're always running off investigating some other country and coming back reporting the shape it's in. Well, some European woman (I think she was French) has been looking us over and reported our condition to the League of Nations.

Course what she says don't listen so good to us, but the old gal is about right at that. Our so-called prosperous times taught us bad habits and this depression has left us using cheap substitutes for expensive bad habits.

Yours,
Will Rogers.

1492   MR. ROGERS DISCUSSES A GUESS
       ON HOW TO END THE DEPRESSION

BEVERLY HILLS, Cal., May 5. — There is one thing about this depression. It has offered every man, woman and child in America 100 guesses as to how to end it.

President Hoover used up one of his guesses yesterday when he told one of those "men's sewing clubs" (Chamber of Commerce, by the way, I think this was the mother lodge). He said we would "have good times if everybody disarmed."

Why, that's the only people that are drawing salary now, is the army and navy. What does he want to do, put them among the unemployed?

Yours,
Will Rogers.

1493   WILL ROGERS SEES A REASON
                 FOR MELLON NOT BEING SO PERT

HOLLYWOOD, Cal., May 6. — Uncle Andy Mellon don't blather at these luncheon club fiestas very often and when he does things ain't looking so good and he is sent in as a pinch-hitter to bat for confidence. But even him they couldn't get to promise us much. He did say that things were worse in '73. Now if we can get much nourishment out of that, let's do it.

Course Mr. Mellon feels mighty bad over his books not balancing for the first time in years. We are just nine hundred million in the red. So you can't blame him very much for not feeling any too pert. Think of how you'd feel if you counted up at night and found you was nine hundred million short.

                                  Yours,
                                  Will Rogers.

1494   MR. ROGERS FINDS PALM SPRINGS
                 STILL A-TWITTER OVER WALKER

PALM SPRINGS, Cal., May 7. — My wife was just prowling around out here in the desert and ran into Jimmy Walker's old hide-out.

They advertise this as the place "that even cured Mayor Walker of staying out nights," and another ad reads, "If you are troubled with investigations and Republicans, come to Palm Springs for a tan that when you get home they can't tell who you are."

There is over a hundred Mayors here now. They are selling thousands of sheets that Walker had his picture taken in.

                                  Yours,
                                  Will Rogers.

1495   ROGERS SEES OUR MOTHERS
                 SAFER IN INDIA OR AFRICA

TUCSON, Ariz., May 8. — Well, here we are in Tucson, the champion humane town of America. Its climate has prolonged more people's lives than any single place. It has a fine university, and the best college polo team in the U. S. This up-to-date little city is just situated near enough to Mexico to get a touch of liberty.

I was reading a nice thing in this morning's local paper. It was of a dinner in New York of a lot of fine women: Mrs. Theodore Roosevelt Sr., Mrs. Hoover, Mrs. Lindbergh, Mrs. Sloan and Kermit Roosevelt's wife, all to arouse not only interest but horror in our unbelieveable death rate from child birth—16,000 a year, the highest in the world.

The way we lose 'em here it would be safer if you are figuring on having a baby to go to some uncivilized country like India or Africa to do it.

Yours,
Will Rogers.

1496   MR. ROGERS, ON MOTHER'S DAY,
         TAKES 'MA' FOR A 7-MILE WALK

CARLSBAD, N. M., May 10. — Celebrating "Mother's Day" by giving "Ma" Rogers a vacation. Picked her a white desert flower and walked her for seven miles through the celebrated Carlsbad Caverns.

I thought the biggest hole in the ground was when you were drilling for oil and struck a dry hole, but this is bigger than even that. It's just the Grand Canyon with a roof over it.

Then, when you get inside it's got all the cathedrals of the world in it, with half of 'em hanging upside down.

If a "drunk" suddenly woke up in that great hall in there, he would think he had died and gone to heaven, for that's the nearest thing to his imagination of the place.

Yours,
Will Rogers.

1497   MR. ROGERS FINDS IN THE WEST
         AN INCUBATOR OF POLOISTS

ROSWELL, N. M., May 11. — You have heard of great preparatory schools where they turn out great football talent for the large universities. Well, right here in Roswell, N. M., the prettiest little city you ever saw, is situated the New Mexico Military Academy, and their kid polo teams are famous. It's the incubator for coming international polo. Think of a preparatory school with 120 kids out to make the team.

This country is all doing fine. They have already charged off and started in on a new basis of values, the same as the whole country has got to do. Up to 1929 was a nightmare and they have just forgot it, and everybody is happy.

Yours,
Will Rogers.

1498   MR. ROGERS WAXES ENTHUSIASTIC
       OVER THE BEAUTIES OF THE WEST

WINSLOW, Ariz., May 12. — You folks that think a desert country is terrible should see Arizona and New Mexico now. The whole States are covered with hundreds of the most beautiful kinds of flowers.

Saw the petrified forest again. What's these Baptist that think the whole world started with Noah going to say about a thing like that. Just another miracle, I reckon.

Wild buffalo fed the early traveler in the West and for doing so they put his picture on a nickel.

Well, Fred Harvey took up where the buffalo left off.

For what he has done for the traveler one of his waitress's picture (with an arm load of delicious ham and eggs) should be placed on both sides of every dime. He has kept the West in food and wives.

Yours,
Will Rogers.

1499   MR. ROGERS TOUCHES LIGHTLY
       ON A FEW OF THE DAY'S EVENTS

BEVERLY HILLS, Cal., May 13. — Here's about all I can find in newsprints today.

Spain is in a mess. Now we know they are becoming a regular republic.

Hawks got in his plane in Europe yesterday, so naturally he broke a record.

Prince of Wales lays England's depression to not advertising enough. We lay ours to overadvertising. We were such good salesmen we sold to each other and went broke.

Secretary of the Navy Adams, of the Pepsin gum Adamses is out here on the ocean watching maneuvers. He is the only Secretary our Navy has had that could stay on deck long eough to see anything.
Yours,
Will Rogers.

1500   MR. ROGERS DECIDES THE SLUMP
WAS FORESEEN BY ONLY TWO MEN

BEVERLY HILLS, Cal., May 14. — Today ought to be a day of consolation to folks that have made bad investments. Here George F. Baker, who is supposed to have not less than a half billion, winds up with one eighth of that. And he was supposed to be the smartest financial man we had. The thing busted right in his face. So what chance did anybody else have?

I tell you, and I believe it as strong as I ever believed anything in my life, Calvin Coolidge was the only man in America that saw this whole thing coming, and got from under. He just says to himself: "Folks have bought everything in the world, for a dollar down, under me, now let 'em pay for 'em under Herbert. I will see you again when things pick up, so long."

Name me another man in America that saw it coming, unless it was Al Capone. I hate to class a fine upstanding citizen like Mr. Coolidge with Capone, but facts is facts, and Cal and Al are the only two out of 120,000,000.
Yours,
Will Rogers.

1501   WILL ROGERS COMMENTS
ON THE POPE'S BROADCAST

BEVERLY HILLS, Cal., May 15. — I guess our country holds the record for dumbness. The Pope spoke to the world this morning in three languages and we didn't understand a one of 'em. But the minute he finished and the local stations got back to selling corn salve and pyorrhea tooth paste we were right up our intellectual alley again.

A real prince of Japan will visit Los Angeles tomorrow, but he picked a bad time to come, for on the same day Aimee gets in here from one of her pilgrimages, and any time Aimee returns home from anywhere, even if it's just from the desert, why this town goes practically ga-ga.

Yours,
Will Rogers.

1502   Mr. Rogers Reports Activity Of A Certain Kind Out West

SANTA MONICA, Cal., May 17. — Mighty exciting week-end out here in this land of sunshine and second mortgages, with Aimee getting home and Clara Bow's life story starting in the papers in the morning.

But, do you know that I never saw people moving around as much. Every one of us is hustling from bank to bank trying to renew our notes. A man has to be mighty careful nowadays or he will burn up more gasoline trying to get a loan than the loan is.

One fellow paid the bank his interest out here the other day and the police heard about it, followed him, and, sure enough, he had been in some of the late robberies.

Yours,
Will Rogers.

1503   Mr. Rogers Appears To Doubt The Wisdom Of Legislators

MOJAVE, Cal., May 18. — When I come through North Carolina the other day they were trying every means known to devilment and science to get their Legislature to resign.

Well, California's finally exhausted yesterday. Thirty-five hundred bills were introduced, 1,450 unsuccessfully (that many passed).

Now, no State can possibly have that many things wrong with it. And, of course, they turn down the only modern, up-to-date and sensible one of the whole 3,500. It would have gotten the State more favorable comment than all the others put together. That was to get Governor Rolph an airplane. In a big State like this how do they expect him to get around—on a bicycle?

Yours,
Will Rogers.

1504   MR. ROGERS DECIDES THE WORLD
         HAS A BAD CASE OF NERVES

BEVERLY HILLS, Cal., May 19. — League of Nations in Geneva just gets started in on some big scheme when a Russian gets up and proposes something and the rest of the congregation don't know if he is "kidding" or on the level.

Russia don't do as much harm to the rest of the world as they just worry 'em. She just loves to put a thumb in the soup and let the guests see it's in there.

The whole world's nerves are "jumpy," anyhow, right now. Anybody with a sheet over their head can run the world home and under the bed.

                              Yours,
                              Will Rogers.

1505   WILL ROGERS PUTS IN A WORD
         FOR THE VETERANS' POPPY DAY

SANTA MONICA, Cal., May 20. — Was at the government hospital out here in Sawtelle and all the disabled boys were working hard making poppies which they sell on Poppy Day which is next Saturday, the twenty-third. It's a great cause, and don't pass 'em up Saturday.

Asking our small aid one day a year is not exactly having our soldiers impose on us. Nobody can sell anything else nowadays, and this starting in buying a poppy might be the turning point.

So buy one, and you will feel so good you are liable to buy a coat to pin it on before the day is over.

                              Yours,
                              Will Rogers.

1506   MR. ROGERS BEGS TO ANNOUNCE
         THAT LOS ANGELES HAS ARRIVED

BEVERLY HILLS, Cal., May 21. — Los Angeles used to be considered by her critics as just a great big overgrown country town with none of the big city business methods like Chicago and New York.

But, they can't say it any more. We are important in a modern way now. We have attracted America's greatest and biggest industry. We got racketeers, too.

We got big enough that the "on the spots" and the "take 'em for a ride boys" are not just using the old pueblo as a whistling post. No more importing high-priced men from Chicago to help supervise a gangster picture, just use the ones that are working here. We are a modern American city at last.

Yours,
Will Rogers.

1507   THAT MAYOR OF LOS ANGELES
          IS HAILED BY WILL ROGERS

HOLLYWOOD, Cal., May 22. — There is a band of Mayors of American towns eating their way free through Europe. Well, leave it to the Los Angeles Mayor to do the right thing at the right time. At a banquet given in their honor wine was served, and he just did the manly thing and got up and walked out.

I hope when the French Mayors return the visit and we put on a couple of robberies and maybe a murder during their meal that they will have the good common decency toward their mother country to get right up and walk out, too.

Yours,
Will Rogers.

1508   MR. ROGERS PROPOSES A FUND
          TO BRING THOSE MAYORS HOME

HOLLYWOOD, Cal., May 24. — "Ill-will" Mayors' trip to France was in another mess yesterday. The bells of Rouen played "The Star-Spangled Banner," but the Southern Mayors wouldn't move till they played "Dixie." Los Angeles held out for "California, Here I come" and Maine for the "Stein Song."

We better start a fund to get those boys back home and out of the banquet tables before July the Fourth or they will have us in another war.

This little article of mine is used in the Paris Herald, so the funds will easily be raised by patriotic Frenchmen, and bring Chaplin home with 'em, too.

I want to hereby apologize for our Los Angeles Mayor. He was not discourteous in not touching the glass to his lips. He just couldn't trust himself with it that close.

Yours,
Will Rogers.

1509   MR. ROGERS'S OWN VERSION
         OF ONE OF THOSE RAPIDAN CHATS

BEVERLY HILLS, Cal., May 25. — It used to be quite a friendly and social distinction for a Cabinet member to be asked to "week-end" on the Rapidan but it's nothing to brag about nowadays.

Invitations read, "You are requested to attend a 'wake' in honor of Mr. Mellon's late lamented 'overdraft.' Don't bring fishing tackle; bring your department's salary list. Yours, Sir Boss."

Next scene on the Rapidan:

"Mr. Postmaster General, how much does it cost to run your 'racket'?"

"Eight hundred and thirty-eight million, Mr. President."

Mr. Hoover: "Yeah?"

"That's with strict economy and getting all the Congressmen's free mail to the voters on time."

Mr. Hoover: "Yeah? Well, you lop off the 38 million. We got to get Andy out of the red by November, '32."

Yours,
Will Rogers.

1510   MR. ROGERS IS GETTING FED UP
         ON THIS CONFERENCE BUSINESS

BEVERLY HILLS, Cal., May 26. — A conference in London on what to do about the world's surplus wheat broke up as usual. They even eat cornbread during the conference.

Russia proposed export wheat on a quota basis. We would not agree to it, so another conference breaks up with us being the "goat."

Will we ever quit sending delegations off to conferences? We just wait for a conference to get in wrong with somebody. There should be a heavy export duty on "good-will" groups and delegates to conferences.

We have had so many conferences that we are even sore at each other here at home.

Yours,
Will Rogers.

1511 MR. ROGERS HEARS OF A NEW KIND
OF 'WEEK' IN HIS HOME STATE

BEVERLY HILLS, Cal., May 27. — We have all kinds of various "weeks"— "Eat an apple week," "Don't shoot your husband week," "Don't cuss the Republicans any more than you can help week."

But, Claremore, Okla., the home of the great radium water, is having this week one of the most practical and useful ones, "Take a bath week." They can't relieve the present depression but they relieve the tissues. Even the Rotarys, Kiwanis, Lions, Apes and Chamber of Commerce have joined in the novelty of the thing and it bids fair to become a yearly event.

My old friend Governor Murray and myself have been cordially invited to attend.

Yours,
Will Rogers.

1512 MR. ROGERS CONDONES MURDER
IF IT CURTAILS RADIO SPEECHES

BEVERLY HILLS, Cal., May 28. — Last week we had quite an unusual murder out here (and it's getting very hard to put on anything unusual in the way of a murder).

A well-known politician was killed and at first they could find no reason. Then it was discovered that he was on the verge of financing a preacher in establishing a radio broadcasting station.

So, now the murderer will surrender and show that his deed was to save the public and he will be acquitted with honors, and his services will be in demand everywhere.

The regret is that this hero didn't start his life's work earlier.

Yours,
Will Rogers.

1513   ROGERS OFFERS AN ANALYSIS
        OF WALL STREET'S PROBLEM

BEVERLY HILLS, Cal., May 29. — A couple of years ago no business seemed to be up to date unless it had its "holding company." The title "holding" seemed like you had something, so the suckers went for it, but now the stockholders find out that all they were holding was the bag.

So that's what's the matter with your Wall Street. You can't go out now when your business ain't doing so good and merge with something else that's doing worse and form a "holding company" and issue more stock. What you got nowadays you got to "hold" yourself. The buyers are looking in the bag now before they hold it.

    Yours,
    Will Rogers.

1514   MR. ROGERS THINKS OUR PLIGHT
        IS WORSE THAN WASHINGTON'S

SANTA MONICA, Cal., May 31. — President Hoover made a mighty fine and very sincere speech Saturday at Valley Forge. He found somebody that was worse off than we are, but he had to go back 150 years in history to do it.

He claims that George Washington was in just about as bad shape with his army then as Mellon is with his deficit now.

But George only had to worry about getting through the Winter. We got to worry about getting through the Summer, then the Winter, then another Summer before the Democrats can possibly do anything for us.

    Yours,
    Will Rogers.

1515   MR. ROGERS IS MOVED BY PLIGHT
        OF TEXAS GUINAN IN FRANCE, BUT —

BEVERLY HILLS, Cal., June 1. — Poor Texas Guinan and her gang was just unfortunate. She happened to hit France right after the American Mayors, so France says, "One show troop at a time is enough for us."

Give Tex credit. She wouldn't have delivered a Chamber of Commerce speech at the Unknown Soldier's tomb.

But there is not much sympathy for Tex. Anybody that makes a living off "suckers" should never have to leave this country in a professional capacity.

> Yours,
> *Will Rogers.*

1516   MR. ROGERS HAS A SUGGESTION
FOR THE SOUTH ON PROSPERITY

HOLLYWOOD, Cal., June 2. — Just had an election out here today for new Councilmen and new sewers and more people got their crosses mixed up.

This is "cotton week" all over the South. They have laid by their skills for a week, and at all the luncheon clubs the speeches are to be about "cotton." That will perhaps disgust all the listeners with ever wearing cotton again.

What the South needs is a week called "Steal the farmers' cotton seed week." If the South was robbed of all its cotton seed for five years they would be loaning Mellon money.

> Yours,
> *Will Rogers.*

1517   MR. ROGERS REPORTS ON ELECTION
THAT RESULTED AS HE EXPECTED

BEVERLY HILLS, Cal., June 3. — Yesterday our municipal election ran true to political form. The sewer was defeated, but the councilmen got in.

In our big murder case out here the fellow they are trying for a double killing come pretty near being elected to the office of judge. Looks like if he had bumped off three instead of two he would have been elected.

I was telling you the other day about what a lot of "hooey" this college "honorary degree" is. Well, my contention was upheld. Didn't you see where Wickersham got one at Syracuse University?

> Yours,
> *Will Rogers.*

1518   Mr. Rogers Finds The Slump
Has Taught Him Something

HOLLYWOOD, Cal., June 4. — We used to always be talking and "sloganing" about "back to normalcy." Well, that's right where we are now, and where we are going to stay, so we might just as well get used to it.

It's taught us one important fact, that we haven't got as many "big men" as we thought we had. We used to think every head of a big organization was a "big man," and he was as long as everything was running in spite of him, but when old man "get-back-to-earth" hit us in the jaw, why we didn't have an industry that shrunk like the "big man" industry did.

Big men are just like stocks now, they are selling at just what they are worth, no more.

Yours,
Will Rogers.

1519   Will Rogers Sees Reason
For Coolidge Quitting Writing

BEVERLY HILLS, Cal., June 5. — Can't you see a little political foresight in Mr. Coolidge's quitting writing? No country would be cuckoo enough to nominate a columnist for President.

Mr. Coolidge's great following was built by not talking and not by saying something every day. He took it up through necessity and not preference.

When will this country that wastes billions on everything finally do justice to a retiring President and allow him for life at least two-thirds of his Presidential salary? It ought to be worth that much to the taxpayers for the privilege we take in crucifying 'em while in office.

Elect 'em for a six-year term, not allow 'em to succeed themselves. That will keep their minds off politics and the life salary will relieve 'em of any worry of the future.

Yours,
Will Rogers.

1520   MR. ROGERS MAKES A MOTION
           AND IS AWAITING A SECOND

BEVERLY HILLS, Cal., June 7. — About all that was in the papers this morning was about "debts." Every nation, and every individual, their principal worry is "debt."

What would be the matter with this for relieving practically everybody's "depression"— just call all debts off?

There can't be over a dozen men in the world that are owed more than they owe, so you wouldn't be hurting very many and besides if you do give them some worry, that's what they had everybody else doing for years.

It's not supply and demand its old man interest that's got the world by the ears.

This would give great temporary relief to 99 per cent and wouldn't hurt the others long for they would soon have it back again.

I make it a motion. Do I hear a second?
                        Yours,
                            Will Rogers.

1521   MR. ROGERS MAKES NOMINATION
           FOR SECRETARY OF THE TREASURY

BEVERLY HILLS, Cal., June 8. — The government floated an eight hundred million dollar loan the other day and Al Capone took most of it himself. There is the guy that should be Secretary of the Treasury. Just turn him over the country and split the profits with him.

I see by today's statistics of what the soldiers have done with their late bonus money that a big item is second-hand cars. Sorry to hear that. We haven't got twenty men in America that are well off to support one.
                        Yours,
                            Will Rogers.

1522   MR. ROGERS IS A BIT BEARISH
           ON THIS CONFERENCE BUSINESS

BEVERLY HILLS, Cal., June 9. — Mr. Mellon and Mr. Stimson are going over to London to another conference.

We say we are not going to cut down on the debt payment. We could write and tell 'em, but we like to get in wrong personally.

We have another delegation at Geneva on dope. We want to limit the output. We don't manufacture it and the other nations do, so you know where the conference will end.

We get nothing at a conference only the trip. It looks as if the depression would hurt the conference business, but it don't. They can always dig up enough to go and get in wrong.

Yours,
Will Rogers.

1523   Mr. Rogers Finds A New Kind
         Of Charity, And A Worthy One

HOLLYWOOD, Cal., June 10. — Out here in Los Angeles it was suddenly brought to public attention the other day that when school was out children that had been given their lunch because their parents could not afford it would be without it.

Well, the response by everybody was wonderful, but you know that's a situation that's liable to exist in a lot of towns. They might just forget that because school was out there was no reason to keep up the lunches, and there is not a town or city that won't gladly do it.

People are marvelous in their generosity if they just know the cause is there, so just in case your town might have overlooked it. Out here it was the parent-teachers that did it. Some towns might not have that.

Yours,
Will Rogers.

1524   Mr. Rogers Has A Bit To Say
         About Oklahoma's Sheriffs

BEVERLY HILLS, Cal., June 11. — Well, Oklahoma sheriffs broke a record. They finally found a car with no liquor in it, but it had to be occupied by Mexicans to do it, so they shot two of 'em for being unusual.

The sheriff's excuse was that the car had a Kansas license on it (Kansas adjoins Oklahoma). Does a foreign license in Oklahoma bring out the gendarmes, or is it the name Kansas that makes you shoot on sight? If he had showed his badge instead of his gun, the whole thing wouldn't have happened.

Well, it's lucky for Mr. Pershing, for if the conditions had been reversed, he would have been marching into Mexico today "to clean that country up and make 'em civilized."
                                          Yours,
                                               Will Rogers.

1525   ROGERS COMMENTS ON SCHOOL
             AND THE STUDY OF ENGLISH

BEVERLY HILLS, Cal., June 12. — My daughter graduated yesterday at a girls' preparatory school. They read off what course each girl had taken. When they said, "Mary Rogers, diploma in English," I had to laugh at that. One of my children studying English why it's just inherited. You don't have to study it in our family.

Doug Fairbanks had a niece graduating, Wallace Beery had a relation, Frank Lloyd, the great director, a daughter, and all four of us just sat there and purred like four old tomcats basking in a little reflected sunshine and secretly congratulating ourselves on choosing a profession where education played no part.
                                          Yours,
                                               Will Rogers.

1526   MR. ROGERS TRIES TO LIVE DOWN
             THE PAST, BUT TATTLERS TELL

BEVERLY HILLS, Cal., June 14. — No part of a person's private life is free from the eagle eye of that bird Brisbane.

I am as ashamed of my early years spent at Eton and Oxford as all the rest of their alumni is. But if any of us can conceal it and get away with it, why don't he give us credit, and let us go on living it down? But no! He has got to "blab" it to the world.

By the way, if you think this ain't going to be the worst Winter for unemployment we ever had, just count the number in these college graduation classes. Immigration is not our biggest problem, it's surplus diplomas.
                                          Yours,
                                               Will Rogers.

1527   Mr. Rogers Appears Disturbed
         By The New Crop Of Lawyers

BEVERLY HILLS, Cal., June 15. — Did you read how many thousands (not hundreds) but thousands of students just graduated all over the country in law? Going to take an awful lot of crime to support that bunch.

A man naturally pulls for the business that brings him in his living. That's just human nature. So look what a new gang we got assisting devilment, all trained to get a guilty man out on a technicality and an innocent one in on their opposing lawyer's mistake.

This is the heyday of the shyster lawyer and they defend each other for half rates.

Yours,
Will Rogers.

1528   Will Rogers Pays A Tribute
         To Late President Harding

BEVERLY HILLS, Cal., June 16. — Mighty glad to see Mr. Hoover and Mr. Coolidge finally (after years of delay) go out and dedicate the Harding Memorial. Too bad they waited till Ohio looked politically doubtful, and the odd thing about it is that they both owe their Presidency to this man's death. If he had lived one would have retired as an ex-Cabinet member and the other as just another ex-Vice President. They ought to have been just standing waiting for it to be finished in order to do their part for there was certainly nothing to be ashamed of in being there.

Harding was the most human of any of our late Presidents. There was more of the real "every day man" in him. If he had a weakness it was in trusting friends, and the man that don't do that, then there is something the matter with him sho nuff.

Betrayed by friendship is not a bad memorial to leave.

Yours,
Will Rogers.

1529   Will Rogers Remarks

BEVERLY HILLS, Cal., June 17. — Just heard Mr. Hoover over the radio at Lincoln's Tomb. He is making a monumental tour of the country visiting the tombs of dead Republicans, and incidentally to count the lives ones left. You'd be surprised the amount of good Republicans dead. Poor Franklin D. Roosevelt, when he launches his campaign, can't find enough Democratic monuments to get his policies over.

Yours,
Will Rogers.

1530 Will Rogers Sees A Good Break
    For The Harassed Mr. Capone

BEVERLY HILLS, Cal., June 18. — The government has finally been able to arrange an "armistice" with Al Capone.

He is to go to jail "in person" for two years (which term he named himself). His lieutenants are to carry on his business and deliver the receipts to him at the jail every day.

In return the government is to feed, clothe and protect him from harm and release him just about the time business turns the corner.

The government is remodeling Leavenworth now for him.

Yours,
Will Rogers.

1531 Rogers Sees Some Good Luck
    Due To Break For Mr. Hoover

BEVERLY HILLS, Cal., June 19. — Poor Mr. Hoover, if things ever do turn, and start breaking right for him, he will be a good man to string with, for he ought to have a long streak of luck. Of all the things that's gone against him, the worst one happened this week. His speech run 15 minutes overtime, and he took up Amos and Andy's time on the radio.

That was a vote loser sure enough. That did him more harm than even the Wickersham report. I never saw radio fans so worked up. That will be a lesson to all presidents.

Yours,
Will Rogers.

P. S.—The old West is deteriorating. In Reno they are shooting cartoonists with empty guns.

1532   WILL ROGERS REPORTS HIS ACT
        HAS BEEN STOLEN BY HOOVER

BEVERLY HILLS, Cal., June 21. — Mr. Hoover is stealing my act. He wants to postpone international debts for a year. Two weeks ago I had the same scheme, only I took more territory, I wanted to cancel everybody's, and every nation's debt, and the only persons that fell for my plan was two guys that owed me. They immediately agreed and canceled.

It's not government debts that's worrying us. Ramsay MacDonald, Hindenburg and Andy Mellon are the only ones worried about government debts (and we pay them to worry). It's individual debts that's got the 119 million by the nape of the neck.

We can always manage to dig up our taxes. It's old man interest that hurts.

Yours,
Will Rogers.

1533   MR. ROGERS DOESN'T BANK MUCH
        ON THIS 'MORAL LEADERSHIP' TALK

BEVERLY HILLS, Cal., June 22. — Here we go again! America is running true to form, fixing some other country's business for 'em just as we always do. We mean well, but will wind up in wrong as usual.

When some nation wants us to help 'em out they use the same old "gag," that we should exert our "moral leadership" and, like a yap, believe it, when, as a matter of truth, no nation wants any other nation exerting a "moral leadership" over 'em even if they had one.

If we ever pass out as a great nation we ought to put on our tombstone, "America died from a delusion that she had moral leadership."

Yours,
Will Rogers.

1534   MR. ROGERS'S FAVORITE AMERICAN
        IS LOADED DOWN WITH DEGREES

BEVERLY HILLS, Cal., June 23. — Every time I pick up a paper I see my favorite American citizen, Dwight Morrow, getting a degree from some more universities. He has played a regular circuit of 'em. He has been in his cap and gown more than he has his pants this Spring.

You know it's awful hard for these universities to get a good headliner to draw the crowds and publicity, so when they get a real one like Mr. Morrow they just weigh him down with "hokum" degrees.

We are living in an age of publicity. It used to be only saloons and circuses that wanted their name in the paper, but now it's corporations, churches, preachers, scientists, colleges and cemeteries.

Yours,
Will Rogers.

1535   MR. ROGERS DESPAIRS OF SCHEMES
        PROPOSED TO SAVE THE WORLD

BEVERLY HILLS, Cal., June 24. — There is one big advantage about proposing plans and schemes for the world's solution now. None of them can be acted on till Congress meets in December and by that time all of the ones proposed now will be forgotten and a new batch will be brought out.

We can't maintain excitement over any one thing over a couple of weeks at the most. The world ain't going to be saved by nobody's scheme. It's fellows with schemes that got us into this mess. Plans get you into things, but you got to work your way out.

Yours,
Will Rogers.

P. S. — Vanderbilt and his wife are having a duel and the public hope it will be successful.

1536   MR. ROGERS MARVELS AT THE JUMP
        THAT THE PRESIDENT HAS MADE

BEVERLY HILLS, Cal., June 25. — I never saw a man jump into a hero's berth as quick as President Hoover did. Why, this time last week he was in as bad as a Democrat. Now, he is proposed for the Nobel peace prize.

Wall Street has broke out on another rampage. Course the unemployed here ain't eating regular, but we will get around to them as soon as we get everybody else fixed up O. K.

I still claim as I did a month ago that all debts should be canceled, but my scheme didn't hit the international banking group with the same gusto that Mr. Hoover's did. I was appealing to the wrong class.

Yours,
Will Rogers.

1537   WILL ROGERS SEES TOUGH JOB
         FOR MR. MELLON IN PARIS

BEVERLY HILLS, Cal., June 26. — Mr. Mellon has got a tough job. He has to go to Paris and explain to the French that it's better if Germany didn't pay anything for a year. Now, when you start in telling France something about Germany, that's kinder like explaining politics to Calvin Coolidge. It can't be done.

France will say, "That's fine, Mr. Mellon, from a Pittsburgh angle, but we happen to live right across the river from 'em and we know what's going to happen to us soon as they are able again. What are you trying to do, shorten our lives one year?"

Yours,
Will Rogers.

1538   THE FIRST GOOD NEWS OF THE 1932 CAMPAIGN!
       MR. ROGERS SAYS HE WILL NOT RUN FOR ANYTHING

SANTA MONICA, Cal., June 28. — Will you do me one favor? If you see or hear of anybody proposing my name either humorously or semiseriously for any political office, will you maim said party and send me the bill?

Life magazine and I had a lot of fun last time by running for office, but am certainly not going to try and impose the same comedy twice.

My friend on Collier's (George Creel, it is, by the way, that writes that clever "Keyhole Column" in Collier's) says that I am taking this running serious. George, that's the worst slam you ever took against my sense of humor.

I certainly know that a comedian can only last till he either takes himself serious or his audience takes him serious, and I don't want either one of those to happen to me till I am dead (if then).

So let's stop all this damned foolishness right now. I hereby and hereon want to go on record as being the first Presidential, Vice-Presidential, Senator or justice of peace candidate to withdraw. I not only "don't choose to run" but I don't ever want to leave a loophole in case I am drafted, so I won't use "choose." I will say "won't run" no matter how bad the country will need a comedian by that time. I couldn't run anyhow, because I can't make up my mind which side to run on, "wet" or "dry." I don't know which side the most votes is on and I can't straddle it, for that's where all the rest of the candidates are now.

I hope in doing this that I have started something that will have far reaching effect. Who will be the next to do the public a favor and withdraw? What is there to worry anybody over the next nominations anyhow? It's one year away, but the candidates will be Hoover and Curtis versus Franklin D. Roosevelt and some Western or Southern Democratic Governor as Vice President.

Campaign literature of the Democrats should read "that in case of success that Owen D. Young would be Secretary of the Treasury." Big business has kept the Republicans in for ten years just to get Mellon.

Well, he ain't got anything on Owen Young when it comes to talking sense with big money.

Oh, yes, Collier's also said "that I could get a very liberal campaign fund." Well, none has shown up to now, so that's really the reason for this early withdrawal. Politics has got so expensive that it takes lots of money to even get beat with nowadays.

I have looked politics and the movies both over and, while they have much in common I believe politics is the most common, so I will stay with the movies. Will Hays didn't make any mistake. It's hard to give up the old White House, but it would be much harder to take politics serious. So long, boys.

Will Rogers.

1539 Mr. Rogers Waxes Enthusiastic
    Over The Post-Gatty Flight

BEVERLY HILLS, Cal., June 29. — No news today as big as this Post and Gatty that are making this world of ours look like the size of a watermelon.

This pilot Post is an old, one-eyed Oklahoma boy. He has just got that good eye glued on the horizon and he is going to find that horizon if it meets the earth anywhere, and Gatty, this reformed Australian "brumby and wombat" (you boys that didn't go to Oxford are lost in another maze of intellect) well, this Gatty, just give him a compass and one peek at the Giant Dipper and he can tell you where you are even if you ain't there.

This is one ship I would have loved to been a stowaway on.

Yours,
Will Rogers.

1540   MR. ROGERS'S CHIEF INTEREST
        IN THE NEWS IS IN THE FLIERS

BEVERLY HILLS, Cal., June 30. — No news outside those fliers making a sucker out of the world.

Southern Methodist Conference out here passed resolution asking Congress to exempt them from war. Don't know what claim they have over other denominations unless it's that they are always fighting so much among themselves that two wars at once would be a hardship on 'em.

Mellon is still coaxing the French. Looks like he will have to give 'em a "bonus" to accept his plan.

Yours,
Will Rogers.

1541   MR. ROGERS IS PLEASED GREATLY
        WITH NEW HEAD OF TEACHERS

BEVERLY HILLS, Cal., July 1. — America is a land of opportunity and don't ever forget it.

Yesterday out here in Los Angeles (where our local papers say people are dying from heat by the thousands in the East) out here we are just dying but for no particular reason at all, well there was elected to a very high office, president of the Educational Association, just a plain pleasant looking fat (and enjoying it) common sense woman. She is head of the rural schools in Maine and when you are rural in Maine you are rural. Now she is head of all the teachers in our land.

I guess from her name, "Miss," that she is an old maid, but, darn it, I just liked her looks in the paper this morning and I believe she could teach these young modern heathens of ours some sense.

Yours,
Will Rogers.

1542   WILL ROGERS PAYS A TRIBUTE
         TO AN EX-CONGRESSWOMAN

BEVERLY HILLS, Cal., July 2. — You remember I told you there was some awful good dead Republicans. Well, the finest woman one of 'em all went yesterday, ex-Congresswoman Alice Robertson of Oklahoma.

Nick Longworth told me this story: When they was voting on the soldiers' bonus she didn't believe in it in her own heart and she told why and told that her action would mean her finish in Congress. She told how she loved 'em and had fed 'em and spent every cent she ever had on 'em (and she had), but that she wouldn't vote against her conscience just to stay in Congress.

Nick said every man in the room went to her and complimented her on her bravery, then went over and voted the way the most votes were back home. She was a fine old soul, too fine for politics.

Yours,
Will Rogers.

1543   WILL ROGERS PAYS TRIBUTE
         TO WORLD FLIERS AND BACKER

BEVERLY HILLS, Cal., July 3. — The Governor of Australia (Gatty's home) cabled "Australia is proud of Gatty and I am sure Gatty is proud of Post." Now beat that for beautiful and diplomatic wording, and, say, let's give a great big hand to Hall that financed and made the thing possible. Never has a promoter remained so much in the background. If some other men had backed that trip, they would have had Gatty and Post riding in the jump seat parading in New York.

It was a great combination, a great flier, a great navigator and modest backer.

Yours,
Will Rogers.

1544   MR. ROGERS WOULD LIKE TO SEE
         THOSE FLIERS REALLY MAKE GOOD

BEVERLY HILLS, Cal., July 5. — I got my first thanks this morning for ever saying a nice thing about some man, and I do lots of times brag on our prominent men, but always take it as a matter

49

of fact. But the old Oklahoma oil man that backed the flight come through.

"Many thanks for your kind notice, and the best I can do in return is to take Post and Gatty to visit Claremore, Okla. Advise if you want us."

Now, here is a chance for these two boys to really make good. If Gatty can navigate enough to find a field there, I'll say he is a Columbus, and if Post can land on the field, I'll say he is a magician. I have always had to use a parachute.

Yours,
Will Rogers.

1545   WILL ROGERS POINTS THE WAY
       TO REAL SAFETY ON THE FOURTH

BEVERLY HILLS, Cal., July 6. — When the Fourth of July and a Sunday come together there just ain't anything to do on Monday but send flowers.

Fireworks killed and maimed everybody that had a match. Rip tides in the ocean just wait for a holiday to get their quota, and autos got what was left.

About the only sure way to keep from being hurt on the Fourth of July is to participate in one of our heavyweight prize fights.

Yours,
Will Rogers.

1546   MR. ROGERS IS HONORED BY A CALL
       FROM A HEAD MAN IN CONGRESS

BEVERLY HILLS, Cal., July 7. — Now I can't be so truthful about these Congressmen in Washington, for yesterday the head one of all of 'em drove out with Congressman Crail to my igloo to see me.

Tilson, the Republican majority leader (who will perhaps be the next Speaker). We talked over old times when we used to meet and tell jokes in Longworth's room.

He was called in to consult on Mr. Hoover's debt plan. It was well thought out and no politics involved, as he fed quite a few Democrats during the huddle.

Tilson says, "We are over the worst" Let's hope he is right. Even a Congressman can be right occasionally.

       Yours,
        Will Rogers.

1547   Mr. Rogers Finds Enterprise Still Lives In Oklahoma

BEVERLY HILLS, Cal., July 8. — Show you what enterprise will do. Claremore was one of the few towns that was built up so solid that it had no landing field. Even the adjoining country was one mass of suburban homes.

Well, overnight, in order to get our great Oklahoma pilot, Post, and his famous partner, Gatty, to come there, they just tore down and blasted out blocks of homes, and now they got the best landing field in the world (outside of the Templehof Field in Berlin) just ten minutes' drive from the heart of Claremore.

Course (due to a constant Republican administration) most of these destroyed homes were mortgaged, but at that it shows what a real town can do.

My friend Frank Hawks has suggested making a landing field out of New York City. I knew somebody would think of a useful use for that ground some day.

       Yours,
        Will Rogers.

1548   Mr. Rogers Tells Why France Is Better Off Than The Rest

BEVERLY HILLS, Cal., July 9. — Editorials have been blaming France for not falling over themselves to cancel the debt.

Well, France receives $95,000,000 more than she pays out to England and the United States. France is better off today than all of them. Why? Because of hard work and watching the pennies.

France is a good deal like Amos on the radio, "Now wait a minute, Andy, that scheme of yours sounds mighty big and fine now, but in the end where is we gettin' off?"

The United States is exactly like Andy. Anything comes up, "Oh sho, sho, send it over C. O. D. We will pay fur it or sumpin. Come on, Vanilla, les go fishin'."

Yours,
Will Rogers.

1549   BUY RANCH AND LIVE FOREVER
        IS THE ADVICE OF WILL ROGERS

SANTA BARBARA, Cal., July 10. — Dude ranches were the economic salvation of the Northwest. Wyoming may be king of the dude ranches, but Santa Barbara, Cal., is daddy of the rich "dudes'" owning ranches and enjoying 'em, and it's a great thing from every angle. They improve 'em, give lots of employment, raise fine horses and keep themselves out of a lot of worse devilment.

So buy a ranch somewhere in the West. All your life every man has wanted to be a cowboy. Why play Wall Street and die young when you can play cowboy and never die?

Yours,
Will Rogers.

1550   MR. ROGERS REPORTS TROUBLE
        IS CONFRONTING SANTA BARBARA

SANTA BARBARA, Cal., July 12. — Germany's got her problem, Mr. Hoover his Farm Board, England her "dole," but Santa Barbara has got real trouble.

The "Crusader," anti-prohbition float, won the prize in the parade. The drys claim it was all right to enter it provided it didn't win anything. Now they are going to have the parade held over again with different judges. If the drys win the next one, the finals will be held in neutral territory, perhaps Canada.

Mr. Hoover and Vice President Curtis are together today on the Rapidan, rehearsing signals for the big game next November.

Yours,
Will Rogers.

1551   WILL RUSHES BY PLANE
          TO SEE POST AND GATTY

TULSA, Okla., July 13. — Breakfast in Santa Monica and dinner in Claremore. Rushing home to help welcome Post and Gatty, who are going to visit our metropolis tomorrow. I thought if they could fly clear around the world and come to Claremore I ought to make this hop. Besides I am just anxious to see those guys. Flew Western Air to Amarillo, Tex. Now I am flying 9000 feet at 170 an hour in one of these fast low-wing Lockheeds belonging to the Bowen Line.

It's my first trip in one where they bundle the wheels up inside the wings. They say they sometimes forget to put 'em down. Believe me Pilot Lee will be reminded of it when we start to land. The wheels are under the wings and the passenger can't see if they are down. I am going to do a little wing walking and go out and see for myself tonight.

Yours,
Will Rogers.

1552   MR. ROGERS FLIES IN FAMOUS SHIP
          AND HOBNOBS WITH REAL FLIERS

CLAREMORE, Okla., July 14. — Well, this was a great day for Gatty and Post. It was just an ordinary day for Claremore, but it was a big thing for those boys. They never saw a town like ours.

We built a real airport in four days just to welcome 'em. I was with 'em in Tulsa last night and flew over here in the Winnie Mae with them today. It's the combination of the two that make 'em so great. I'd bet on 'em going around the world endways and cross both poles.

In all the excitement and rushing about, you know when they sleep? At the banquets. They said if it wasn't for banquets they wouldn't have any time to sleep at all. Smart fellows.

Yours,
Will Rogers.

1553   MR. ROGERS REPORTS ON WHAT
          IS HAPPENING HERE AT HOME

CHELSEA, Okla., July 15. — Around big cities nowadays you read of nothing but the plight of Germany and how their finances can be saved, but when you get out here in the agricultural region you read of what's happening at home.

53

Another drought looks like it's going to kill off the corn crop. Oats 15 cents a bushel. If food is not cheaper than it ever was then somebody is making money, and it ain't the farmer.

The farmer can't abandon the farm. He ain't got enough to move to town on.

Some of our optimistic after-dinner-speaking financiers of the East ought to try making a living and those speeches on 35-cents-a-bushel wheat.

Yours,
Will Rogers.

1554 Mr. Rogers Sees The Country And Discovers A New Salad

PHOENIX, Ariz., July 16. — If you want to see lots of our country in one day and all kinds of it leave Fort Worth in the morning from their fine new airport across Texas. (And, brother, you will know you crossed something.) Abilene, Big Springs, El Paso, Douglas, Tucson, Phoenix, and you will be in Los Angeles at 7.

Had a great new dish last night. Open all the cans of tomatoes you have, all the cans of cove oysters, lots of sliced onions, raw, mix 'em in a big bowl.

It's a sort of soup salad. It's called "we have scraped the bottom salad." You get it at Shady Oak Farm, Fort Worth.

Yours for the latest,
Will Rogers.

1555 Rogers Pays Last Tribute To A Real Hollywood Actor

BEVERLY HILLS, Cal., July 17. — He had been in movies for years, just about the best real cowboy out there, the most graceful roper I ever saw. You fans, didn't know him, for he didn't get to do much but the rough stuff and the skilled stuff, but when any director wanted anything done right on a horse it was "Ha, Pedro, do this for this high-priced 'dummy' and he can take the close-up." Great smile, great teeth, great disposition.

You have gone now, Pedro, to where, when you do something, your name will be on the bills. "Pedro Leon en persona un muy bueno hombre." You was a Mexican vaquero to some, but a real man to those who knew you. Adios, mi amigo.

Yours,
Will Rogers.

1556   MR. ROGERS TAKES UP THE DEBTS,
        CABLE TOLLS, RACE HORSES, &c.

SANTA MONICA, Cal., July 19. — Our two finest race horses seem to have taken up the same racket as our prizefighters and wrestlers. "You win this time, and I'll win the next. Let's take it easy and look at the dough we can get."

If Mr. Hoover wanted to call a Cabinet meeting nowadays, he would have to hold it in Europe. He is the only member in the United States.

If we had just donated to 'em the price of our long-distance telephone and cable calls, they woudn't have needed any more help. Clarence Mackay made enough on it already to afford to marry a prima donna.

Yours,
Will Rogers.

1557   MR. ROGERS SYMPATHIZES A BIT
        WITH TWO PERSONS IN THE NEWS

BEVERLY HILLS, Cal., July 20. — This is sorter "give the down and out a chance day."

They pounced on Ma Kennedy (Aimee's mother) after the poor soul had tried to scare up some fun and amusement. They started to examine her sanity, but they couldn't find any one in Hollywood capable of making the test.

Can't see much satisfaction (only for the politicians to have something to point to with pride in years to come) in sending old man Fall to the pen. He got the $100,000, but he evidently did not put up oil lands for security, for he has lost the ranch to Doheny for the same $100,000.

Course everything wasn't exactly on the up and up, but that is one case that was tried entirely by politics.

Yours,
Will Rogers.

1558   MR. ROGERS PENS A SAD PICTURE,
        LONG RANGE, OF LONDON PARLEY

BEVERLY HILLS, Cal., July 21. — This conference in London ought to be called "a hard luck testimonial meeting." It had no more than opened than each nation jumped up and told how poor they were before the others even had a chance to ask 'em for anything.

Ramsay MacDonald (a Scotchman), the host and toastmaster, before he finished he had 'em all in tears with England's condition.

France brought their own lunch (and not much of it).

Even "Uncle Andy" Mellon, to stave off a possible touch, joined the spirit of the thing and wore a Pennsylvania homespun suit and no sox.

It wound up by Germany offering to loan them what little she had left.

Yours,
Will Rogers.

1559   MR. ROGERS SEES NOTHING NEW
            IN OUR PLAN TO AID GERMANY

BEVERLY HILLS, Cal., July 22. — This new scheme of Mr. Hoover's to Germany "that all short-time credits shall be extended, and converted into long-time credits," why that ain't new. That's our old standby gag of "renewing your notes."

Why, half of our traffic is folks going or coming from renewing our notes.

I sho' do hope Mr. Hoover gets 'em straightened out. He had made every conscientious effort to help 'em, but helping one country in Europe is like helping one bee in a hive. You may help him (or her as the sex may be) but you will know you have been to a helping.

Yours,
Will Rogers.

1560   MR. ROGERS STILL IS YEARNING
            FOR THE LIFE OF A STOWAWAY

BEVERLY HILLS, Cal., July 23. — Two trips I would like have been on. One was stored away in the tail of Post and Gatty's ship, and the other is with Bernard Shaw and Lady Astor in Russia (maybe stored away in Bernard's beard). The laughs there will be on that trip, for Lady Astor can hand 'em out about as fast as old "apple cart" can.

Well, it's fine if they have fixed it so Germany will pull through. There is one debt they ought to wipe out entirely, for it had no reason ever existing, and that's for the "armies of occupation." That was just like sitting over the grave of a dead man for a year to see if he was coming to life and then charging his family the price of the sitting.

Boys brought home enough fine fat German girls to pay for that trip.

Yours,
Will Rogers.

1561   Must Be Hot, Says Will Rogers, When California Admits It

BEVERLY HILLS, Cal., July 24. — This must have been an awful hot spell. California papers are printing their own heat prostrations.

If it hadn't been for Secretary Mellon and Stimson and O. O. McIntyre, there wouldn't have been an American tourist trade this Summer.

The financial depression is so bad that American millionaire polo players are having to play on American horses.

I didn't know it till I was reading the statistics the other day, but the Argentine republic furnishes us over 90 per cent of our tanned hides and gigolos.

Yours,
Will Rogers.

1562   Mr. Rogers Finds Another Thing That Is Against This Country

SANTA MONICA, Cal., July 26. — A fellow was just up here telling me that one of the causes of the extreme heat was that the Japanese Gulf Stream was in closer to us this year and that the water was much warmer, hence warming the land. Even the ocean is against us. Did you ever see as many cockeyed things that could happen to one country all at once?

Ex-President Calles has declared that you can use silver to pay your debts instead of gold. He is trying to get silver back where it belongs. That's fine. Mexico has got the silver, but what about us? We will have to start paying off with potatoes and watermelons.

Yours,
Will Rogers.

1563   Mr. Rogers Notes The Downfall
            Of Another Boastful Leader

BEVERLY HILLS, Cal., July 27. — Lots of countries are breaking the monotony of their depressions with little home-talent revolutions.

A big amateur dictator in Chile had said, "Nothing could harm me; I am under divine protection." Well, yesterday the bullets got to getting so close he commenced figuring maybe he had kinder overestimated his partnership with the Almighty.

There's no leaders in any country now that look like they are getting any divine aid.

Did you read about some women getting held up in China? Well, they was the female kinfolks of Harry Carr, the best writer on the Coast. He wrote an awful nice piece sympathizing with the bandits.

                     Yours,
                     Will Rogers.

1564   Mr. Rogers Hears The Rumblings
            Of War And Prepared For Call

BEVERLY HILLS, Cal., July 28. — I was pretty worried last week. I am a Colonel on Alfalfa Bill Murray's Oklahoma "fighting staff." I thought he overmatched hisself. Take on Kansas till we get in practice, then Texas in the finals.

When I heard "Old Bill" hisself had hid a long squirrel rifle under his mustache and gone to the wars "in person," I said to myself, "Col. Rogers, you better go into rehearsal."

So, I got myself a chemist and we started to work. The only way to lick a Texan is with bad liquor. Any State that can make worse liquor than Texas can lick 'em, but it's hard to make worse. That's why Texas licked Mexico. Texas had the worst. They fattened on Mexico's "tequilla."

                     Yours,
                     Will Rogers.

1565   Mr. Rogers Is For Digging A Lot
            Of Canals Even If We're Broke

BEVERLY HILLS, Cal., July 29. — Been reading of our army survey of a new canal by Col. Dan Sultan, but what you haven't read is the wonderful work that he and his crew did during the Nicaragua earthquate.

He moved in with his whole outfit, among which were some splendid doctors, and they worked day and night there. They and the marines were in the right place at the right time that time.

He explained the canal to me down there. For folks that like to dig canals, there is a good place to dig. One there cost $700,000,000, but Lord, the way we are going what's seven hundred more million in hock for us?

We are sunk anyhow, so let's get a series of canals, then save the best one.

Yours,
Will Rogers.

1566   Mr. Rogers Finds Grasshoppers
Do More Harm Than Farm Board

BEVERLY HILLS, Cal., July 30. — I been getting some papers sent to me from the Northwest, and I am telling you, from the pictures, these grasshoppers have laid that country lower than the Farm Board.

They just swarm onto a place like farmers at a free barbecue, and leave about as little.

There is one thing to be said for the grasshopper—he has generally operated in Republican territory. Kansas has been ruined by 'em as often as by their politicians, so that's why the Democrats have never paid the bugs much attention, in fact, kinder urged 'em on. But they never even prayed for anything like this to happen.

Yours,
Will Rogers.

1567   Rogers Now Expects Capone
To Sue U. S. For Defamation

BEVERLY HILLS, Cal., July 31. — That was funny in Chicago yesterday that judge not knowing anything about the U. S. Government having a special treaty with Al Capone to let him off easy. This backwoods judge was trying to treat him like a criminal. Now the whole thing has got to go to court and he will win and perhaps sue the government for defamation of character.

If all of our navigators ever get as reliable as our engines half our people will be spending their weekends at Mars and Venus (perhaps Venus). Those old boys that went to Turkey did a mighty fine job. Just the idea of going there was as original as the feat itself.

Yours,
Will Rogers.

1568   MR. ROGERS ADOPTS A WET PLANK;
              WOULD TRADE WHEAT FOR BEER

SANTA MONICA, Cal., Aug. 2. — Somebody said we had a chance to sell Germany some wheat and cotton on time.

Sure, let 'em have all they want, and take the pay out in good German beer. Then pass a law that if you found a man drinking whiskey he gets ten years.

If everybody had all the beer they wanted they would naturally be against the whiskey drinker and would help enforce the law against him. Then you would have a popular law.

Put a good tax on the beer and that would take care of the unemployment fund.

A bushel of wheat for a big "growler of wusberger"' wouldn't be a bad trade.

That's about all the ideas I got today.

Yours,
Will Rogers.

1569   MR. ROGERS SUDDENLY DISCOVERS
              THAT THERE IS A DEARTH OF NEWS

BEVERLY HILLS, Cal., Aug. 3. — No news any more in the depression, and no more news than truth in optimistic predictions.

We not only cured our "big men" from predicting, but we just about cured 'em from thinking they was "big."

Debts are about all canceled but our own, heat is dying out, grasshoppers are starving out. Nobody running for President on either side in '32 but Mr. Hoover, and even he may lose his passion for punishment by then.

So it just looks like nothing ever happens in our country but interest and taxes.

Yours,
Will Rogers.

Will Rogers as "Lemuel Morehouse" in the motion picture Young As You Feel, an adaptation of George Ade's play, Father and the Boys (Fox Film Corporation, 1931).

1570   Mr. Rogers Is In The Field
            For A Job As Ambassador

BEVERLY HILLS, Cal., Aug. 4. — See by the paper this morning they have formed, away out here in Sacramento, Cal., a Draft-Dwight Morrow-for-President Club.

Well, I hope he makes it. All I want out of it is the Ambassadorship to Mexico. (Don't laugh, you haven't seen all our Ambassadors lately, have you?)

I could get away with that job, for Morrow could tell just what to do and who to do it to. I could attend the dinners and bull fights and make speeches to both, and listen without laughing (much) to the Americans saying we got to take this country over and civilize it like ours. Like ours, ha! ha!

                       Yours,
                       Will Rogers.

1571   Mr. Rogers Is Kept Quite Busy
            By The Wars In Oklahoma

BEVERLY HILLS, Cal., Aug. 5. — Say these wars is getting to be tough. I had no more than got home from the battle of Red River in which, with my old commanding general (I am a Colonel on the staff of Bill Murray), we licked Texas and "made bridges free for Oklahomans" to cross, even if they had no business on the other side. Today my old general calls me back into the trenches.

(Let's see who we are fighting this week?) Oh, yes, the Standard Oil and the octopuses. We want $1 oil, and we ain't going to quit shooting till we get it.

Old Bill's been right every time, and I am still with him. Next week we are going to fight for 20-cent wheat.

                       Yours,
                       Will Rogers.

1572   Mr. Rogers Sums Up The News
            Of The Day And Is Uninspired

BEVERLY HILLS, Cal., Aug. 6. — Tough day for news.
China had a flood.
Mae Murray, film actress, decided to retain same husband.
Ain't heard a word from Russia since Shaw left it.
Even a Wickersham report would read good today.

Wheat went so low that even the grain speculators are being driven into legitimate business.

All that saved the day was Jack Dempsey announcing that he was going to fight again and Grace Coolidge getting her hair bobbed. I'll bet Calvin will sneak off where the voters can't see him and get a manicure.

I hope something unusual happens before tomorrow. Maybe Lindbergh's radio will work.

Yours,
Will Rogers.

1573   ROGERS DISCUSSES HONOLULU,
        JIM REED AND VACATIONS

BEVERLY HILLS, Cal., Aug. 7. — My wife and daughter just off the boat today from Honolulu with a ukulele under one arm and a surf board under the other. They claim it's a great vacation spot. They visited some of the big cattle ranches. That and that hula stuff would hit me better than trying to stand on my head on a board.

Saw my old friend Jim Reed of Missouri, and Jim generally knows what he is talking about, says the government is in the bootlegging business. Lord, as far behind as the treasury is now they got to get into something that pays.

Our Governor of California wants everybody to take a six days' vacation. That won't affect over 10 per cent of our people.

Yours,
Will Rogers.

1574   WILL ROGERS SEES A DARK PLOT
        IN THAT FLIGHT OVER JAPAN

SANTA MONICA, Cal., Aug. 9. — Say, some more of our girls ought to get married and retire for a while. Look at our Helen Wills Moody. Bless her lamp-shaded form, she just went out and brought the tennis championships back to the white race.

Two of our pilots flew over Japanese fortifications and now it looks like they will be hung. When a Jap is serious over some fool thing he can be the most foolishly serious of all the two-legged folks.

Well there you go, Hoover secretly sending these boys over there to get a line on all this. Just shows you he ain't thinking about us here at home, only worried about whipping Japan.

Yours,
Will Rogers.

1575   MR. ROGERS SEES NEW TROUBLE
         FOR HOOVER AS HE GROWS OLDER

SANTA MONICA, Cal., Aug. 10. — Today is our President's fifty-seventh birthday. I look for him to come in for a lot of censure for allowing himself to get that old. If ever a man should be wished well it should be him.

We think everything has happened to us when nothing has happened to us. Mr. Coolidge and Wall Street and big business had had their big party, and was just running out of liquor when they turned it over to Mr. Hoover. He arrived at the picnic when even the last hardboiled egg had been consumed. Somebody slipped some Limburger cheese into his pocket and he got credit for breaking up the dance.

Prices and everything is getting back to normalcy—all but the people; they are the last to see it.

Yours,
Will Rogers.

1576   WILL ROGERS HAS SOME IDEAS
         ON USES FOR THOSE WINE BRICKS

BEVERLY HILLS, Cal., Aug. 11. — Here is what the Prohibition Director decided about this pressed grape bricks you have been reading so much about; "They will turn to wine if handled properly, but it's not illegal to buy 'em; we would have to prove that he was going to handle 'em properly." Well, that's fine. That a gal Mabel, and I hope you get the government loan. By the way, a few sample bricks would reach me at the above address, only, mind you, for paving and heaving purposes. I got a cat on my back fence I want to throw 'em at. Of course, if they turn to wine before I hit him I will be disappointed and humilated beyond words, because the cat don't like wine.

Send instructions what to do in case I make up with the cat.

Yours,
Will Rogers.

1577   MR. ROGERS HAS A KIND WORD
         FOR WICKERSHAM COMMITTEE

BEVERLY HILLS, Cal., Aug. 12. — Say, you know this Wickersham report that we all been kidding about. That thing has dug up a lot of mighty valuable dope at that. About everything they went into they found was "cockeyed."

Our deportation of non-citizens—they found we had sent everybody away that we shouldn't and none that we should.

Now they show up this "third degree," where they beat you till you admit to anything that has been done, even if it happened before you was born.

All we got to do in this country to find out anything is wrong is just to investigate it.

Anyhow, him and his gang wasn't loafing.

Yours,
Will Rogers.

1578   WILL ROGERS FINDS WIDOWS
        ARE PREY FOR SWINDLERS

BEVERLY HILLS, Cal., Aug. 13. — One of the most astonishing things I ever read was in the paper today publishing facts and figures that there has been over $300,000,000 swindled by fake stocks and mines, proposals of marriage and all sorts of schemes, just from mostly widows, alone here in Los Angeles.

Now there is no harder earned money in the world than earned by a wife, and then to be simple enough to let some guy talk her out of it. They say it's worse in California than anywhere. It's either the climate, or widows are dumber.

About the only way I see to lick these malesharpers is not to leave your wife anything. That will get even with those slicks.

Yours,
Will Rogers.

1579   WILL ROGERS PAYS TRIBUTE
        TO A GENEROUS GESTURE

SANTA MONICA, Cal., Aug. 14. — Say, you talk about a people and a place being appreciative of what was done for them when they was in trouble. Remember England, Ark., that had all the trouble during the drought last fall? Well there is a coal-mining section of Oklahoma (same as the coal mines everywhere) they were mighty hard up. Well, this England, Ark., just loaded up thirteen heaping truck loads of food and sent them to Henryetta, Okla. Now that's remembering, ain't it?

England is in a mighty fertile country, and this year they have really raised something. Course they can't get nothing for it, but ain't it nice they help others out with it?

Yours,
Will Rogers.

1580 WILL ROGERS WOULD EXTEND
THE FARM BOARD'S NEW PLAN

BEVERLY HILLS, Cal., Aug. 16. — Farm Board destroying every third row of cotton is the nub of a great idea. What would give more relief than extinguishing every third Senator, every third congressman, every third committee, every third stock broker, every third law. Make a third of the vice presidents of concerns go back to work. Turn the cows back into every third golf course. Convict every third gangster arrested. One-third of all millionaires that issue optimistic reports from aboard yachts. Too many banks, bump off a third. Stop up every third oil well and every third political speaker.

Destroy one-half the newspaper columnists, and last, but the main thing, the matter with the whole world is there is too many people. Shoot every third one. This whole plan is inexpensive and a sure-fire scheme back to prosperity.

Yours,
Will Rogers.

1581 ROGERS EXPLAINS WHY FRANCE
IS WELL OFF IN THE DEPRESSION

BEVERLY HILLS, Cal., Aug. 17. — Wasn't much happened over the week-end outside of Texas put on a little earthquake which California papers brought up to giant proportions.

Winston Churchill made the front page by hanging on to Bernard Shaw's whiskers and Nancy Astor's petticoat. He is stepping out of his class of wits with those two. He has misfit into too many prominent positions in England to shoot at those two successes.

Borah says that France is better off than any nation today. Well, if you remember, they are the only one that went to work and saving the minute the war was over. We are just starting now.

Yours,
Will Rogers.

1582   WILL ROGERS THINKS CONGRESS
IS DUE TO HELP UNEMPLOYED

BEVERLY HILLS, Cal., Aug. 18. — What's all the scandal today? Good deal of talk of Congress meeting early on account of the unemployed. Well, I believe if I was unemployed and hungry I would want a little more substantial help than just the thought of "our boys" being gathered in Washington. In fact, I believe a man can get just as hungry with them there as he can if they are investigating the Philippines or France or somewhere else, and I am sure Mr. Hoover ain't bringing the lads in just because he has missed 'em so. But Congress might do something. They are about due.

Yours,
Will Rogers.

1583   WILL ROGERS FEARS WE MUST
SAVE OURSELVES ACCIDENTALLY

BEVERLY HILLS, Cal., Aug. 19. — Every day brings new schemes in the papers for relief. The Russians have got a five-year plan. Maybe it's terrible but they got one. We been two years just trying to get a plan. The latest two came from Mr. McKelvie of the North and Governor Long of the South. Neither one helps the corn raiser or the city fellow. One wants to give all the surplus wheat to the unemployed (that has been suggested more times than there is bushels.) Long wants to plant no cotton next year. Both good schemes, but neither don't put anybody to work. So we are still in the market for a plan.

We will just about have to save ourselves accidentally. That's the way we stumbled on prosperity.

Yours,
Will Rogers.

1584   WILL ROGERS CALLS GIFFORD
A BIG MAN FOR A BIG JOB

BEVERLY HILLS, Cal., Aug. 20. — Mr. Hoover has named another man to look after the jobless. The latest one is Mr. Gifford, the very efficient head of the American Telephone and Telegraph Company. That's a terrible position to wish on anybody. "Here, you go out and find six million work." Well, if Gifford can't give you a job he can at least put you on a phone so you can call up your other idle friends, or he can use these six million to keep that other six million off the line while you are trying to talk.

Anyhow, we got a big man in a big job, and if he gets away with it he is our Moses.

Yours,
Will Rogers.

1585   WILL ROGERS HAS HIS SAY
         ON NEW HOOVER COMMISSION

BEVERLY HILLS, Cal., Aug. 21. — No matter how bad the depression gets and how short we become of the necessities of life we never seem to run out of material to put on a commission. Mr. Hoover just got ahold of a book called "Who's Who for no Reason at All" and appointed sixty men. That breaks his own record for quantity if nothing else.

He picked every bank president and corporation head who have handled their own affairs so ably in the last year and a half that it is their stockholders that constitute the present needy.

Yours,
Will Rogers.

1586   WILL ROGERS EXTOLS COUZENS
         FOR HIS GIFT TO UNEMPLOYED

SANTA MONICA, Cal., Aug. 23. — Best news in a whole bale of Sunday papers was from a Senator.

Wouldn't think it, would you?

Senator Jim Couzens offered a million to Detroit's relief fund. A few examples like that early before the cold sets in will have great effect. Young Insull in Chicago is doing some fine work.

That's the best thing about Mr. Hoover's big committee. It's what they will give themselves and get their friends to give that will make them valuable. Our rich are mighty liberal when the real showdown comes.

So thank you Jim, we will cable your friend Andy about this.

Yours,
Will Rogers.

1587   WILL ROGERS LISTS SURPRISES
                AND DISAPPOINTMENTS IN NEWS

     HOLLYWOOD, Cal., Aug. 24. — Did you ever see as many things happen to a country in one year? One disappointment after another. Had Al Capone headed for jail and then he notified us that he didn't care to attend this semester. Ramsay MacDonald was our only friend in England, now he is "on the dole." When Uncle Andy Mellon, the missing link between finance and government, pulled up one billion lame that was a shock. We knew our financial "giants" had failed to giant. We knew our laws had crumbled. We knew the weather was against us, but to have Lindy keep a reception committee waiting one month, that was our last straw.

                          Yours,
                              Will Rogers.

1588   ROGERS SAYS LINDBERGHS FOUND
                NEW ISLANDS FOR THE JAPANESE

     HOLLYWOOD, Cal., Aug. 25. — See where the Japanese jury returned a verdict of "not guilty" against Lindy. They not only freed him but complimented him for finding some islands that they didn't know they had themselves. Funny how they guard those forts and I don't reckon there is a fort in the world that all other nations don't know more about it than the one that owns it.

     The Labor Government of England fell because it wanted to cut the salaries of those that wasn't laboring. Now they got a coalition government. That's one they have when there is nothing left to divide up.

                          Yours,
                              Will Rogers.

1589   WILL ROGERS DOUBTS ACCURACY
                OF LOS ANGELES WEATHER MAN

     HOLLYWOOD, Cal., Aug. 26. — Everybody in Los Angeles can die of the heat but one lone man, and he will stagger to the typesetting machine and report "temperature 96 degrees." Their thermometer is in a Frigidaire.

Sixty shots were fired in Mexico's Congress while it was in session, and they were only able to totally eliminate one member, and then people ask "What's the matter with Mexico?"

After reading what tonsils did for Estelle, Dempsey will get his divorce.

Yours,
Will Rogers.

1590   ROGERS PRESIDES AT PARLEY
            ON A HOLLYWOOD MOVIE LOT

BEVERLY HILLS, Cal., Aug. 27. — A lot of different nationalities were working with us on a movie set yesterday, all representatives of different countries. We all sit around and gabbed between scenes. The Chinaman: "My country very bad, what will be the end?" The Russian: "Poor Russia, what hopes can it have?" The Englishman: "We were never in such a bad way; who knows how we will come out?"

I said: "Boys, I sure would like to tell you, and I will just as soon as I find out where we're going ourselves."

Yours,
Will Rogers.

1591   ROGERS SAYS BIG MONEY GOES
            TO PARTY THAT SUPPORTS IT

BEVERLY HILLS, Cal., Aug. 28. — No wonder the Republican party in this country is careful to do nothing to interfere with big banking interests. Look over in England. The Labor party was in but they had no money. They get out and a different bunch in New York and Paris banks loaned 'em a half billion dollars.

Big money only goes to the party that supports big money. I am entering no crusade to end it. I am just telling you how it is. You go ahead and change it.

Yours,
Will Rogers.

1592   WILL ROGERS THINKS AIR RACES
            ARE AMERICA'S GREATEST SHOW

SANTA MONICA, Cal., Aug. 30. — Post and Gatty and their families were out to spend the day with us today. They are mighty modest, fine boys. Gatty thinks we have pilots and engines that will take us anywhere; that it's up to navigation now.

They are leaving at once for the Cleveland air races. Post won the race from here there last year. This year Jimmy Doolittle has a very fast new plane that should win. That ought to be the greatest show in America, for there is nothing new in any kind of a show nowadays but aviation.

Yours,
Will Rogers.

1593   WILL ROGERS IS A BIT CAUSTIC
            ON THE NEWS OF THE WEEK-END

BEVERLY HILLS, Cal., Aug. 31. — Not much news over the weekend, as we look at news nowadays. Flood in China drowned a million. We take that with as little concern as a New York gang killing or the fifty people killed in autos over the week-end. Mr. Mellon is today's headliner, borrowing one billion one hundred million at 3 per cent. Could have got it at about 1½, but wanted to give the boys a break. This means they are going to finance by borrowing instead of increased taxes on those able to pay.

It's too close to election to antagonize the big boys.

Yours,
Will Rogers.

1594   ROGERS SEES MORE INTEREST
            IN GOLF THAN IN UNEMPLOYED

BEVERLY HILLS, Cal., Sept. 1. — This country is not entirely over the "cuckoo" stage yet, for every day there is more printed in the papers about the new and old golf ball than there is on unemployment. When the dimensions of a golf ball is our greatest worry, we still got a long way to go to get back to normal. Five thousand people followed Bobby Jones and watched him watch the golf championship. We ought to get Bobby to sit in Washington and watch it. That might revive interest in our present form of government.

Yours,
Will Rogers.

1595   WILL ROGERS SAYS PRESIDENT
               PUT OWEN YOUNG ON THE SPOT

BEVERLY HILLS, Cal., Sept. 2. — California will stay ahead in everything or bust, even depression. A guy out here yesterday robbed the poor-farm.

I think Mr. Hoover had overlooked Owen D. Young on his first relief committee and all the papers commented on it, and to make up for it he appointed him on a special one. Asking a Democrat to feed the country is almost a "believe it or not." Young is in a tough spot. If he feeds 'em through the Winter, he will only be keeping 'em alive to vote the Republican ticket next Fall. Voters can't remember back over two months.

                     Yours,
                     Will Rogers.

1596   WILL ROGERS FINDS EVERYBODY
              OCCUPIED SPREADING RUMORS

BEVERLY HILLS, Cal., Sept. 3. — We got one thing to be thankful for anyhow. The country is not in as bad shape as the rumors have it. If ever a land was rumored to death it's us. There is not a bank in America that is not closed a thousand times a day by whispers. In fact there is no unemployed. We got one hundred and twenty million people working overtime just repeating rumors. If we did pass out as a great nation our epitaph should read "America died from fright."

                     Yours,
                     Will Rogers.

1597   WILL ROGERS FINDS LARNIN'
              SPOILS ONE FOR REAL WORK

BEVERLY HILLS, Cal., Sept. 4. — The papers today say that illiteracy has decreased. The more that learn how to read the less learn how to make a living. That's one thing about a little education, it spoils you for actual work. The more you know the more you think somebody owes you a living.

Chic Sale was just out to see me, an old friendship we started in vaudeville together many, many years ago. We are very fond of he and his fine family. We both wrote a book, but I foolishly wrote mine on politics, a subject nobody was interested in.

            Yours,
            Will Rogers.

1598   ROGERS FOLLOWED OUIMET
      36 HOLES TO LEARN NAME

SANTA MONICA, Cal., Sept. 6. — This trip of Wilkin's will sure discourage a man from ever buying a second-hand submarine. I don't see why he don't try the thing under water, it sure won't float on top. Unless he has made arrangements to have a whale tow him he ain't got much chance ever getting far.

I don't know anything about golf, but I do know We-met that won the championship yesterday. He is a great friend of Fred Stone, and about the only time I ever followed a man was him and Fred. It's just about like following a man plowing all day. I had to follow him thirty-six holes to find out how to pronounce his name, We-met.

            Yours,
            Will Rogers.

1599   MR. ROGERS COMES FORWARD
     WITH DEMAND FOR NEW TAXES

SANTA MONICA, Cal., Sept. 7. — When will they quit taxing farmers' land regardless if it made anything? Or selling people's homes for taxes?

Not till they get a sales tax small on necessities and large on luxuries; then a stiff inheritance tax on the fellow that saves and don't spend.

That will get him either way.

A tax paid on the day you buy is not as tough as asking you for it the next year when you are broke.

It's worked on gasoline. It ought to work on Rolls Royces, cigarettes, lipstick, rouge and Coca-Cola.

            Yours,
            Will Rogers.

1600   MR. ROGERS REVIEWS THE NEWS
        AND MAKES A BOW TO BORAH

BEVERLY HILLS, Cal., Sept. 8. — No dullness over this weekend's news.

King of England and the Prince of Wales set a fine example and get a merit badge.

Our Bill Murray made a good speech, and when everybody has had their say on a subject, Senator Bill Borah says something. That "It's all right to say the government don't support the people, but who got the people in the shape they are if it wasn't the mismanagement of the government?"

Them's true words, Willie. No wonder they won't run you for President.

Yours,
Will Rogers.

1601   MR. ROGERS TELLS WHY LEAGUE
        DOESN'T INVITE US TO JOIN NOW

BEVERLY HILLS, Cal., Sept. 9. — Mexico just joined the League of Nations. Since we went broke we have never been invited in.

If the South don't raise any cotton next year it will just be their luck to have the boll weevil change its diet and switch over to something else.

With no cotton in the South next year the people can devote all their time to politics instead of just two-thirds of it.

Wilkins is bringing the Nautilus home to get a new tow rope.

Yours,
Will Rogers.

1602   MR. ROGERS THINKS OUR WOMEN
        WILL KEEP ONE RECORD FOR US

BEVERLY HILLS, Cal., Sept. 10. — We had quite a mix up over an international speed boat race.

I know Gar Wood and I don't think he is that kind of a sportsman, but whether he did or did not, we know the Englishman had the fastest boat, the same as they have the fastest auto and the fastest plane.

But I believe our women have got it on 'em for speed. They are about our last hope to hold a speed record.

Yours,
Will Rogers.

1603   MR. ROGERS LIKES THE MANNER
        IN WHICH ENGLAND DOES THINGS

BEVERLY HILLS, Cal., Sept. 11. — You can't beat that England. She don't look good till they get in a hole, then watch her.

They wasn't afraid to put an additional tax on big incomes. They forget politics when they are in a tight place.

Republicans can't tax big incomes over here for they haven't got next year's campaign budget yet. Democrats still owe for their last three elections.

Somebody said that Al Smith wouldn't run next year, but Al says it wasn't him that said it.

Yours,
Will Rogers.

1604   MR. ROGERS HOLDS OUR MAYOR
        HAS AT LEAST ONE DISTINCTION

SANTA MONICA, Cal., Sept. 13. — France gave Jimmy Walker the Legion of Honor because he didn't bring nineteen other mayors with him.

Every time the Republicans start to pin a rosette of poison ivy on him in New York he is sipping a stein of beer with Hindenburg, shooting craps with Premier MacDonald, or doing an adagio dance with Mussolini.

No man was ever so investigated on one hand and dined on the other. He keeps just three decorations ahead of the investigating committee.

Yours,
Will Rogers.

1605   WILL ROGERS ANNOUNCES
A SHIFT OF HIS AFFECTIONS

BEVERLY HILLS, Cal., Sept. 14. — Sister Aimee McPherson had just yesterday sent an advisory out to invite me as her special guest to her new musical play based on the Bible, words by Moses, music by McPherson.

Now she has gone and got married on me, so I am going to switch my affections over to "Ma" Kennedy.

Hollywood may not keep you young, but it sure keeps you marrying.

Los Angeles's fiesta was a big success, all but the "Native Sons" parade, and not enough entries came from Frisco to make it worth while.

                                Yours,
                                Will Rogers.

1606   WILL ROGERS PAYS A TRIBUTE
TO A 'SKINNY LITTLE FELLOW'

BEVERLY HILLS, Cal., Sept. 15. — London has had lots of conferences. There was enough fuss made over the disarmament one to fix the whole world for years.

Our delegates went by special boat. Dressmakers worked for months before, but a skinny little fellow with nothing but a breechcloth, a spinning wheel and an old she-goat goes there representing more humanity and with more authority than all the high hats in the world.

It's sincerity versus diplomacy.

Viva Gandhi.

                                Yours,
                                Will Rogers.

1607   MR. ROGERS'S COMMENT RUNS
CHIEFLY TO NEWS OF GANDHI

BEVERLY HILLS, Cal., Sept. 16. — So Mayor Walker stood Mahatma Gandhi up and went to a night club instead. As our southern mothers always said, "Raising will tell."

Gandhi, on viewing Buckingham Palace all illuminated, said: "What an extravagance for a country trying to balance its budget!"

Mr. Hoover has just appointed a "home building conference." Why not call a moratorium on the mortgages of the ones we got?

Every McPherson marriage unearths a batch of old worn-out sweethearts.

Yours,
Will Rogers.

1608   MR. ROGERS REVIEWS THE BOUT
        BETWEEN HUEY LONG AND TEXAS

BEVERLY HILLS, Cal., Sept. 17. — Texas had just lost a war to Governor Murray, so when Governor Long said they had been influenced by the lobbyists, why they called him a "liar," by resolution. (That's like calling you a liar by mail.)

Nothing makes a man or a body of men as mad as the truth. If there is no truth in it they laugh it off.

Now Texas is going to raise all the cotton she can and be worse broke next fall than this, just to spite Long, because he had the only real cotton idea that's been suggested.

Yours,
Will Rogers.

1609   ROGERS THINKS AMMUNITION
        THE ONLY WAY TO FREEDOM

BEVERLY HILLS, Cal., Sept. 18. — Poor little Gandhi, he is becoming discouraged with the London Conference. He says they only talk. I wonder if he thought a nation got independence over a conference table and not over a gun barrel. Where would we have been if Washington had conferred instead of confiscating? Didn't a Missouri Senator set the Philippines free this Summer? And Pat Hurley went over and annexed 'em again. Ammunition beats persuasion when you are looking for freedom.

Yours,
Will Rogers.

1610   Mr. Rogers Sets Forth His Views
         On The Far East Row And Polo

SANTA MONICA, Cal., Sept. 20. — Japan has been trying to match a war with China for years. Looks like they finally made it. Russia is rehearsing to get in. This Manchuria must be a pretty valuable country. Now we will see how strong the League of Nations are.

Did you read what that Argentine polo team did to America? Andrada, a real cowpuncher, was the whole show. It was a great thing for polo. The social register has had its last hold on the game. The next American team will know no more about pouring tea than a marine.

Yours,
Will Rogers.

1611   Mr. Rogers Thinks It Is Time
         That A Smart Man Came Along

BEVERLY HILLS, Cal., Sept. 21. — Something has happened to England's gold standard.

I don't know any more about it than a prominent man knows about relieving depression. I know you can't get any gold out of the Bank of England even with a check from the King indorsed by Gandhi.

We got all the gold over here and look how pretty we are sitting. "Yeah?"

It looks like the financial giants of the world have bungled as much as the diplomats and politicians. This would be a great time in the world for some man to come along that knew something.

Yours,
Will Rogers.

1612   Mr. Rogers Gives His Version
         Of What Happened At Detroit

BEVERLY HILLS, Cal., Sept. 22. — The American Legion did themselves mighty proud by giving the President such a fine reception.

They made him feel he alone was not entirely responsible for the war in China, England's dole, fog over Alaska and Whataman's "it."

He told 'em truthfully that the taxpayers couldn't stand another cash bonus and the boys said:

"O.K., chief, we don't want to cause the taxpayers any hardship, but do you think a glass of beer would be asking too much for our service rendered?"

         Yours,
         Will Rogers.

1613   WILL ROGERS EXPRESSES
     SYMPATHY WITH RAILROADS

ROSWELL, N. M., Sept. 23. — It's two days and two nights here by rail. Flew in here in seven hours in Hal Roach's (the movie comedy producer) private plane, Captain Dickson piloting.

I shouldn't say anything that would in any way be detrimental to the poor railroads, for they are having tough enough sledding. The only thing "riding" the R. R. is the government (with restrictions). If they would lay off and let 'em run 'em their own way maybe the public would come back.

This is the prettiest little town in the West.

         Yours,
         Will Rogers.

1614   MR. ROGERS FLIES INTO A LAND
     OF CONTENTMENT AND PLENTY

OOLAGAH, Okla., Sept. 24. — Flying all morning over stopped-up oil wells, while Venezuala is shipping it in tariff free by the shiploads. Now explain that, here in my old home section. Bins full of wheat and cribs full of corn, fat steers bring what a fat hog used to.

Nobody's got much money, but smoke houses all full of meat, woodpiles are high, Bill Murray to look after our troubles so nothing to do this winter but hibernate and listen over the radio to Wall Street wailing.

         Yours,
         Will Rogers.

1615   WILL ROGERS IS PINCH-HITTING
            FOR ALFALFA BILL MURRAY

CHELSEA, Okla., Sept. 25. — I am in Oklahoma pinch hitting for Governor Murray. He is in St. Louis today fixing the unemployed, tomorrow he is in Little Rock fixing the cotton situation, and I am just waiting around here till sometime when I catch him passing through Okahoma.

He is the Jimmy Walker of Governors.

Middle West never gets very stirred up over prohibition, but they figure now that a man has to have some drinks to go with these prices of farm products.

Yours,
Will Rogers.

1616   MR. ROGERS SINGS: 'HOME FOLKS
            ARE THE BEST FOLKS AFTER ALL'

WINSLOW, Ariz., Sept. 27. — Accompanied by a couple of my kids and a nephew, we are flying back to old Orangejuiceville after a happy day yesterday at a big celebration in Claremore.

It sure was fine to meet all the old home folks. After all, it's the best people that stay at home. It's just the tramps that leave and do the bumming.

It broke all records for an enjoyable day. There wasn't a speech made, and you just can't imagine how glad everybody was. The Chamber of Commerce and some politicians were broken-hearted not to be able to say something, but we kept 'em still.

Yours,
Will Rogers.

1617   MR. ROGERS IS READY TO USE
            MOST ANYTHING FOR MONEY

HOLLYWOOD, Cal., Sept. 28. — To show you what our smart men know, they led us to believe the world was coming to an end when England lost her gold standard. Now we come to find out that things are picking up on what they thought was a calamity.

Other nations are going to silver voluntarily. Sure, use silver for money, use as many things as you can for money, and the more trading and business will be done.

Astor made a fortune trading chewing tobacco for skunk skins.

Poor Bryan, he ran for President just thirty-eight years too soon!

Yours,
Will Rogers.

1618 Mr. Rogers States His Position
On Taxation Of Big Incomes

YUMA, Ariz., Sept. 29. — They are trying to find a scheme to raise more money without hitting big incomes.

Republican's theory is that if you tax big incomes too much you will discourage a man from making so much for himself. Didn't discourage him during the war when income tax ran as high as 70 per cent. Some of the biggest fortunes were made at that rate of income tax.

Any guy that's been lucky enough to have a bucket of water during this two-year drought shouldn't kick on handing out a drink.

Yours,
Will Rogers.

1619 Mr. Rogers Begins To Feel
A Bit Sorry For The Wets

EL PASO, Tex., Sept. 30. — In the old days in a prohibition fight the money used to be with the wets, but nowadays it's all on the other side.

In addition, the great bootlegging interests (which is no longer just a racket but an industry) have joined with the W.C.T.U. Now yesterday's statistics show some new allies. Candy sales have jumped from $150,000,000 to $400,000,000, soft drinks from $50,000,000 to $275,000,000 and ice cream from $55,000,000 to $305,000,000.

So, the poor wet has nothing on his side but his thirst.

Yours,
Will Rogers.

1620   Mr. Rogers Is Entering A Land
That Is Not 'Modern' But Happy

EL PASO, Tex., Oct. 1. — I always send these telegrams from the very place I am, but I am heading down into the wilds of old Mexico and will leave this and a couple of more here as I will be out of touch with what we humorously call civilization.

They don't even have a daily lecture on pyorrhea or know what cigarette will raise or lower your Adam's apple. They're so primitive they have never tasted wood alcohol or know the joys of buying on credit.

They are evidently just a lot of heathens that are happy.

Yours,
Will Rogers.

1621   Will Rogers Offers New Idea
On Cancellation Of Debts

EL PASO, Tex., Oct. 2. — These old big boys work fast and away ahead of time. Big bankers are coming down from New York daily to show President Hoover that the debt moratorium should be extended, maybe a year, maybe five years. They didn't know which, but they were sure they should be canceled entirely. In that way it would make it easier for them to collect the money that was owed them personally.

Mr. Hoover ought to have told 'em, "Boys I will cancel half they owe us if you cancel half they owe you." That would have checked their philanthropy.

Yours,
Will Rogers.

1622   Mr. Rogers Thinks Of One Use
To Which We Can Put Our Gold

EL PASO, Tex., Oct. 4. — Say, what if all the nations go off the gold standard and decide that silver is a metal, too?

This fellow Calles, the ex-President of Mexico, started all this when he declared silver was their national dish. Now all of 'em are joining in.

A nation has the right to declare anything it wants for money—poker chips, possum hides, empty gin bottles, niblicks or canceled Congressmen's checks to bootleggers, as it looks like us and France will have to take our gold and fill our teeth with it.

         Yours,
         Will Rogers.

1623   WILL ROGERS FINDS MEXICO
      READING COOLIDGE'S REFUSAL

EL PASO, Tex., Oct. 5. — Talk about big ranches and a great cattle country, you ought to see this Hearst Babicora ranch in Old Mexico.

Takes a week to even fly over it. Lot of grain, grass and tens of thousands of fat cattle.

The first news of the outside world I have seen was a Mexican sitting under a mesquite bush reading the Saturday Evening Post about Coolidge's not running. His refusals are getting longer every year.

         Yours,
         Will Rogers.

1624   WILL ROGERS FINDS IN MEXICO
      AN EXAMPLE OF REAL LOYALTY

EL PASO, Tex., Oct. 6. — Coming in from the Hearst ranch on one of America's unique railroads, the Mexico Northwestern. Been pillaged and robbed by bandits for eighteen years, yet the same people have stayed with it through all this. They could teach many of our concerns a lesson in loyalty.

Here is a queer coincidence. Away down in the wildest part of Mexico, I was told this morning by a peon of the death of Dwight Morrow whom I had met in Mexico and who I had come to think more of than any man in public life I ever met. That's all they are talking about all up the line today. They all say "amigo de Mexico," friend of Mexico.

Yes, and a friend of humanity, too. What a loss!

         Yours,
         Will Rogers.

1625   WILL ROGERS FINDS THAT NEWS
OF REAL INTEREST TRAVELS FAST

EL PASO, Tex., Oct. 7. — News can travel when it's of real interest to the people among whom it travels.

I hadn't heard a thing for eight days—no world series, no word from Al Capone, didn't know Wall Street had shook the small klinkers out, another conference had been held, but the only real thing of future importance that had happened in the eight days was Dwight Morrow's death, and I heard that in the heart of Mexico (and from the heart of Mexico).

I am sorry Mr. Hoover is too busy to attend the funeral. This fellow Morrow was quite a fellow.

Yours,
Will Rogers.

1626   MR. ROGERS IS IN THE FIELD
WITH HIS TICKET FOR 1932

BEVERLY HILLS, Cal., Oct. 8. — Here, why didn't you tell me what this fellow "Pepper" Martin from Oklahoma was doing?

I had been in Mexico all this time and hadn't heard a thing. I would have flew clear there to see that fellow Oklahoman operate. Why, I can't hear a thing of Hoover, Borah, Coolidge, Aimee, Capone or Gandhi.

Well, there was never a time when a man that would "do something" is more appreciated, or a novelty than he is today.

It looks like Governor Murray and Martin in '32.

Yours,
Will Rogers.

1627   WILL ROGERS NOW KNOWS
WHAT A FROZEN ASSET IS

BEVERLY HILLS, Cal., Oct. 9. — After "Pep" Martin fell down on me so hard today there just ain't much to talk about but Mr. Hoover and his "relief for frozen assets." We had heard of all kinds of relief, drought, grasshoppers and potato bug, but the general run of us didn't know that these frozen assets were in such bad shape till this plan came along. In fact, we didn't know what a frozen asset was, but now everything is clear.

If you got a little frozen asset in your house, why the Federal Reserve will take it over.

Everything's "jake" now.

Yours,
Will Rogers.

1628   Mr. Rogers Gives His Version
Of Hoover And The Bankers

SANTA MONICA, Cal., Oct. 11. — Mr. Hoover has had many a tough break during the many weeks he has been in, but just kinder looking it over from all angles, I believe that this last week was his most successful one in a long time. I think he just rounded all those big bankers up and said:

'Now listen, this thing has got past a joke. You birds got to get in here and help me do something. I been helping you out long enough. Now if big business wants a Republican administration, big business better start helping a Republican administration, or else!"

Yours,
Will Rogers.

1629   Mr. Rogers Is Willing To Take
Scents And Berets On The Debt

BEVERLY HILLS, Cal., Oct. 12. — If I had suggested such a "nut" thing I doubt if even my own papers would have run it, but somebody in official life done it on the level—suggested that England pay us her debts in battleships, that they had more than we have.

Now, can you see England bringing over a couple of big dreadnoughts to us and turning the sailors loose on the "dole?"

Why not let Italy pay in spaghetti and France in perfume and berets?

Yours,
Will Rogers.

1630   MR. ROGERS GIVES HIS OPINION
         ON THE POWER OF THE LEAGUE

HOLLYWOOD, Cal., Oct. 13. — Every morning some nation issues Japan an ultimatum to quit fighting China, and every time she gets another ultimatum she sends in another army.

Poor League of Nations! They have written Japan so much they have run out of stationery. She don't even open their notes any more.

That League was a great thing to make the little fellow behave, but when the big fellows want to get away with anything it has no more power than a Senate investigating committee.

Yours,
Will Rogers.

1631   MR. ROGERS FINALLY REVEALS
         WHAT HAS BLIGHTED HIS LIFE

BEVERLY HILLS, Cal., Oct. 14. — As soon as the government lawyers had shown that Al Capone wore silk underwear, why they rested their case. They looked at the jury and figured that would be the most damaging evidence they could bring before 'em.

I don't know if that's the worst charge against Capone, but that about sizes up the condition of the rest of the country. We haven't been any more used to the silk underwear than Capone was and his old cotton is scratching us and that's what we are beefing about.

Yours,
Will Rogers.

1632   WILL ROGERS APPROVES OF MOVE
         TO MAKE MRS. MORROW SENATOR

BEVERLY HILLS, Cal., Oct. 15. — See where Mrs. Morrow has been offered her husband's seat in the Senate if she wants it.

Now, in most cases those positions are offered the wives just out of courtesy, but Mrs. Morrow is just about as unusual a woman as her husband was a man. She was a tremendous item in Mr. Morrow's Mexico success. She learned Spanish and became a great favorite with the Mexican people.

If she goes in there she will know what the Senate is all about. Well, of course, not exactly, but as near as it can be found out.

       Yours,
       Will Rogers.

1633   Rogers Thinks Those 13 Votes
     Significant In The Bid To Us

BEVERLY HILLS, Cal., Oct. 16. — Mexico's whole Cabinet retired whole.

Headline says "Chicago electrocuted four gangsters." Their limousine must have crossed a live wire.

"Harvard bars Aimee from the campus." Harvard must have some smart men to think up all the fool things that school does to get notoriety.

Thirteen nations asked us to join the League to try and help make Japan behave. That number 13 ought to be the tipoff right there to stay out of there.

       Yours,
       Will Rogers.

1634   Mr. Rogers Sees Some Hope
     In The Conviction Of Capone

SANTA MONICA, Cal., Oct. 18. — See where they convicted Al Capone on five counts silk underwear and four others.

Now comes the out on bail, new trial, change of venue, habus corpus, stay of execution and twenty-one other things that the law has invented to hinder justice.

This case is a great boost for Mr. Mellon and his deficit, for if bootleggers and robbers are liable for an income tax, why our treasury will be richer than France.

       Yours,
       Will Rogers.

1635   Will Rogers Remarks

BEVERLY HILLS, Cal., Oct. 19. — Best Edison joke I know was on me. He and Mrs. Edison used to always come to Ziegfeld Follies and I played directly to him with my little jokes for four years before I knew he was deaf. Owen D. Young was making a flowery speech about him at Ford's great dinner at Dearborn. We all got to laughing. Young was mystified. It was Edison making faces and pantomiming that what Young was saying was "hooey." Ford moved his old invention shop to Dearborn, even brought the red New Jersey clay. When Edison first saw it he also noticed the clay. "Gee Henry, where did you get this?" He'd been a great old man even if he never invented anything.

      Yours,
      Will Rogers.

1636 Mr. Rogers Thinks Cornwallis Did His Nation A Good Turn

 BEVERLY HILLS, Cal., Oct. 20. — Been having a big celebration down at Yorktown. The State of Virginia is celebrating their taking over the thirteen colonies from England, eventually losing the management of them to Pennsylvania and Mellon.

 I bet if Cornwallis was alive today he would have entered into the spirit of that celebration, for he just looked ahead 150 years and lost that war on purpose.

 Look at the Philippines. If one of our generals would lose them for us he would be our great national hero.

      Yours,
      Will Rogers.

1637 Mr. Rogers Reports A Deluge Of Praise On His Job Speech

 HOLLYWOOD, Cal., Oct. 21. — I can't answer all the telegrams and letters, but I want to take this means of thanking the most people that ever wired or wrote me on anything—my little speech over the radio for the unemployed—and will send them copies as soon as I can think of what I said. Dozens of community chests want to use it as an ad. Sorry it wasn't the usual "hooey" on the subject, for some paper would have published it and saved me all the trouble.

 What made me feel kinder proud was that while I got after the "big men," yet it was the big men that sent me the fine wires. Mr. Gifford, head of American T. and T. Owen D. Young said, "It was the best speech ever would be made on the subject." Edsel Ford wants a copy for his father.

 I am going over to the flying field to get my good friend, Pat Hurley. Going to try and make him stay all night with me.

      Yours,
      Will Rogers.

1638   Mr. Rogers Interviews Hurley
          On The Big Issues Of The Day

BEVERLY HILLS, Cal., Oct. 22. — Scene in box stall in Rogers home: Secretary of War Hurley eating Rogers's "fodder."

"Mr. Hurley, this is not for publication, but should the Philippines have their freedom?"

"Will, this is a good administration, you see if it ain't."

"Now, Pat, you was in both China and Japan. Just what is their troubles?"

'I'll tell you, Will, Hoover is a very warm, sympathetic man when you know him."

"Mr. Secretary, will that Russian plan work?"

"Listen, Will, they haven't got a soul they can run against us."

So I just fed him and slept him for nothing. The next Cabinet officer pays his board.

Yours,
Will Rogers.

1639   Will Rogers Sees Influence
          Of A Woman On Bernard Shaw

BEVERLY HILLS, Cal., Oct. 23. — Bernard Shaw came out this morning in favor of prohibition. He is also a vegetarian. Shows you what the influence of a good woman will do even on a writer. Lady Astor, a staunch believer in prohibition, accompanied Shaw to Russia.

I read a story of Edison's funeral and I said this is the making of this writer for it was a masterful bit of human reporting. Then I saw it was by Arthur Brisbane.

Well, that was one funeral where you could use up all your eulogies, and then you would only have a few introductory remarks.

Yours,
Will Rogers.

1640   Mr. Rogers Reviews The Events
          Of Recent Days In Washington

HOLLYWOOD, Cal., Oct. 25. — This man Laval, who is mighty ably representing the great French nation, is said to be a self-made Frenchman. (And we thought only Americans were self-made.)

Well, he was just getting along great with Mr. Hoover, as they had said that they had no "real business" to transact.

But then, unfortunately for Monsieur Laval, he run into our Prime Minister, Mr. Borah, who has charge of our foreign affairs. Typical Frenchman had met a typical American. And mere compliments ceased.

          Yours,
          Will Rogers.

1641   Mr. Rogers Takes Cognizance
      Of A New York State Issue

 BEVERLY HILLS, Cal., Oct. 26. — Governor Roosevelt of New York was sponsoring a bill in the State for reforestation and Al Smith said it was unwise, wrong in principle, entirely without precedent, wholly undesirable, misleading, confusing and badly drafted.

 He didn't exactly want to find fault, but he just couldn't hardly reconcile himself to agree with it in its entirety on account of them both being members of the same great political party.

 Well, Laval is gone. His trip was a success. He had never seen Washington before.

          Yours,
          Will Rogers.

1642   Mr. Rogers Gives Expression
      To A Few Navy Day Thoughts

 BEVERLY HILLS, Cal., Oct. 27. — Well, this was Navy Day. We celebrated it this year by lopping off its appropriations.

 Wake up some morning with a war on our hands, then the mad rush will be on to build ships. Give the companies big bonuses to get 'em done quick. Then, we will have to go through that silk-shirt buying period again.

 England is a pretty wise old bird. She relinquished her world's financial supremacy, but she didn't relinquish any ships. Shows which she thinks is the most valuable to a country.

          Yours,
          Will Rogers.

1643   Mr. Rogers Sees In Britain
              A Lesson For The G. O. P. Here

BEVERLY HILLS, Cal., Oct. 28. — Father O'Donnell, head of the great Notre Dame University, did me the honor of a visit out to the "lean to" here yesterday, and, by the way, he says constant usage makes a thing correct and that "Notre Dame" is O.K., and the ones that try to say "Notrey Dom" is all wet. He says Anderson is doing a great job of coaching in Rockne's place.

No business or school is bigger than the head of it, and you just have to meet this fellow and chat with him to see why that school prospered.

See what happened in England. No matter what government or party is in, if you have your election during the hard times they will throw 'em out on their ears. The Republicans have just got from now till next Summer to make things look better or out in the alley they go.

                              Yours,
                              Will Rogers.

1644   Mr. Rogers Is Out To Round Up
             2 Strays From The Home Corral

DOUGLAS, Ariz., Oct. 29. — Early in the autumn, Mrs. Rogers and I sent two sons away supposedly to schools. (We got tired trying to get 'em up in the morning.) One went north, here in this State; another to New Mexico. Since then we have received no word or letter.

We have looked in every football team all over the country. Guess they couldn't make the teams, knew their education was a failure and kept right on going.

Any news from any source will be welcome.

I am flying to Mexico City today. The big one spoke Spanish, so maybe he is there. The little one didn't even speak English, but he loved chili and hot tamales, so he may be there, too.

                              Yours,
                              Will Rogers.

1645   WILL ROGERS, AFTER AIR TRIP,
FINDS MEXICO LOOKS 'FINE'

MEXICO CITY, Oct. 30. — Hal Roach, Eric Pedley, the great international polo player; Captain Dickson and I had a wonderful flight here from Los Angeles in Mr. Roach's plane. I sure do like this country, and this is one of the greatest cities in the world.

Am mighty glad to report everything here looks fine. A few changes in cabinet positions but no disturbances whatever.

Going out right now to visit my old friend ex-President Calles. He is still here, quite a bit here. When Mr. Morrow and myself sized him up here four years ago we said he was not only the strongest man in Mexico, but pretty near anywhere.

                                      Yours,
                                        Will Rogers.

1646   MR. ROGERS FINDS A NEW LOW
ON HIS VISIT TO MEXICO CITY

MEXICO CITY, Nov. 1. — Did you ever spend a lonesome hour in a strange town?

You all think you have, but you haven't. The lonesomest hour in the entire world is in Mexico City and Madrid, Spain, on Sunday afternoon between the hours of 4 and 5 when everyone has gone to the bull fights.

I am not against it. Every nation for their own affairs and own sports. Some nations like to see blood and some to see their victims suffer from speculation. It's all in your point of view.

They kill the bull very quick. Wall Street lets you live and suffer.

                                      Yours,
                                       Will Rogers.

1647   MR. ROGERS FINDS THAT MEXICO
IS DOING PLENTY OF THINGS

MEXICO CITY, Nov. 2. — Following Dwight Morrow is not my idea of a soft job, but this American Ambassador Clark we got here is doing it, and great, too. They like him here.

He thinks Mexico is in better shape politically than in many years, and say, it's not all bullfights here.

Mexico's famous university plays Tulsa Saturday, Memphis' baseball team is here and the Mexican army is sending a great polo team to California.

Studios are making their own movies.

Yours,
Will Rogers.

1648   MR. ROGERS IS BACK IN THE STATES
         AND HEARS OF A NEW COMMISSION

SAN ANTONIO, Tex., Nov. 3. — Just flew in here from Mexico City by two good lines, the Pan American to Brownsville and American Airways to here.

That's a great valley down in that lower end of Texas, but did you know there is a mess of Republicans down in there? The rest of Texas is ashamed of 'em and got 'em segregated away off down there to themselves like some towns do vice.

I been away a few days, but I see by the papers Mr. Hoover's got a new commission. This is one of the most unique ones of all. He has appointed it to find out "if he storied about the navy or if he didn't."

Yours,
Will Rogers.

1649   MR. ROGERS FINDS THREE TOWNS
         THAT ARE NOT STANDARDIZED

SAN ANTONIO, Tex., Nov. 4. — I aways told you that there was just three towns in the whole of America that was different and distinct, New Orleans, Frisco and San Antonio. They each got something that even the most persistent chamber of commerce can't standardize.

Say, what do you know about the Democrats walking away with the next Congress? I am going to try and get out here in the mesquite brush about eighty miles at Uvalde, Texas, and see an old prairie dog, Jack Garner, that is going to be the next Speaker of the House, and funny thing, he was Nick's best friend.

Yours,
Will Rogers.

1650   Mr. Rogers Finds A Real Ranch
               And Real Cow Hands In Texas

KINGSVILLE, Tex., Nov. 5. — Down on the great King ranch, biggest in the whole Southwest, and I did my best acting today trying to look and act like a cowboy on Bob Kleberg's best cutting horse, and hanging on by my teeth.

Both Kleberg girls dragged calves up to the fire faster than I ever could.

This is a real outfit. If you think there ain't any more real cowboys in this country, you're crazy.

Flew down here with the flying Laphams and Frank Hawks. Mother Lapham flying her own plane, Papa Lapham his, Baby Lapham his, each Lapham servant their own.

                            Yours,
                            Will Rogers.

1651   Rogers Visits Jack Garner,
               And Learns About Pecans

NORTH UVALDE, Tex., Nov. 6. — Here I am in this beautiful little western town. Flew in here from the King Ranch to spend the afternoon with a man who you are going to hear more of in the next few months than any man in America. That's just plain Jack Garner, who will almost surely be the next Speaker of the great House of Representatives.

I never did go in much for this typical American stuff, but this fellow in his career and his home life will come pretty near living up to what we think one is. His only regret, and this is no bull either, in going back to Washington this time is how he and his wife will miss Nick Longworth. That alone almost keeps him from being typical anything. He raises famous soft-shell pecans. He gave me some and I just found out what a soft-shell pecan is. It's one you can crack with just a small hammer.

When I got here he was practicing with a gavel.

                            Yours,
                            Will Rogers.

1652   MR. ROGERS FINDS WE ARE BACK
         WHERE WE STARTED ON THE NAVY

BEVERLY HILLS, Cal., Nov. 8. — Mr. Hoover's navy jury set him free. Mr. Gardiner's jury set him free. Now we are right where we are in all our investigations. Just where we started from.

The only way we will ever find out who is right is to have a war. If we are ready for it, Hoover is right; if we are not, Gardiner is right. And wars are just like depressions, they come when you least expect 'em.

We lost a lot of common sense and a lot of well needed humor in the Senate when we lost Caraway of Arkansaw. It was a pleasure to watch him walk up and down the aisle, like Felix the Cat, and then bump the Republicans off with just one short remark.

Yours,
Will Rogers.

1653   MR. AND MRS. ROGERS GET, AT LAST,
         THE USUAL WORD FROM THE BOYS

HOYLWOOD, Cal., Nov. 9. — Well, I got home and we heard from the boys. Yes, on the first of the month they remembered us. They arrived at their schools O. K. If their remittance is in proportion to their grades I am not going to have such a tough year at that.

And, here is a warning to the world at large. Please quit sending me by either mail, telegram, booklet, volumes or word of mouth schemes to end the depression. Just go ahead and end it without any aid from me and then you can wire me word collect that you have done it.

Yours,
Will Rogers.

1654   MR. ROGERS IS A BIT PUZZLED
         BY THE FAR EAST'S NEAR-WAR

BEVERLY HILLS, Cal., Nov. 10. — We can't tell from this morning's press which nation has declared war on the other, China or Japan. Each wants to make it appear that the other was the aggressor. It always helps out in your recruiting and your patriotism if you can make your own people believe you was the one pounced on.

I think the only real diplomacy ever performed by a diplomat is in deceiving their own people after their dumbness has got them into a war.

Yours,
Will Rogers.

1655   WILL ROGERS SAYS

BEVERLY HILS, Cal., Nov. 11. — Old Hollywood is just like a desert water hole in Africa. Hang around long enough and every kind of animal in the world will drift in for refreshments.

Yesterday there came a mess of newspaper men from all over our destitute land on their yearly periodical. There wasn't an odorless breath in a carload. They are supposed to be holding business meetings, but the meetings are with our female scream scars. The "moulders of public opinion" have been moulded into the "orgies" of Hollywood.

Yours for a respectable press,
Will Rogers.

1656   MR. ROGERS HAILS A DEMOCRAT
         WHO BOBS UP WITH 'GOOD IDEAS'

BEVERLY HILLS, Cal., Nov. 12. — Barney Baruch, about the lone sole survivor of what was once our boasted "big-men period," and along with Calvin Coolidge being the only two men that knew the "bubble" was going to bust right in our face, advocated in a speech Wednesday "increase in income tax in the higher brackets," "sales tax on all but necessities," "no debt cancellation."

These Democrats are always bobbing up with some good ideas.

Yours,
Will Rogers.

1657   WILL ROGERS SEES REHEARSAL
         FOR A REAL WAR IN MANCHURIA

BEVERLY HILLS, Cal., Nov. 13. — Somebody foolishly invited the newspaper editors from all over to come out here and now we can't get rid of 'em.

Vice President Curtis is still prowling around here from one studio to another. I can't tell if he wants to get in the movies or is just trying to find a Republican.

The Japanese and Chinamen haven't officially declared war yet. All this killing and fighting is just rehearsing in case war should be declared. If you get killed now it don't count.

                        Yours,
                        Will Rogers.

1658   Mr. Rogers Cites The Difference Between Grandi And Gandhi

SANTA BARBARA, Cal., Nov. 15. — Japan has picked China out an emperor for Manchuria. That's about like Al Capone picking out prohibition enforcement officers for Mr. Hoover.

Gandhi gets in today. Don't get Grandi mixed up with Gandhi. Gandhi has practically no wardrobe and carries his own goat for milk. Grandi is dressed like a diplomat, including whiskers, and carries his own grape vine.

Gandhi went to England to get liberty for his country. Grandi comes to get —?—?—?— from Hoover. Both missions will be equally successful.

                        Yours,
                        Will Rogers.

1659   Will Rogers Tells Of A Way To Enjoy Nap And Aid Idle

BEVERLY HILLS, Cal., Nov. 16. — Watch your local movie theatres for the date they are giving their unemployment benefits, with the proceeds going to your own locality. That's a big thing, and should raise a lot of money. Go, even if it's my picture and you have to sleep through it. I always holler at the end of each one, so it wakes everybody up and let's 'em know it's over.

Say, this new home building idea of Mr. Hoover's sounds good. They are working out a lot of beneficial things. The only thing is it took 'em so long to think of any of 'em. We ought to have plans in case of depression, just like we do in case of fire, "Walk, don't run, to the nearest exit."

                        Yours,
                        Will Rogers.

1660   MR. ROGERS HAS HIS OWN IDEAS
        REGARDING THE GRANDI VISIT

BEVERLY HILLS, Cal., Nov. 17. — The steamship lines must be giving tourist rates to foreign diplomats. There is no other way of accounting for 'em all coming over. Poor Washington, D. C., can't hardly tell what flag to hang out.

This fellow Grandi, I remember him from the London disarmament conference last year. He just sit there and watched France. Now he is here to find out if Laval got anything for France. If she didn't, why he don't want anything, but if she did he wants a helping out of the same dish.

You talk about actors being jealous. You haven't seen any jealousy till you watch diplomats work.

Yours,
Will Rogers.

1661   WILL ROGERS GIVES HIS OWN OPINION
        AS TO WHAT IS INTERESTING NEWS

BEVERLY HILLS, Cal., Nov. 18. — Of all the items we had in the papers this morning, including "China Attacks Japanese Troops", "Japanese Attack Chinese Troops," "Grandi and Hoover Confer Informally," "American Exports Hit by Prince of Wales's Appeal to Use Only British Goods," "United States Congressmen Visiting Canada Highly Endorse Sales Tax and Other Canadian Customs," the one lone item that appealed to everybody was that poor fellow with the hiccoughs.

Everybody is more interested in him than the League of Nations, disarmament and the investigation of Jimmy Walker.

Yours,
Will Rogers.

1662   MR. ROGERS' THOUGHTS POLITICAL
        AS HE FLIES INTO A SNOWSTORM

MEDFORD, Ore., Nov. 19. — Breezing along over the snow-capped mountains of Northern California. Breakfast in Beverly, dinner in Seattle. There is nothing more beautiful in America than looking down on this redwood highway.

Say, Texas has got a chance next Tuesday to put the Democratic Congressional majority over the top and cinch Garner for Speaker if they elect Kleberg at San Antonio. I would like to see a real cowpuncher get in there, even if he was a Republican.

Say, we are running into a snowstorm and may have to set her down at Medford, but you can always trust a good airline pilot. This one has flown this route five years.

Yours,
Will Rogers.

P. S. And we did set her down here.

1663   WILL ROGERS DECIDES TO GO ON, KNOWING THREE CHINESE WORDS

SEATTLE, Wash., Nov. 20. — I was just handed a special press dispatch by the Centralia Daily Chronicle at Centralia, Washington, that China and Japan had agreed to an armistice in Manchuria. I told you if I went over there I could have the boys out of the trenches by Christmas, but I didn't think I could do it by Thanksgiving.

I have already learned to pronounce two towns and one General's name, so I am not going to turn back now. Besides I will just get there for the "after-war prosperity." Remember ours?

Yours,
Will Rogers.

1664   MR. ROGERS TELLS OF POSSIBILITY OF A WAR ON THE HIGH SEAS

S. S. EMPRESS OF RUSSIA, Via San Francisco, Nov. 22. — On the Empress of Russia, the Soviet perhaps call it now Lenin's ferry, with my old friend Floyd Gibbons. If I had the world to pick from there is no one I would rather go with. I met him in Warsaw, Poland, in '26 when we were covering Pilsudski's revolution.

On the train with Floyd crossing Canada from the East was twenty-two Chinamen going home on this boat. When I saw old Field Marshal Gibbons with twenty-two Chinamen I appointed myself master of ceremonies of twenty Japanese who are also on the boat going home.

We may have some news for you any day now as this Gibbons-Rogers war is not under the supervision of the League of Nations.
Yours,
Will Rogers.
P. S. — Bless this ocean for being quiet today.

1665   MR. ROGERS FINDS HIS 'ARMY'
OUTNUMBERED AND PLANS A COUP

ABOARD S. S. EMPRESS OF RUSSIA, Nov. 23. — Floyd Gibbons, being a real newspaper man, he don't get up. He naturally thought that his 22 Chinamen were the only ones passengers.

Well, I got to stirring around and I found 225 more, making nearly 250 in all against my 20 Japs. So, I am going to trade commands with him before he knows about these extra Chinese.

Everything is pretty peaceful so far except some Chinese college boys that lost on Notre Dame.

We got some missionaries on here going out to make all the world good and pure like us.
Yours,
Will Rogers.

1666   MR. ROGERS FINDS FAN TAN
IS THE OLD CHINESE ARMY GAME

ABOARD S. S. EMPRESS OF RUSSIA, Nov. 24. — I went below decks to drill my Chinese army today but I couldn't get 'em away from a fan tan game.

We call 'em heathen, eh? You play with 'em and see how heathen they are. They will have these missionaries' red underwear before they get to Shanghai. Clara, this would have been no game for you. And speaking of movies, I see by this morning's paper you can pretty near tell who is the highest-priced female screen star of each year by seeing who the Marquee de Coudray is married to.

Say, cable me who won the Texas election today and tell me which one of my friends will be speaker, Tilson or Garner.
Yours,
Will Rogers.

1667   Mr. Rogers Comes Pretty Near
         Not Having A Thanksgiving Day

ABOARD S. S. EMPRESS OF RUSSIA, Nov. 25. — When you reach the 180th meridian west you lost a whole day. Don't ask me why. It's all Wickersham to me.

If you come back this way you get it back. If you don't you just lose it. The way days are now it don't look like it's worth coming back for.

We go to bed tomorrow night, Thursday, and wake up Saturday, maybe. We come pretty near losing Thursday, Thanksgiving. Guess lots of folks wish they could skip this Thanksgiving. Getting less cause for it every year. It's just about a bust with everybody that don't raise turkeys or cranberries to sell.

Yours,
Will Rogers.

1668   Will Rogers Learns A Lot
         In A Storm On The Pacific

ABOARD S. S. EMPRESS OF RUSSIA, Nov. 27. — You know I told you we was going to lose a day for no other reason than to make somebody's calendar come out even. Well, we lost a day. We gained a typhoon. We lost a lifeboat and I lost my whole internal possessions. An old Oklahoma prairie product has no business on this ocean when it's washing away lifeboats. Brother, you get quite a spring freshet.

Gibbons was broken hearted when we got through it alive, for it spoiled a good story for him.

I already found out enough on this trip to warrant coming, and that is that if America will stay home and take care of our own business we need never fear Japan if she has to cross this ocean to get to us. If we can't lick a seasick soldier then we deserve to lose.

Yours,
Will Rogers.

1669   Mr. Rogers Discusses The News
         Of Walker And The Mooney Case

ABOARD S. S. EMPRESS OF RUSSIA, Nov. 29. — I been reading where Mayor Jimmy Walker was trying to get Tom Mooney out of jail. I believe if I was in jail and winter like this coming on I would whisper to my friend, "Get me out, but not till Spring."

Jim ought to get Mooney out of jail. Mooney got Jimmy out of New York. But Jimmy don't have to be afraid of a Republican investigating committee in New York. One has never yet been able to find out even where the committee was meeting at.

Yours,
Will Rogers.

1670   MR. ROGERS IS ADDLED A BIT
          BY THE COURSE HE IS TAKING

ABOARD S. S. EMPRESS OF RUSSIA, Nov. 30. — Yesterday we lost a whole day, so the argument has come up when is it back home? We not only don't know what hour it is back there but we don't know what day it is, and some of us are even doubtful about the week, and Gibbons don't know what year it is.

It's Sunday here. We just come from services on the boat but they say it's only Saturday at home. Everybody is at civil war arguing over it, so please wire what time it is at home.

Everything is cockeyed to us, anyhow, for here we are traveling straight west to get to the Far East. Japan, the land of the rising sun, is where it sets.

Yours,
Will Rogers.

1671   MR. ROGERS IS REALLY GLAD
          DAWES HAS STOPPED THE WAR

ABOARD S. S. EMPRESS OF RUSSIA, Dec. 1. — This ocean is just as innocent looking today, just like it hadn't done a thing.

We have followed the great circle route and swung away up north. If we had gone ashore I would have been telling my Republican jokes to an Eskimo, and I expect the Republicans wish they was with the Eskimos about now.

This morning's wireless reports Mix better, which is good news. He has given many a grown-up and all kids a thrill. In 1905 at Madison Square Garden Tom and I made our New York horseback debut with Zack Mulhall's Wild West.

Sure glad Charley Dawes has stopped this war and I can change it into a kimona shopping tour of Japan and China.

Yours,
Will Rogers.

1672   Mr. Rogers Thinks Of A Job,
        Just A Chore, For Congress

ABOARD S. S. EMPRESS OF RUSSIA, Dec. 2. — Look on your map and find Kamchatka. It's part of Siberia. Well, we was just grazing it all day yesterday.

There ought to be a law against making an ocean this wide. That's something Congress can take up at the next session, as they won't have anything to settle much, outside of unemployment, two billion deficit, arrange extra taxes where they will do least harm next November, relieve Wall Street and think up something new to promise farmers.

Narrowing an ocean will be just a chore for this Congress.

Yours,
Will Rogers.

1673   Mr. Rogers Sends First Story
        On The War From Shipboard

ABOARD S. S. EMPRESS OF RUSSIA, Dec. 3. — Here is the best war story and it happened on this boat.

This Fall a Chinaman working on the boat who evidently knew how big China's population was asked about the war from a radio man, "How she go war?"

The radio guy, kidding him, said, 'Yesterday Chinese lost 500 men, Japanese three men."

Next day the Chinaman was back again, "Catchem mo news?"

Sure, Chinese lost 600 men, Japanese two men."

Third day: "What air say bout war today?" The answer was, "Chinese lost 700, Japanese lost one man."

The Chinaman was pleased and said, "Pletty soon be no Japanese left."

Yours,
Will Rogers.

1674   WILL ROGERS IN JAPAN TO STUDY
        GEISHA GIRLS AND DIPLOMATS

ABOARD THE S. S. EMPRESS OF RUSSIA, Dec. 4. — Now don't get me mixed up on this Oriental pilgrimage with this fellow Floyd Gibbons. He is a war man and is over to tell you about them. That ain't my business over here at all. I am a peace man. I haven't got any use for wars and there is no more humor in 'em than there is reason for 'em. Get your war news from Gibbons and your Geisha girl news from Rogers.

I am over here "scouting for Ziegfeld's Follies" and I want to see where they train these Japanese diplomats that go to an international conference and bring home everything but the desk that the treaty was signed on.

That's all we got to show for the Washington disarmament conference was the desk, and we will perhaps lose it at the next one.

Yours,
Will Rogers.

1675   MR. ROGERS, A REAL COUNTRYMAN,
        LIVES UP TO ALL EXPECTATIONS

TOKYO, Dec. 6. — Well, sir, yesterday on the boat before we steamed into Yokohama, I got the first indication that the depression had really turned the corner.

A professional Scotch golf player deliberately and with malice aforethought drove six golf balls from the deck away out into the ocean.

Talk about a "rube" in town. I got off the boat last night standing rubbering at everything with my mouth open and got run over by a ricksha. That's a taxicab propelled by a man.

Yours,
Will Rogers.

1676   WILL ROGERS FINALLY SIZES UP
        THE SITUATION IN MANCHURIA

TOKYO, Dec. 7. — After drinking at least two barrels of tea and wanting to be fair, here is about how Manchuria looks to me:

Will Rogers (center) with Governor General of the Philippines Dwight Filley Davis and eldest daughter, Alice Davis (left), during travels to Japan and China in December, 1931.

China owns the lot. Japan owns the house that's on it. Now who should have the policemen? China is trying to save its country, Japan is trying to save its investments, the League of Nations is trying to save its face.

Now somebody has got to lose.

Yours,
Will Rogers.

1677   WILL ROGERS FLIES OVER JAPAN
       ON HIS WAY TO MANCHURIA

OSAKA, Dec. 8. — Flying from Japan to Manchuria.

Every man, woman and Democrat in the world have seen pictures of Japan's famous mountain peak with the snow on the top, Mount Fujiyama, but think of flying around him. We come by him this afternoon, and what a beautiful country this is to fly over.

I didn't know Japan was so mountainous. Had old Gibbons rubbering for a landing field but there wasn't any.

This is just one of the villages of Japan. It only has two million. The papers here tonight predict a fight at Chinchow.

Yours,
Will Rogers.

1678   MR. ROGERS LANDS IN A COUNTRY
       NEW TO HIM AND FINDS ODD HATS

KAIJO, Dec. 9. — Well, here we are in a whole different country—Korea, and this is the capital. Flew down the inland passage from Kobe to Nagasaki, and it was beautiful; then from Japan to the mainland of Asia, across the Sea of Japan, about 150 miles, and oh say, I found people that have funnier hats than the Princess Eugenie kind you are wearing back home. It's the Korean men, the peasants. It's a sort of old black cab driver's derby, but it's made of screen netting like the thing we used to keep over cheese in the Claremore grocery store.

Yours,
Will Rogers.

1679   WILL ROGERS REACHES DAIREN
AND SEES RELICS OF OTHER WARS

DAIREN, Dec. 10. — Gibbons quit me and took the locomotive. These Japanese pilots were flying too close to the tops of the rice fields to suit him.

Had a great flight in here to Dairen, the most modern city and port you ever saw, and spent the afternoon visiting historic old Port Arthur of Russia-Japanese war fame, the birthplace of Japan and the graveyard of old Russia.

If I can't find this present war I can find where some of the others were fought. I am only two wars behind.

Yours,
Will Rogers.

1680   ROGERS FINDS COLD WEATHER
BUT NO WARFARE IN MUKDEN

MUKDEN, Dec. 11. — This is the famous Mukden in Manchuria where all your news comes from. The Chinese army evacuated the city and the American newspaper men moved in. They have been here so long and times are so tough that about half the banditry committed is by them.

They got no American news until I mushed in over the snow today. They did not know old General Ma Garner, with 220 Democrats had marched on Washington.

No war today, cold weather.

Yours,
Will Rogers.

1681   MR. ROGERS BEGS TO ANNOUNCE
THAT HE HAS THE WAR STOPPED

MUKDEN, Dec. 13. — I got this war stopped if the League of Nations don't start it again.

I am leaving this afternoon for Harbin in North Manchuria. That is supposed to be the liveliest and most unique town in all the Far East. It's in Chinese territory and a Soviet railroad headquarters, also the refuge of the old Czar Russians.

And, say, do you know this whole country of Siberia looks just like Oklahoma and the farmers are just as bad off?

Yours,
Will Rogers.

1682   MR. ROGERS FINDS IN HARBIN
          THE REAL CAUSE OF THE WAR

HARBIN, Dec. 14. — This is Harbin. It's 32 below. Horses wearing snowshoes. Vodka is not a beverage, but a necessity. Wild dog fur is kolensky. The American consul-general is the emperor of Manchuria.

I got on a fur hat that looks like Daniel Boone. And what do you think I found? A war? A revolution? No! "Abie's Irish Rose." Played by Russians and Chinese combined. What more cause could there be for a war?

But don't miss this town.

Yours,
Will Rogers.

1683   MR. ROGERS OFFERS TO RELIEVE
          LEAGUE OF BIG JOB AT HALF PAY

MUKDEN, Dec. 15. — League of Nations is sending here a commission to look over the ground. That's like a sheriff examining the stall after the horse has disappeared.

Now, I am here on the ground and can do that and for half the money and will send in the same report they will, only shorter.

By the way, up in Harbin Saturday I was offered the governorship of North Manchuria by General Ma, so if the League wants me they will have to act quick, which, of course, they can't.

Yours,
Will Rogers.

1684   MR. ROGERS IS PESSIMISTIC
          ON THE MANCHURIAN MUDDLE

MUKDEN, Japan, Dec. 16. — America could hunt all over the world and not find a better fight to keep out of.

There is only two things certain out here. The Manchurian problem won't be settled this year or next. The second certainty is any commission that tries it will wind up in wrong with both sides.

We don't belong to the League. They are the ones that are refereeing it, and we have yet to referee a fight successfully. But, of course, we will join 'em and get in wrong. It's too big an opportunity to lose.

Yours,
Will Rogers.

1685   Mr. Rogers Takes No Chances
            With Those Chinese Brigands

DAIREN, Dec. 17. — Good joke on me. I had my ticket all bought today to go from Mukden to Peiping on the railroad, but that's the one the bandits have been working on. I figured my jokes wouldn't go so good out in this snow waiting for Claremore, Okla., to ransom me out, so I am taking roundance on 'em with a boat.

I am going to join those students in China if I can find some of my old Oxford fraternity pins.

This war ain't quite over yet. Wait till you read about next week at Chinchow. Now, remember that.

Yours,
Will Rogers.

1686   Soya Beans And Cabinets
            Point To A Moral For Rogers

DAIREN, Dec. 18. — Plenty of excitement in these countries. Japan's Cabinet resigned, China's resigned. It's funny we can't ever have any luck like that.

Human nature and intelligence is about the same. Chinese have planted a new, big crop of soya beans and they haven't sold the last two years' crop. Don't that sound exactly like the wheat and cotton farmers at home? Yet we call these heathen. Yeah!

Yours,
Will Rogers.

1687   Mr. Rogers's Disillusionment
            Increases As He Gets About

DAIREN, Dec. 20. — They got a new gag in Europe now to help along their argument that America should cancel the debts. They are appealing to our egotism (and they figure we are not short on it).

The new gag is "America won the war and she should pay. We admit that it was America coming in when she did that determined the destiny of the World War. Therefore, she is answerable for present European conditions, and should put them right."

Now, ain't that a hot one? No matter what you do, you are wrong. If you help 'em lose it you are wrong, if you help 'em win it you are wrong.

There just ain't any such animal as international "good-will." It just lasts till the loan runs out.

Yours,
Will Rogers.

1688 WILL ROGERS FINDS A COUNTRY
      THAT IS WORSE OFF THAN OURS

TIENTSIN (via Tokyo), Dec. 21. — My Peiping press cards are no good in China so the Advertiser is relaying this through Tokyo.

Been bobbing around for the last three days on one of China's oceans in a boat just six inches longer than a Ford, trying to get from Manchuria here.

Run into a storm and had to turn back and go into Port Arthur harbor for the night, but did get here and finally found a country worse off than we are. How's that for an accomplishment? And, for the same reason as us, overproduction.

Pardon me for trying to get humor from a serious situation, but when a country bigger and more fertile than the whole State of Texas changes hands, yet war is not declared on either side, and five months later the League sends a jury out to see how it was done, now there is a laugh in there somewhere.

Yours,
Will Rogers.

1689 MR. ROGERS FINDS A CRYING NEED
      IN THE CHINESE SCHEME OF THINGS

PEIPING, Dec. 22. — Vice-President Marshall found what America needed. I can tell you what the Orient needs.

Don't bring a lot of clothes. You can get anything here, toilet articles, cigarettes, shoes, Scotch, and all American standard equipment.

But for mercy sakes bring a pillow—one with feathers in it. These out here are stuffed with rice, which wouldn't be so bad if they had cooked it first.

Yours,
Will Rogers.

1690   Mr. Rogers Finds An Argument
For Preparedness In China

PEIPING, Dec. 23. — The American missionaries have taught the Chinese to not fight but rely on the Lord. The Chinese diplomats have taught the people to rely on the League, but now they feel that both have fallen down on 'em.

This is a time in the history of the world when you better be pretty well prepared or you won't get anywhere.

Yours,
Will Rogers.

1691   Mr. Rogers Is A Big Navy Man
After Looking Around In China

PEIPING, Dec. 24. — Get a lot of British news over here in the papers. She may be off the gold standard but she has got a navy that will make the other nations think a long time before they start throwing rocks at her.

When a British warship steams into these ports she anchors just close enough in to give the local Congress and Senate a real view of what a dreadnaught is. When you see those guns pointing at you you don't ask whether they are on a gold, silver, waste paper or zinc basis.

With that navy Nicaragua could go on a banana basis and still be cock of the walk.

Merry Christmas.

Yours,
Will Rogers.

1692   Mr. Rogers Looks Into Future
Of Two Nations Of The Far East

PEIPING, Dec. 25. — Had a long talk with the young Marshal Chang Si Liang. He was the war lord of Manchuria and all Manchuria, spoke English and was a very pleasant young fellow.

One thing you got to say about these Chinese. They are good losers. There is no yapping or excuses.

He thinks that China will eventually absorb the Japanese the same as they absorbed the Mongolians who captured China so much they got tired.

> Yours,
> *Will Rogers.*

1693   MR. ROGERS FINDS CHRISTMAS DAY
IN CHINA IS A DREARY AFFAIR

SHANGHAI, Dec. 27. — I didn't know that Christmas did mean so much till you have to spend one away off like this from home.

I don't know when these Chinese have Christmas but it wasn't on the twenty-fifth. Course, Shanghai, where I am now, is supposed to be the livest town east of Suez, but all the false whoopee in the world don't make up for the old Christmas tree at home and there is thousands of 'em out here feel the same way.

> Yours,
> *Will Rogers.*

1694   MR. ROGERS FINDS THE JAPANESE
RUN THEIR WAR ON SCHEDULE

SHANGHAI, Dec. 28. — Papers says the Japanese are marching on Chinchow.

Didn't I tell you last week they was going to take it about Xmas time? When these Japanese run a war they run it on schedule.

That's not a bad Xmas present. This new part they are taking is as big as Oklahoma.

This washes your League of Nations up. This slapped them right in the face.

> Yours,
> *Will Rogers.*

1695   MR. ROGERS GETS THE USUAL GIFT
        FROM SANTA CLAUS IN CHINA

SHANGHAI, Dec. 29. — Got the usual father's or husband's Xmas present from my wife with this card, "You can go to China or Manchuria, but you can't escape the Xmas handkerchief."

Get this for a laugh. Have had a date to interview three different high government officials, and they were all kicked out before I got to 'em.

China is the only country in the world strong enough to have withstood fifty years of misgovernment in a row that the foreigners haven't gobbled up.

But their own educated ones have and it keeps right on being just China.

                              Yours,
                              Will Rogers.

1696   MR. ROGERS FINDS HE KNOWS
        TOO MUCH ABOUT CHINA NOW

SHANGHAI, Dec. 30. — Trouble with me I been in China too long. If I had only stayed a couple of days I would have had a better idea of China. The more folks you talk to, the more you see and the less you know.

Always dodge the "expert who has lived in China and knows China." The last man that knew the Chinese was Confucius, and he died feeling that he was becoming a little confused about 'em.

                              Yours,
                              Will Rogers.

1697   MR. ROGERS LEAVES THE WAR FLAT
        AND THINKS THAT ALL IS SETTLED

ABOARD S. S. PRESIDENT TAFT, Dec. 31. — See by the papers they are evacuating Chinchow without a fight.

That's a good joke on every twenty newspaper boys who have been waiting in Mukden for two months just for this last fight. And, they wanted me to stay over. Goody!

Well, this winds up the war. Japan has got all they want of China and China has certainly got all they want of Japan and the League has got all they want of the whole mess.

                                    Yours,
                                        Will Rogers.

DAILY TELEGRAMS — 1932

1698   WILL ROGERS COULD NOT FIND
              ANY CHOP SUEY IN CHINA

ABOARD S. S. PRESIDENT TAFT, Jan. 1. — Shanghai was a knockout. It's Brooklyn gone English. Say, where did they get this Chinese chop-suey stuff? I have run the legs off every ricksha motorman in China, and nobody ever any more heard of it than Nevada did of Volstead.

Another hoax was that a Chinaman's word was as good as his bond. Well, that goes with the chop suey. That might have been in the old days, but not since the missionaries and business men come in. Chinese are just as human as anybody now.

                         Yours,
                         Will Rogers.

1699   MR. ROGERS FINDS THE CHINESE
              AND THE DEMOCRATS ARE ALIKE

S. S. PRESIDENT TAFT (via San Francisco), Jan. 3. — I just found out who China is like. It's the Democrats at home. Individually they are smart, likeable and efficient, but let two get together and they both want to be President.

Formed a new government at Nanking yesterday and nobody would let the other be head man, so they called it a committee government. Now everybody is President.

There's a new idea for you Democrats.

                         Yours,
                         Will Rogers.

1700   MR. ROGERS OFFERS A NEW PLAN
              FOR HANDLING THE PHILIPPINES

ABOARD S. S. RAWALPINDI, Jan. 4. — There's few prettier sights than steaming out of beautiful Hongkong Harbor.

I wanted to go by and set the Phillippines free, but being a friend of Hurley's maybe we better let Pat keep 'em awhile.

I am in favor of giving the Philippines their freedom and then us go under their protectorate. That's the only chance I see of us maybe getting an improvement in the government.

>   Yours,
>   *Will Rogers.*

1701   MR. ROGERS, AT SEA, WORKS OUT
            A BRAND NEW TAX PROGRAM

ABOARD S. S. RAWALPINDI, Jan. 5. — What are they doing over home about the sales tax?

That's the best and most equitable tax there is. The gasoline tax, which is nothing but a sales tax, has proven painless, productive and punitive.

Now, if a tax on gasoline keeps up all the roads why wouldn't a tax on light wines and beers keep up the House of Representatives, one on Coca-Cola and Jamaica ginger and Camembert cheese keep up the Senate, White Rock and cracked ice the State Legislatures, and so on on everything that we have to have or hire and make each stay within the budget.

For instance, if people wasn't drinking much beer, we wouldn't have many Congressmen; if toothpaste and facial creams had a slump, why cut the President's salary in proportion.

It looks like a good scheme from over here.

>   Yours,
>   *Will Rogers.*

1702   MR. ROGERS, ASTRIDE THE EQUATOR,
            TRIES A NEW COOLING SYSTEM

SINGAPORE, Jan. 6. — You heard about the equator. Well, here is a town that is straddle of it.

It runs right through my hotel room and in all the beds here they have a long narrow pillow that lays longways. It's supposed to be some aid to you in keeping cool and it's called Dutch wife.

This used to be a wild port, but this Dutch wife is the extent of its devilment now.

>   Yours,
>   *Will Rogers.*

1703   MR. ROGERS FINDS RUBBER FARMS
        AS CHEAP AS KANSAS WHEAT LAND

SINGAPORE, Jan. 7. — Americans used to holler about England having the rubber business.

Well, Uncle Henry Ford and Uncle Harvey Firestone, instead of going in Liberia and Brazil, if you will just cable me an order to check on you I can get you enough rubber ranches here to supply all the punctures for years. They are cheaper than wheat farms in Kansas. Great opportunity!

So, Hen, you and Harvey cable quick.

Yours,
Will Rogers.

1704   ROGERS FINDS GOLD STANDARD
        HURTS OUR FAR EAST SALESMEN

PENANG, Jan. 8. — The gold standard is all Greek to me. But if you want to sell any goods anywhere outside of home you better either cut your prices down to where they would be if you were off the gold or get off.

Our salesmen say they haven't sold anything out here since other nations' stuff went off the gold, and got cheaper.

Salesmen are even smoking their own cigarettes and burning up their own gas they can't sell.

Yours,
Will Rogers.

1705   WILL ROGERS GIVES HIS VERSION
        OF AN UNREPORTED CONVERSATION

PENANG, Jan. 10. — Since the big epochal gastronomical meeting of Democrats nobody knows what Al Smith and Franklin D. Roosevelt has been saying to each other. But it's about like this:

"Listen, Al, give me a chance. I been nominating you for years, now you do the nominating and let me do the running, won't you? Come on, Al, be a good fellow."

"Now, Frank, just give me one more crack at 'em. Then if I don't do anything, why you can have 'em. I had tough luck last time.

Hoover was hot. But he has cooled down now, and I believe it's my year. So just give the old boy one more crack at 'em, won't you, Frank? That's a good fellow."

      Yours,
       Will Rogers.

1706   Mr. Hoover Finds Another War
     That Seems A Bit Hampered

  ALLAHABAD, India, Jan. 12. — Forced down with broken piston. Jails so full may have to call this war off. How is Stimson vs. Japanese war going?

      Yours,
       Will Rogers.

1707   Mr. Rogers Promises To Return
     With A Lot Of Information

  KARACHI, Jan. 13. — Twelve hundred miles flight today across the heart of India.

  Tomorrow Persia and the Sultan. That ought to be good.

  There is lots of things I can tell you later that I can't tell you now. Savvy?

      Yours,
       Will Rogers.

1708   Mr. Rogers Yearns For News
     Of The Old Home Country

  S. S. RAWALPINDI, Jan. 14. — Will somebody wire me c.o.d. something that's happened at home since Nov. 21, my day of sailing.

  Did the Democrats take Congress? Did Jimmy Walker get Mooney out? Who won the football game in Pasadena?

  All I hear is "Culbertson won five rubbers," "Culbertson won three rubbers." Who is Culbertson and who is rubber? If he is that important there let's run him on the Democratic ticket. That will cure him of rubbering.

On an English boat and I have misplaced by dress suit and letters of introduction so I haven't eaten anything or met any one.
                               Yours,
                                    Will Rogers.

1709   ROGERS FLIES OVER JERUSALEM,
         THE DEAD SEA AND BETHLEHEM

CAIRO, Jan. 15. — Today saw Jerusalem, Dead Sea and Bethlehem. Never catch me traveling over here again unless I have read the Book. First, these Pyramids. Mexico's got bigger. And the Sphinx, Coolidge has got him licked to death.

Tomorrow 600 miles of ocean flying in a land plane to Athens; see if the Greeks got a word for that.
                               Yours,
                                    Will Rogers.

1710   MR. ROGERS FINDS THE NEAR EAST
         HAS SOME GREAT OPEN SPACES

BAGDAD, Jan. 15. — Finally found a telegraph. Persia was a hot sketch.

You Bible students, stockmen and hunters better note this. Flew low all morning between Euphrates and Tigris. It's all level prairie and uncultivated.

Most animals I ever saw were there, thousands of cattle, donkeys, camels, water buffalo, deer, wild boar.

Now over Jerusalem and Holy Land and Bagdad.
                               Yours,
                                    Will Rogers.

1711   WILL ROGERS IS ENTHUSIASTIC
         OVER WORLD'S LONGEST AIR LINE

ATHENS, Jan. 18. — This is the longest airplane route in the world, from Java to Amsterdam. Ten thousand miles with the same pilot, same crew, same plane all the way.

Holland line tomorrow from Athens to Rome in eleven hours. Old Plato and Caesar would have liked to have prowled that fast.

Just had a wonderful chat with Premier Venizelos. He is not only of Greece, but he is Greece.

Yours,
Will Rogers.

1712   MR. ROGERS REJOICES AT SIGHT
OF LAND RULED BY A DICTATOR

ROME, Jan. 19. — Flew over from Athens today and circled old Vesuvius. That is the only way to see her.

Mussoliniland sure looks like pie and cake after coming out of those Indias and Chinas and Mesopotamias.

They call this old boy a dictator, but he has done more with less to work on than any man in the world.

Yours,
Will Rogers.

1713   MR. ROGERS SENDS A WARNING
REGARDING THE DEBT PROBLEM

PARIS, Jan. 20. — Flew over Corsica Island today. No wonder Napoleon left there.

Now here is a warning. All Europe is looking for us to do all the debt cancelling. So don't send delegates with hardened arteries, as usual, but get some with hardened hearts, for these people are even rehearsing their crying now.

Yours,
Will Rogers.

1714   MR. ROGERS MAKES A PREDICTION
ON THAT LAUSANNE AFFAIR

LONDON, Jan. 21. — Flew from Paris today. Americans always make this trip, but won't fly at home. Yet, we have twenty lines as good.

I sure miss Charley Dawes. The trouble is, there is not enough of Dawes to go around everywhere we need him.

I bet you they call the Lausanne reparations conference off as we are not there. You can't have a picnic lunch unless the party carrying the basket comes.

Yours,
Will Rogers.

1715   WILL ROGERS OFFERS HIS VIEW
OF THE FEDERAL RELIEF BILL

LONDON, Jan. 22. — See where Congress passed a two-billion-dollar bill to relieve bankers' mistakes and loan to new industries. You can always count on us helping those who have lost part of their fortune, but our whole history records nary a case where the loan was for the man who had absolutely nothing.

Our theory is to help those who can get along even if they don't get it.

Yours,
Will Rogers.

1716   WILL ROGERS REMARKS

LONDON, Jan. 24. — Got the dope on these international bankers that are crying for us to cancel. Every American trade commisioner and business man over here tell of the flock of bankers' representatives over in Germany and Europe in the last few years. Hotel lobbies full of 'em offering all kinds of commissions to help put over loans for American banks. The loans were forced over here as much as the sales of 'em forced over home. Now they want the government to cancel to make up for their mistakes. Now if this is not the real low down on it then Borah is a Republican.

Yours,
Will Rogers.

1717   MR. ROGERS HAS RELIEF PLAN:
STOP BORROWING FOR 5 YEARS

LONDON, Jan. 25. — The President signed another loan bill. This one for only $125,000,000 for land banks. Then last week $2,000,000,000. You can tell this is an election year from the way these appropriation bills are passing. It will take the taxpayers fifty years to pay for the votes in this election.

Our only solution of relief seems to be to fix it so people who are in a hole through borrowing can borrow some more. Borrowing, that's what's the matter with the world today. If no individual or country could borrow a dime for five years that would be the greatest five-year plan ever invented.

Yours,
Will Rogers.

P. S. But what about Morgan & Co.? That would be discriminating against them, wouldn't it. Well, we won't do it then. Just let it go.

1718 WILL ROGERS FINDS EUROPE
       BLAMES US FOR EVERYTHING

LONDON, Jan. 26. — I would like to stay in Europe long enough to find some country that don't blame America for everything in the world that's happened to 'em in the last fifteen years—debts, depression, disarmament, disease, fog, famine or frostbite.

If the dog had two pups and they were expecting more they will show in some way where the debt settlement was directly responsible for this canine delinquency.

But the other day was the best one, they had a prison mutiny and so every paper said it was American movies and American influence that give their prisoners this unusual idea.

The birth rate is falling off so I am going to get out of here before we get blamed.

Yours,
Will Rogers.

P. S. — What ever become of our disarmament troop. I can't hear of 'em over here.

1719 WILL ROGERS PUTS IN A CLAIM
       FOR SOME OF THAT TWO BILLION

PARIS, Jan. 27. — Got a real flying partner. Mrs. Rogers, who joined me in London and flew over here this afternoon, is another Frank Hawkes. We come in a big four-motored, thirty-four-passenger plane, a bar, hot meals, two stewards and everything.

Say, our American disarmament band is lost somewhere on the high seas. Well, no matter how late they are, they will get here before anybody disarms.

What's this I hear about my two best Democratic friends, Jesse Jones and Harvey Couch, going to be allowed to distribute some government money? This can go on record as being my application for some.

Yours,
Will Rogers.

1720   MR. ROGERS STILL CONTENDS
        THAT IT'S A GREAT OLD WORLD

PARIS, Jan. 28. — Some queer things are going on in the world if you just happened to have been there and seen 'em. Japanese warships are ready to bombard China because China insists on boycotting Japanese goods. England puts 500 more of Gandhi's bunch in jail because they boycott and picket against English goods.

Here you have China and India, who constitute five-eighths of the world's population, practically at war because they can't do what they want to, yet signboards all over England say "Buy British."

It's a great world even if you are just looking at it for comedy purposes.

Yours,
Will Rogers.

1721   MR. ROGERS HAS SOME THOUGHTS
        ON SAVED NATIONS AND OTHERS

PARIS, Jan. 29. — Flying to Berlin in the morning to see the country that there has been so much talk about saving. I can't see the difference nowadays when a country has been saved and when it hasn't.

American delegation gets in tonight. On the same boat are 400 barrels of gold coming from home and on another boat 500 barrels. We always thought barrels were just to send apples or potatoes in. Then they talk about canceling the debt. Say, if we don't run out of barrels we won't have enough gold left at home to fill our front teeth.

Yours,
Will Rogers.

1722 MR. ROGERS DOESN'T CONSIDER
THE PEN SO MIGHTY THESE DAYS

PARIS, Jan. 31. — Bad flying weather today kept us out of Berlin.

We had better quit writing notes to Japan or she will have all China. Every time they get a note they take another town that they hadn't thought of till our note give 'em the idea. Quit writing and warning 'em what not to do. Wait till they do something that will really affect us.

This war was originally private just between them and China. The way we got in the last war was through notes. We send so many that nations can't tell which one we mean.

Our wars ought to be labeled "Entered on account of too much penmanship."

Yours,
Will Rogers.

1723 WILL ROGERS GETS A LAUGH
AND A NEW HOPE AT GENEVA

GENEVA, Feb. 1. — Well, we are all here ready for disarmament. The first laugh was when the Japanese delegates arrived. I don't know, but it just struck everybody funny. They have a large bunch and everybody expects to see 'em take over the city and have it under martial law by morning. The younger members of their delegation that started out to the conference have been called back for military service.

Our female delegate, Miss Woolley, is the outstanding novelty. I had an hour and a half chat with her this afternoon. Didn't know whether to call her Miss, Mrs. Professor, Doctor or what, so I just called her Doc, and Doc and I got along great. I had taken an interpreter but I didn't need him, but some of my stuff had to be repeated to her.

She is very plain, likeable, broad in mind and body, feet and plenty of 'em right on the ground. You would like her. She is not the type for a college president at all.

Thirty million women of the world have hope and faith in her common sense versus diplomacy. It's no joking matter getting the world to disarm. Maybe a woman can do it. It's a cinch men can't. So good luck to you, "Doc."

Yours,
Will Rogers.

1724   Mr. Rogers Finds Every Nation
With Fare And A Gun At Parley

GENEVA, Feb. 2. — This is the hash of nations. There is sixty-five nations represented here. You see, this is land disarmament, too, so every nation with railroad fare and a gun is here. The smaller the nation the bigger the delegation.

If you disarmed the delegates you would have disarmed over half the countries represented.

Turkey is here not to disarm but to try and book some wars for the coming season.

The conferences open tomorrow alphabetically with Abyssinia the keynote speaker.

There is lots of nations here willing to throw away two spears and a shield for every battleship we sink.

Went into another huddle today with Doc Woolley. I am strong for Doc.

The American delegation held a skull practice today with the American press. Each delegate spoke. All bemoaned the fact that both Congress and the Senate had disarmed the American delegation of $150,000, leaving them only $300,000 to argue on.

So our delegation on account of this opens about half sore at the world anyhow.

Yours,
Will Rogers.

1725   Mr. Rogers Finds Human Nature
Is Only Obstacle To Disarming

GENEVA, Feb. 3. — Disarmament conference was held up for one hour yesterday while we all went to the League of Nations meeting to demand of Japan that she quit shooting while the opening session was in conference.

That meeting was much more dramatic of the two. Japan has been winning hands with a pair of jacks for four months, and finally they caught 'em at it. It was England that called the turn on 'em when they read a list of battleships that was on the way there. Japan realized they wasn't dealing with chopsticks then.

The biggest laugh, of course, was uttered unintentionally by the Japanese when he spoke of Chinese aggression. Well, that like to broke up the meeting.

The conference is off to a flying start. There is nothing to prevent their succeeding now but human nature.

Yours,
Will Rogers.

1726   WILL ROGERS SEES ONE REASON
       FOR HOPE IN THE ARMS PARLEY

ABOARD S. S. EUROPA, Feb. 4. — Well, got the disarmament conference off to a good start. Can't say it wasn't running smooth when I left. No meeting today on account of the war in China. They have to disarm between shots.

Now I am going to make you a prediction. I believe that conference will get somewhere. You know why? Just because nobody thinks it will. I believe they will just accidentally do something. I have been to all of 'em and they all started out expecting big things, and then busted. At this one every delegate enters with an apology, so I kinder got some hopes.

I give "Doc" Woolley her parting instructions and I am coming home to Cuckooland. God bless it. He hasn't lately, however, but He will when we deserve it.

Yours,
Will Rogers.

1727   MR. ROGERS EXPRESSES THANKS
       FOR MR. MELLON'S SERVICES

ABOARD S. S. EUROPA, Feb. 5. — This is just a little note to "Uncle Andy" Mellon, the first man to step down in order to take the Ambassadorship to Great Britain. Mr. Mellon, you saved us taxes and you made us money, and we will like a lot of "yaps" went and blew it in. When it was all gone we took it out on you. The thing busted in your face the same as it did in ours.

This is a crisis where the bigger you were the harder you fell. We are mighty poor losers if we can't remember what you did and thank you, and wish you well. So good-by Andy, take care of yourself. If you put on knee breeches be sure and put on long woolens underneath and always remember if we had saved what you saved for us we wouldn't need saving now.

Yours,
Will Rogers.

1728   WHAT MR. ROGERS THINKS ABOUT
        ON A SUNDAY ON THE HIGH SEAS

ON BOARD S. S. EUROPA, Feb. 7. — The Europa, Berengaria and Paris racing over to bring back more barrels of gold to France.

Got Ambassador Edge of France on here with me. He is about the only ex-Senator that made good.

On the Paris is the League of Nations Manchurian delegation. You remember they was appointed last fall to go out and see how much country Japan had captured.

Well, Japan asked 'em not to come till they had captured enough to make the trip worth while. If Japan keeps expanding the delegation will meet the Japanese army at about Reno or Salt Lake.

                    Yours,
                        Will Rogers.

1729   ROGERS SAYS 16,000,000 VOTES
        GIVE SMITH RIGHT TO TRY AGAIN

ABOARD S. S. EUROPA, Feb. 8. — I went clear around the world to keep from coming back across that Pacific, and here this ocean is worse than it was. We are pulling in a day late. Even the oceans have depressions. If this boat don't hurry up and get in I will be too late to vote for Al.

I always kinder thought he was coming out—well when you get sixteen million votes it does kinder lead a man to think he has some license to believe that he is not just some outsider butting in.

                    Yours,
                        Will Rogers.

P. S. — That warning the League of Nations sent just seems to whetted Japan's appetite more than the notes we used to send 'em single handed.

1730   MR. ROGERS, IT SEEMS, IS HAPPY
        JUST TO BE BACK HOME AGAIN

NEW YORK, N. Y., Feb. 9. — Oh, boy, I was glad to set my old big feet on American soil, even if it has got a second mortgage on it,

127

Had the greatest trip I ever had in my life and I believe if everybody made it they might come back poorer but better off in the feeling toward our country.

I know business is off, they say 60 per cent. Well, that still leaves us 30 per cent ahead of anywhere I have seen.

If we can just let other people alone and let them do their own fighting. When you get into trouble 5,000 miles away from home, you've got to have been looking for it.

Yours,
Will Rogers.

1731   WILL ROGERS LOOKS IN AGAIN
ON WASHINGTON ACQUAINTANCES

WASHINGTON, D. C., Feb. 10. — Appropriations were just flying every which way today here in Congress, but I couldn't seem to get my hands on any of it. Heard Borah in the Senate make what the press boys all said was one of his best speeches. Visited my old friend Speaker Garner. Even all the Republicans say he is doing a great job with his handling of this Congress.

Had long chat with Mrs. Longworth, who still knows what all the shooting is about. Heard 'em approve Ogden Mills in the Senate as our new Secretary of the Treasury. Everybody is very high in their praise of his ability and he went through without a murmur.

Yours,
Will Rogers.

1732   MR. ROGERS CALLS ON PRESIDENT
AND WINDS UP ON A COMMISSION

WASHINGTON, D. C., Feb. 11. — Safeguarded and protected by the Secretary of War, I just been in and had a long chat with Mr. Hoover to report on Manchuria, Shanghai, Hollywood, Claremore, and to ask for small dole for international bankers.

President was in fine humor and he told jokes. Said Pennsylvania, the second richest State, was the only one that had passed the tin cup for relief from the federal government. He laughed and got a kick out of this.

"They paid 12 per cent of the taxes. Under the relief program they would receive only 3 per cent. So all they would lose by government relief, instead of relieving themselves, would be 9 per cent. Now, there is one that would do justice to you, Will."

He is worried about this money hoarding and asked me, "Write a joke against these hoarders. Humor might show 'em how foolish they are. Now go do that."

So after all my kidding about Hoover commissions, I am finally on one, "the Hoover anti-hoarding joke commission."

So anybody knowing any anti-hoarding jokes, send 'em to me. I want to be one commission to make good.

Yours,
Will Rogers.

1733   ROGERS WOULD FORCE CONGRESS
        TO PROVIDE THE MONEY IT VOTES

NEW YORK, N. Y., Feb. 12. — The worst thing that has happened to us in a long time is that this is an election year. Every statesman wants to vote appropriations, but is afraid to vote taxes. The oratory of Washington is on "reconstruction," but the heart of Washington is on November 4, 1932.

We never will get anywhere with our finances till we pass a law saying that every time we appropriate something we got to pass another bill along with it stating where the money is coming from.

Yours,
Will Rogers.

1734   MR. ROGERS VISITS HEREABOUTS
        AND JOTS DOWN A FEW ITEMS

NEW YORK, N. Y., Feb. 14. — Had a fine day today over with the Morrow family in Jersey. The more difficulties pile up on us the more we realize what this country lost when we lost him.

The Lindbergh baby is the cutest thing you ever saw, walking, talking, and disgraced the Lindbergh name by crying to come away with Mrs. Rogers and I in the car.

Say, just left Ring Lardner. There is a man that has forgot more humor than all the rest of us try to write. He is working on a new baseball series that's bigger news to America than if the Japs evacuated Chu-Chin-Chow.

Had lunch and a two-hour chat with Al Smith yesterday. He took me up on top of his building, the highest in the world. He can pretty near see Washington from there—well, as near as anybody else can, anyhow.

Yours,
Will Rogers.

1735   MR. ROGERS, IN THE CAPITAL, FINDS SIGNS OF NEW LIFE

WASHINGTON, D. C., Feb. 15. — Down here in Washington to see Mr. Ziegfeld's latest and greatest show, "Hot-Cha."

Now, about this war that we are all excited about. Had a long chat today with Secretary Stimson and he gave me his side of the thing. He feels that it is going to quiet down over there and they will come to some terms.

The Japs are not so cocky as they were. They figured on taking Shanghai for lunch and it's been seventeen days and they haven't got it yet.

Had fine visit with Mr. Dawes and his money-loaning gang. J. P. Morgan and eighteen international bankers were in line ahead of me to get in.

But the whole place here has a spirit of better feeling. Anyhow, the corpse is showing life.

Yours,
Will Rogers.

1736   MR. ROGERS REACHES CLEVELAND ON AN AERIAL HITCH-HIKE HOME

CLEVELAND, Ohio, Feb. 16. — Flew here from Washington, 320 miles, in one hour and thirty minutes, piloted by Dave Ingalls, Assistant Secretary of the Navy. I "bummed," or rather, "thumbed," my way here, so I think that's a record for speed for a hitch-hiker.

This Ingalls is a very remarkable young man in more ways than flying. In fact, he is the only Republican I would trust my life with.

Say, just had a chat with Newton Baker. A pleasanter fellow you never met, and of course we know his ability. Instead of talking about himself he was singing the praises of John Garner. That's no way for a candidate to do.

The Democrats have got so many good men this year they can even make a mistake and still be right.

Yours,
Will Rogers.

1737   Mr. Rogers Helps Mr. Ford
          To Size Up The Situation

CHICAGO, Ill., Feb. 17. — Just flew in here tonight from Detroit. Spent the day there with Mr. Ford.

When the world is in a hole I go to Ford and ask him. More common sense than all of 'em. Then, too, I know there is more people interested in the new Ford than there is interested in Manchuria; they ain't going to get into Manchuria, but they are going to get in these Fords.

I think what he feels is what the country needs is a good eight-cylinder car at the price of the old four and a new four at the price of a good baby buggy.

He drove me around in everything he had. It's a real tonic to visit a man that has more money invested all over the world than any five men, and more.

He said, "Will, you never was as funny purposely as some of our prominent and rich people are acting these days. This is not a panic. It's a side-show, watching folks and seeing how scared they can get."

Yours,
Will Rogers.

1738   Will Rogers Finds Chicago
          Is Thriving Despite Knocks

CHICAGO, Ill., Feb. 18. — Chicago, the more they knock it the bigger it gets.

Due to a mix-up in taxes, they don't get any, so the city is just like a modern human being, it has to exist on borrowed money.

But, it's like China. It's so big nothin' can stop it.

Going to see Jack Dempsey in his first big comeback fight tonight. Us old timers got to pull for each other.

Surprised at the war talk you hear? Well, if we do get in, we will have broken a world's record. We will have gotten into a war for less reason than any nation in the history of the world.

If we are out upholding downtrodden nations, it will take a bookkeeper to keep track of our wars.

Yours,
Will Rogers.

1739 MR. ROGERS SAYS KEEPING DOWN
PAY WON'T KEEP AIRPLANES UP

TULSA, Okla., Feb. 19. — Just flew in from Chicago. Was going over to Claremore tonight, but the hotels are all so full, going to have to stay here in the edge of town.

I see where some line is going to make aviation pay by taking it out of the pilots' salary. When they start hiring cheap pilots I will stop flying. That's what built up what confidence in aviation we have is the experience, character and dependability of our pilots. I think they are just about the highest type bunch of men we have.

I am interviewing all the candidates to see what they are running on, if anything, just outside a desire. So I got to see our Governor, Bill Murray.

Yours,
Will Rogers.

1740 MR. ROGERS BEGINS FUNCTIONING
AS A HOOVER COMMISSIONER

CHELSEA, Okla., Feb. 21. — About time for my anti-hoarding joke commission to start operating.

I am picking the best of my commission. I got Mr. Wickersham on it. I believe he deserves another chance to make good on a commission, so it's the Rogers-Wickersham committee, but Rogers is chairman.

Out on the Rogers ranch at Oologah, where I spent yesterday, Herb McSpadden, my nephew, had to take a milk stool and whack an old cow over the rear end. She was hoarding her milk.

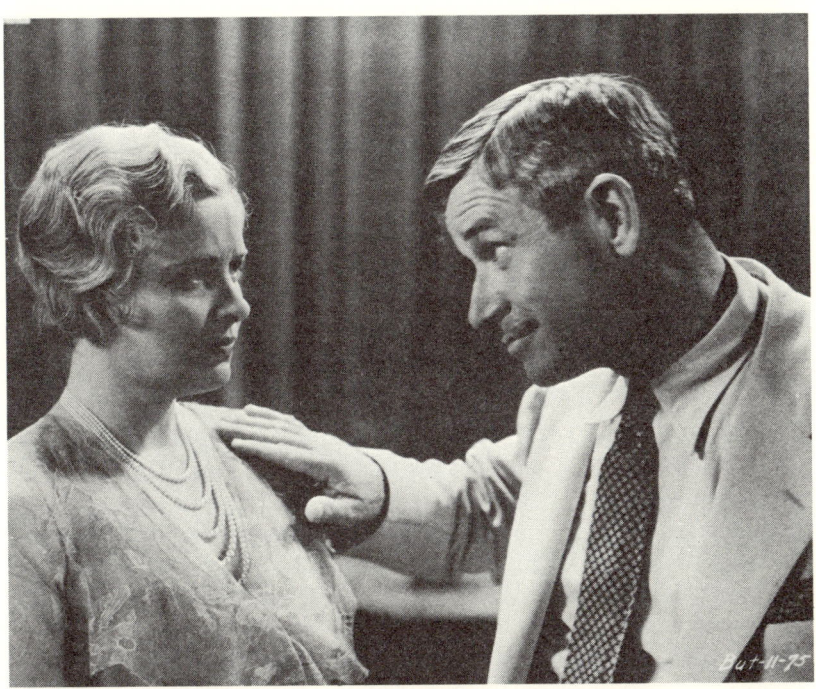

Will Rogers as "Earl Tinker" in scenes from the motion picture Business and Pleasure, *an adaptation of Booth Tarkington's novel,* The Plutocrat (Fox Film Corporation, 1931).

A Jewish farmer at Claremore named Morris Haas hid $500 in bills in a barrel of bran and a cow ate it up. He has just been able to get $18 of it back, up to now.

This hoarding don't pay.

Yours,
Will Rogers.

1741   WILL ROGERS IS MISTAKEN
FOR THE FATHER OF A CROONER

ALBUQUERQUE, N. M., Feb. 22. — I have made this trip by air 100 times, but I never saw such mobs at the fields. Rudy Vallee is on our ship. I am just as excited as they are, and say, he is a very modest, likeable young fellow. I was even flattered when the folks at Amarillo thought I was his father.

Was in Oklahoma City last night and my old friend Bill Murray liked to talk to me all night. He is sure a smart old bird. He knows more about things than any one I ever saw.

Yours,
Will Rogers.

1742   WILL ROGERS THINKS THE NEWS
FROM SHANGHAI IS EXAGGERATED

BEVERLY HILLS, Cal., Feb. 23. — There is two things I think you will find out about this war in China.

One is that it is rather over "press agented." All these writers were in Manchuria when I was, and I know they naturally being writers had to kinder exaggerate it all to keep it readable. So they naturally are putting it on pretty thick in Shanghai.

The other is you always want to look at your date line and see if the dispatch is headed Shanghai or Tokyo. Then which ever one it is discount it at least 50 per cent in favor of the other side. For both places have their government censorships and you can't send anything out that is not colored in their favor.

Yours,
Will Rogers.

1743   Mr. Rogers Reveals The Cause
            Of The Crowding In Washington

BEVERLY HILLS, Cal., Feb. 24. — You can't get a room in Washington. Every hotel is jammed to the doors with bankers from all over America to get their "handout" from the Dawes commission.

And I have asked the following prominent men in America this question: "What group have been more responsible for this financial mess—the farmers, labor, manufacturers, tradesmen, or who?"

And every man, Henry Ford, Garner, Newt Baker, Borah, Curtis and a real financier, Barney Baruch, and everyone of 'em without a moment's hesitation said: "Why, the big bankers."

Yet they have the honor of being the first group to go on the "dole" in America.

                     Yours,
                     Will Rogers.

1744   Mr. Rogers Has His Own Ideas
            About The "Big Board's" Value

BEVERLY HILLS, Cal., Feb. 25. — Mr. Whitney, the man in charge of all the "faro and roulette tables" of the New York Stock Exchange, threw a scare into Mr. Hoover and some Congressmen yesterday by telling 'em if they stopped speculators selling something "they haven't got"—why, it would stop the Stock Exchange, and people with stocks would have to sell 'em like folks with horses, or cows, or wheat, for just what they are worth.

Now you can just imagine the terrible consequences of that exchange being closed. Why, it would be terrible!

At least 115,000,000 out of the 120,000,000 would put on a celebration that would make Armistice Days look like a wake.

                     Yours,
                     Will Rogers.

1745   Will Rogers Flies 210 Miles
            To Ranch In Seventy Minutes

SAN SIMEON, Cal., Feb. 26. — Talk about moving. Breezed up here to this wonderful Hearst ranch, 210 miles from Los Angeles, in an hour and ten minutes in Hal Roach's new Lockheed plane—one of those that when it starts off it tucks its legs inside it. All you have to worry about is "are they going to let down when we get there." Mountains go by just like telephone posts in a Ford. Got their own lighted air field here on the ranch.

Here's one rich man that hasn't hoarded his money. There is more people working, and building, on this the most beautiful and gigantic of American estates than there is international bankers trying to get that two billion away from Dawes.

Yours,
Will Rogers.

1746   WILL ROGERS FINDS A HAVEN OUT WEST FOR MAN AND BEAST

SAN SIMEON, Cal., Feb. 28. — Up here at Mr. Hearst's ranch you get dozens of long typewritten pages of all the news that comes over all the press wires. Lots of this is never printed in the papers, only what you are supposed to read.

If you have missed anybody from any part of the United States and can't find 'em they are here guests of this ranch.

He has the most wonderful wild animal collection all over these mountains. I guess this place has more different kind of animals and more different kind of guests than any place outside Leavenworth. Calvin Coolidge and Polly Moran had a great time together.

I have just held a political argument with the president of Oglethorpe University with Paul Block refereeing.

Yours,
Will Rogers.

1747   WILL ROGERS SUGGESTS A WAY TO GET NEW TAXES FAIR TO ALL

BEVERLY HILLS, Cal., Feb. 29. — Every time Congress starts to tax some particular industry, it rushes down with its main men and they scare 'em out of it. About the only way I see for 'em to do, so it would be fair to everybody, would be for Congress to go into secret session, allow no telephones, no telegrams, no visitors, so no outside lobbyists can get at 'em, then tax everything they want to, and should tax, then announce, "Boys, it's all over; there is no use shooting at us now."

As it is now, we are taxing everybody without a lobby.

Yours,
Will Rogers.

1748   MR. ROGERS CONSIDERS THIS WAR
       AN 'OFF AGIN, ON AGIN' AFFAIR

BEVERLY HILLS, Cal., March 1. — In one column of our morning papers the war had been called off, but they hadn't notified the other column.

The Japanese say they don't want China, and it's a cinch the Chinese don't want Japan. The Japanese say if the Chinese would get back twenty miles from Shanghai that they would quit fighting. The Chinese say if the Japanese would go back home, where they belong, they would quit fighting.

So nobody really knows what they are fighting over. It's almost like a civilized European war in that respect.

Yours,
Will Rogers.

1749   WILL ROGERS RECALLS A GOLDEN-HAIRED BABY
       TODDLING ABOUT IN THE LINDBERGH NURSERY

BEVERLY HILLS, Cal., March 2. — Why don't lynching parties widen their scope and take in kidnappings? They are ten times more premeditated and performed by more normal people.

It wasn't enough for that Morrow family to lose the most able, fairest and broadest of our public men then have to be saddled with this. I am sure nothing could carry more sympathy.

What a shock to everybody. But how much more of a one it is when you have seen the baby and seen the affection of the mother and father and the whole Morrow family for the cute little fellow.

Two weeks ago Sunday Mrs. Rogers and I spent the day with them. The whole family interest centered around him. He had his father's blonde curly hair, even more so than his dad's. It's almost golden and all in little curls. His face is more of his mother's. He has her eyes exactly.

His mother sat on the floor in the sun parlor among all of us and played blocks with him for an hour. His dad was pitching a soft sofa pillow at him as he was toddling around. The weight of it would knock him over. I asked Lindy if he was rehearsing him for forced landings.

After about the fourth time of being knocked over he did the cutest thing. He dropped of his own accord when he saw it coming. He was just stumbling and jabbering around like any kid 20 months old.

He crawled up in the back of the Morrow automobile that was going to take us home, and he howled like an Indian when they dragged him out.

I wish we had taken him home with us and kept him.

Yours,
Will Rogers.

1750 WILL ROGERS FINDS THE NATION
HAS BUT A SINGLE THOUGHT

BEVERLY HILLS, Cal., March 3. — Did you ever see such a day? Nobody don't feel like doing anything, taking any interest in anything.

The attention of the world is on a little curly haired baby. Till he is found we can't get back to normal.

Never since the two days and a night that this same kid's father was out over the Atlantic has the attention of everybody been centered so completely on one thing.

The greatest single "kick" that a whole nation got, outside of the signing of the armistice, was when the news was flashed that Lindbergh had landed in Paris.

The next one we hope and pray will be when this baby is delivered safely home.

Yours,
Will Rogers.

1751 WILL ROGERS HAD FORGOT TO WRITE
A SON WHO HAD FORGOT TO WRITE

ROSWELL, N. M., March 4. — Eight hundred and twenty-five miles in less than five hours, and part of it in a snowstorm, with Captain Dickson doing a fine job of piloting Hal Roach's fast plane. Meeting Mrs. Rogers here coming out from the East. Hope the Lindberghs have as good luck as we did. We finally found one of our boys here that we hadn't heard of in months.

He has learned to play polo here, but hasn't learned to write. Asked him why we never hear from him. Said he had forgot our address.

Cattle country looks fine, lot of rain, no prices. If Wall Street men had these old cattlemen's nerve and "tripe" you would have never heard of this panic. Cattle are so cheap that cowboys are eating beef for the first time in years.

Yours,
Will Rogers.

1752   MR. ROGERS TURNS BOOK CRITIC
          AND HIGHLY RECOMMENDS ONE

SANTA MONICA, Cal., March 6. — Don't tell me we got people that can read, and they haven't read Pearl Buck's great book on China, "Good Earth."

It's not only the greatest book about a people ever written, but the best book of our generation. Even in China, the Europeans, and the Chinese say it's absolutely true, and there is few books written about people where they say it's good themselves.

I had an engagement to fly up and meet her, but it stormed that day, and I missed the treat.

So go get this and read it. It will keep you out of some devilment and learn you all about China, and you will thank me.

Yours,
Will Rogers.

1753   LINDBERGH STAND IN CRISIS
          COMMENDED BY WILL ROGERS

BEVERLY HILLS, Cal., March 7. — Out of 120,000,000 people if Lindbergh had had as much advice on how to fly the ocean as he has on this case, he would have cracked up in St. Louis. I think the boy has used splendid judgment in this, the same as he has in everything he has done since we first heard of him. Remember it was his sober judgment that first suggested "get the baby back at any cost," and then start worrying what the punishment would be if they caught 'em.

And remember there is other kidnapped ones out that are just as dear to their folks as this baby of his, so get all the folks in that's kidnapped, then make some new laws and start over again.

Yours,
Will Rogers.

1754   ROGERS HAILS SOUSA'S TUNES
         AS HIS ENDURING MONUMENT

BEVERLY HILLS, Cal., March 8. — He was in life rather small of stature. Not particularly impressive, very modest and unassuming. Yet he produced something that any hour of the day or night can quicken the blood and thrill the nerves of every American man, woman or child. His tunes were the Lincoln's Gettysburg address of music.

"El Capitan," "Washington Post" and "Stars and Stripes Forever" is a monument that needs no concrete. It's for the soul, and not for the eye.

Our little March King is dead, but his marches will be marched-to down through the ages.

Yours,
Will Rogers.

1755   WILL ROGERS ASKS FUND TO AID
         FORGOTTEN ARMS DELEGATIONS

BEVERLY HILLS, Cal., March 9. — The poor old disarmament conference at Geneva, it's just dropped plum out of the papers. It just shows you how we can get all excited about something, and think that life and death depend on it, and in six weeks nobody can remember it.

Those poor delegates, they was fairly well known a month ago, now their own folks don't know where to send them mail. I am going to ask for contributions for funds to build a home for delegates who have been sent off to conferences and forgotten.

Yours,
Will Rogers.

P. S. — What a wise guy that Charley Dawes was to escape that burial alive.

1756   WILL ROGERS REMARKS

BEVERLY HILLS, Cal., March 10. — In one of my little poems I said the bankers were the first to go on the "dole." The "wrath of the mighty" ascended on me. Even the Wall Street Journal (Wall street's house organ) editorially said I should confine my jokes to some semblance of truth. Now I want to be fair, even with the bankers, for they are pretty touchy now. I have had critics come out and say "As an actor old Bill is not so hot." Well, I just wanted to come out and call him a liar, but in my heart and conscience I knew he was right. So I know how you "boys" feel. Now if you will take this money and loan it out to a lot of the little fellows that need it you bankers got a chance to redeem yourselves. But I am not kidding you. People are not "pointing with pride" to your record in this crisis up to now. Will be glad to reprint any alibis.

Yours,
Will Rogers.

1757   WILL ROGERS REMARKS

BEVERLY HILLS, Cal., March 11. — My good old friend Arthur Brisbane sure put one over on me, showing the difference between a good reporter and a punk one. Two weeks ago I had two hours with Al Capone. (That raises Arthur one hour.) He told me all that I read today he told Mr. Brisbane and more. But there was absolutely no way I could write it and not make a hero out of him, and even as superb a writer as Mr. Brisbane couldn't either. Everybody you talk to would rather hear about Capone than anybody you ever met. What's the matter with an age when our biggest gangster is our greatest national interest. Part is the government's fault for not convicting him on some real crime. Now will somebody please suggest what to do with the story I got bottled up with me and be fair to everybody.

Yours,
Will Rogers.

1758   WILL ROGERS HAS TWO VISITORS
            WHO SHOW A VERY RARE QUALITY

HOLLYWOOD, Cal., March 13. — Well sir, had a couple of mighty interesting and charming callers out at the ranch Friday afternoon, Secretary Kellogg and Senator Gillette of Massachusetts, a couple of mighty fine old men that have played quite a part in our history the last few years.

The thing I liked about their visit was they had no opinion to offer on "when we had scraped bottom." Most every man you meet can tell you who will be our next President, but these ignorant, uninformed gentlemen had no idea.

I have always believed that if the very, very proper inducements were presented that you could smoke Calvin out. Mr. Gillette thought no, Mr. Kellogg yes.

I have told many alleged jokes on both of them, and it was gratifying to know I could do so and still retain their friendship.
Yours,
Will Rogers.

1759   MR. ROGERS SEES LESSON FOR ALL
       IN THE VICTORY OF HINDENBURG

BEVERLY HILLS, Cay., March 14. — It was gratifying to read in the press this morning that Germany "went sane" in their primary election yesterday.

Hindenburg is assured of re-election April 10. He must be a grand old character, the only man that the whole of Europe produced that they followed in war and followed in peace.

Hitler had some swell sounding ideas, but this depression has lasted so long it has given the people a chance in all countries to know that nobody can fix it overnight with an idea.

Nobody knows exactly where it came from, and nobody knows exactly where or when it's going from here. Hindenberg had no solution and was re-elected.

So, why don't everybody do like him and quit lying about it.
Yours,
Will Rogers.

1760   MR. ROGERS HOLDS THAT CONGRESS
       DID NOT VOTE ON PROHIBITION

BEVERLY HILLS, Cal., March 15. — Dry Congressmen voted yesterday, not on prohibition, but voted in favor of keeping the people from voting on it.

Now the wets are not as sore at prohibition as they are the fact that they was never in their lives allowed to vote on it. The drys can win at a general election now, but let the thing drag on for four more years and they will lose.

So it looks kinder short-sighted on the drys' part not to let the people vote while the going is good. But it's one of those things that are out of the hands of the people now and into the hands of the politicians.

The wets have got a hand full of drinks, and the drys think they got a hand full of votes.

Yours ignorantly on the subject,
Will Rogers.

1761   MR. ROGERS DESIRES TO DODGE
        ANY ARGUMENT ON PROHIBITION

BEVERLY HILLS, Cal., March 16. — Yesterday I finished my little poem, "the wets have a hand full of drinks, and the drys think they have a hand full of votes." Well, I meant to put, but I forgot it, the words "or visa versa."

But I don't want to get mixed up in that argument. No person has ever convinced another on prohibition. People's minds are changed through observation and not through argument.

John Hays Hammond, the great mining engineer, but through somebody's oversight never became President, was out to see me today. He and Maj. Frederick R. Burnham, the author of that great book "Scouting on Two Continents." We talked of South Africa where we had all prowled about at one time or another.

Yours,
Will Rogers.

1762   MR. ROGERS THINKS THE ELECTION
        THE NATION'S BIGGEST HANDICAP

BEVERLY HILLS, Cal., March 17. — I see where a bunch of 'em are trying to defeat the sales tax. Canada and everywhere that have tried it have found it absolutely satisfactory.

The idea that a tax on something keeps anybody from buying it is a lot of "hooey." They put it on gasoline all over the country and it hasn't kept a soul at home a single night or day. You could put a dollar a gallon on and still a pedestrian couldn't cross the street with safety without armor.

We are three billion in the hole and will be three more next year, and not a Congressman has got the nerve to ask voters to pay part of it. You can talk hoarding, you can talk lack of confidence, but the biggest handicap to a return of prosperity is that there is an election this Fall.

Yours,
Will Rogers.

1763   WILL ROGERS FINDS DIVERSION
            IN THE PROCEEDINGS AT GENEVA

BEVERLY HILLS, Cal., March 18. — One of the funniest things I have read in a long time was the disarmament conference in Geneva took a month off to rest. That's like a vice president of a bank or a night watchman asking for time to recuperate.

The Japanese have started evacuating Shanghai. They claim they won a moral victory by driving the Chinese twelve miles back from Shanghai. What good did that do? That would be just like the Irish driving the Jewish folks twelve miles out of New York. What would the answer be at the finish?

Yours,
Will Rogers.

1764   WILL ROGERS GIVES CONGRESS
            A RATING OF NEARLY '4 OUT OF '5

SANTA MONICA, Cal., March 20. — Congress, with an eye, not on the budget, but on November 4, put a tax as high as 72 per cent on some incomes. That's three-fourths.

Congress almost tied pyorrhea. It only gets "four out of five," and Russia only gets half.

Course a man to give up three million out of four is tough; but, on the other hand, 90 per cent of our people would be willing to give up 990 per cent of a million if allowed to make one.

The crime of taxation is not in the taking it, it's in the way that it's spent.

Yours,
Will Rogers.

1765   Mr. Rogers Sadly Points Out
One Record We Still Hold

BEVERLY HILLS, Cal., March 21. — Phar Lap sounds like a mouth wash, but runs like a race horse.

All American horses saw of him yesterday was his tail and his dust. England, which holds a mandate over Australia, already had the auto and aeroplane records, and Williams of Canada won the Olympics. Now this race horse makes a sucker out of us.

But the good old U. S. A. still holds one international record. Our international bankers have loaned more of other people's money to foreign countries, on less security, than was ever loaned before, even on security.

Now, there is a record we want to see beat, but no other bankers are dumb enough to beat it.

Yours,
Will Rogers.

1766   Mr. Rogers Backs Block-Aid
As Charity Beginning At Home

BEVERLY HILLS, Cal., March 22. — Has your town or city investigated this great scheme called "block-aid" that they have in New York City?

Each person with a job that lives in that block is asked to contribute a dime, quarter or not more than a dollar per week. Now your block is so organized that each block helps itself. It's practical and it works.

Every city, town and even country townships should organize and use it. You know absolutely where your money is going, it's helping your next door neighbor. That's one trouble with our charities, we are always saving somebody away off, when the fellow next to us ain't eating. Same thing wrong with the missionaries. They will save anybody if he is far enough away and don't speak our language.

This is a time when I don't care where you live, you can't throw a rock without hitting somebody that needs help worse than you do. Here is a scheme where charity begins at home.

Yours,
Will Rogers.

1767   MR. ROGERS AIRS SOME VIEWS
ON CONGRESS AND TAXPAYERS

BEVERLY HILLS, Cal., March 23. — Congress knocked the rich in the creek with a 72 per cent income tax, then somebody must have told 'em "Yes, Congress you got 'em while they are living. But what if they die on you to keep from paying it?"

Congress says, "Well, never thought of that, so we will frame one that will get 'em, alive or living, dead or deceased."

Now they got such a high inheritance tax on 'em that you won't catch these old rich boys dying promiscuously like they did.

This bill makes patriots out of everybody. You sure do die for your country if you die from now on.

                       Yours,
                       Will Rogers.

1768   MR. ROGERS ARISES TO APPLAUD
SOME STARS OF YESTERYEAR

BEVERLY HILLS, Cal., March 24. — John J. McGraw gave a little dinner last night. These and many more were present:

Jim Jeffries, who was champion when you had to fight.

Tod Sloan, whom Kings have dropped their monocles applauding.

Barney Oldfield, the originator of giving Americans a thrill.

Chief Meyers, who hit home runs when the ball wasn't rubber.

Mike Doulin, who, with his wife, Mabel Hite, received the biggest reception I ever heard on a stage.

All passing over the horizon of popular clamor, but never forgotten by McGraw. Yet, if all these men's combined applause and cheers had been recorded in sound and run nowadays, it would make our present-day celebrities envious.

I'm raving. I guess I'm getting old. But I want you kids to know that in your dad's time there was men.

                       Yours,
                       Will Rogers.

1769   MR. ROGERS SEEKS INFORMATION
ON JUST WHAT IS A SALES TAX

BEVERLY HILLS, Cal., March 25. — This thing of a political party controlling the House or the Senate is not always exactly what it's cracked up to be. The Democrats defeated the sales tax. By about next November, when it's percolated into a lot more people's minds that it's only tax, why some of these boys are going to have the privilege of staying home for the next four years.

Why should a sales tax work on gasoline and cigarettes and not work on anything else? If people use as much tooth paste as they are advised to over the radio, a small tax on it would just about pay our national debt, to say nothing of lip rouge.

Yours,
Will Rogers.

1770   MR. ROGERS NOTES THE WISDOM
            OF OUR NATIONAL STATESMEN

SANTA MONICA, Cal., March 27. — Mr. Calvin Coolidge had a mighty instructive article on finances in last week's Sat-Eve-Post.

We got a long-sighted government. When everybody has got money they cut the taxes, and when they're broke they raise 'em. That's statesmanship of the highest order.

The reason there wasn't much unemployment in the last ten years preceding '29 was every man that was out of a job went to work for the government—state or city.

It costs ten times more to govern us than it used to, and we are not governed one-tenth as good.

Yours,
Will Rogers.

1771   WILL ROGERS THINKS THE NEWS
            FROM VIRGINIA ENCOURAGING

BEVERLY HILLS, Cal., March 28. — That baby news from down in Virginia sounds the most encouraging there has been.

Of course, this is a case where everybody wants to get in on it and claim they know something. But if we can trust those prominent men like that to know what they are doing, look what it would mean to give all this hope falsely.

Why, it would just show you how some folks could be either misled, or to what means they would go to get publicity.

But I believe they know something, and we will all get some good news, and the world will look brighter to everybody.

Yours,
Will Rogers.

1772   Mr. Rogers Detects A New Art
           In The Matter Of Paying Loans

BEVERLY HILLS, Cal., March 29. — No matter what the poor old dumb government tries to do, the "big boys" have a scheme that beats it.

Now the big bankers have got a new "racket." Instead of them going direct to the new finance commission for dough, they send the folks that owe them. He gets it from the government and then pays them off. That don't leave a single soul out snipe hunting with a sack but the government.

And, brother, when one of those "big babies" transfers one of his loans over to Uncle Sam, it's not a "frozen asset," it's a "petrified persimmon."

Yours,
Will Rogers.

1773   Mr. Rogers Is Hurt And Demands
           Some Mercy For The Taxpayer

BEVERLY HILLS, Cal., March 30, — Wait a minute here now. It's all right for Jack Garner's reformed Congress—

To pour it onto the rich with income taxes;

To fine a man for dying;

To put a tax on malt till they make it cost like beer, even if it don't taste like it;

To refuse to pass a sales tax, then turn around and tax everything that is sold;

To put a tax on matches and drive the U. S. to the insane asylum trying to make cigar lighters work—

All these fool things come under the heading of Congressional employment.

But, when they put a tax on chewing gum, the only thing left for a poor man to chew, that's going too far.

Yours,
Will Rogers.

1774   Mr. Rogers Tries To Follow
           The Gyrations Of Congress

BEVERLY HILLS, Cal., March 31. — Congress turned down the sales tax claiming that it was unconstitutional, undemocratic and even unhealthy, that it was a tax on the poor in favor of the rich. Then they turned yesterday and put a tax on matches.

Well, I never saw a poor man that didn't at one time during his life, no matter how poor, have to light a match. Got a tax on candy, but not on crude oil from Venezuela.

You see these things that they are taxing now, they are not a sales tax. No! No! Entirely different!

This is just a tax on things you have to buy.

Yours,
Will Rogers.

1775   MR. ROGERS SEES A BABY'S PERIL
        AGAIN TOUCHING NATION'S HEART

BEVERLY HILLS, Cal., April 1. — It takes a baby to stir the sympathy and interest of a hard-boiled nation. Yesterday that baby that fell in the drill hole—till we got this morning's paper to see if they had saved him, why we didn't care any more what Congress did than they do themselves.

And maybe this means a good omen for the Lindbergh baby. And anyone else that has a clue, don't mention it to the press or public till after you got the baby. You will get enough publicity after that to last a lifetime.

Yours,
Will Rogers.

1776   MR. ROGERS REPORTS THE HORSE
        IS DOING A REAL COME-BACK

SANTA MONICA, Cal., April 3. — Major Chamberlin and his troop of crack riders of our army were just up here at the ranch. They are our representatives in the Olympics. They are at San Diego working day and night on their horses. Major Chamberlin has represented us in previous games and he says that the horsemanship events are the most popular on the whole program.

You talk about something coming back. Say, the old horse is coming back in a high lope. Thousands of people are riding a horse today that five years ago couldn't sit in a Ford with all doors locked.

Polo, racing and horse shows all doing great work to help the farmer and rancher to raise better horses.

Legalize racing in every State. Sure people will bet, but they get to see the horses run, and you certainly can't see General Motors and General Electric and General Utility run when you bet on them.

Yours,
Will Rogers.

1777   MR. ROGERS IS CONVINCED NOW
        THAT EVERYTHING IS ASKEW

BEVERLY HILLS, Cal., April 4. — I see where Secretary Stimson is going to take a vacation. He is going to the disarmament conference in Geneva. I was there at the opening. Certainly was a picnic that day.

By the way, wonder what ever became of "Doc" Woolley that was a member of the original cast. She was as pleasant a nice soul as I ever met. I hated to see her banished to Siberia like that.

I tell you the whole world is "cockeyed," and we mustn't be surprised at anything. Mr. Coolidge, who never said an unkind word against anybody—in fact talks less than anybody—he pays $2,500 for talking too much. I look to see John D. Rockefeller Sr. arrested for vagrancy.

Yours,
Will Rogers.

1778   MR. ROGERS GIVES HIS VIEWS
        ON FREEING THE PHILIPPINES

BEVERLY HILLS, Cal., April 5. — Congress yesterday gave forty minutes to Philippine independence—gave forty minutes, but no independence.

Democrats all voted for it. They are in about the same fix the Philippines are.

Sugar and immigration were the things they were voting on. The freedom of a race of people never entered into it.

We better give 'em their freedom while we got 'em. The only reason we ever held 'em this long was because the Japanese didn't use sugar in their tea. But they are liable to start using it any day.

Yours,
Will Rogers.

1779   WILL ROGERS PAYS A TRIBUTE
          TO PHAR LAP AND AUSTRALIA

BEVERLY HILLS, Cal., April 6. — Australia, a great horse country, finally produced what looked like the "superhorse." He came 10,000 miles and won in a gallop. He received as great an ovation as he had ever received winning at home. He is dead.

Horse lovers the world over sympathize with Australia. Mr. Wolfe, the Australian sports writer who accompanied him here, was out to see me last week. He talked of him like he was human.

No one could possibly have brought on his death. Our foreign friends can accuse us of lots of things, but not giving a foreign contestant, be he man or animal, a fair chance is not one of them.

It's too bad, Australia. Phar Lap was just a horse, but he brought you honor and represented you nobly. For you never saw a good horse grow where a good man didn't grow.

Yours,
Will Rogers.

1780   MR. ROGERS DISCUSSES MILLS,
          THE BUDGET AND A SMART FLIER

BEVERLY HILLS, Cal., April 7. — This Ogden Mills that is now treasurer of the deficit, nobody has accused him of being "the best treasurer since Alexander Hamilton." But, I have heard Jack Garner himself say that Mills was "a mighty able and conscientious man."

Congress bases her estimate of the budget on "what the people ought to make in 1932." Mills says, "Yes, they ought to make that much, but who are they going to make it out of?"

Word just came that Frank Hawks was hurt. Frank is like one of our family, but the hospital tells me that it's not dangerous. He is a fine, intelligent fellow. That's one profession I have never met, a "dumb" aviator.

Yours,
Will Rogers.

1781   ROGERS SEES WAY TO STOP
          THE WOMEN PIPE SMOKERS

BEVERLY HILLS, Cal., April 8. — At a luncheon yesterday a Congressman's wife couldn't read President Hoover's handwriting and Mrs. Hoover had to interpret it for her. Now that can mean various things. Can a Congressman's wife read? Can't Mr. Hoover write? (All of 'em being Republicans.) The chances are that both of the above are right, and that the reason Mrs. Hoover could read it was she remembered what she told the President to say in the message to the women.

Headline says, "Society Women of New York Smoking Pipe." The only way to break 'em from it is not to watch 'em do it.

Yours,
Will Rogers.

1782   MR. ROGERS RATES SOVIET AHEAD
         OF CONGRESS AS WONDER WORKER

SANTA MONICA, Cal., April 10. — Didn't you see a headline in this morning's papers saying that "Russia is going to extract the snow from the clouds before the clouds reach Moscow, thereby relieving the city of having snow"?

Now that sounds silly, don't it? We all say "Those darn Russians, they always got some crazy ideas."

Then, in the next column it says "Hoover and a Congressional committee propose to take two hundred million dollars from government expenditure."

Well, I'll bet you the Russians get the snow out of the clouds before Hoover and Congress gets any government employees out of their swivel chairs.

But both things sound good in print.

Yours,
Will Rogers.

1783   WILL ROGERS REMARKS

BEVERLY HILLS, Cal., April 11. — After Wall street had been dead for a couple of years and everybody that had so generously contributed to the funeral was just about to go to work and forget about it, why now the United States Senate, that investigates everything after it's dead, is going to dig up the body and hold an autopsy. They will find out exactly what everyone else already knows, "deceased died from overgorging while the gorging was gorgeous."

Yours,
Will Rogers.

1784   WILL ROGERS REMARKS

BEVERLY HILLS, Cal., April 12. — The Senate grand jury which is in session now couldn't get much nourishment yesterday out of this fellow Whitney that's head of the "Wall street gang." There is one kind of noble thing about our modern racketeers, they will go to the electric chair before they will give away any of the workings of their organization. At first we thought when they had this investigation we was going to get the names of our "big men" who were betting the country would never amount to anything. Oh! Yeah!

Yours,
Will Rogers.

1785   MR. ROGERS HEARS OF THINGS
         HE MISSED IN THE FAR EAST

BEVERLY HILLS, Cal., April 13. — Floyd Gibbons been out here telling me all that I missed in China. The night before I would leave all the towns I would make a speech to all the assembled Americans. Then the war would break out.

Then on top of all Floyd's valuable information, why today a chat with Sir Victor Sasoon, who knows more about China and India than any man, for he is to those countries what J. P. Morgan is to us. We have to get his O. K. to see if we can have sugar with our coffee.

Gibbons and Sasoon both feel that Japan is holding Manchuria till Russia is in shape to take it over. China returns to civil war now till some other outsider shows up.

So pacifists haven't much to look forward to in the Far East.

Yours,
Will Rogers.

1786   WILL ROGERS SEES DEMOCRATS
         DOING THEIR BEST FOR HOOVER

HOLLYWOOD, Cal., April 14. — The Democrats met Wednesday night to consciously drink a toast to Thomas Jefferson, and unconsciously elected Herbert Hoover.

It's been the same every year, only this fall it's going to be harder for the Democrats to elect a Republican than it's generally been.

The reason it's tough is, there are hundreds of people this year that are going to vote the Democratic ticket in spite of the Democratic party.

    Yours,
    Will Rogers.

1787   ROGERS TELLS THE STORY
          OF A NEGRO BULLDOGGER

BEVERLY HILLS, Cal., April 15. — A little small, good-natured, likeable Negro died last week in Oklahoma, named Bill Pickett. Don't mean a thing to you, does it? Well, he was the originator of a stunt that has thrilled millions. It was the rodeo stunt of "bulldogging."

When they arrest a cowboy for cruelty to animals in bulldogging, they arrest the wrong participant. More men get hurt than steer. He worked with white cowboys all his life and never had an argument or enemy. Even the steer wouldn't hurt old Bill.

    Yours,
    Will Rogers.

1788   MR. ROGERS DEVOTES HIS SPACE
          TO A STAGGERING OBSERVATION

SANTA MONICA, Cal., April 17. — Mr. Hoover wants to put in the "stagger system." That don't sound like a dry.

He says we can save eighty million a year by "staggering." we have always thought "staggering" was a shame, but now it's a blessing.

But what he means by the "stagger" is you "stagger" to work today, then "stagger" home and lay off tomorrow, and I "stagger" over and work in your place that day, then you "stagger" back the next day.

The man who is employing you don't know just who is going to "stagger" in to work for him on any given day, but it gives more people days to work and more people more days to "stagger," so the plan is well worth "staggering" into.

    Yours "staggeringly,"
    Will Rogers.

1789 Mr. Rogers Mentions One Lobby
    Of Which He Never Has Heard

BEVERLY HILLS, Cal., April 18. — Every time the government suggests putting a tax on something the manufacturers of that object rush to Washington like "Coxey's army," demanding that it's an injustice.

No matter what the tax is put on, the man that makes it don't pay. It's the bird that buys it. But, we have never yet heard of a "purchasers' lobby" rushing down.

Course, the auto makers feel that they are being discriminated against, and it looks like they are.

Everything we buy should have its equal proportion of tax, outside of cheap food and cheap clothes.

There won't finally be anything left of Congress's tax bill but the envelope they sent it over to the Senate in.

         Yours,
         Will Rogers.

1790 Mr. Rogers Sums Up Findings
    In Wall Street Investigation

BEVERLY HILLS, Cal., April 19. — Today's news featured two items in the same column "Monte Carlo fails to pay dividend for first time" and "Wall Street investigation still carried on."

Senate has been investigating Wall Street for ten days and all they have found out is that the street is located in the sharp end of New York City, that not only the traders but the street itself is short, that neither end don't lead anywhere.

         Yours,
         Will Rogers.

1791 Mr. Rogers Sees A Chance
    To Effect A Bit Of Economy

BEVERLY HILLS, Cal., April 20. — Talk about economizing and cutting out all unnecessarys, what's the idea of holding the Chicago Republican convention?

This morning's papers announced Mr. Hoover's campaign plan, the route, the towns, who he would shake hands with, and what he would wear.

And as for the platform, it will be the same one they have read for forty years but have never used.

And the speeches will be the same ones delivered for forty years but never listened to.

Yours,
Will Rogers.

1792   MR. ROGERS'S DAILY POTPOURRI
             INCLUDES A BIT OF BOOSTING

HOLLYWOOD, Cal., April 21. — Country's been full of jokes at the expense of the radio announcers, but have you caught any of these political speakers that are desecrating the ether? Why you actually want to kiss the announcer when he comes on after one of those.

Took three years of solid depression to get the truth out of dear old Charley Schwab.

Thirty-eight aeroplanes with mail and passengers come and go daily from Los Angeles airports.

Congress is just like us individuals. They are finding it tough to dig up the money they spent last year that they didn't have.

Yours,
Will Rogers.

1793   WILL ROGERS GIVES HIS VIEW
             OF THE STOCK MARKET INQUIRY

HOLLYWOOD, Cal., April 22. — Did you read that Senate Wall Street investigation? The Senate sent out and got a fellow named Gray. Well, he didn't ask the usual Senate questions. Gray knew where the body was buried, and poor Mr. Whitney, who had a cinch on the stand up to then, why it looked like he was going to break down and confess. Twenty-four thousand patriotic Americans, and some splendid friends from France, was all betting against the country, and we used to arrest men for just saying something against it.

Morgan kept his German bonds up to ninety, till he got 'em all peddled. Now they are thirty-five. "Hot-cha."

Yours,
Will Rogers.

1794 MR. ROGERS REVIEWS THE NEWS
      FROM WASHINGTON AND LONDON

SANTA MONICA, Cal., April 24. — This fellow Gray has brought investigations back on the front page. Some of that rich bunch will hire him.

Wall Street will live this down, for the more we find out about anything the less we ever do about it. But, they never will live down Charley Dawes calling 'em a "peanut stand."

A bunch of women are after Mellon because he is going to give the Britishers a drink. Most of America don't care how many he gives 'em, just so he don't take enough himself so he will cancel the debt.

Yours,
Will Rogers.

1795 MR. ROGERS TAKES PASSING NOTE
      OF LATEST WORD FROM DOORN

HOLLYWOOD, Cal., April 25. — See where the Kaiser in a statement says, "I would do the same very thing over again."

Well, if he would he is about the only one connected with the war that would. Many a nation and many an individual would like to have had a second guess at it.

That lawyer Gray for the Senate must have lost some dough on the Street and he's out to locate the guy that got away with it.

There is no quicker way in the world to have folks lose interest in a murder trial than to call in alienists.

Yours,
Will Rogers.

1796 WILL ROGERS REMARKS

HOLLYWOOD, Cal., April 26. — When you think you have heard all the devilment about anything, why you haven't heard anything till a little Italian Congressman (and a Republican, too, strange to say) from New York City, La Guardia, he's always got the evidence. He dragged in a trunkful of canceled checks yesterday that brokers had given financial writers.

You know it's too bad everybody was so busy getting in on it, that no one had time to investigate Wall street before '29, when the horse was being stolen.

Yours,
Will Rogers.

1797   WILL ROGERS SEES A LESSON
            IN RESULTS OF THE PRIMARIES

HOLLYWOOD, Cal., April 27. — Say, I bet Al Smith threw a scare into some of these wise politicians that they won't forget for some time.

Whoever advised Roosevelt to enter that primary anyhow? Running against Smith in Massachusetts is like trying to win a debate with Sister Aimee on her grounds.

And, Smedley Butler in Pennsylvania. He used fine judgment. He run as a "dry" instead of as a marine.

There is one thing you can bet on this year. No voter is going to do anything that a politician thinks he will do. The way most people feel they would like to vote against all of 'em if it was possible.

Yours,
Will Rogers.

1798   MR. ROGERS RISES TO DEFEND
            THE HIGH INCOME TAX RATES

HOLLYWOOD, Cal., April 28. — The big writers are hollering now that Congress "soaked the rich" by raising the rate after it passed $1,000,000 to 45 per cent.

Why the holler? A man making $20,000 pays almost twice the rate as one making $10,000. So, why not the man making $200,000 pay twice the rate of one with $100,000, or why not pay more on your second million than on your first?

You can't legitimately kick on income tax, for it's on what you have made. You have already made it. But, look at land, farms, homes, stores, vacant lots. You pay year after year on them whether you make it or not.

Every land or property owner in America would be tickled to death to pay 45 per cent of his profits, if he didn't have to pay anything if he didn't make it.

Yours,
Will Rogers.

1799   WILL ROGERS FINDS AVIATORS
            EARN THEIR GOVERNMENT PAY

HOLLYWOOD, Cal., April 29. — The Congressman that suggested cutting government aviators' salaries to help balance their overspent budget didn't get far with his bill. In fact, he wasn't able to "take off" and leave the ground with it. Taxpayers know that an aviator risks his life every day, and a politician only on Nov. 4 every two years.

The other day Henry Ford visited Mr. Hoover and told him that what the country needs was a "new eight" and a garden. Most people got no room for a garden, so what Mr. Ford will do is put out a car with a garden in it. Then you hoe as you go.

Yours,
Will Rogers.

1800   WILL ROGERS OFFERS A WORD
        OF ADVICE TO HIS UNCLE SAM

SANTA MONICA, Cal., May 1. — Well, about all you can see in the papers is Honolulu. The whole thing just proves that the islands haven't got any use for the navy and the mainland.

Course I guess I am all wet, but I never have seen any reason why us, or any other nation, should hold under subjection of any kind any islands or country outside of our own.

We say we have to have it to protect the Pacific. Why don't we have to have the Azores to protect the Atlantic? We are going to get into a war some day either over Honolulu or the Philippines.

Let's all come home and let every nation ride its own surfboard, play its own eukaleles and commit their devilment on their own race.

Yours for remaining on the home grounds.
Will Rogers.

1801   MR. ROGERS PUTS IN A WORD
        FOR HIS FAVORITE CANDIDATE

BEVERLY HILLS, Cal., May 2. — Tomorrow is primary day out here in California. Course, it's all cut and dried with the Republicans, but the old Democrats out here in Orangejuiceville have got a chance to name the next Democratic nominee.

Al Smith's big spurt in the East has shown that Governor Roosevelt can't possibly go to the convention with enough to nominate. Give Garner California and Texas and he will be sitting prettier than any of the three, for there is one thing about a Smith delegate, he is sure loyal to Smith, and won't go for any one else at the finish only who Smith tells 'em to.

The Democrats always beat the man that goes to the convention with the most votes, McAdoo at Madison Square Garden when he had a big majority. Champ Clark at Baltimore when he had 600, so California can win with Jack.

Yours,
Will Rogers.

1802   MR. ROGERS IS TERRIBLY UPSET
BY WHAT HAPPENED TO THE ATOM

BEVERLY HILLS, Cal., May 3. — Let's give a great big hand to those two Governors, Rolph of California and Balzar of Nevada, for making the flight clear across our country in a day. Too many won't fly because of their regard for their country and the shape it would be left in, in case of accident.

See where two English scientists were able, the headline said, to "split the atom." The world was not bad enough off as it was; now they go and split the atom. That's the last straw.

We expect the Democrats to split, the country to split over prohibition, but we always felt that the old "atom" would remain intact. It was certainly a big disappointment to me.

Come on, boys, let's up and atom.

Yours,
Will Rogers.

1803   MR. ROGERS DOES NOT THINK
THE PRIMARIES PROVE MUCH

HOLLYWOOD, Cal., May 4. — About all these primaries prove around the country is that the Democrats have got three good men and the Republicans only one. It looks to me like any man that wants to be President in times like these lacks something.

Wall Street is being investigated, but they are not asleep while it's being done. You see where the Senate took that tax off the sales of stocks, didn't you? Saved 'em $48,000,000.

Now, why don't somebody investigate the Senate and see who got to them to get that tax removed? That would be a real investigation.

Yours,
Will Rogers.

Rogers gathers material for a daily telegram while he relaxes in the hectic surroundings of a movie set.

1804 MR. ROGERS NOW IS CERTAIN
      THAT SPRING HAS ARRIVED

HOLLYWOOD, Cal., May 5. — Spring has been late arriving this year, but this morning on our front page she got here.

It was the old familiar figure Citizen Calvin Coolidge wading in the creek. When that distinguished weather mark takes his hip boots out of dry dock and launches forth with rod and cigar into the very bowels of a Spring freshet, America knows she can then shed her woolens and enjoy her depression in the open air.

The picture showed he had a little "perch" in his hand and the same grin on his face that he wore on that memorable day in Washington when he, with due premeditation and malice aforethought, slipped the custodianship of these whole United States into the innocent hands of Herbert Hoover.

You can't blame him for grinning, if he never caught a fish.

Yours,
Will Rogers.

1805 WILL ROGERS SEES HOOVER
      FINALLY ON THE WAR PATH

HOLLYWOOD, Cal., May 6. — Our heretofore docile Quaker President went on the warpath yesterday and cut loose with both barrels at Congress and the Senate, and his message was loaded with votes. It was on government economy.

He told the court in his own way what was happening. "You guys are not going to do anything about cutting down. You are afraid, because every one you fired has got a vote, so if you are afraid to shoot the bear, give me the gun and I will do it and take the consequences."

Somebody has been feeding Herbert raw meat, and if he keeps up that diet and builds up those corpuscles he will be elected by acclamation.

Yours,
Will Rogers.

1806 MR. ROGERS REVEALS THE DIARY
      OF A BUDGET-BALANCING SENATE

SANTA MONICA, Cal., May 8. — Diary of a United States Senate trying to find $2,000,000,000 that they have already spent but didn't have.

Monday — Soak the rich.

Tuesday — Begin hearing from the rich.

Tuesday afternoon — Decide to give the rich a chance to get richer.

Wednesday — Tax Wall Street stock sales.

Thursday — Get word from Wall Street, "Lay off us or you will get no campaign contributions."

So Thursday afternoon — Decide "We was wrong about Wall Street."

Friday — Soak the little fellow.

Saturday morning — Find out there is no little fellow. He has been soaked till he is drowned.

Sunday — Meditate.

Next week — Same procedure, only more talk and less results.

Yours,
Will Rogers.

1807   WILL ROGERS GIVES HIS VIEWS
OF DARROW AND W. J. BRYAN

BEVERLY HILLS, Cal., May 9. — That fellow Massie and his wife had a tougher time getting out of Honolulu than they did while there. I didn't read about anybody trying to stop Darrow, but I bet at that he made a lot of friends over there.

I have known Darrow a good many years, and always go to see him in Chicago. I knew William Jennings Bryan many years. Both men lived ahead of their times, Bryan in government and Darrow by believing that the under dog, in any fight, had his side.

And, I bet they both had great admiration for each other.

Yours,
Will Rogers.

1808   MR. ROGERS'S HEART GOES OUT
TO OUR ENVOY TO ST. JAMES'S

BEVERLY HILLS, Cal., May 10. — Poor Mr. Mellon is just finding out what an Ambassador's business to England is. It's to introduce American mothers' daughters to the King and Queen.

You ought to hear Charley Dawes tell about his experiences with those ferocious mothers. They try everything from bribery to blackmail, and politics to poison. They drove poor Charley pretty near "nutty."

I doubt if a charging elephant, or a rhino, is as determined or hard to check as a socially ambitious mother.

I see there is just as many this year. Even depression can't stop 'em.

Don't you envy "Andy," "Charley?"

Yours,
Will Rogers.

1809   WILL ROGERS FINDS NEW YORK
         ISN'T AHEAD IN EVERYTHING

BEVERLY HILLS, Cal., May 11. — New York, which always thinks it's ahead in everything, is going to "walk for beer." The rest of the country don't have to walk for it.

Dave Ingalls of Cleveland, Ohio, our naval ace in the World War, is nominated on the Republican ticket for Governor of his State. His ticket was "let the people vote on whatever they want to, whether it be prohibition, knee breeches for diplomats, or shall Mickey Mouse be allowed to produce sex dramas."

The Democrats have already started arguing over "who will be speaker at the convention." What they better be worrying about is "who is going to listen to the 1,150 delegates that will speak."

Yours,
Will Rogers.

1810   WILL ROGERS PAYS A TRIBUTE
         TO THE AKRON TRAGEDY HERO

BEVERLY HILLS, Cal., May 12. — They were all just young recruits, told to hold on and they did. Two met death because they had no hand hold, or no chance. The other did have one chance in a million and he took it.

Now, we all want to hang onto him like him to the Akron. He lives just twenty-five miles as the Ford flies from my home, the glorious old State of Oklahoma, where a rope is not just an implement, it's a tradition.

Our history has been built on citizens dangling in the air by a rope and some escaped the dangling that would have made better history.

But, we are proud of this boy. Unlike his early ancestors he tied his own knots, and saw that they wasn't around his neck.

Yours,
Will Rogers.

Rogers and Assistant Secretary of the Navy for Air Dave S. Ingalls. Ingalls flew Rogers over the country on many occasions.

1811   WILL ROGERS EXPRESSES
         SORROW OF THE COUNTRY

BEVERLY HILLS, Cal., May 13. — One hundred and twenty million people lost a baby, 120,000,000 people cry one minute and swear vengeance the next. A father who never did a thing that didn't make us proud of him. A mother who, only the wife of a hero, has proven one herself. At home or abroad they have always been a credit to their country. They have never fallen down. Is their country going to be a credit to them? Will it make him still proud that he did it for them? Or in his loneliness will it allow a thought to creep into his mind that it might have been different if he had flown the ocean under somebody's colors with a real obligation to law and order?

America goes further into debt, and the debt is to the Lindberghs.

Yours,
Will Rogers.

1812   MR. ROGERS REVIEWS FROM AFAR
         THE VARIOUS BEER PARADES

SANTA MONICA, Cal., May 15. — The big news in the papers today was the different "beer parades" held over the country.

New York, the originator of this unique entertainment, had 100,000 in line. Then there was 500,000 sitting in "speaknaturallys" that was drinking beer and watching humorously the 100,000 that was perspiring and marching.

Washington, D. C., had one. Theirs was an "inaugural parade." They were inaugurating 23 new Congressional places.

Chicago broke the record. They only had one man in their "beer parade." It was learned afterwards he was a stranger in the city. Marching for beer is exactly like taking an umbrella with you in bathing.

Yours,
Will Rogers.

1813   MR. ROGERS TAKES UP A QUESTION
         THAT IS DISTURBING EVERY ONE

BEVERLY HILLS, Cal., May 16. — The Senate slept on the tax bill over the week-end. But the birds that are going to have to pay it didn't sleep any.

Some Senators say that no man should be allowed to earn over $75,000 a year. They forget that a man that earns that much, or more, works for a different kind of an employer from the one Senators work for.

Suppose you got $100,000 a year for working for a firm and you spent $200,000,000,000 of their money that you didn't have and you didn't know where you was going to get it, how long would you be working for that firm?

Yours,
Will Rogers.

1814   MR. ROGERS PUTS IN A BOOST
        FOR A FELLOW OKLAHOMAN

BEVERLY HILLS, Cal., May 17. — Any time our Governor "Prairie Hay" Bill Murray gets in an argument with the federal government over what a State can do with its own products you can bet "Bill" will win. He knows more about State rights than any man in the country.

Just going out now with our popular Governor Rolph to accept the gift to the State of California of the biggest Arabian horse ranch in the world, given by Mr. Kellogg of Battle Creek.

The Governor knows good breakfast food and I know good horses. I don't want to detract from what may be mighty fine morning "fodder," but I am a ham and egg man myself.

Yours,
Will Rogers.

1815   WILL ROGERS COMMENTS A BIT
        ON THE COUNTRY'S GULLIBILITY

HOLLYWOOD, Cal., May 18. — Well, of all the fool things to hit the country in the face with is this guy's story.

He was supposed to be a reputable business man. That should have been a tip-off to us right there, for being no business now, there can't possibly be any business man.

Then he was heartily indorsed by a preacher and an ex-admiral. Well, we know that a preacher will fall for anything, and a retired admiral is not exactly a William Pinkerton.

Now, you can't blame poor Lindbergh, for in his position he was grabbing at every straw, but the rest of us were just carrying out America's reputation for being— Well, add your own last word.

Yours,
Will Rogers.

1816   MR. ROGERS APPEARS A BIT COOL TO THE CLAMOR OF THE WETS

BEVERLY HILLS, Cal., May 19. — See a lot of pictures of Mrs. Vincent Astor and society women of New York taking up nickels on the street to aid the anti-prohibition campaign.

Such antics as that are sure to win the small town and the farm women over. Yes sir, right over to the opposite side!

I'll bet there is more fool things done for publicity's sake that defeat their own purpose than ever aided it.

There is but one reason that prohibition won't be repealed, and it's not numbers either. It's because the wrong people want it repealed.

Yours,
Will Rogers.

1817   WILL ROGERS SEES CONGRESS SEEKING A SECOND MORTGAGE

BEVERLY HILLS, Cal., May 20. — Congress is human for the first time in years. They are broke, just like everybody else, and are running around in a circle trying to pay what they owe.

They got an eighteen-billion-dollar first plaster on the country, and now they are pop-eyed trying to get a second mortgage. They will eventually find out they are just like other folks; they will have to cut down.

No taxpayer is going to make 'em a loan if they are going to keep as much help as they always have.

Yours,
Will Rogers.

1818   MR. ROGERS EXPLAINS HIS 'GAG'
        ABOUT REPEAL OF PROHIBITION

SANTA MONICA, Cal., May 22. — The other day I wrote a little "gag" about the main thing that handicapped repeal of prohibition was the wrong people are for it.

I still claim it's true. Prohibition is not a party issue. It's not a wet and dry issue. You will find it is country against city. Your city's wet and the country is against it more because it's the city dictating to them what to do. And, if you don't think it's that way, you wait till you count the votes.

Country folks know the whole thing won't work, but they are not going to let "town folks" tell 'em so.

That's why I say the wrong people are for it to get it through.

Yours,
Will Rogers.

1819   MR. ROGERS TAKES OFF HIS HAT
        TO A 'DOWNTRODDEN WIFE'

BEVERLY HILLS, Cal., May 23. — I don't suppose there is any country, unless it be India, where the wife is more downtrodden than they are in the United States.

Amelia Putnam flew across the Atlantic Ocean and then had to call up her husband to see if he thought it would be safe for a married woman to venture into London alone.

But, by golly, us old scared males, our hats are off to Amelia. Her bravery is only surpassed by her skill.

But, there is no use kidding ourselves. It does make a "sucker" out of us men. While the men are playing bridge and arguing over their golf scores, the women are flying the ocean.

Yours,
Will Rogers.

1820   MR. ROGERS DECIDES THIS YEAR
        IS A TOUGH ONE FOR EVERYBODY

BEVERLY HILLS, Cal., May 24. — The whole country, including Nicholas Murray Butler, been knocking the Senate so much lately till they just had a session yesterday and held a clinic over their own body.

And, do you know they couldn't find a thing wrong with themselves. Both parties just spent the session scratching each other's back, and us paying for the manicure.

But give the devil his due. They have had their troubles. Every time they went to tax something a voter would rise up and say, "Yeah?"

It's been a tough year to be a Senator. It's been a tough year to be anything. Even Capone has a tough year, so what can you expect from other industries?

Yours,
Will Rogers.

1821   WILL ROGERS IS IN FAVOR
OF HUMORING CONGRESSMEN

BEVERLY HILLS, Cal., May 25. — Congress and the Senate are wondering if they will be through in time for their various conventions.

Now the question arises in our time, the same as in Shakespeare's (or some other old timer), "to be in session or not to be in session, that is the question; whether it is better to suffer with or without Congress and the Senate."

Most folks say, "Let them suffer like they made us suffer." But to keep a politician away from his convention is just like taking ice-cream away from a kid. It's liable to make 'em so mad there is no telling what they will pass.

Yours,
Will Rogers.

1822   WILL ROGERS HAS HIS SAY
ON THE NEW YORK SITUATION

BEVERLY HILLS, Cal., May 26. — They ought to take that Jimmy Walker investigation out on the road and charge admission.

Jimmy was in great form. Those Republicans are always going to find out something on old Tammany, and the more they find out about 'em, the less they prove. They get everything on 'em but the evidence.

There is only one conclusion to draw, Tammany is either the slickest thing back there, or the Republicans are the dumbest.

Yours,
Will Rogers.

1823   Rogers Draws A Contrast
         And Suggests A Moral

BEVERLY HILLS, Cal., May 27. — Bands playing, soldiers marching, orators orating telling you it's your duty to "buy Liberty bonds." Fifteen years later, no bands, no marching, no orators, just a patriotic girl, or a broken piece of human frame trying to sell a "poppy" for a few cents. Made by even a more unfortunate brother in one of our fifty-five hospitals.

Given fifteen years to think it over, war has degenerated from the price of a Liberty bond to the price of a "poppy."

Six millions of these boys, regular customers, are disabled this year, too, and from the same war, so those that have will have to try and make up for these, by buying more.

There is only one sure way of stopping war, that is to see that every "statesman" has the same chance to reflect after it's over that these boys making "poppies" have had.

Yours,
Will Rogers.

1824   Mr. Rogers Recalls That No Boy
         Pitied Him When He Was Mayor

SANTA MONICA, Cal., May 29. — Paul Block, the wealthy newspaper man of New York is an old acquaintance of mine, and I knew he had a boy, but I had no idea the boy was so interested in downtrodden mayors.

At that time, I was Mayor of Beverly Hills, and I know I was worse off than Mayor Walker. I had to furnish my own car and got pinched in it, and received no salary at all, and had to keep my screen stars out of devilment.

Course, there was always a lot of people out here claimed I was overpaid.

Yours,
Will Rogers.

1825   Will Rogers Wants A Decision
         On The Sales Tax Proposal

SANTA MONICA, Cal., May 30. — Now the sales tax thing is going to pass.

May not pass this year, for all the boys are up for election and they want to show their voter where he is not to pay anything.

171

But, as soon as election is over, and when they get back in, they will go ahead and pass it, for its the fairest and easiest to collect. No nation that ever tried it ever abandoned it.

What's the difference between a lot of taxes put on a lot of articles and a few taxes put on everything but the cheapest necessities.

So come on Herbert, make up your mind.

Yours,
Will Rogers.

1826   WILL ROGERS EXPLAINS SPURT
OF CONGRESS ON THE TAX BILL

BEVERLY HILLS, Cal., May 31. — Looks like Garner and Hoover are not going to wait till November 4 to have it out. They are going to do it now.

Hoover calls Garner's plan of relief a "pork barrel." Garner can't come back at him and say, "your reconstruction finance was also a pork barrel." For the bankers that money helped didn't eat pork. So poor Jack has got to dig up another slogan.

We are living in a great age. The Senate has got to tax something right away, for the conventions will be here, and no matter what taxpayer is shot in the back the Senators must have the pleasure of being at the convention.

Yours,
Will Rogers.

1827   MR. ROGERS GOES A-TRAVELING
AND JOTS DOWN A FEW NOTES

SAN FRANCISCO, Cal., June 1. — When a Los Angeles guy comes up here to Frisco, it's just a country boy going to town. You have to take your spurs off here. You can't explain Frisco. It's just the Greta Garbo of the West.

Just come up through Stanford University at Palo Alto and my son, a student there, couldn't tell me where Herbert Hoover's home was. He is either just dumb or a Democrat, could be both.

See the Senate took your money and balanced their budget. The whole thing is supposed to be based on what we all earn this year. Somebody is going to get fooled.

Yours,
Will Rogers.

1828   Mr. Rogers Finds Palo Alto Sign
            That He Considers Significant

PALO ALTO, Cal., June 2. — Back here again today looking for Mr. Hoover's house. Saw a sign "to let" on it, so that don't look any too nourishing for you Democrats.

Had a talk with Herbert this morning, not Herbert Hoover, but "the" Herbert, Herbert Fleischacker, who is the J. P. Morgan, Owen Young, Carter Glass and Andy Mellon, all combined, of the Pacific Coast.

And, he is one rich man who didn't start out by saying, "Well, I am an optimist." He said "I don't know any more what's the matter with us, or what is going to happen to us, than the U. S. Senate does."

Imagine a big banker admitting to that?
                            Yours,
                            Will Rogers.

1829   Will Rogers Urges Sales Tax
            To Care For The Unemployed

BEVERLY HILLS, Cal., June 3. — Congress politically, but not economically, turned down the sales tax. Well, even out of the mouths of babes may come a good idea. Ham Lewis, a Senator from Illinois, suggests this: "Put a sales tax on now (on objects not taxed under the present bill) and use that additional money just for the aid of the unemployed."

Now there is some sense to a scheme like that, for it provides where the money is coming from before it's spent; there is not a soul (unless it be a politician) that would object to paying a few cents more for an article, if he knew it was going to some one who needed it worse than him.

So come on, a manufacturers' tax for the unemployed.
                            Yours,
                            Will Rogers.

1830   Will Rogers Sums Up The News
            Of The Day As It Looks To Him

SANTA MONICA, Cal., June 5. — The Senate voted a 10 per cent cut in government civilians' wages. Surprised they didn't vote themselves a raise.

173

Chile is the first country to return to normalcy. Last Saturday they had two dictators and one president, and returned the country to the Democrats.

The Crown Prince is trying to get back in power in Germany. A man has either got to be conceited or looney to purposely want to be the head of any country nowadays.

Congress is working fast now, so they can attend the convention, and the payers of the tax can attend the poorhouse.

Yours,
Will Rogers.

1831   MR. ROGERS GREETS THE RETURN
OF TWO OLD CAMPAIGN FIGURES

BEVERLY HILLS, Cal., June 6. — We never realized that elections were so near till we saw by the papers this morning that each political party has "some" plan of relieving the unemployed.

They have been unemployed for three years, and nobody paid any attention to 'em, but now both parties have discovered that while they are not working there is nothing in the Constitution to prevent them from voting.

So Democratic Campaign Leader "Hooey" and Republican Leader "Baloney" say:

"We have to do something about this, Miss Secretary, reach in the bag and get out some of those old campaign promises. We will dust 'em off and use 'em again this year, and remember no matter what the other side promises, see their promise and raise 'em two more."

Yours,
Will Rogers.

1832   MR. ROGERS HAS NEW CANDIDATE
FOR PRESIDENTIAL NOMINATION

BEVERLY HILLS, Cal., June 7. — Got a new suggestion for Presidential candidate. Found a prominent man who can make up his mind.

This fellow Rockefeller jumped right out of the Sunday school room into the hearts of his countrymen with the most plain, straightforward and lucid statement that's been issued not only on prohibition but that's been said on any subject since the panic. Even the rabid drys will applaud his honesty and frankness.

Stop to think it over, this fellow would make us a fine President, if we could persuade him to take over a little, small, run-down outfit like ours.
Yours,
Will Rogers.

1833   W<small>ILL</small> R<small>OGERS</small> C<small>OMMISERATES</small>
               W<small>ITH</small> T<small>HE</small> N<small>ATION'S</small> B<small>ANKERS</small>

BEVERLY HILLS, Cal., June 8. — "The Bankers Institute" (who call themselves the educational end of banking) are holding a big convention out here. Every one of 'em carry American Express money orders. There is not a checkbook in a carload.

I hope they go back by Canada and see how it is that Canada has only had one bank failure in ten years. The idea evidently is not copyrighted.

But we can't alibi all our ills by just knocking the old banker. First he loaned the money, then the people all at once wanted it back, and he didn't have it. Now he's got it again, and is afraid to loan it, so the poor devil don't know what to do.
Yours,
Will Rogers.

1834   M<small>R</small>. R<small>OGERS</small> A<small>GAIN</small> N<small>OMINATES</small>
               A P<small>RESIDENTIAL</small> C<small>ANDIDATE</small>

BEVERLY HILLS, Cal., June 9. — I tell you this country is upside down. Didn't Iowa nominate a radio announcer for Senator?

Mr. McAdoo wisely says the Democratic platform should allow you to vote on the prohibition or any other amendment you can think of.

Charley Dawes would make the best President of anybody in the whole country, but he wouldn't stay with it. The minute the new had worn off and he had the thing on its feet, he would want to switch to Sultan of Morocco, or Eva in Aimee's Temple. Why, he is as nervous as a cigarette smoker.
Yours,
Will Rogers.

1835   Mr. Rogers Notes Each Splash
As Drys Dive Off Springboard

BEVERLY HILLS, Cal., June 10. — Why, the drys are diving off the springboard so fast there won't be any room in the water for the original wets.

Will H. Hayes, the old Presbyterian circuit rider, went off the sixty-foot board into the deepest part yesterday. Bishop Cannon is just trying to find a bathing suit now that will fit him.

When everybody gets through saying everything in the world about a subject, why then Calvin Coolidge comes along and says what should have been said in the first place. In these times of everybody guessing and alibiing, Calvin can still see clear. But, that's why he is where he is, because he could always see ahead.

Yours,
Will Rogers.

1836   Will Rogers Reaches Chicago
By Train—Disgraced, Insulted

CHICAGO, Ill., June 12. — Well here I am right at the stage door waiting to see all the actors in this great comedy called "a convention held for no reason at all."

I have the distinction of being the first Democratic white child to arrive at the Republican fiasco. Breakfast at home Saturday morning, dinner in Kansas City, then into Chicago for breakfast Sunday, but disgraced myself by making the last hop on the train, as there was no regular plane. Guess I am getting old, going back, be taking up golf next.

A newspaper man spoiled my whole convention by asking me if "I was an alternate." Now a delegate is bad enough, but an alternate is just a spare tire for a delegate. An alternate is the lowest form of political life there is. He is the parachute in a plane that never leaves the ground.

Yours,
Will Rogers.

1837   WILL ROGERS SEES DEMOCRATS
                 FACING TROUBLE ON WET ISSUE

CLAREMORE, Okla., June 17. — Well, I was the first Democratic white child to escape from the Republicans. Just flew in here from Chicago in four hours.

Saw all of 'em leaving Chicago last night. Alice is coming back for the Democrats—said this one was misrepresented and wasn't a convention. Pat Hurley went away grinning like a possum. The real wets all went away mad, the real drys went away sorer than the wets. The Democrats seem more pleased with it than the Republicans, but they must not crow too quick. Wait till they get there and try to frame up a prohibition plank that will please all, and they will begin to realize what these birds were up against. So they are liable to come out of there with one that reads more different ways than the Republicans did.

                               Yours,
                               Will Rogers.

1838   MR. ROGERS, BACK IN CALIFORNIA,
                 SEEMS A LITTLE PESSIMISTIC

SANTA MONICA, Cal., June 19. — Mr. Hoover says he is not going out and lectioneer for the job. That's kinder like a pitcher saying, "I don't need to even warm up against this team."

I believe if some one of the Democratic candidates would say the same thing, he would be nominated. For the Democrats have lost many an election between June and November.

This is one year the more a man promises the less he will be believed. Voters are not going to vote for a man this year with any hope of him helping 'em any. They are just going to vote for him for——?. Well, I don't believe they will even go to the trouble of voting. They have lost everything else so they are afraid they might lose their vote.

                               Yours,
                               Will Rogers.

1839   MR. ROGERS IS LOOKING FORWARD
                 TO A GREAT SHOW NEXT WEEK

BEVERLY HILLS, Cal., June 20. — Everybody asks, "Who are the Democrats going to nominate?"

"If the Democrats nominate a good man." Where do they get that "good man" stuff? The Democrats haven't got anything else. And, if you don't believe it you just listen in on the radio next week.

Flew through Fort Worth, Texas, the other day and home over the splendid American Airways. Texas is sending more folks to Chicago than they did to Houston. Special trains, bands, all for little Jack Garner.

The wets out this way are hollering for Ritchie.

It's going to be a great show—1,100 real delegates, and not a postmaster in the hall. Nobody knows what any one of 'em is liable to do.

Yours,
Will Rogers.

1840   MR. ROGERS SUFFERS A CHANGE
OF HEART TOWARD CONGRESS

BEVERLY HILLS, Cal., June 21. — Say, you all got to quit knocking Congress. Didn't you see what they did yesterday? Passed a bill to cut their own salaries. Come on, let's give the boys a great big hand. That was mighty good of 'em at that.

Well, how did your taxes work today? This was the first day of the new taxes. Everybody is wondering how they come to tax the articles that they did. Well, I found out how it was done. They give each member permission to bring in the name of some article that he particularly didn't like personally, and they put a tax on for him.

Yours,
Will Rogers.

1841   MR. ROGERS IS A BIT SARCASTIC
REGARDING THIS NEW ARMS MOVE

BEVERLY HILLS, Cal., June 22. — You are, from now on, going to hear every imaginable scheme brought out to get America to cancel the debts.

In fact, a "wow" of a one has just been showed up. "We are to cancel the debts if Europe will not arm."

That's original! The Liberty bondholders of America bribe Europe to disarm!

We pay 'em five billion dollars if they promise us they just struggle along on what guns they have and not be rash and spend their money foolishly on armaments.

You can't hire a nation from buying a gun if they think they need one any more than you can bribe folks not to carry an umbrella on rainy days.

And, by the way, what are they going to pay us for not arming?
Yours,
Will Rogers.

1842   WILL ROGERS DESERTS POLITICS
          FOR A MORE IMPORTANT ISSUE

BEVERLY HILLS, Cal., June 23. — Mr. Hoover issued a splendid disarmament program, but he was unfortunate enough to issue it on the same day the "square deal" boxing commission disarmed Max Schmeling.

So, naturally, nobody paid much attention to Mr. Hoover's plan. It was the New York plan that attracted all the attention.

Poor Sharkey, nobody feels that he was in any way responsible for it. And, of course, Max was gained by it. Make it clear to foreigners that in the Olympic Games that no boxing commission has anything to do with 'em.

And, ask the radio announcers if the next fight is not so "hot" to tell us so. Sounded like Dempsey and Fitzsimmons were battling it out at the height of their careers.
Yours,
Will Rogers.

1843   MR. ROGERS EXPRESSES THANKS
          FOR ATLANTIC AND PACIFIC OCEANS

BEVERLY HILLS, Cal., June 24. — Well, Mr. Hoover's disarmament plan fell just like all of 'em have. Nations that have none say it's "fine," but the ones that are well armed say it's terrible.

I have been to every one of those disarmament conferences both here and in Europe, and if there is one thing that has been absolutely proved that can't be done it's to get countries to agree on what constitutes protection.

We can make fine proposals over here, for Mexico and Canada are not so strong, but you put us over there in the midst of that mess, and, brother, we would go out and buy another gun, too.

We ought to set by a day of thanksgiving, blessing the Atlantic and Pacific Ocean for their splendid judgment in locating where they did.

Yours,
Will Rogers.

1844 Mr. Rogers, Down In Oklahoma,
   Still Hears Democratic Noises

CLAREMORE, Okla., July 3. — Flew down here to recuperate from one straight month of speeches. Heard a mule braying a while ago out at the farm and for a minute I couldn't tell who he was nominating.

Roosevelt made a good speech yesterday and he gave aviation the biggest boost it ever had. Took his family and flew out there. That will stop these big shots from thinking their lives are too important to the country to take a chance on flying.

But it was a good thing the convention broke up. Times was hard. Some of the delegates had started eating their alternates. Cannibalism was about to be added to other Democratic accomplishments.

Keep the following records straight. It was California that sold out and not Texas. Texas was for sticking even after California had quit 'em.

I have one thing to be thankful for. I am the only defeated candidate that didn't have a band left on my hands to ship back home.

Could an artist paint a more pitiful picture than a poor defeated candidate waking up the morning after the vote and seeing thirty-five horn tooters that had, on account of the humane laws, to be delivered back home. It's enough to discourage candidates but it never does. Four years later they are back again, same ones.

Yours,
Will Rogers.

1845 Mr. Rogers Recalls The Victory
   Of The Rural Boys At Chicago

NOWATA, Okla., July 4. — The Democratic Convention was a victory of the country boys over the city slickers.

New York and Chicago come there thinking that on account of being uninstructed Tammany was no more for Smith than Smith is for Tammany.

Well, they thought they would be in a position to stop Roosevelt, sell out to the highest bidder and go home driving the band wagon.

Great idea. All that went wrong with it was that the old orange squeezers from California thought of it first, sold out and was on their way West with the loot before New York and Chicago jiggigos could get their cards marked.

It was a lesson in rural politics.

Yours,
Will Rogers.

1846   WILL ROGERS IS IN THE THICK
         OF AN OKLAHOMA FREE-FOR-ALL

CLAREMORE, Okla., July 5. — Today is primary day here in town, both Democratic and also Republican (if any one was humorous enough to run on such ticket here).

There is more Democrats here in Rogers County running for office than in both Chicago's "fiascos."

Looks like the taxpayers in the U. S. are the only folks hiring any help nowadays. A private business when it don't do any business, don't use anybody. But the less business the public has the more we hire to tend to it.

There is but one county institution that needs enlarging, and that's the insane place, put us all in there till we know enough to vote to cut out at least 50 per cent of our governing expenses.

Yours,
Will Rogers.

1847   MR. ROGERS FINDS DOWN IN TEXAS
         A NICE, HOMEY LITTLE PLACE

VERNON, Tex., July 6. — Yes, ranches are all gone. Yeah?

Well, I am on one right now of 600,000 acres, belonging to W. T. Waggoner, with 25,000 cattle and some of the best horses in any State. He is one cowman that was smart enough to solve the low prices of cattle and make ranches pay. Every cow has got her own oil well.

The town this will be sent from is Vernon, an old-time cow town, but now a place that is a real modern Claremore. Court house bigger than Garner's Capitol in Washington.

Garner is the talk of everybody in Texas. These people down here don't know that there is a guy named Roosevelt that is mixed up with him in this new enterprise. The ticket down here is "Garner and Garner."

Yours,
Will Rogers.

1848   Mr. Rogers Would Rather Look
At Cattle Than At Delegates

VERNON, Tex., July 7. — No papers away out here on the prairie where I am, so I don't know what has happened.

By golly, to people away out on farms and ranches, where people make a living off what you are supposed to make it off of, why it don't make much difference what happens. The "market could have closed strong," or closed forever, and it wouldn't matter to a big bunch of Americans.

It sure is a lot prettier sight to look at thousands of white-faced cattle than thousands of bald-faced delegates in one corral howling like mad and milling for nothing.

They brand the cattle so you can tell 'em, and have to put bandages on the delegates, so there's not much difference after all.

Yours,
Will Rogers.

1849   Will Rogers Tries His Hand
At Roping Some Live Calves

MULESHOE, Tex., July 8. — Down here at the Mashed O, my old friends the Halsell's ranch, branding thousands of calves. I have been roping at 'em all day and they just look around and say go on comedian and do your stuff on the stage, but don't try a real cowboy's racket.

I'll catch one of the little rascals yet if I have to bribe him.

Say, I've been so interested in real things I just quit reading the papers. What is Congress doing and why did Aimee's husband establish his good name? A rancher just rode out to the round-up and said the happy warrior had decided to leave the war and be happy again.

Did you know that hogs went up $2 a hundred while the two conventions were in session? Make your own joke.

Yours,
Will Rogers.

1850   WILL ROGERS FINDS THAT THINGS ARE LOOKING BETTER OUT WEST

MULESHOE, Tex., July 10. — Well sir, don't you think things are looking better? They are among the stock raisers and farmers.

I have always maintained that the Republicans this Summer before election would with all their influence and money power create an amateur prosperity enough to make folks think things were on the upgrade and not to change horses.

You know it's not going to take much to make us think we are doing fine. No breast, or white meat, just the wing and old back will taste like a banquet to us now.

I think too just promising the people some beer made everybody feel better, even if they know they will die of old age before they get it.

Yours,
Will Rogers.

1851   WILL ROGERS GIVES WILL ROGERS BOOST IN HIS RACE FOR CONGRESS

ALBUQUERQUE, N. M., July 11. — A nap in Chicago cost me the Presidency. Now I find that while I was down in Texas trying to rope a calf my namesake in Oklahoma brought home the bacon.

Well, I am for him. He has shown more ingenuity already than any candidate I ever heard of.

They are trying to "hog" him out of it now. Well, that's politics for you. They say that he was a Republican eight years ago. My goodness, the whole State of Oklahoma was Republican just four years ago, so he saw what was coming four years before they did. I tell you this bird is smart. In fact, he will be plum out of place in Congress.

So let's all get behind "Will Rogers for Congress."

Yours,
Will Rogers.

1852 MR. ROGERS IS FOR CONTINUING
      TO OWE THE SAME FELLOW

BEVERLY HILLS, Cal., July 12. — Say, the more you read of that bill for relief that the President vetoed the more you can see he was right.

It was going to loan money to individuals. Now it's right to have the government feed and help get jobs, but to loan everybody money that needs it to pay off somebody else that they owe, well, in the words of my old friends, the two Black Crows, "You can't do that."

Besides, borrowing from one fellow to pay another one don't do any good. Just keep on owing the same fellow. He has got used to "carrying" us by now.

In other words, let's don't change creditors while crossing a stream.

Yours,
Will Rogers.

1853 MR. ROGERS INTERPRETS THE STAND
      OF THE REPUBLICAN WOMEN WETS

BEVERLY HILLS, Cal., July 13. — Here is a funny situation. The women anti-prohibitionists said, "We will support the party that comes out for direct repeal."

And they would if it had been the Republican party. But, as luck would have it, it was those "mangy" Democrats instead.

Now, most of these women are wealthy Republicans. And they are having a time now trying to get out of it.

The ladies want prohibition repealed all right, but not bad enough to repeal the Republican party with it. They want it wet, but not wet enough to be Democratic.

In other words, politics is thicker than beer.

Yours,
Will Rogers.

1854 MR. ROGERS FISHES AROUND A BIT
      AND DISCOVERS THE REAL ISSUE

BEVERLY HILLS, Cal., July 14. — Well, let's see what was staring us in the face from the papers today.

Will Rogers as "Pike Peters" in scenes from the motion picture Down to Earth, based on a story by Homer Croy (Fox Film Corporation, 1932).

Nurmi, the great Finnish runner in the coming Olympics, run in here yesterday from New York. The other Finns arrive by plane this afternoon.

Roosevelt has actually started his Presidential campaign. I see pictures all over the front page today of him fishing. Are we never to get an original candidate? Well, as least, he didn't stand in the creek with rubber boots on.

This campaign will be settled on fish. Do you want a deep sea fisherman in the White House, flounders and cod, or a big trout and perch man?

Yours,
Will Rogers.

1855   WILL ROGERS NOW SEES BEER
LINED UP AS POLITICAL LOOT

BEVERLY HILLS, Cal., July 15. — Prohibition originally started out with us as a moral issue. It was either good or bad for you to drink. Then it drifted to economics: Did people save more when not drinking? Then into racketeering. But now it's drifted into the worst angle of any, that is politics. American history records no return of anything once it got into politics.

The vote in the Senate the other day shows that morals, economy, less taxes, nothing entered their minds; only "how can my party get part of the beer and all the credit?" Beer has lined up with the post offices as political loot.

Yours,
Will Rogers.

1856   WILL ROGERS SEES JUBILATION
AT ADJOURNMENT OF CONGRESS

EAST BAKERSFIELD, Cal., July 17. — Was up to Stanford Saturday to see the American athletes try out for the Olympic Games. Talk about different nations competing, say they were competing there the white race against the colored. Why, all you had to do there to win a race or a jump was just have a dark-complexion man show up as competitor. In fact, I got to believing that I could "black up" and go in there and win something myself. Talk about Finns running, you watch Booker T. Washington's boys.

I never saw a country as happy as the United States was yesterday when they read Congress would adjourn. People just felt that the depression couldn't end till those birds quit appropriating and got home.

Yours,
Will Rogers.

1857   WILL ROGERS SAYS CONGRESS
        WENT DOWN APPROPRIATING

BEVERLY HILLS, Cal., July 18. — Well, Congress adjourned, but they went down appropriating, and some of them are going to find in November that they have just appropriated themselves out of a job.

They killed the sales tax; now, what alibi are they going to offer for that? It's proving a life-saver for Mississippi. They keep building more roads, certainly not for the automobiles. Guess it's just to provide room for folks "thumbing" their way somewhere.

America used to use their forefinger to "point with pride." Now it's their thumb, to register hope.

Yours,
Will Rogers.

1858   ROGERS FINDS ABUNDANCE
        OF JAPANESE AT OLYMPICS

BEVERLY HILLS, Cal., July 19. — If any country wants to pounce on Japan, now is the time, for every able-bodied Japanese, man, woman and child, is here to compete in the Olympics. There is hundreds of 'em; the big Swedes and Germans can't step without tramping on dozens of 'em. And they all got kodaks.

I asked a nice little Japanese girl if her father and mother was on the team, too.

"No, they didn't have a kodak."

Visiting the studio today was Matthew Brush, not "late" of but "still" of Wall Street.

187

Three years ago he saw America going over Niagara Falls, and sold everything "short" but barrels. Such foresight was naturally investigated by the Senate, so he was, and has pronounced clear of at least "astigmatism."

Yours,
Will Rogers.

1859   ROGERS FINDS CONFERENCES FINE FOR STIRRING UP HATE

BEVERLY HILLS, Cal., July 20. — I see where Mr. Mellon is coming home "bringing the data on the economic conference." "A conference." "A conference." That's all we have had for years. The world has just conferred itself into bankruptcy.

There hasn't been a conference since the beginning of the war that hasn't stirred up more hate, and done more harm than it has good. A conference is just an admission that you want somebody to join you in your troubles.

The world can't improve till it gets so poor that it can't send delegates to a conference. Then it will begin to improve by depending on itself.

Yours,
Will Rogers.

1860   WILL ROGERS SAYS MUSSOLINI KNOWS HOW TO RUN A CABINET

BEVERLY HILLS, Cal., July 21. — Mussolini has got the right idea. When a Cabinet officer resigns, he fills the post himself. When the Cabinet holds a meeting, Mussolini just talks to himself under an assumed name.

See they are sending the bonus boys home at just what it actually costs, but they give the Congressmen 10 cents a mile to get rid of them.

Mr. Hoover is not to "open the games here," which means his political advisers have assured him that the State is "safe." Well, he will not only miss some votes, but will miss some awful good running and jumping. Maybe he has seen enough of that in Washington.

Yours,
Will Rogers.

1861   WILL ROGERS OFFERS A MIRROR
AT $1.80 TO CONFOUND AN ARTIST

BEVERLY HILLS, Cal., July 22. — An artist in New York, because his sale of antiques didn't turn out so hot, got hostile at us. He said a "William and Mary" mirror only brought the paltry $400. Well, my boy, William hasn't got any mirror, but my daughter Mary has, and if I can get her away from the front of it I will be glad to add Bill's name to it and let the "Rogers William and Mary" go for $1.80. I will show that bird what depression really is.

He says America is a "race of children and rogues, governed by morons." Well, that last part is just what the Democrats are trying to remedy.

                              Yours,
                              Will Rogers.

1862   WILL ROGERS PAYS TRIBUTE
TO A GREAT MAN OF THE STAGE

BEVERLY HILLS, Cal., July 24. — Our world of "make believe" is sad. Scores of comedians are not funny, hundreds of "America's most beautiful girls" are not gay. Our benefactor has passed away.

He picked us from all walks of life. He led us into what little fame we achieved. He remained our friend regardless of our usefulness to him as an entertainer. He brought beauty into the entertainment world. The profession of acting must be necessary, for it exists in every race, and every language, and to have been the master amusement provider of your generation, surely a life's work was accomplished.

And he left something on earth that hundreds of us will treasure till our curtain falls, and that was a "badge," a badge of which we were proud, and never ashamed of, and wanted the world to read the lettering on it, "I worked for Ziegfeld."

So goodbye, Flo, save a spot for me, for you will put on a show up there some day that will knock their eyes out.

                              Yours,
                              Will Rogers.

1863   WILL ROGERS SAYS PEOPLE
JUST DON'T CANCEL DEBTS

BEVERLY HILLS, Cal., July 25. — My good friend Senator Borah canceled the debts over the radio Saturday night and they hadn't any more than announced the tooth paste company that sponsored it than the boys commenced shooting at him. Borah canceled 'em because I guess he knew he wasn't going to get 'em.

But if a man owes you some money and he is having hard sledding you won't go to him and say, "Well, that's all right buddie, here is the note, I will just tear it up." No, sir, that's not done. In fact he never asks or expects that. He always understands that he is to pay when he gets it. An individual couldn't single-handed assemble that much nerve. It takes nations to concentrate that much.

Yours,
Will Rogers.

1864   WILL ROGERS FINDS ELECTION
HAS ALREADY COST BILLIONS

BEVERLY HILLS, Cal., July 26. — You remember during the war when we would read that the Liberty bond issue had been oversubscribed. Well, the other day Congress voted that they was going to loan folks something like $2,000,000,000, well you talk about a thing being "oversubscribed," why the whole issue was spoken for before sundown. Why I honestly believe they could have loaned twice that much, and they perhaps will when they meet again, for that was the loaningest" and "appropriationist" Congress that ever was.

Be a good joke on 'em, if after loaning all that money, they then go home and get beat, had all their "loaning" for nothing. The coming election has already cost the taxpayers billions of dollars.

Yours,
Will Rogers.

1865   WILL ROGERS SAYS A WORD
FOR THE SMALL-TOWN EDITOR

BEVERLY HILLS, Cal., July 27. — We have a great bunch out here prowling around. It's the National Editorial Association, composed of editors in smaller towns and weekly publications. They are just eating their way around the country, having a good time, and getting a lot of pleasure out of it. And giving every one that meets 'em a close-up of just about as representative gang of Americans as would be possible to band together—intelligent, well read, and no national advertising controls their pages.

They are not conceited enough to think they "mold public opinion." They just go along serving their community with the most indispensable article that it has. And yet their real power is greater than all your metropolitan dailies combined. Any person that don't read at least one well-written country newspaper is not truly informed.

Yours,
Will Rogers.

1866   WILL ROGERS SAYS EVERYBODY
        WANTS TO MOVE SOMEBODY ELSE

BEVERLY HILLS, Cal., July 28. — See where Mr. Hoover and almost his entire Cabinet held a meeting to decide where to move the bonus army. The Democrats are holding a meeting to decide where to move Mr. Hoover and his Cabinet. Everybody wants to do something with somebody else.

I see by this morning's paper where "living" has decreased 70 per cent since December. In figuring these statistics, (and by the way who is it that figures up all these fool things?) well, anyhow, you might live that much cheaper, but that don't figure in the worry. If worry is worth anything, we never was living as expensive.

Yours,
Will Rogers.

1867   WILL ROGERS GIVES THE VIEW
        OF 15,000 HUNGRY VETERANS

BEVERLY HILLS, Cal., July 29. — Too bad about this affair in Washington. Personally, I think the whole idea of this pilgrimage was ill advised, and no doubt did their cause harm, but they have their side of it too. They have the same right there as any other "lobbyist." They at least were not paid. They were doing it for themselves, which placed 'em right away about 90 per cent higher in public estimation than the thousands of "lobbyists" that are there all the time.

But no matter how you feel about the whole thing, you have got to admire the fine way that big body of hungry men acted while they were there. They hold the record for being the best behaved of any fifteen thousand hungry men ever assembled anywhere in the world. They were hungry, and they were seeing our government wasting thousands and millions before their eyes, and yet they remained fair and sensibe.

Would 15,000 hungry bankers have done it, 15,000 farmers, 15,000 preachers? And just think what 15,000 clubwomen would have done to Washington even if they wasn't hungry. The Senate would have resigned and the President committed suicide.

It's easy to be a gentleman when you are well fed, but these boys did it on an empty stomach. So we at least owe 'em a vote of thanks. And it was too bad their fine record was marred at the finish by somebody blundering.

Yours,
Will Rogers.

1868   WILL ROGERS VIEWS THE SCENE
AT THE OPENING OF OLYMPICS

BEVERLY HILLS, Cal., July 31. — Get this for a laugh. First event on the Olympic program, weight-lifting, both light and heavy. Each event won by a Frenchman; one was a dancing teacher, the other a dealer in a gambling house.

The best showing at opening was by Canada, second by Italy, third Argentine, and today 105,000 people are looking for the ladies' milliner that put those French "berets" on our American boys. Those "boudwoir caps" are bad enough on a Frenchman, but on an American athlete they are a scream.

Only test of endurance at the opening was 10,000-meter prayer. A man with a short prayer could get a booking for life just at these national events.

Yours,
Will Rogers.

1869   ROGERS SAYS BOTH PARTIES
REALLY NEED THE JOBS NOW

BEVERLY HILLS, Cal., Aug. 1. — Everett Sanders, the very able head of the Republican campaign, went clear up to the old boss's home at Northampton to try and get Mr. Coolidge to help keep the Democrats from getting their "bonus" this Fall.

The army drove the soldiers out. Now they want Coolidge to help drive the Democrats out of Washington. Both armies are equally destitute, in fact the soldiers have worked since the Democrats have.

This is not an election of parties or policies this Fall, it's an election where both sides really need the work. In fact, I think if you would split the salaries between every two candidates running, they would call off the election.

Yours,
Will Rogers.

1870   WILL ROGERS FINDS THE HORSE
IS INDISPENSABLE IN WARTIME

BEVERLY HILLS, Cal., Aug. 2. — Saw an event this morning that took real nerve. Twenty-six army officers from ten different countries had to ride four miles up and down hill over twenty-two jumps, high and solid if a horse hit 'em, they drew 'em just as they started, and started at five-minute intervals. No one, including the three Americans, had ever seen the horses. He had to be his own judge of the speed his horse could stand up under.

Now you talk about nerve, and no nation has any monopoly on it, they were all great, and our American Army horses were fine. You would have been proud of 'em.

Don't let Brisbane or anybody else who is going to fight the whole next war entirely with planes and poison gas do away with the cavalry. There is certain things you can't replace the horse in, and war is one of 'em.

Yours,
Will Rogers.

1871   WILL ROGERS FINDS ATHLETES
OUTRUNNING THE POLITICIANS

BEVERLY HILLS, Cal., Aug. 3. — It's awful hard to get your mind on such insignificant things as Republican or Democratic candidates with 1,500 picked athletes of the world breaking records under your nose. If an athlete wins an event and don't break a world's record we hiss him out of the arena.

Incidentally, the man that brought the first slaves to this country must have had these Olympic Games in mind, for these "Senegambians" have just about run the white man ragged. Every winner is either an American Negro or an American white woman.

Wait till we get to golf, bridge, or cocktail shaking, then the American white man will come into his own. Everybody out here is predicting this California recordbreaking to continue right up till after Nov. 4, when Roosevelt will outrun Hoover, Tolan, Metcalfe, and maybe Babe Didrikson.

Yours,
Will Rogers.

1872   WILL ROGERS SAYS ROY CHAPIN
        GOT JOB IN TIME FOR SALARY CUT

BEVERLY HILLS, Cal., Aug. 4. — One of the very able men of the automobile industry goes into the Cabinet, Roy Chapin. He arrived on his new job just in time to get his salary cut 15 per cent. You can get some awful good men now to work for mighty little money.

In the bicycle events out here in the Olympics, our riders couldn't get there in time to change a tire for the foreigners. Too many Fords parked outside our school houses for our young folks to even know how to ride a bike.

Folks had nothing laid up when this depression hit us, but it looks like they think autographs will save 'em next time.

Yours,
Will Rogers.

1873   ROGERS FINDS A WAY TO TELL
        DEMOCRAT FROM REPUBLICAN

BEVERLY HILS, Cal., Aug. 5. — Every year it gets harder and harder to tell the difference between a Republican and a Democrat. (Course outside of the looks.)

Their platforms and policies become more and more alike. But I believe I have found out the sure way to tell one from another this year. It's just the way they talk. The Republican says, "Well, things could have been worse," and the Democrat says, "How?"

Yours,
Will Rogers.

1874   ROGERS CALLS MARKET RISE
PLOT TO DEFEAT DEMOCRATS

BEVERLY HILLS, Cal., Aug. 7. — Been telling you for a year what these Republicans would do with that market just in time to knock the poor inoffensive Democrats out of their hard-earned votes in November.

Now they are all just a buying and selling among themselves in stocks that haven't shown a cent of increased earning power. That shows the thing is kinder "cockeyed." The earnings should come first and then the raise in price of the stock.

Like everything that is prearranged, it's being kinder overdone. As dumb as we are we know we can't get prosperous that quick.

But one good thing about it all is that it might have a lasting result. But don't forget the original idea of it was to beat the poor old Democrats, who never did anybody any harm in their lives.

Yours,
Will Rogers.

1875   ROGERS FINDS OLYMPIC GAMES
THE GREATEST SHOW OF THE AGE

BEVERLY HILLS, Cal., Aug. 8. — You folks all over the United States that thought these Olympic Games was just some real estate racket of Los Angeles and didn't come, you have been badly fooled. You have missed the greatest show from every angle that was ever held in America.

Regardless of hard times, there has been from 70,000 to 105,000 people every day. Regardless of this old town's boosting and blowing, they certainly come through beautiful.

It was dignified, impressing and thrilling, and you have just missed something you won't get to see again during our lifetime.

And say don't worry about the Japanese flying over here in case of war, those birds will swim over.

The Argentine won the marathon, 26 miles long. He could stand it, but fainted during his Argentine's national anthem. That is the longest tune in the world and was written to be played during a marathon.

Yours,
Will Rogers.

1876   ROGERS SURPRISED A HAY-FIELD
SHOULD WORRY MR. COOLIDGE

BEVERLY HILLS, Cal., Aug. 9. — Mr. Coolidge's excuse for not going to the White House to attend the notification ceremony is that "it would irritate his hay fever." Now Plymouth Notch, Vermont, where he is now, is right in the middle of a hayfield. And there hasn't been any hay cut in Washington, D. C. since October, '29.

These politicians if they ain't a lot of prima donnas! Senator Dickinson, the Republican keynote speaker, accuses Roosevelt of being a bad sport by holding the Mayor Walker investigation the same day of notification. "Now don't you have your party on the same day I have my party, or that will split the newspaper space." I suppose if a war or an earthquake showed up on that day, Dickinson would claim it was a Democratic trick.

Yours,
Will Rogers.

1877   MR. ROGERS NOTES A SURPRISE
IN STORE FOR MR. HOOVER TODAY

BEVERLY HILLS, Cal., Aug. 10. — Well, tomorrow is the big surprise day for Mr. Hoover. He is to be notified, not beatified, just notified. They are going to tell him that he is to have the extreme pleasure of having nothing on his mind for the next four years but this country.

A poor man who has had more hard times thrust on him than any man that ever occupied that high position, then to have a bunch come who were endeavoring to sentence you for four more years, that almost comes under the heading of a blow.

By the way, Jimmie Walker is to have his notification tomorrow, too. And, oh, yes, Japan is sore at Stimson again. Poor Japan, Stimson has kept those little fellows worried worse than they have our swimmers.

Yours,
Will Rogers.

1878   WILL ROGERS HAS HIS SAY
ON THE STOCK MARKET RISE

BEVERLY HILLS, Cal., Aug. 1. — Here yesterday was a good illustration of how these market boosters can pull a bad one. Yesterday farm machinery went up on the stock market.

Now there is not a farmer in the United States that can pay his taxes, or his groceries. Now how is he going to buy any farm machinery. He has no more credit. If he wanted to he couldn't get a garden hoe much less a threshing machine. He can plow with a forked stick and raise more than he can sell. So that raise don't look so hot. That's like Christmas trees going up at New Years.

Everybody is trying to tune in on Seabury being investigated by Walker. Our investigations have always contributed more to amusement than they have to knowledge.

Yours,
Will Rogers.

1879   WILL ROGERS THINKS THE DRY
         IS NOW THE "FORGOTTEN MAN"

BEVERLY HILS, Cal., Aug. 12. — Well he did it. Mr. Hoover held his handkerchief up and saw which way the old "noble experiment" was blowing and joined in the parade. You can talk "morals" and all that, but when the votes lay the other way, why they sho go with 'em.

Now the question is where are the "drys" going? Both sides are wet and the poor old dry hasn't got a soul to vote for. He is Roosevelt's "forgotten man."

Yours,
Will Rogers.

1880   ROGERS CONTRASTS WIND NEEDED
         BY ATHLETES AND POLITICIANS

SANTA MONICA, Cal., Aug. 14. — Just witnessed the closing of the most impressive and successful Olympic Games ever held. Every part of our country either contributed a runner, jumper or a spectator.

It was the best managed and attended big affair you ever saw. Seeing or reading about the exploits of the youth of the whole world for the last few weeks has been a good thing for everybody.

Now we go from that into three straight months of political "hooey." Records will be broken there, too. You will hear speeches that require more wind than the marathon race. Both sides will commit enough fouls on each other that if they were in a game of sportsmanship they would be disqualified before election. A politician will never see the day he can lose with as good grace as these boys and girls did. Not an alibi among two thousand athletes.

Yours,
Will Rogers.

1881   WILL ROGERS SEES A LESSON
IN AN OLD NEGRO'S SENTIMENT

BEVERLY HILLS, Cal., Aug. 15. — You can always depend on the real old American Negro to say the apt thing in a few words. Up here at the ranch the other day a Negro private of the famous Tenth Cavalry (who are taking care of the American horses) was leading a tired horse around that had lost in his particular competition. He didn't know any one was in hearing distance, but we heard him say:

"Never mind, old boy, you didn't win nothing, but I loves you."

Now let some educated diplomat think of a more fitting thing to say to our foreign and native competitors than that.

Never mind what boy or girl, what State or what country, come and was defeated, "we loves you."

Yours,
Will Rogers.

1882   MR. ROGERS SUGGESTS A WAY
TO END THE FARM PROBLEM

BEVERLY HILLS, Cal., Aug. 16. — This Mayor Walker investigation would be a great money-taker if they would just move it around and make a one-day stand in each town. That would be a touring "Olympics" with the Mayor as "Babe" Didrikson.

The farmers are on a strike in Iowa. Instead of selling their stuff for nothing, they just eat it themselves and that saves 'em the expense of hauling it to town. Funny they never thought of that before.

I have always claimed that if every farmer would eat all that he raised that he would not only get fat himself but farm products might "probably" go up.

Course, on account of this not being an economist's idea, it might not work.

Yours,
Will Rogers.

1883   MR. ROGERS FAVORS NOMINATING
       A REAL FISHERMAN FOR PRESIDENT

BEVERLY HILLS, Cal., Aug. 17. — Things are picking up politically. "Mr. Hoover caught a fish three feet long."

As the last two Presidents seem to have been judged as much by their fishing as any other accomplishment, why it's funny we don't nominate one of those whaling captains and get a real fisherman in the White House.

Just think of the relief of a movie audience looking at a weekly "President Gustavos Svenson landing a 200-ton whale. It looks like whale oil will replace banana oil in public office."

I have read all Presidential speeches on both sides up to now, and the winner is the man smart enough to not make any more. There is a great chance for a "silent" third party.

Yours,
Will Rogers.

1884   WILL ROGERS FALLS A VICTIM
       TO THE MANIA FOR PARADES

SANTA BARBARA, Cal., Aug. 18. — This is "fiesta" day in Santa Barbara. The other days in Santa Barbara are "siesta" days. (If you don't speak all these languages it's not my fault.)

Hundreds and hundreds of beautiful horses in the parade, and a man without a silver-mounted saddle up here is a vagrant. Everybody in Spanish costumes. These big blond Iowans look kinder funny in 'em, but they have 'em on (sometimes backwards).

Every town should have some kind of yearly celebration. (I am writing like Brisbane.) Didn't Rome have its annual bathing festival? Didn't Cairo have some kind of female rodeo? Albany, N. Y., is going to make the Walker investigation a yearly Fall festival.

So think up something for your town to celebrate. Have a parade. Americans like to parade. We are a parading nation. "Upluribus paraditorious" (some paraders).

Yours,
Will Rogers.

1885 Will Rogers Declares Drys
    Finally Have A Candidate

 SANTA BARBARA, Cal., Aug. 19. — The notification committees have been around notifying everybody that something has happened to 'em, well, they finally caught up with my old "Injun" friend, Charley Curtis yesterday. And they warned him that there was a possibility that he would have to listen to four more years of the same speeches that he had heard for the last four.

 Mr. Curtis kinder stalled a Ford right in the middle of the road on prohibition. That is going to bring up a kind of curious situation, as he is the only Presidential or Vice Presidential candidate that is dry. So the drys have finally got somebody to go to at last.

 "Keep the country dry with Curtis in the Vice Presidency."

        Yours,
        Will Rogers.

1886 Will Rogers Pays Tribute
    To A Remarkable Woman

 SANTA MONICA, Cal., Aug. 21. — We have a very remarkable woman out here in Los Angeles at the present time, the head of the world's greatest and most useful organization, Evangeline Booth of the Salvation Army.

 Now, she says that "things are better." That really means something. What could be a greater barometer of the affairs of the unfortunate than her Army?

 All the men who offer predictions deal in money. She deals in people. They look at the stock market for an answer. She looks at the notches in the belts.

 The Salvation Army is proof of how respected and useful an organization can get if you keep it out of politics.

 So, when Evangeline Booth says something about "folks" it means something, for she seeks nothing from us but our down and out. She takes care of our big men's blunders.

        Yours,
        Will Rogers.

1887 Mr. Rogers Offers An Analysis
    Of The Campaign To Date

 BEVERLY HILLS, Cal., Aug. 22. — Well, the old gentlemanly game of politics is just starting to hit her stride.

Roosevelt in his Ohio speech gave seven points where he would remedy things. The Hoover bunch are trying to get the market up seven points so this is a seven-point campaign.

The minute one side makes a speech, the humorously called "strategists" on the other side go into a huddle to pick it apart, which all don't mean a thing.

There is not a voter in America that twenty-four hours after any speech was made could remember two sentences in it.

Politicians amuse more people than they interest.

Yours,
Will Rogers.

1888   MR. ROGERS ADMITS CANDIDLY
       THAT HE CAN'T PICK THE WINNER

BEVERLY HILLS, Cal., Aug. 23. — I just come to the conclusion that I am the "dumbest" guy in America.

Everybody I meet and talk to can tell me exactly who is going to be elected President. I never saw a time where there was as many confident people on both sides. Why, when I talk to either a Republican or Democrat and even ask them, why they look at me like I was crazy, or kidding 'em, that I don't already know.

Brisbane says that "Hoover won't carry six States." Will H. Hays says "Roosevelt will only get one county in Georgia and the Virgin Islands."

So, I guess I am the only person that don't know. But I am going to be honest, I just don't. Voters are mighty unreliable. You got to become a liar before you become a voter.

Yours,
Will Rogers.

1889   MR. ROGERS PICKS OUT A SPOT
       TO SPEND HIS DECLINING YEARS

MOJAVE, Cal., Aug. 24. — The old desert; the more you see of it the more you can understand folks really loving it.

It's a great health giver to many a disabled soul. It's just like a lot of folks. It never had a chance. The minute you give it any water it grows more stuff than all your fertile land.

These old boys sitting away out here don't look like they have to worry whether Mr. Hoover's letter to the drys will keep them in line or Mr. Roosevelt's retaining Walker will help hold Tammany in tow. Their living has got to come from a well and a pump and not from any political patronage, so these fellows escape all that political "hooey" that hits us every four years.

Yes, sir, when we retire from active life, it's the Senate or the desert, and by golly I believe I will go to the desert.

Yours,
Will Rogers.

1890   MR. ROGERS FINDS A PLACE
        FREE OF POLITICAL STRIFE

BISHOP, Cal., Aug. 25. — Ten years ago this was a wonderful valley with one-quarter of a million acres of fruit and alfalfa. But Los Angeles had to have more water for the Chamber of Commerce to drink more toasts to its growth, more water to dilute its orange juice, to water its geraniums for the tourists, while the giant cottonwoods here died.

So now this is a valley of desolation, but wherever you find privation and oppressed people, you find Democrats always bucking the giant octopus. Last night the local Democrats held a rally. Everybody in town including the lone Republican (who of course is postmaster) attended. He agreed to change his politics in return for his present office.

It was unanimously passed, all adjourned. The politics is settled here for the next four years.

Yours,
Will Rogers.

1891   MR. ROGERS MAKES A DISCOVERY
        THAT SOLVES AN OLD MYSTERY

BISHOP, Cal., Aug. 26. — I guess there is no two races of people in worse repute with everybody than the international bankers and the folks that put all those pins in new shirts.

Owing to this Wall Street boom only having reached us by newspaper reports, I been buying some fifty-cent blue work shirts, and you know I found out something. They haven't got any pins in 'em. No sir, they are made so solid they don't have to pin 'em up till you get 'em home.

Pins in shirts have caused more profanity than putting. But now you know the reason. It's to keep 'em from falling apart.
Yours,
Will Rogers.

1892   MR. ROGERS, FROM AFAR, SIZES UP
        THE DEMOCRATS' SEA GIRT RALLY

BISHOP, Cal., Aug. 28. — Well, I see where Mr. Roosevelt in New Jersey had a big Democratic rally and mosquito rodeo.

There was 100 Democrats there applauding, or fighting mosquitoes, you couldn't tell which. A few Republicans were there to cheer the insects on in their good work.

The original Roosevelt used to call it "pussyfooting." This one took in the whole cat. He called it "pussycatting."

Charlie Chaplin says he is afraid his boys will grow up and find out they were actors once. Charlie, actors are like politicians, they never grow up. My company has to watch me every day to keep me from playing Little Lord Fauntleroy.

There is nothing as "kittenish" as an old senator campaigning. You got to watch him, or he will parade right out on the rostrum with rompers on.
Yours,
Will Rogers.

1893   MR. ROGERS TAKES TIME OUT
        TO PAY A TRIBUTE TO TEXAS

BISHOP, Cal., Aug. 29. — Well, sir, away up here in the mountains working on the movies.

The latest papers tell me of the struggle in Texas of two of my good friends, Governor Sterling and "Ma." Sterling has made a good Governor; but this is a year that, as the Black Crows used to say, "Even if you are good we don't want any more of you." This is a year when we all are just looking for somebody to lay our ills onto.

Texas is a great State. It's the "Old Man River" of States. No matter who runs it, or what happens to it politically, "it just keeps rolling along."
Yours,
Will Rogers.

1894   Mr. Rogers Is Tempted To Go
         Into Business For Himself

BISHOP, Cal., Aug. 30. — California always did have one custom that they took serious, but it amused the rest of the United States. That was in calling everything a "ranch." Everything big enough to spread a double mattress on is called a "ranch."

Well, up here in these mountains where there is lots of fishing, why every house you pass they sell fishing worms, and it's called a "worm ranch."

Well, I aways did want to own a ranch, so I am in the market for a good worm ranch. I never was so hot as a cowboy, but I believe I would make a good "worm herder."

If I can land our Presidents as clients, I could made it sound like England when they sell to the King, "Rogers's Worm Ranch, Purveyor to His Excellency the President."

Yours,
Will Rogers.

1895   Mr. Rogers Finds An Industry
         Not Hit By The Depression

BISHOP, Cal., Aug. 31. — In a Los Angeles bank robbery last week, due to the bravery of a bank official and the efficiency of the police, two robbers were killed. They caught all the rest. I think it was four captured.

Well, I wish you could read the crime and jail records of all those six men. They had been pardoned or paroled from every institution in the State at least once a month for the last fifteen years.

Their records read like they had just played a series of one-night stands in each jail. They wasn't prisoners. They were traveling men, making hotels out of jails, and that's not an unusual case in any State.

Pardoning has been one industry that hasn't been hit by depression. When have you read anywhere of a crime being committed by an amateur?

Yours,
Will Rogers.

1896   MR. ROGERS TAKES UP THE NEWS
          AND DRAWS A FEW CONCLUSIONS

BISHOP, Cal., Sept. 1. — Everybody has been denying that they saw this fellow Norman, the head of the Bank of England. Hoover says if he saw him it was under an assumed name. Mellon says he never heard of him, so the whole thing is just a rumor. Mr. Norman wasn't in America at all.

The orange squeezers out in California went for the Democratic ticket here the other day like they did in the old days when they was Republicans.

The rest of the country certainly got even with California. They had an eclipse, and if you ever saw a thing leave any one flat, it left us. The Chamber of Commerce has already taken it up. New England got the whole thing. It's their first show since the Plymouth Rock "fiasco."

Yours,
Will Rogers.

1897   MR. ROGERS GIVES HIS VIEWS
          ON TWO POLITICAL OCCURRENCES

BISHOP, Cal., Sept. 2. — Away up here in the mountains we got news last night by Indian runners that "Little Big Chief" Mayor Walker had resigned. Now how is New York going to tell when Mayor Walker has resigned and when he ain't? They can't tell from his actions.

Moccasin talk just tells me that "Ma" Ferguson is probably nominated. I would like to ask a favor of my friends, no matter where they be, if they have any flowers, old wreaths or crepe bows, to please send 'em to Amon G. Carter of Fort Worth, Tex. It's rather a pathetic case. He had always staid clear of politics, but the summer heat got him, and he started to actively campaign against "Jim" Ferguson. One hundred and twenty million, and he picks out "Jim" to argue politics with! It would be like me arguing lip rouge with Greta Garbo. So send the poor devil any consolation you can.

Yours,
Will Rogers.

1898   Mr. Rogers Finds That Hoover
       Is Losing Ground In The Sierras

BISHOP, Cal., Sept. 4. — I bought my worm ranch. The man is to turn over two thousand yearling worms, two thousand two-year-olds, five hundred bull worms and the rest a mixed herd.

Now, I find in these Sierra Nevadas they are fishing with grasshoppers, so got a grasshopper ranch adjoining. Am going to do a Luther Burbank, cross my grasshoppers and worms and produce an animal that if the fish don't bite at him, he will bite the fish, so you get your fish anyhow.

I am no fisherman and hope I never get lazy enough to take it up. I am in these mountains on an essential industry (ask Bill Hayes), but these loafers up here tell me that the fish are not biting this year, and you would be surprised the votes Hoover is losing.

Yours,
Will Rogers.

1899   Mr. Rogers Tours The Desert
       And Sees Some Ghost Towns

BEATTY, Nev., Sept. 5. — Had a wonderful day today.

Started out early this morning at Tonopah, the famous old silver mining town, then down to Goldfield, the gold town. There, Labor Day, 1906, was the start of Tex Rickard.

I stood on the ground today where twenty-six years ago today Battling Nelson and Joe Gans fought forty-two rounds. They had fighters in those days, as well as promoters.

Then out to Death Valley Scotty's castle. Arabian Nights never conceived anything like that on the desert. Then to Beatty, and the famous old Rhyolite and Bullfrog towns.

If they should ever momentarily get sensible and make silver a money, all this would come back.

Now for Las Vegas, Nev., and the Boulder Dam. Water costs more than gold in this West.

Yours,
Will Rogers.

1900   Mr. Rogers Makes A Report
On The Hoover-Boulder Dam

BEVERLY HILLS, Cal., Sept. 6. — Don't miss seeing the building of Boulder Dam. It's the biggest thing that's ever been done with water since Noah made the flood look foolish.

You know how big the Grand Canyon is. Well, they just stop up one end of it and make the water come out through a drinking fountain.

They have only been bothered with two things. One is silt and the other is Senatorial investigators. They both clog everything up.

It's called the "Hoover Dam" now, subject to election returns of Nov. 8.

The dam is entirely between Nevada and Arizona. All California gets out of it is the water.

Yours for the latest dam news.

                Yours,
                Will Rogers.

1901   Mr. Rogers Is Glad One Fog
Of Doubt Has Been Dispersed

BEVERLY HILLS, Cal., Sept. 7. — The doubtful are gradually falling into line.

Calvin Coolidge has had everybody on the anxious seat for months as to who he would support in the November handicap. Campaign managers and politicians have been dogging his rubber-booted footsteps. But it took, not a politician, but a commercial-minded gentleman (proprietor of America's biggest nickelodeon), Mr. George Horace Lorimer, not with words, or editorial persuasion, but with his signature on a small piece of paper, payable at one of the few banks left open, to break Mr. Coolidge's dogged doubt.

His printed endorsement of the Republican party is perhaps the biggest paid advertisement (in favor of any purely commercial product) since Amos and Andy sold themselves "down the river" for toothpaste.

                Yours,
                Will Rogers.

1902   Mr. Rogers Reviews The News
            As He Got It In The Far East

BEVERLY HILLS, Cal., Sept. 8. — These made news today:

Something in the paper about disarmament. I don't know what it was but I know it wasn't about disarming.

Al Smith is coming out with a statement in the Outlook magazine as to who he is supporting. Getting so we have to wait for magazines to come out to get all the latest news.

Rudy Vallees decided to go back together till after the depression.

Iowa farmers are doing pretty good with their strike. They are stopping the trucks and eating what the other farmers send to town. In that way the farmer only has to haul it half as far.

Yours,
Will Rogers.

1903   Will Rogers Commemorates
            A California Anniversary

BEVERLY HILLS, Cal., Sept. 9. — Eighty-two years ago today California entered the Union, on a bet. The bet was that the country would eventually be called California and not America.

We took it away from Mexico the next year after we found it had gold.

When the gold was all gone, we tried to give it back, but Mexico was too foxy for us. In '49 the wayward sons of ten thousand families crossed the country, and the roads was so rough they couldn't get back.

Just when the mining had petered out, soembody discovered a moving picture camera, and the old days of '49 were on again. Now child prodigies come by the bus loads. Fords are packed with literary geniuses. My pictures alone have been the means of bringing every hard-looking old "bird" in the world out here.

It's a great old State; we furnish the amusement to the world; sometimes conscientious, sometimes unconscientious, sometimes by our films, sometimes by our orators, but you can't beat it.

Yours,
Will Rogers.

1904   WILL ROGERS IS NOT SURPRISED
        TO HEAR OF WALKER'S VOYAGE

SANTA MONICA, Cal., Sept. 11. — Every time you read of some Republican campaign speech, it was made at just a meeting of some kind, but every time you read of a Democrat making one it was at a dinner. The old Democrats are going to be sure they get something out of the speech, anyhow.

No wonder Mayor Walker went to Italy. Did you see that new Mayor's picture? He's got it on Jimmy for looks, and he mastered and taught Latin, Greek, and English.

And, of course, with those foreign accomplishments, he does not belong to Tammany Hall.

Yours,
Will Rogers.

1905   WILL ROGERS REMARKS

BEVERLY HILLS, Cal., Sept. 12. — The last right of a citizen has been taken away from 'em. You can't even commit suicide in private any more. The press digs up the body, and the public, instead of the Coroner, heads the investigation. "What's the big idea killing yourself around here and not notifying the press?" "What's the idea leaving a note that nobody but your wife can understand?" "Don't you know this is a free country and the public has got as much right to know everything as your family?" "Who did you love, and when, and why?" "Have you got any old love letters, or birthmarks on you that we haven't seen. We'll teach you to try and sneak off and die and not let us in on all the reasons. Now get up and pose for the photographers, and give us the whole confession. And don't let it happen any more."

Yours,
Will Rogers.

1906   MR. ROGERS WOULD DISCIPLINE
        THE HEAD OF THE FLYING FAMILY

HOLLYWOOD, Cal., Sept. 13. — They found the flying family. They ought to left the father out there a couple of more days just to throw a scare into him for taking those children.

See where some more took off for Rome. A nurse with "million-dollar legs." Over that ocean is one place where legs is not good to you, no matter what price they are.

Who said being Secretary of War wasn't a hazardous business? Mr. Hoover drafted Pat Hurley to pinch hit for him and face the American Legion and try and get some Republican votes.

Pat's speech sounded like the Kingfish's over the radio. "Now, remember, we is all brothers in that great fraternity, de Mystic Knights of de Sea."

Pat got away with his life, but no votes.

Yours,
Will Rogers.

1907   MR. ROGERS APPEARS TO BE HAPPY
       OVER WHAT HAPPENED IN MAINE

BEVERLY HILLS, Cal., Sept. 14. — What do you know about Maine going sane? And "as Maine goes, so goes the postoffices."

Why, four years ago they imported a Democrat into the State just to show around at the fairs.

Even Wall Street got plumb discouraged at the news. "You mean to tell us this booming and trading we been doing among ourselves here has all gone for naught?"

Mr. Hoover wired to Everett Sanders to "tighten the lines, enlighten the people, our cause is right."

Roosevelt just grinned, and even the original couldn't a shown more teeth.

The old campaign is getting hot. God help a man out looking for re-election on a night like this.

Yours,
Will Rogers.

1908   MR. ROGERS HAS A 1-POINT PLAN
       FOR THE RELIEF OF THE FARMER

BEVERLY HILLS, Cal., Sept. 15. — Roosevelt got into the farm relief business yesterday. They all do.

Now nobody can promise the farmer whether his wheat or potatoes will sell for a nickel or a dollar. Supply and demand, and not a political speaker, determines that.

The only relief you can give the farmer is through his taxes. Work it like the income tax. If he makes it he pays on it, and if he don't make it he don't pay.

A thousand shares of stocks or bonds make nothing, you pay nothing, but on a thousand acres of land you pay enough to support half the community who own no land and pay no taxes.

But, the farmer will spend the rest of the fall just running from one speaker's platform to another listening to schemes to relieve him of nothing but his vote.

Yours,
Will Rogers.

1909   WILL ROGERS GIVES THE NEWS
          HE THINKS IS FIT TO PRINT

BEVERLY HILLS, Cal., Sept. 16. — Well, let's see what's in the news that's fit to reprint today? Al Smith had one of the finest and most fearless articles in this week's S. E. Post. Why is it he is about the only politician on either side that can write on a subject and you can tell where he stands?

Roosevelt is headed West. Says he is "just out to meet the folks." But he will give preference to any one of legal age and a registered voter.

Mr. Hoover, who originally wasn't going further West during the campaign than the Potomac, has started looking at time tables.

Politicians, in order to hold the real dyed-in-the-wool radio nut, are crooning their speeches.

Yours,
Will Rogers.

1910   MR. ROGERS OFFERS A 1-POINT
          SUGGESTION TO THE RAILROADS

SANTA MONICA, Cal., Sept. 18. — Big forest fire been burning out here for two weeks. That certainly won't do Hoover any good, letting that happen right here in his home State.

France says they are "willing to disarm," but they didn't say so till Germany went home from the conference and announced they were starting to build some more of those vest pocket cruisers.

Both political parties are trying to help the railroads. The railroads could help themselves if they would make the fares what they were in the days when they used to make money.

If they would compete with a bus and truck instead of just cussing 'em, they wouldn't need all this help.

Yours,
Will Rogers.

1911 MR. ROGERS DISCUSSES POLITICS,
CALIFORNIA FOG AND CARROTS

BEVERLY HILLS, Cal., Sept. 19. — I been out of town working and missed an old friend that was out here, Josephus Daniels. He was out here spreading some Roosevelt bait. He is a grand old man, is "Uncle Joe," and he ought to know Roosevelt, for he worked for him six years.

Did see Mayor Curley, however. He runs the great city of Boston without an investigation. Curley sincerely believes Roosevelt will carry forty-eight States.

I haven't heard from my good friend Amon Carter of Texas. I am afraid he is taking politics too serious, for he was awfully able and entertaining before.

California's having more fog than ever in its history. I arrived here during a Democratic administration and it was sunny and bright, so there goes Hoover again, fire, fog, and lack of rain is liable to lose him the State.

Some guy invented "vitamin A" out of a carrot. I'll bet he can't invent a good meal out of one.

Yours,
Will Rogers.

1912 MR. ROGERS FIGURES THAT SILENCE
WILL WIN THE COMING ELECTION

BEVERLY HILLS, Cal., Sept. 20. — Say, I got a whole new slant on this election racket today. I run into a Republican.

You see, on account of my low social standing I haven't been able to meet anybody but Democrats. But this Republican tells and shows me where this thing is going to be a real race. These windy Democrats had led me to believe that the thing was going by default.

Mr. Hoover made a move yesterday, that if I had been one of his advisers, I would never have let him make it. He wants "to put more orators in the field." I think, and hope, that it was a typographical error. It should read: "We want more orators under the field."

As I told you all before, I seem to be the only person in America that has no idea who will win this election, but I do know one thing, it will be the side with the fewest "orators." Yes, or even speakers.

Yours,
Will Rogers.

1913   Mr. Rogers Presents His Views
            On The Disarmament Question

BEVERLY HILLS, Cal., Sept. 21. — Well, we are off again at our old trail. We are not supposed to meddle in foreign affairs, so we don't tell Germany she "can't arm"; we "advise her not to."

Now, there is nothing that makes a nation or an individual as mad as to have somebody say, "Now, this is really none of my business, but I am just advising you."

They never will get anywhere with this disarmament, for no nation can tell another nation what they need to defend themselves. That's a personal affair.

If I sleep with a gun under my pillow, I don't want somebody from across the street to "advise" me that I don't need it.

Yours,
Will Rogers.

1914   Mr. Rogers Seems A Bit Dazed
            By Some Reversals Of Form

BEVERLY HILLS, Cal., Sept. 22. — Wisconsin did something or other in the papers this morning. I don't know what it was as they are always doing something that nobody can figure out.

The stock market did something yesterday, too. I don't know what it was. It's always doing something that nobody can't figure out.

Looks like this fellow McKee, the acting Mayor of New York, is doing some mighty good acting, and is liable to be cast for the part permanently. Walker wasn't as smart as I figured him. I would have never let an understudy like that get a chance to "go on" if I had been Jimmy.

Had a great night last night. There was static on the radio and you couldn't hear a single political speech.

Yours,
Will Rogers.

1915   Will Rogers Says Voting
            Is Sole 1932 Job For Many

BEVERLY HILLS, Cal., Sept. 23. — We all out here in Los Angeles are going to wake up in the morning with nothing on our hands but a Presidential candidate.

Mr. Roosevelt, a very fine highclass man, win, lose or draw, is out here shaking these lemon trees, to try and bring down some Republican fruit that might fall in the Democratic basket among the oranges.

This is a year that will bring out lots of votes, for the voter has nothing to do but vote; his 1932 employment consists entirely of voting.

This is Mr. Hoover's home State, and we want to welcome him too, in case he decides to come out in any rebuttal testimony.

Yours,
Will Rogers.

1916   MR. ROGERS FINDS THE DEMOCRATS
             ARE PRETTY HARD TO DISCOURAGE

SANTA MONICA, Cal., Sept. 25. — Well, Mr. Roosevelt has come and gone. Seemed mighty cheerful and happy.

That's one thing about a Democrat. They never are as serious as the Republicans. They been out of work so long they got used to it.

The Democrats take the whole thing as a joke and the Republicans take it serious, but run it like a joke.

So there's not much diference.

Yours,
Will Rogers.

1917   WILL ROGERS HONESTLY BELIEVES
             REPUBLICANS HAVE REFORMED

BEVERLY HILLS, Cal., Sept. 26. — Politics pretty quiet over the week-end. Democrats are attacking and the Republicans are defending. All the Democrats have to do is promise "what they would do if they got in." But the Republicans have to promise "what they would do" and then explain why they haven't already "done it."

I do honestly believe the Republicans have reformed and want to do better. But whether they have done it in time to win the election is another thing. The old voter is getting so he wants to be saved before October every election year.

Yours,
Will Rogers.

1918   Mr. Rogers Finds A Bit Of News
               Of Great Interest To Husbands

BEVERLY HILLS, Cal., Sept. 27. — The government is suing an old "injun" from Oklahoma. They claim he was "out of his head" because he gave his wife money, and they want her to give it back, not to the Indian, but to the government.

There is a case that's of great interest to all married men. If the government wins this, the next case you hear of will be: "The U. S. Government vs. Mrs. Will Rogers, in behalf of another Indian ward of the government, Will Rogers, who has been out of his head at various times since November, 1908." (I think that's the year.)

If the government gets anything back from her, I am willing to split with 'em on the usual government basis, U. S. taking 80 per cent, citizen 20 per cent.

Yours,
Will Rogers.

1919   Mr. Rogers Finally Is Rewarded
               For His Patience With The Radio

BEVERLY HILLS, Cal., Sept. 28. — It was good today to hear our old friend DeWolf Hooper recite his epic, "Casey at the Bat." It was good to hear Graham McNamee, who has remained pre-eminent as an announcer during all these years. Ted Husing was good, as usual.

The old radio pays for itself every fall during the world series. We listen to ads, crooners and politicians all year just to hear: "The count is three and two on Babe Ruth and the pitcher is winding up."

That's America's greatest suspense. Babe is the only man in the world that was ever "tuned out on" when he stepped up to that old home-plate microphone.

Yours,
Will Rogers.

P. S. — Gandhi is eating again; Democrats still fasting.

1920   Mr. Rogers Offers A Plan
               For Fixing Postal Rates

BEVERLY HILLS, Cal., Sept. 29. — Babe Ruth and Lou Gehrig chased both candidates and all their accomplices right off all the pages again today.

See there is some chance of going back to 2-cent postage. Every time we get a good law we change it. The postoffice loses millions a year just because the politicians are afraid to charge a voter as much as it does to carry all the unnecessary letters and folders and junk that goes through the mail.

There ought to be a law that the postoffice could open a letter, and if it's important it should be sent for nothing, and if it's like 99 per cent of the letters that everybody gets, the postage should be a dollar.

Letter writing is a mania and not a necessity.

Yours,
Will Rogers.

1921   WILL ROGERS DOUBTS JAPAN
       CAN BEAT US AT HIGH DIVING

BEVERLY HILLS, Cal., Sept. 30. — Coast papers are all excited because "Japan has bought more ammunition in the last month than in years—gun cotton, nitrates and scrap iron."

Why worry about a little thing like that? Not being satisfied by making turtles out of us in swimming, they hired our best diver after the Olympics, and in the next games may beat us in that. But here is one thing they didn't reckon on. Our high diving is inherited from our politicians. Our public men do nothing but high dive. They climb up the ladder on promises, just before election, then dive off after they are elected.

No, sir, Japan, you got a lot of diving to learn to catch us.

Yours,
Will Rogers.

1922   MR. ROGERS FINDS SUNDAY OFFERS
       NO RELIEF FROM SPELLBINDERS

SANTA MONICA, Cal., Oct. 2. — See where the Prince of Wales is visiting Sweden to see if he can't drag Greta Garbo out of seclusion. That would be a great match for both countries.

After finishing listening to the world's series, I figure on account of it being Sunday I could leave it turned on and not have to listen to some politician, but what do I get? Four preachers, all at different places. What was they doing—saving the sinner? No. Two of 'em was saving the Republicans and the other two was saving the Democrats.

The old sinner won't get much consideration till after November 4.

Yours,
Will Rogers.

P. S. — All during the world's series all we could hear was "the ball trickled through so and so's fingers." This was the "tricklinest" series I ever heard.

1923   MR. ROGERS OFFERS AN ANALYSIS
       OF THE FAR EASTERN PROBLEM

BEVERLY HILLS, Cal., Oct. 3. — Been reading lot of editorials and everything about what the world was going to do about Japan taking over Manchuria.

Last December Floyd Gibbons and I flew from Japan to Mukden, Manchuria. At the hotel was gathered from newspapers all over the world about twenty star writers. Floyd asked 'em, "What's going to happen here in Manchuria?"

I will never forget their answer, it was so unanimous. They were all Far Eastern writers and knew what they were talking about. "Say these Japanese are in here to stay. League of Nations? World Court? Kellogg pact? Nine-Power treaty? America? Russia? Or anybody else. Who's going to put 'em out?"

Now, you got the whole Manchurian problem right there. So you just as well quit talking about it, if you ain't going to take a gun with you.

Land don't change hands by treaties; land changes hands by arms.

Yours,
Will Rogers.

1924   WILL ROGERS JOINS CALIFORNIA
       IN WELCOMING THE BANKERS

BEVERLY HILLS, Cal., Oct. 4. — Guess who is out here holding a convention, that you would never thought would show their faces again? Yep, "The Bankers." The Reconstruction Finance Corporation fixed 'em up so they could make the trip.

They are likeable rascals, and now that we are all wise to 'em, and it's been shown that they don't know any more about finances than the rest of us know about our businesses (which has proved to be nothing), why, they are geting just as human as the groceryman, the druggist or the filling station man.

This panic has been a great equalizer, it's done away entirely with the smart man.

So, the bankers are here having a good time. They don't feel that they have any position to uphold. They are just a lot of Elks.

Yours,
Will Rogers.

1925 MR. ROGERS CONSIDERS THE BURIAL
OF THAT HATCHET WAS TIMELY

EL PASO, Tex., Oct. 5. — I read Mr. Hoover's speech, every word of it.

Now, he may be dry, but somebody sure slipped him a couple of nips and told him, "Go out there and tell those birds something. Deliver 'em a speech so they won't think it's Hoover."

And, I want to tell you he took right after 'em. Course, another thing was in his favor. A man can put a little more into a speech when it means his job.

Some men will stand for a lot of things, but you start taking their woman or job away from 'em, and you are going to get something besides platitudes.

I'll tell you Al and Franklin didn't make up a day too soon. They made up, going to bury the hatchet. Decided to bury it in Hoover.

Yours,
Will Rogers.

1926 WILL ROGERS STILL MARVELS
AT THE IMMENSITY OF TEXAS

SAN ANTONIO, Tex., Oct. 6. — I been flying, train riding, automobiling, horseback and buggy riding over Texas for thirty-three years and I've never seen a tenth of it.

If it had been in Europe eighty wars would have been fought over it. There is single ranches here bigger than France, counties bigger than England, saddle horse pastures as big as Alsace Lorraine.

The lakes of Switzerland would be buffalo wallows in Texas. It's located between Mexico and the United States to keep Mexico from annexing the United States.

It's so far to town that the cowboys started in to vote for "Teddy" arrived in time to register for Franklin.

It's sole industry is internal politics. It's so big that no one Governor can handle it. They have a man and his wife.

It's the only State where a Republican has to have a passport to enter.

Yours,
Will Rogers.

P. S. — They would use California for a telephone booth down here.

1927   WILL ROGERS THINKS MEXICO
THE MOST CIVILIZED COUNTRY

MEXICO CITY, Mexico, Oct. 7. — Well, here is Mexico, my pet foreign country. They just had a change of Presidents here. Not a shot fired, not a speech made, not even a radio address. Country not all divided against itself. I tell you this is the most civilized country in the world.

Our Ambassador, Mr. Clark, is just carrying out the Dwight Morrow plans and our relations were never better with Mexico. In fact, Clark was the adviser of Morrow while he was here.

Calles is still the strongest man on the Western Continent. Rodriguez, the new President, is very able.

If you want to see excitement, go to Texas; half want a man and half want a woman.

Yours,
Will Rogers.

1928   MR. ROGERS RECOGNIZES A NATION
THAT WASHINGTON TURNED DOWN

SAN SALVADOR, Oct. 9. — This is San Salvador. The U. S. don't recognize this government because it's supposed to have come in during a revolution, something like Washington did in America.

They miss something by not recognizing it. It's a beautiful country, so I am recognizing it in behalf of Huey Long, Jim Ferguson and Bill Murray, the three "American musketeers."

Those three old boys would not recognize anything unless it had had a fight to get in.

I am a "joint commission," going through South America for Hoover and Roosevelt "jointly."

Yours,
Will Rogers.

1929   MR. ROGERS PREFERS REVOLUTIONS
            TO THE DIN OF POLITICAL BATTLES

SAN SALVADOR, Oct. 10. — I am leaving for everything south of the equator. Revolutions are thicker down there than Roosevelt Republicans. Am flying down the west coast by Chili, then to Argentina for a week, and up the east coast by Brazil.

I will see more in a week than a New York gossip artist can see in five years of keyholes. South America is our coming country, so it's good to know where it's at.

I want to get back just before election, not to vote, but just to see the show. I think people would like to read something in the papers besides "Hoover said this" and "Roosevelt says that."

I think it's a good time to go.

In fact I am gone.

Yours,
Will Rogers.

1930   MR. ROGERS COVERS 5 COUNTRIES
            IN A DAY'S TRAVEL BY PLANE

COLON, Oct. 11. — This big three-motored Ford Pan American Airways passenger breezed through some country today, San Salvador, Honduras, Nicaragua, Costa Rica and Panama, with stops in each place.

Mr. Gerald Dempsey of Long Island and Santa Barbara, Cal., is aboard, headed for Chili. I am not headed for anything, just headed for home by the way of Cape Horn.

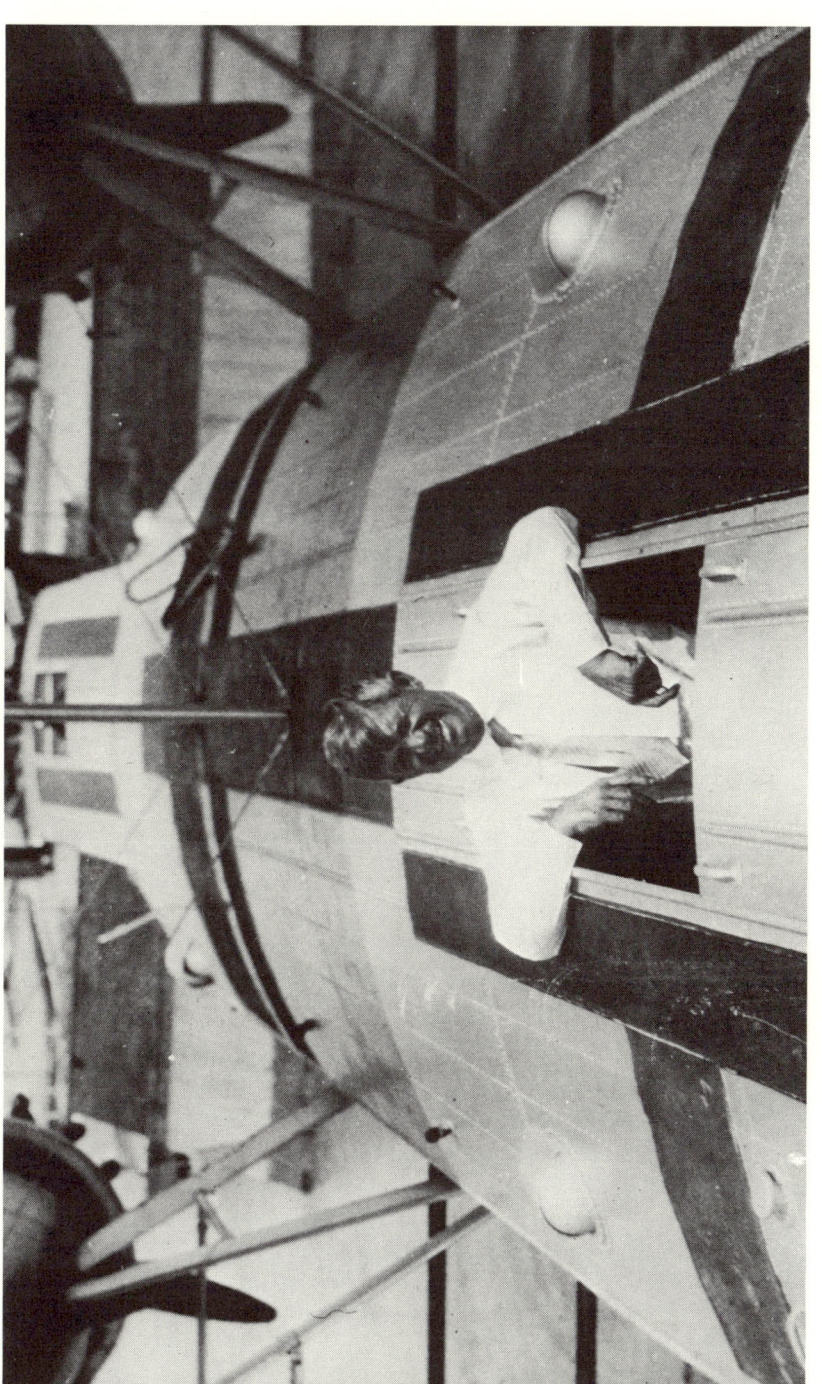

Rogers in an early ocean-going airplane, called a Clipper (ca 1932).

It was good to visit Managua, Nicaragua, again. I camped there with the marines right after the earthquake. The town has done wonderful in rebuilding.

Saw Mr. Hanna, our Minister there. He says that every marine was to leave on Jan. 1. That will be as good a move as the one sending 'em in was a bad one.

Yours,
Will Rogers.

P. S. — Rain? Brother, you never saw rain.

1931   MR. ROGERS DROPS A FEW LINES
              AS HE SKIMS OVER COLOMBIA

BUENA VENTURA, Columbia, Oct. 12. — Well, here we are breezing down the west coast of South America. If there ever was a country that the airplane was a godsend to it's this.

The American Consul just told me they get 367 inches of rain. He said a year, but I think it's a month.

We are kinder getting into the revolution neighborhood. Almost every two South American countries are paired off. I have been promised reserved seats at all that I will attend. I am stealing a march on Floyd Gibbons this time.

Well, the plane is whistling to leave.

Yours,
Will Rogers.

1932   MR. ROGERS FINDS PERU'S VOTERS
            HEARD COOLIDGE PLEA FOR HOOVER

LIMA, Oct. 13. — Colombia, Ecuador and Peru today. Lima, Peru, is the oldest city in the western world. It's worth a trip alone.

Flew across the equator yesterday morning. The Pan-American Grace Line hands you a diploma or certificate proving you have been across the line.

An old man at a little Peruvian village where we stopped for gas today came up to me and said, "Did you hear Calvin's speech last night on the radio?"

Here, I have had a fine radio at home and never got anything outside of Los Angeles county.

Well, the race must be getting hot if they have drafted Calvin. I'll bet Calvin will be all broke up when he hears he wasted his speech on people away down here that can't vote.

Yours,
Will Rogers.

1933 ROGERS FINDS TACNA-ARICA
AND WONDERS WHAT ABOUT IT

ANTOFAGASTA, Chile, Oct. 14. — You remember such a fuss one time over a country between Peru and Chile called Tacna Arica? Well, I was there today. It takes an airplane to find it. It would be just like us going to war with somebody over Death Valley, California. They said there today that I was the only American ever there that wasn't sent by the United States government as a commission to settle it.

This is the heart of the great nitrate region of Chile. We are right at this moment as I am writing this flying over some of the mines. They are not mines, they are right out on a flat prairie desert and they just scrape it almost off the top of the ground. It's just like plowing up potatoes. I can get some mighty cheap, and both political parties was needing it mighty bad when I left.

Was I talking about rain the other day? Well, we have had two thousand miles of solid desert where it never rains. That's a fact. It was never known to rain. It's drier than my old friend Upshaw's platform.

Peru is the Inca country. In fact every country has become the Inca country—red inka. Excuse me for that one, but remember we are flying at 13,000 feet. It's the altitude that makes you light-headed.

Yours,
Will Rogers.

1934 MR. ROGERS IS A BIT PUZZLED
BY A SOUTH AMERICAN WAR

SANTIAGO, Chile, Oct. 16. — Here is one for Ripley. Peru and Colombia are going to war over a boundary, the usual reason down here, but get this:

The land in dispute is so isolated that neither nation can get to it, so they are arranging to have the armies meet at some convenient place and fight over a piece of ground that the winner can't get to after they have won.

Chile has had five Presidents this fall. One inaugural parade started out with one President and wound up at the White House with another, so they inaugurate two Presidents for the price of one. The man that's in now is afraid to send out his laundry.

When you read this at breakfast in the morning I will be flying the Andes, a long ambition realized.

Yours,
Will Rogers.

1935   MR. ROGERS GETS A REAL THRILL
IN A FLIGHT OVER THE ANDES

BUENOS AIRES, Oct. 17. — Say, had a great trip over those Andes Mountains.

Our highest altitude was 21,500 feet. They have oxygen tubes at each seat, but I guess I am so windy anyhow that I didn't use any.

I kept prowling up forward and talking and looking with the pilot, an American boy named Wagoner. They are all American pilots on this whole trip. We could see the railroad, thousands of feet below winding its way over and through, but high tariffs between each country have killed off the trade and it's not running any more, so that's one way to help the railroads.

It's just the starting of spring down here now. Flew over hundreds of miles of checker-boarded green fields, like Kansas or Iowa, and the fattest and biggest cattle you ever saw.

Yours,
Will Rogers.

1936   MR. ROGERS IS ENTHUSIASTIC
OVER A SOUTH AMERICAN CITY

BUENOS AIRES, Oct. 18. — Say, you talk about a city, this Buenos Aires is as big as Chicago, as live as Paris, beautiful as Beverly Hills and as substantial as Claremore, Okla.

Like all countries, the President is just in from day to day. He may be on the same plane with me going out. I have met 'em going and coming down here so much that the traveling man you meet is not a drummer, he is an ex-President escaping to the brush somewhere.

To be unemployed nowadays is terrible, but it's not as bad as it is to be unemployed if you are working for the people.

Yours,
Will Rogers.

1937   MR. ROGERS FINDS NO NEWS OF US
         IN SOUTH AMERICA'S PRESS

BUENOS AIRES, Oct. 19. — You folks might think you are big folks up there as a nation, but you don't mean anything down here.

I haven't seen one word of news printed about the United States since I left Brownsville, Texas, and that includes Spanish or any kind of paper.

The Englishmen have got this country tied up tighter than Borah has Idaho.

Has the election been called off, or just what has happened?

The big news down here is the argument between Ireland and England. There is a big mess of both of 'em down here.

Yours,
Will Rogers.

1938   WILL ROGERS FINDS SOMETHING
         TOO FAST FOR HIM TO LASSO

BUENOS AIRES, Oct. 20. — Well, had a great day today. Saw the real Argentine gauchos do their stuff right out on one of the big estancias.

We flew out to this big ranch. This whole country is a landing field. Had some of the American polo players along.

These bolos that you hear about 'em throwing they use for ostriches. We chased ostriches all afternoon. They are the fastest things I ever saw run. I never got close enough to one to even holler at him. Got the bolos tangled up around my own neck. These gauchos are sure wild.

It's the most fertile country I ever saw and has the most cattle and horses per acre in the world.

Yours,
Will Rogers.

1939   WILL ROGERS FINDS A COUNTRY
         THAT CAN PLAY REAL FOOTBALL

RIO GRANDE DO SUL, Brazil, Oct. 21. — Say, they got a little country down here named Uruguay, with Montevideo the capital. Did you know that before the world depression that a dollar in their money was worth a dollar and three cents of ours. Even now it's the highest priced money in South America.

Saw their big football stadium. For five straight years they have had the champion football soccer team in the world, and they play any country. The referee stays inside a big wire net where the spectators can't get at him.

Down here the people vote on whether they will hold a football game or a revolution, both equal in casualties.

Yours,
Will Rogers.

1940 MR. ROGERS FINDS CONSOLATION
IN SANTOS FOR THE REPUBLICANS

SANTOS, Oct. 23. — Say, this Brazil is beautiful along this coast. Thought the plane was going to reach Rio Janeiro tonight, but Old Man Head Wind hit us right in the face all day.

If you read this in the morning take another swig at your coffee. Here is where it's all raised and this is the biggest coffee port in the word.

This town is just sweeping up the streets from a revolution two weeks old, but down here the President stayed in, so the Democrats couldn't dislodge him. That might be the first consolation the Republicans at home have had.

Yours,
Will Rogers.

1941 MR. ROGERS FINDS THAT BRAZIL
IS A LAND TO INSPIRE BRAGGING

PARA, Oct. 24. — Brazil ought to belong to the United States. We like to brag about everything "big."

We been flying up its coast line for five solid days and still got another day.

If any of you see the Rockefellers, kiss 'em for me. There is not a mosquito up this coast. If they can just hear of one trying to get a start down here there is ten Rockefeller Foundation men got him singing the blues before sundown. No sir, you got to wait till you get to "God's country" to get eat up by insects.

Rio Janerio is the prettiest city in the world from the air. We are just circling Para where we land for the night. It's right at the mouth of the great Amazon River.

Up from here is where Mr. Ford's rubber plantation is but somebody sold him all male trees and they are having a little trouble getting 'em to bear. I bet they couldn't fool him on carburetors but he didn't know sex life in the forest.

Yours,
Will Rogers.

1942   Mr. Rogers Spends The Day
       Flying Across The Amazon

PORT OF SPAIN, Oct. 25. — If you think that Amazon River ain't big!

We was from just daylight to after lunch ferrying over it in an aeroplane. There is an island in it as big as New York State.

Don't you all remember looking on a map and seeing three little countries called French Guiana, Dutch Guiana and British Guiana? Well, we found and stopped at all three of 'em today.

We also flew by (but not too close) to Devil's Island, the famous French prison off French Guiana where Dreyfus was.

I couldn't see any inmates playing football so I will take mine with my good friend Warden Lawes of Sing Sing.

Tonight we will stop in Trinidad, Port of Spain, an English possession and a beautiful spot.

Yours,
Will Rogers.

1943   Mr. Rogers Sets Forth Clearly
       His Status As A Polo Player

SAN JUAN, P. R., Oct. 26. — Finally got hold of a U. S. paper. Said I went to buy polo ponies. That must have handed my banker a laugh. Thank somebody for the compliment.

Old age and depression hit my polo same year. Type of polo I always played, I could get my horses off a merry-go-round. Besides, if I wanted good horses I would never leave America for 'em, and if they will let 'em race in every State we will have better ones everywhere.

Just stopped for gas at our Virgin Islands. Looks like Roosevelt got it tonight.

Stopping in San Juan, Puerto Rico. Just looking down now on the wreckage of that hurricane one month ago tonight. It's hard to tell who needs money the worst nowadays, but I believe you could send some here through the Red Cross and feel that it's going to the most needy place.

Yours,
Will Rogers.

1944   MR. ROGERS DISPOSES OF AN ISSUE THAT LONG HAS BEEN IN DISPUTE

CORAL GABLES, Fla., Oct. 27. — Winter is coming and tourists will soon be looking for a place to mate.

Now let's get this Florida and California thing settled. I can afford to be fair, for I can't sell my lots out there, anyhow.

Hotels, even. Both have wonderful ones.

People, even. Both equally windy.

Distance from civilization, even.

Tennis, California; horseshoe pitching, Florida.

Desert and mountains, California; lakes, Florida.

Bathing, Florida wins. We take to the tub about October.

Good roads. Pardon me, Florida, I shouldn't have brought that up.

Millionaire visitors, even. None either place. That's a race of people that has been entirely exterminated by bad judgment.

Florida excels in fish and Democrats. Outside of Catalina Island we can't touch you on fishing.

So, if you like to fish and look at Democrats, Florida is your onion.

But you've got to come to California to see Janet Gaynor, Sally Eilers, Clara Bow and the great Garbo.

Are you listening?

Yours,
Will Rogers.

1945   WILL ROGERS IN FLYING HERE FINDS WASHINGTON DESERTED

NEW YORK, N. Y., Oct. 28. — Had a fine trip in here today from Florida, over the beautiful country of Florida, Georgia, South and North Carolina, Virginia, Maryland and New Jersey. Was going to stop in Washington, but the newspaper boys said there wasn't a soul there.

"Ain't Mr. Hoover here?"

"No, he has gone to save Indiana."

"Well, I know my old Injun' friend Charley Curtis is here."

"No, he is saving Kansas."

"Well, then I will just drop up and see some of the boys in the Cabinet."

"Why, there is none of the Cabinet that's been here since early in the Spring."

"Well, who is running the country?"

"Why, nobody, that's why things are kinder picking up."

Yours,
Will Rogers.

1946   WILL ROGERS, BACK TOO EARLY,
FINDS A RODEO OF APPLESAUCE

NEW YORK, N. Y., Oct. 30. — I have had the most terrible disappointment. I never do look at a calendar and I naturally thought election came around the first day or so of November. So I was timing my South American jaunt to arrive back here after the speeches was over and here I go and make a week's mistake in my time, and arrive back in the midst of the most colossal rodeo of applesauce in the history of our national pastime.

I would have rather made a forced landing in the Andes, or purposely stood straddle of the Equator another week if I had known this. From now on you will never catch me without a calendar.

I honestly believe there is people so excited over this election that they think the President has something to do with running this country.

Yours,
Will Rogers.

1947   MR. ROGERS FINDS THE GUESSES
HERE ON THE ELECTION CONFLICT

NEW YORK, N. Y., Oct. 31. — Mrs. Rogers and I just looked out of our window and Mr. Hoover was coming into our hotel for the night. He is on some Chautauqua circuit and is speaking in some hall here tonight.

Wall Street is betting two and a half to one on Roosevelt. That's a bad omen for the Democrats, for Wall Street hasn't been right in three years.

You can hear anything you want around here about the outcome, depending on who you talk to, Democrat or Republican.

Tilson, Republican leader of the House, told me "We got everything east of the Ohio River and north of the Line" (meaning Mason and Dixon).

Admiral Grayson says: "Only way the Democrats can lose is to sell out." So take your choice.

Yours,
Will Rogers.

1948 WILL ROGERS FAVORS CLOSING THE CAMPAIGN RIGHT NOW AND LETTING THE BOYS GO FISHING

NEW YORK, N. Y., Nov. 1. — There should be a moratorium called on candidates' speeches. They have both called each other everything in the world they can think of. From now on they are just talking themselves out of votes.

The high office of President of the United States has degenerated into two ordinarily fine men being goaded on by their political leeches into saying things that if they were in their right minds they wouldn't think of saying.

Imagine Mr. Hoover last night, "any change of policies will bring disaster to every fireside in America."

Of all the conceit. This country is a thousand times bigger than any two men in it, or any two parties in it. These big politicians are so serious about themselves and their parties.

This country has gotten where it is in spite of politics, not by the aid of it. That we have carried as much political bunk as we have and still survived shows we are a super-nation.

If by some divine act of Providence we could get rid of both these parties and hired some good men, like any other big business does, why that would be sitting pretty.

This calamity was brought on by the actions of the people of the whole world and its weight will be lifted off by the actions of the people of the whole world and not by a Republican or a Democrat.

So, you two boys just get the weight of the world off your shoulders and go fishing. Both of you claim you like to fish. Now instead of calling each other names till next Tuesday, why you can do

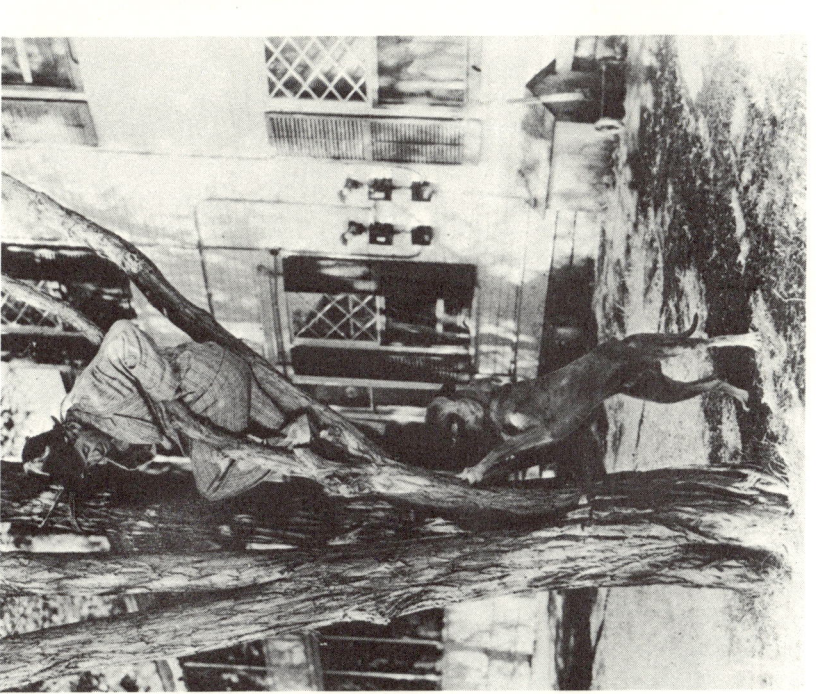

Will Rogers as "Jubilo" in the motion picture Too Busy To Work, *adapted from Ben Ames Williams' story*, Jubilo (Fox Film Corporation, 1932).

everybody a big favor by going fishing and you will be surprised, but the old United States will keep right on running while you boys are sitting on the bank.

Then, come back next Wednesday and we will let you know which one is the lesser of the two evils of you.

Yours,
Will Rogers.

1949   MR. ROGERS IS THOROUGHLY TIRED
          OF PART OF THE AMERICAN SYSTEM

NEW YORK, N. Y., Nov. 2. — Don't you all kinder wish that the President of our country wouldn't have to run around all over the land getting upon a soap box to shout his merits like a backwoods Congressman running for re-election?

That's why a President's term should be six years; no re-election, and be retired for life on half salary. Then he serves with dignity right up to the finish. And don't have to take part in this mess of promises, accusations and ballyhoo.

We thought when the radio was perfected and everybody could hear a speech, that it wouldn't be necessary to drag a President around over the country like a circus. But, no, the State leaders must satisfy their vanity by having him appear "in person" in their State.

But, after all, there is very little dignity, very little sportsmanship, or very little anything in politics, only "get the job and hold it."

Yours,
Will Rogers.

1950   WILL ROGERS FINDS COMEDY
          THE FEATURE OF THE CAMPAIGN

CLEVELAND, Ohio, Nov. 3. — There is comedy in this campaign. Otherwise we would all go "nerts."

Mr. Hoover says that in case of Democratic victory "grass will grow in the streets of American cities." But look at the fun it will be to see every traffic cop pushing a lawn mower.

Last night Secretary of the Navy Adams said "It will bring gloom to a hundred thousand firesides." Yes, but look at the hundred thousand Democratic postmasters whose gloom wouldn't be so noticeable.

Tonight somebody else will be funny over the radio. Don't miss 'em.

Just flew the Alleghenies. Fine trip, plane full of passengers.

Great race for Governor in this State. Good Democrat, and the Republicans' ace of aces, Dave Ingalls, running against him. He is the "class" of the whole Republican stable.

Well, I must hurry to California to welcome Mr. Hoover. He is coming 3,000 miles to vote for himself.

Yours,
Will Rogers.

1951   WILL ROGERS NOW FIGURES
              THE WINNER CAN BE THE LOSER

CLAREMORE, Okla., Nov. 4. — This is a hot campaign. Tempers been lost, gentlemanly conduct is a lost art, but let's just stop and study a minute and give the rascals the benefit of the doubt.

The Republicans have been in since 1920. Twelve years. And you would fight, too, if you was in their places. For it's been their hereditary training since childhood that the Republican party shall rule.

Now take the old Democrat. He is fighting, for he is in sight of the first square meal he has had in twelve years. So we mustn't be too critical.

Neither one of 'em is going to save us. Neither one is going to ruin us. Should Mr. Hoover lose, I don't think there is a person that wouldn't feel downright sorry for him, for he certainly has meant well and did all he could, and I expect it won't be long till we will be feeling just as sorry for Roosevelt.

This President business is a pretty thankless job. Washington or Lincoln either one didn't get a statue till everybody was sure they was dead. I'll bet you that even Cal Coolidge, who retired at the "peak," wouldn't tell you that worry didn't more than offset the glory.

So it's going to be mighty hard next Wednesday after it's over to tell which one to congratulate. If this depression stays with us, the loser Tuesday is going to be the winner.

Yours,
Will Rogers.

1952 MR. ROGERS MAKES UP HIS MIND
NOT TO TAKE SIDES IN ELECTION

SANTA MONICA, Cal., Nov. 6. — Well, I am like Mr. Coolidge. You ain't going to get me taking sides in this election. I am going to write about aviation.

Aviation will save this country someday, and I know no politician is going to do it. Wish we could get our Presidential candidates to travel by plane, but there is no back platform to make the speeches from and there is no plane big enough to carry all their "yes" men.

Had a great night flight from Fort Worth to Los Angeles last night. Night flying is smoother, cooler and the real time saver and it is becoming very popular on the lines.

Back home after 21,000 miles. Through twenty countries. All big, three-motored American planes. All American pilots and co-pilots. A radio operator, in touch with Miami, or Brownsville, Texas, every minute. A steward to feed you. The whole fare was less than $1,600 and made the trip in less than three weeks. No night flying.

You would be surprised at the progress in those countries. Arrive early in the afternoon, then sight seeing wonderful old towns and cities every night. It's got any trip to Europe skinned a mile.

These are the countries we are going to have to get our future trade with.

Yours,
Will Rogers.

1953 MR. ROGERS HEAVES A SIGH
OF RELIEF THAT WORST IS OVER

BEVERLY HILLS, Cal., Nov. 7. — There is only one redeeming thing about this whole election. It will be over at sundown, and let everybody pray that it's not a tie, for we couldn't go through with this thing again.

And, when the votes are counted, let everybody, including the candidates, get into a good humor as quick as they got into a bad one.

Both gangs have been bad sports, so see if at least one can't redeem themselves by offering no alibis, but co-operate with the winner, for no matter which one it is the poor fellow is going to need it.

So cheer up. Let's all be friends again. One of the evils of democracy is you have to put up with the man you elect whether you want him or not. That's why we call it democracy.

Yours,
Will Rogers.

1954   Mr. Rogers Offers Consolation
To Those Who Backed The Loser

BEVERLY HILLS, Cal., Nov. 8. — If your side lost don't take it too much to heart. Remember there is always this difference between us and Italy. In Italy Mussolini runs the country. But here the country runs the President.

As I dispatch this little message along late in the evening, it looks like the only thing can beat the Democrats is honest counting.

Certainly brought out a big vote. There was actually women went to the polls that didn't have a new hat. Humiliation couldn't even stop 'em.

                                Yours,
                                Will Rogers.

1955   Mr. Rogers Sees A Lot Of Balm
For The Loser Of The Election

BEVERLY HILLS, Cal., Nov. 9. — Mr. Hoover, the consolation you have from the whole American people is no doubt greater than that ever shared by a losing President.

There was nothing personal in the vote against you. You just happened to be associated with a political party that the people had just lost their taste for.

There is something about a Republican that you can only stand for him just so long. And, on the other hand, there is something about a Democrat that you can't stand for him quite that long.

We all know that you was handed a balloon that was blowed up to its utmost. You held it as carefully as any one could, but the thing busted right in your hands. Well, there just ain't much you can do in a case like that.

No, it wasn't you, Mr. President. The people just wanted to buy something new, and they didn't have any money to buy it with. But they could go out and vote free and get something new for nothing. So cheer up. You don't know how lucky you are.

                                Yours,
                                Will Rogers.

1956   Mr. Rogers Analyzes Some Odds
And Ends Of The Election News

BEVERLY HILLS, Cal., Nov. 10. — Well, the returns are pretty much all in. All but Kentucky. They got a law they can't count their votes till everybody sobers up, so it will be quite a little bit before we get them.

I was surprised at the vote the Republicans polled in Mississippi and Louisiana. I thought there was more post offices there than there is.

California and several states voted to do away with their local enforcement laws. Now out here liquors and wines are classified as "perishable goods" and are given right away on highways and trains.

Democrats had such a hard time getting money to campaign on, that I doubt if they will have enough to get to Washington on.

Yours,
Will Rogers.

1957   WILL ROGERS SAYS FISHING
WORKED WELL FOR GARNER

BEVERLY HILLS, Cal., Nov. 11. — I advised 'em all to go fishing. Let the people alone and make up their own minds. Jack Garner was the only one that listened to me, he went fishing, made no enemies, had a good time, caught three big "channel cats," a seat in the House of Representatives and the Vice-Presidency.

That's about a record for one catch. He wanted to throw back the smallest of the "catfish" and the Vice-Presidency, and just keep the seat in the House and the other two fish. Garner will be the only man ever went from "Speaker" in the House to "listener" in the Senate.

Yours,
Will Rogers.

P. S. — By the way, what ever becomes of the Roosevelts that claimed they was only eighth cousins to this one?

1958   MR. ROGERS LEARNS THAT OTHERS
PROFIT BY HIS LITTLE AIR JAUNTS

SANTA MONICA, Cal., Nov. 13. — Say, my trip to South America was of some use to someone besides myself. Get this. It's a new one on me.

"Dear Mr. Rogers: Did you know when you left for South America that you took forty-nine fifth grade pupils from Concord, North Carolina, with you? We clipped your daily messages and found the places on the map, and tried to learn all we could of the places. We liked the trip fine. We liked our hop over the Andes with you, Buenos Aires, Rio Janeiro, Santiago, Chili, Lima, Peru, and all of them were beautiful.

"You have made us love South America. Hurry up and go somewhere else. We want to go with you. Fifth grade, Long School, Miss Perberton's room."

I am the Nicholas Murray Butler of Concord.

Yours,
Will Rogers.

1959   WILL ROGERS WOULD LET HOOVER
PEEL DEBT MORATORIUM ONION

CORONA, Cal., Nov. 14. — Herbert has invited Franklin down to see him.

Now, on the face of it, that looks like the last word in hospitality. But let's look that gift horse in the face. Is Herbert just crazy about Franklin? No, "children," prominent men are never crazy about each other.

Herbert's in the hole on these foreign debts. Something has to be done right away. If he gives 'em another year or cuts the amount he will get all the blame. But, if Franklin confers with him and then something is done, why they split the blame 50-50.

Now, maybe, two Presidents can run a country, but if I was Franklin I would say:

"Thank you for the invite, Herbert, but the moratorium is your onion. You will have to peel it. I don't want any of the tears of it in my eyes till I start drawing salary. Going on a little trip to South America. See you March 4. Yours, with best wishes, Franklin."

Yours,
Will Rogers.

1960   MR. ROGERS FINDS BROKEN LINK
IN THE DEBTS PAYMENT CHAIN

CORONA, Cal., Nov. 15. — Germany has always paid each of these other nations more than each of them paid you. But, Germany has quit paying them. Now, they say they can't pay us.

What they mean is that they could pay us, but they would have to use some of their own money to do it with. And, of course, a thing as revolutionary as that never entered their heads.

Now, the big joke is that we had been loaning Germany all the money that they paid them, so that they could pay us. So, it really wasn't Europe that fell down on the debts, it was us. It's all our fault.

It was a wonderful idea, as the Republicans worked it for years, only we run out of money and couldn't keep it going.

But, don't ever lay the fault on Europe for not paying us. They would start tomorrow if we would just loan 'em the money to do it on.

Yours,
Will Rogers.

1961   MR. ROGER'S HEART UNTOUCHED
BY "CAN'T PAY" DEBT PLEAS

CORONA, Cal., Nov. 16. — You couldn't pick up a paper for a year and a half but it told of the millions and millions of gold shipped to France, especially.

Our whole export trade consisted of gold bars to Europe. They tried everything from petty larceny to manslaughter to get us off the gold. If they had been able to do it, their celebration would have been bigger than the Armistice. I was in Europe and that's all they talked of. Then for France to say they can't pay!

Here is the funny part about the whole thing. Why don't they default? Oh, no, they never use that word. They don't want it said they "defaulted."

Yours,
Will Rogers.

1962   MR. ROGERS SUGGESTS A MESSAGE
OF THREE WORDS FOR EUROPE

SANTA MONICA, Cal., Nov. 17. — Well, the old propaganda is working, boys. Every night over the radio, or in big lengthy editorials, it keeps on saying, "What are you going to do? You can't collect, we have got to make some different terms."

One message of three words will make every nation in Europe

dig it up and send it over by plane, they would be in such a hurry to get it here—"Pay or default."

There is not a country in the world that would dare default. It would spoil their credit. They couldn't borrow any money any more.

England will pay you every dollar they promised, you can go bet your cent on that. And, France is five times more able to pay than England, but a Frenchman is not an Englishman.

You can see the whole thing is a frame-up by 'em all "ganging" in with their protests at once.

Yours,
Will Rogers.

1963   WILL ROGERS LINKS TWO ITEMS
        IN THE NEWS ABOUT ROOSEVELT

CORONA, Cal., Nov. 18. — Two very important items in the papers: "Mr. Roosevelt to visit Mr. Hoover" and the other "Mr. Roosevelt takes out a $500,000 policy," I do hope these two items together have no (what is it you call it?) significance. Mr. Roosevelt made his policy payable in favor of his pet and well-deserving project, the infantile paralysis home at Warm Springs, Ga.

See where The Literary Digest missed the election by 2 and 6-100 of a point. That sheet is certainly going back. Why don't the Digest hold one now to see if we are going to get any dough back from "our friends" overseas.

Yours,
Will Rogers.

1964   MR. ROGERS WRITES THE WORDS
        FOR THE WHITE HOUSE PARLEY

CORONA, Cal., Nov. 20. — "Hello, Governor Roosevelt, nice of you to come, knowing your distance for Washington."

"Hello, Mr. President, nice of you to make it possible for me to get to Washington, but let's get right to business. Are those foreigners going to pay?"

Mr. Hoover: "Not unless they have to."

Mr. Roosevelt: "What were your campaign promises?"

Mr. Hoover: "No postponements and no cancellations."

Mr. Roosevelt: "Mine, too. What do you say just for a novelty that both parties keep their campaign promises?"

Mr. Hoover: "That's O. K. with me. Stimson, bring us a cable blank."

"Dear (?) Europe: Your applications of poverty to the U. S. Government for extension on your notes is respectfully denied as the taxpayers at home whom we borrowed the money from are demanding it. If we don't receive it from you, we have no possible way of refunding it to them. We hope this is quite clear.

"Yours respectfully,
"HOOVER AND ROOSEVELT,
Representing U. S. Government."
Yours,
Will Rogers.

1965   Mr. Rogers Hopes For The Best
From That Conference Today

CORONA, Cal., Nov. 21. — Well, as you read this our two Presidents will be as nervous over their meeting as a couple of debutantes. Well, we all hope some good comes from their meeting, and in fact we hope some money comes out of it, too.

Wasn't that too bad about that poor fellow Robins down in North Carolina that just got that way looking for another dry?

I know a hitch hiker out here that is having such poor luck getting a ride that now he is standing in the middle of the road offering to go either way.

Yours,
Will Rogers.

1966   Will Rogers Pats The Backs
Of Some Fellow Writers

LOS ANGELES, Cal., Nov. 22. — Got a thrill this morning, Walter Lippman, a grand writer, that I would no more miss reading than miss breakfast. Also, he made the best radio talk the night of election that was made.

Well, he had actually read something I had written about the debts. I couldn't have been more happy if Mr. Hoover and Roosevelt had slummed over in my literary pasture. Course he didn't agree with me. But, just to be disagreed with by a man like him is a thrill.

Speaking of good writers, Mr. Brisbane is out here. Months ago on my porch he bet Mrs. Ned McClain the Republicans wouldn't carry eight states. I thought he was crazy. He was by two States.

Everything is changing in America. People are taking their comedians seriously and the politicians as a joke, when it used to be visa versa.

Yours,
Will Rogers.

1967   MR. ROGERS HEARS OL' OKLAHOMA
IS GETTING BACK TO NORMALCY

LOS ANGELES, Cal., Nov. 23. — Los Angeles paper the other day took what they thought was a terrible slam at my honorable old State with the following:

"Will Rogers's home State of Oklahoma sold more buggy whips last year than any other."

Well, if it did that means she is leading the United States back out of the mess. Put a buggy whip in every man's hand that's got no business with a steering wheel.

The horses raises what the farmer eats, and eats what the farmer raises. But you can't plow in the ground and get gasoline. You don't have to pay some finance company 10 or 15 per cent to own a horse.

We been moving awful fast the last few years, but when we stopped and checked up we found we would have gotten just as far if we had walked, and wouldn't have owed anybody.

So "bravo" Oklahoma!

Yours,
Will Rogers.

1968   MR. ROGERS OFFERS A DEFENSE
TO BROADSIDES OF CRITICISM

SANTA MONICA, Cal., Nov. 24. — Say, a lot of you birds sure take the hide off me when I am wrong (and that's plenty constant), but give me credit when I do guess right.

You skinned me alive when I said nothing would come of the Hoover-Roosevelt meeting. I said Mr. Roosevelt would say, "It's your onion and you peel it till March 4." How different did it happen from that? And, as for the meeting, maybe there is a doubt in both men's minds if it wouldn't have been better if it hadn't been held.

I don't see how folks figured they could agree. They hold two opposite views on the question. That's why they belong to different parties. Either one of 'em might be right. We know they are both sincere in their beliefs, but how was one man going to tell another man how to run his business, until he, the No. 2 man, come in and started running it for him.

Politics don't have to enter into that. That's just human nature. So don't shoot me, boys, till the returns are all in on all these affairs.

Yours,
Will Rogers.

1969   WILL ROGERS SAYS MCADOO WON'T TAKE A CABINET POST

BEVERLY HILLS, Cal., Nov. 25. — If you think this Democratic victory brought on harmony, you just wait till they start to hand out those postoffices down South. There will be more people killed in the rush than in the flood.

Got some real debt information first hand yesterday and not from an editorial. Mr. W. G. McAdoo was out to visit me. Incidentally, all he did (and this didn't come from him either, it comes from known facts) well all he did was make the next President of the U. S.

He says he will absolutely stay in the Senate, and accept no Cabinet position, even if offered.

Later in the afternoon came out Congresswoman Ruth Bryan Owen, daughter of W. J. She was bred in the purple in politics, and shows it.

It was the first Thanksgiving the Democrats have celebrated since B. C. (Before Coolidge).

Yours,
Will Rogers.

1970 Mr. Rogers Announces A Plan
    To Write On Topics He Knows

SANTA MONICA, Cal., Nov. 27. — Well, all I know is just what I read in the papers.

Never miss my old friend Mr. Brisbane, but I finally caught him on one. He wrote Saturday about Mr. Hearst's 15,000 "Holstein" cattle. Now, a Holstein is an old black and white spotted milk cow. She is a beverage animal entirely. She is raised for her juice, and not for her T-bones. Why even Mr. Hearst hasn't got enough editors to milk old "bossies." Course, what he meant was 15,000 "Herefords," white faces, faces made up like women.

Now here is what we got to do with this writing business. We got to have it divided according to talent. I'll handle the cattle end. He takes disarmament, unemployment, wars past and future, history gone and coming, advantages of living in California and Florida.

And, oh yes, I'll take over discussion of the foreign debts, and give him 10 per cent of all I collect. But, he is to have all the dissatisfied Republicans who blame the loss of the election on ignorance.

       Yours,
       Will Rogers.

1971 Mr. Rogers Finds A Republican
    Who Is Fed Up On Straw Votes

BEVERLY HILLS, Cal., Nov. 28. — Hey Rip, I got a "Believe It or Not" for you.

A fellow in Beverly Hills says The Literary Digest polls should be abolished on account of their accuracy. He don't mind a straw vote if it's not right, but he is "agin" the true ones. He says people read 'em and vote with the majority.

But, here is what he don't explain. What makes the majority in the straw votes?

No, you are wrong. Chaplin didn't write that, or Laurel and Hardy, or Joe Brown. It was my friend, the Republican editor of the Beverly Hills Citizen, in a convincing editorial. It was his contribution to "what can the Republican party do to get their hands back in those U.S. mail sacks again?"

       Yours,
       Will Rogers.

1972   MR. ROGERS IS FOR A TIME LIMIT
ON THANKSGIVING TURKEY BONES

LOS ANGELES, Cal., Nov. 29. — Did you read about the woman up in the Northwest that swallowed a turkey bone four days after Thanksgiving, then got in an airplane, got sick and got rid of the bone?

Well, I was going to try to write a little joke about it, showing how many days it took to reach the old bone of the gobbler. When lo and behold, today, Tuesday, our own cook come dragging in turkey hash. We don't reach the bones till about Thursday.

If I run for something, that would be my platform, "boys, no part of any turkey served later than Sunday night after Thanksgiving."

Yours,
Will Rogers.

1973   MR. ROGERS EXPRESSES SYMPATHY
FOR OUR COLLEGE BOYS AND GIRLS

BEVERLY HILLS, Cal., Nov. 30. — They got a "gag" in these colleges now when they slip up behind an old boy or girl and say:

"What are you going to major in?"

"Oh, Professor, I am not going in the army. I ain't going to do any majoring."

"I mean, what is to be your life's work? Hurry up now. Let me know before noon."

Now, there is nothing they can do, yet they are told to make up their minds what it is. Suppose professors and teachers were told they couldn't teach any more, but to make up their minds what they were going to "major" in?

If somebody took my little jokes and good looks away from me, I know it would take me a right smart spell before I could make up my mind what to "major" in, especially if this Eighteenth Amendment is voted out.

Yours,
Will Rogers.

1974   WILL ROGERS GIVES HIS VERSION
OF WHY LAME DUCKS ARE LAME

BEVERLY HILLS, Cal., Dec. 1. — We haven't got enough work to do to go around, so it looks like they are finally going to try and more evenly distribute it by having a five-day week and six-hour day. I see now where the Federation of Labor and almost every one are for it.

All this after three years of starvation. We are a country that everything has to be proved to us. Look at the sales tax. That is coming just as sure as shooting, but you couldn't get the guys in that last Congress to admit it. We hadn't suffered enough yet.

Well, the lame ducks met Monday and that's why they are lame, is because their constituents were thinking faster than they was.

Yours,
Will Rogers.

1975   WILL ROGERS OFFERS A WAY
            TO TAKE CARE OF INTEREST

BEVERLY HILLS, Cal., Dec. 2. — I have heard every kind of reason given for our hard times, and as causes of our slow recovery. But I have never heard the real one, that's that interest is too high. The world and about everybody in it are broke from paying too high interest.

No man should receive more for the "hire" of his money than he could take it and earn with it himself, and for the last three years there has been nothing that he could have made even 1 per cent on it, outside of loaning it.

The banks all failed because the interest people owed 'em was larger than the principal. What would be the matter with banking on a real percentage of business? The banker receives in interest in accordance to what the borrower makes on the loan. If he don't make anything, he don't pay anything.

Well, that's about all for today. Be busy tomorrow reading wires from bankers.

Yours,
Will Rogers.

1976   MR. ROGERS THINKS THIS CONGRESS
            SHOULD KNOW JUST WHAT TO DO

SANTA MONICA, Cal., Dec. 4. — Everbody is knocking this lame-duck Congress, but do you know those fellows have a chance to make a real name for themselves and make us ashamed that we fired 'em?

They know exactly how the people voted on every question that they will be asked to decide on. They know the majority didn't want prohibition. They know the majority don't want the debt canceled. They know everybody wants government expense cut in half.

So when any questions comes up all they have to do is read the election returns. Course, if they want to still be on the minority side of all these things we will know exactly why they was defeated.

Yours,
Will Rogers.

1977 MR. ROGERS GIVES HIS OPINION
OF LAME DUCKS THAT CANNOT SEE

BEVERLY HILLS, Cal., Dec. 5. — Europe turned out a movie called "Congress Dances," and it pleased everybody. Today our Congress met and pleased nobody.

Forty-four Democrats, mostly lame ducks, were the villains. In November the country went overwhelmingly wet. But 100 Republicans and 44 Democrats figured that the country didn't know what it wanted. So that means an extra session of Congress.

Regardless of what your opinion is on this subject, but when you absolutely know that it will eventually pass, then to purposely hold it up and cost the government all this money, then you are a "lame duck," but not in the leg.

Yours,
Will Rogers.

1978 MR. ROGERS SUBSCRIBES FULLY
TO A 'BUY AMERICAN' CAMPAIGN

BEVERLY HILLS, Cal., Dec. 6. — This country is so hungry this morning they could eat a lame duck.

If you want to really know one of the major things that's wrong with us, go take a nickel and get last week's Saturday Evening Post and read the first article in there. It's by Sam Blythe. Then go out, and before you buy the baby a rattle, your sweetheart a toothbrush, your wife a pair of rubber boots, ask if they were "made in America."

Then you can show your patriotism, and not just keep asking "What's the matter with this country?"

England is doing it; the world is doing it. But our society don't think they smell right unless they been dipped in foreign perfume.

Yours,
Will Rogers.

1979   MR. ROGERS IS TOLERANT AND ALOOF
AS REGARDS EDITORIAL WRITERS

BEVERLY HILLS, Cal., Dec. 7. — I would like to state to the readers of THE NEW YORK TIMES that I am in no way responsible for the editorial or political policy of this paper.

I allow them free reign as to their opinion, so long as it is within the bounds of good subscription gathering.

But I want it distinctly understood that their policy may be in direct contrast to mine.

Their editorials may be put in purely for humor, or just to fill space.

Every paper must have its various entertaining features, and their editorials are not always to be taken seriously, and never to be construed as my policy.

Yours,
Will Rogers.

1980   MR. ROGERS GIVES HIS DEFINITION
OF TERM 'LAME DUCK CONGRESS'

BEVERLY HILLS, Cal., Dec. 8. — An awful lot of people are confused as to just what is meant by a "lame duck Congress."

It's like where some fellows worked for you and their work wasn't satisfactory and you let 'em out, but after you fired 'em, you let 'em stay long enough so they could burn your house down.

You know Ruth Bryan Owen, the Congresswoman who had always been a prohibitionist and was defeated in the primary on it. You got to give her credit. When she saw that the vote was against it, why she held no revenge, but voted with the repealists.

So, there you have a woman with more nerve than a lot of men.

Yours,
Will Rogers.

1981   Will Rogers Compares Ideals
                In Football And In Politics

LOS ANGELES, Cal., Dec. 9. — Notre Dame is here. Notre Dame is here to carry on for Rockne. Wouldn't it be wonderful if we had political leaders who could leave ideals and systems that the young knew were fundamentally right. The difference is that the coach has spent a lifetime teaching co-operation. He knows what he wants. While the political candidate only knows that he wants 'em to vote for him. But from then on he is just guessing.

Imagine a politician inspiring voters with, "give us one more vote boys, for the memory of dear old Senator Jasbo." "Ah hooey, who was old Senator Jasbo, and what did he ever do?" But Notre Dame will do it for Rockne as long as a football is blown up.

                              Yours,
                             Will Rogers.

1982   Mr. Rogers Gives The Inside
                On California And Football

BEVERLY HILLS, Cal., Dec. 10. — Big football game, one hundred thousand of us sit there in the cold and picked up what little pneumonia there was left. Give a Californian a football or an orange and he knows more things to do with it than a Harvard guy does a dictionary.

Notre Dame had a fine team but after taking one look at that California line they should have started 'em throwing forward passes before they got off the train. I would have sent players up in the stands to grab off passes.

Pittsburgh is coming out to play this team New Year's in what we humorously call our "Rose Bowl."

Well, it's a nice trip out here and California will play their Chamber of Commerce against 'em in the first half.

Would have brought Colgate but everybody out here thought they were a toothpaste team of the radio.

                              Yours,
                             Will Rogers.

1983   Mr. Rogers Reports California
                Feels Roosevelt Made Good

BEVERLY HILLS, Cal., Dec. 12. — Well, the Democrats made good out here. I don't know what they promised in the rest of the country, but Roosevelt promised us rain, and, by golly, he made good.

The rest of the country can be excited over prohibition, disarmament, war loans or the new Cabinet, but this is a desert country, and if we don't get rain we are blowed up.

We can show you oranges growing, and flowers, but if you look under the bush you will see a hose. A sprinkling can is our national emblem. Rain is never a nuisance here; it's a miracle.

So the Democrats have made good.

Yours,
Will Rogers.

1984   Mr. Rogers Cannot Understand One Strange Form Of Thrift

BEVERLY HILLS, Cal., Dec. 13. — As you read this tomorrow, an air express line will be inaugurated from coast to coast, nothing but express. We used to think it was too expensive to send anything by air but a postcard, but it's not that way now.

Air mail has fallen off since the costs were raised 3 cents. Here, companies have spent and are losing millions giving the people the greatest air network for mails in the world. Write a letter today, the receiver reads it tomorrow no matter where he is. If a letter is not worth 3 cents more to get there three days ahead, it don't look like it is important enough to write. I would just hand it to some hitch hiker and let him deliver it in the spring.

We used to think mails were terribly important, but if they ain't worth 3 cents, the guy might just as well wait till he meets the other fellow and tell it to him.

Yours,
Will Rogers.

1985   Mr. Rogers Now Confesses He Is No Authority On Debts

BEVERLY HILLS, Cal., Dec. 14 — Got some news for you. Fellow wrote the NEW YORK TIMES (my mother paper), took exception to some fool thing I had written and forgot about.

THE TIMES took it serious and so did people arguing over it. They thought the fellow was some authority. Now what do I find out? He is a young Harvard graduate, Charlton Ogburn Jr., 22 years old.

And, like all Harvard graduates, "Junior" wanted to do something "worth while" for the old alma mater.

But America's sense of humor has taught 'em there is three things they must never take serious—a columnist on any paper, a political speech by any candidate, and a Harvard graduate if he hasn't been out four years. Harvard is an eight-year school—four in and four out. But after then they are just human and fine as any college graduate.

So, don't take the debt thing too serious from either Harvard or O. C. C. (Oklahoma Cow Camp). Their information on the subject is about equal.

Yours,
Will Rogers.

1986   Mr. Rogers Believes England
         Will Be Gainer In The End

BEVERLY HILS, Cal., Dec. 15. — Somebody will finally find a way to run this government yet. An old boy was on the right track the other day. He came into the Congressional Gallery the other day waving a gun and said, "I am for America. All not with me better take to the brush, for I am going to take a shot at 'em."

Well, the place was clear in a jiffy. Now they got a sign in the visitors' gallery, "Don't shoot your Congressman, without first getting a license."

England never stood higher in American opinion than today. That was the cheapest hundred million they ever spent. And they will gain in the end by it.

Yours,
Will Rogers.

1987   Will Rogers Remarks

SANTA MONICA, Cal., Dec. 16. — I bet you France pays. In fact they already started paying. Merchants in Beverly Hills (the best dressed and most cosmopolitan town in the U. S.) said they couldn't sell the "scream stars" a single French importation. Instead of Christmas night perfume, it's "jockey club" made in Des Moines and it don't smell bad at that. The "leading men" have all switched from a French to a New Jersey hair tonic. Every show store is knocking the "French heels" off their shoes. These French "berets" that some "near" men were wearing, they have switched to crocheted boudoir cap. Oh, France is paying.

Yours,
Will Rogers.

1988   WILL ROGERS MARVELS A BIT
AT THE SENATE'S FORESIGHT

SANTA MONICA, Cal., Dec. 18. — The U. S. Senate sentenced the Philippines to twelve more years of American receivership.

Will you tell me one thing? How can one nation tell when another nation is ready for independence? But our government can do it. Yes, sir; there is not a dozen of 'em that's ever been west of the Golden Gate, but they could tell you to a day, twelve years from now, just when the "little brown brothers" would be able to mess up their affairs as bad as ours.

Certainly lucky for us we got our liberty when we did. Suppose the House of Commons in England was holding a clinic over us to decide if we were ready for "self-determination."

Yours,
Will Rogers.

1989   MR. ROGERS BELIEVES FRANCE
HAS ABLE PILOT AND WILL PAY

LOS ANGELES, Cal., Dec. 19. — See where France has Paul-Boncour to form a new Cabinet. Six years ago in Geneva, at a disarmament conference, he was head of France's delegation and I saw quite a lot of him. He is very able. I have always wondered since then why they never used him more.

France will pay, and it can't possibly hurt them as bad as it will some of our writers and American financiers. I never saw people so broken-hearted over our country receiving a little dab of money.

Congress voting on beer again Wednesday. It passed the people. But they can't get it through Congress.

Yours,
Will Rogers.

1990   Mr. Rogers Joins In Dispute
Over Merits Of 'Technocracy'

LOS ANGELES, Cal., Dec. 20. — "Technocracy," is it a new mouth wash, a corn plaster or has the scientists just hired a press agent?

It says you only work four hours a day, and there will be no politicians. That last is the best selling clause it has.

There is not a man in the country that can't make a living for himself and family. But, he can't make a living for them and his government, too, the way his government is living.

What the government has got to do is live as cheap as the people. Then you don't need "technocracy."

Yours,
Will Rogers.

1991   Will Rogers Thinks Hoover
Is A Good Collector, After All

LOS ANGELES, Cal., Dec. 21. — I don't know why Mr. Hoover is all excited over the debt yet. That's all over now.

He did a mighty good job. We was owed about one hundred and twenty-five millions and he collected over a hundred. Anybody who can get four-fifths nowadays is doing a mighty good job of collecting.

And besides, France is going to pay. So it looks like the debt thing is all settled till next December, when it will be Mr. Roosevelt's Xmas present to try and get on our tree.

Time to worry over a debt is before you get it, not after you got four-fifths of it.

So arguing over the debt now is just like arguing over the last election.

Yours,
Will Rogers.

1992   Mr. Rogers Is Still Puzzled
By This Technocracy Thing

LOS ANGELES, Cal., Dec. 22. — This technocracy thing, we don't know if it's a disease or a theory. It may go out as fast as Eskimo pies or miniature golf courses. But people right now are in a mood to grab at anything.

They are sure of one thing, and that is that the old orthodox political way of running everything has flopped.

There is not a man in the whole world today that people feel like actually knows what's the matter. If there was, he would be appointed dictator unanimously by the whole world.

Our "big men" don't admit they don't know. They just keep on hoping they can bull their way through.

The case has simply got too big for the doctors, but the doctors haven't got big enough to admit it.

1933   WILL ROGERS FINDS HOOVER
         NOW ACTING AS HE PREDICTED

LOS ANGELES, Cal., Dec. 23. — Say "Babe" Didrickson scaled over another bunch of hurdles yesterday. This time it was the A.A.U.'s that got down on their all fours and she hopped right over them. It didn't take all this messing around and publicity and ballyhoo. They knew at first if she had been paid for the advertisement or if she hadn't. But the minute they saw those gate receipts slipping out of their hands into hers they did a high jump backwards that beat one of her front ones.

"Babe" has always beat women. This is the first time she has ever entered the male ranks and showed them up.

Yours,
Will Rogers.

P. S. — I told you Mr. Hoover would quit worrying about the debts and leave them alone.

1994   MR. ROGERS FINDS CHRISTMAS
         UNCHANGED BY TECHNOCRACY

SANTA MONICA, Cal., Dec. 25. — This "technocracy" didn't seem to make much difference with Christmas. Father's neckties and sox were done up in the same deceptive boxes they were before the scientists took us over.

People didn't get "beer by Xmas." They just had to struggle along on gin and corn.

Mr. Hoover went fishing in the South but didn't catch anything. He had waited too long, and the fish had all gone back Democratic.

France went into a "huddle" and practiced some of Shakespeare's signals. "To pay or not to pay, that is the question; whether it's better to pay and use the Yanks again? or not to pay and lose 'em?"

Yours,
Will Rogers.

1995 MR. ROGERS RETELLS HIS CHOICE
OF THE CHRISTMAS DAY STORIES

SANTA MONICA, Cal., Dec. 26. — Best story in the paper today, and there was many of fine charitable acts on Xmas.

Away out on the Escalante Desert between Los Angeles and Salt Lake—I have flown over it many times, it's one of the most desolate places you ever saw—one lonely ranch, the father had died and the mother and a whole house full of children live there.

Well, the pilots on the Western air run took up a purse of $80 and got the children clothes and toys, and then flew low on Xmas day and dropped 'em.

What a godsend the plane and the radio is to out-of-the-way places.

Yours,
Will Rogers.

1996 MR. ROGERS WAXES A WEE BIT
SARCASTIC ON THE MACHINE AGE

BEVERLY HILLS, Cal., Dec. 27. — So technocracy wants to do everything by machinery.

Well, if they can invent some machine that will kill more people than automobiles, why their plan will work. Three hundred and eighty over Xmas, and prohibition not repealed. That's more people than died by pestilence during the same three or four days in all the countries combined where we send doctors to teach 'em how to be civilized.

So, machinery is just doing fine. If it can't kill you, it will put you out of work.

Yours,
Will Rogers.

1997   Mr. Rogers Has A Suggestion
            On The 'Lame Duck' Problem

BEVERLY HILLS, Cal., Dec. 28. — Mr. Hoover has gone South fishing and, from what I read in the papers that the Democrats are planning for him, I believe I would just keep right on fishing.

I have always believed he made a mistake by not stepping out and turning the whole thing over to 'em on Dec. 1. There wasn't a chance of him and them agreeing on anything. It would have been a great big thing to have done.

Everybody is against the "lame duck," and this is the last one, anyhow. That would have given Hoover an excellent excuse. They couldn't have accused him of quitting. Work it like President Wilson was going to. There would have been enough "lame ducks" followed his example that we would now be seeing what plans the Democrats had.

As it is now, we have two more months of loggerheading and an extra session of Congress.

I would even leave 'em now and say, "Boys, it looks easy, maybe you can fix everything before March 4."

The Democrats would have to dig up some schemes mighty fast. Mr. Hoover would come out sitting mighty pretty. There wouldn't be a Republican on the Potomac to lay anything onto.

As it is now this is just a grudge Congress, a where-can-we-lay-the-blame Congress.

Yours,
Will Rogers.

1998   Will Rogers Cannot Fathom
            The Income Tax Mystery Yet

SANTA MONICA, Cal., Dec. 29. — Did you see the list of refunded income taxes this morning?

If anything should prove that a sales tax was a fair tax, it is the uncertainty of income tax. Through no one's particular fault people pay in a lot of money, then in a year or two they get it back. Then others think they have paid it all up. Then in a year or so the government wants more. There is no expert living that knows exactly what is, and what ain't allowed.

Remember tomorrow, Saturday, Sunday and Monday are the people's last three days of mind relaxation. Congress meets Tuesday.

Yours,
Will Rogers.

P. S. — Have any of you seen my friend Charlton Ogburn, Jr., late of Harvard?

1999 WILL ROGERS HAS HIS SAY ON A VARIETY OF SUBJECTS

BEVERLY HILLS, Cal., Dec. 30. — Say, good joke on us. We thought Congress had adjourned and here they are in session. Now that's the kind of Congress we want, one where we don't know if they are in session or out of session.

See where Insull is going to do like a movie star. He is going to make a "personal appearance" tour all over Europe.

France loaned Austria almost as much as she was to pay us. But she is wet nursing four or five of those little nations. They don't have to pay her back till the next war. You see in Europe they are already choosing sides. On account of the depression France can get a lot of nations signed up mighty cheap now.

.Yours,
Will Rogers.

DAILY TELEGRAMS — 1933

2000   MR. ROGERS OFFERS A NEW IDEA
IN THE WAY OF COMMISSIONS

SANTA MONICA, Cal., Jan. 1. — Well, New Year is here. Now what are you going to do with it?

I bet you there is not a man in America (yes I will take in more country than that, make it the world). There is not a single person that knows any more about what '33 has in store for us than a billy goat. Ten million people have gone without work for three years just listening to "big men" solve their problems.

I don't know what will be the first commission Mr. Roosevelt will appoint, but millions hope that it won't be the "president of this concern," or "the head of that corporation," but ten men who have been without work; we will at least get an original viewpoint.

If the non-worker has to go to the dogs, he at least should have a voice on the commission that sends him.

Yours,
Will Rogers.

2001   MR. ROGERS SEEMS A BIT BORED
BY THE NEW YEAR PROPHET CROP

BEVERLY HILLS, Cal., Jan. 2. — Same facts, same men issued the New Year "outlook" predictions. It looks like they just stay in business all year to tell "what the new year has in store for us." Every one of them has enough to live on no matter what happens.

But I have never seen a paper print what a poor man thought of the "coming year." Suppose at a hanging in a jail the reporters got statements from the warden and all the spectators, but no one asked the convicted man "what he thought the future had in store for him."

So tomorrow after these others have all been forgotten as usual, I have one from just such a man to tell you.

Yours,
Will Rogers.

2002   MR. ROGERS GETS THAT NEW YEAR INTERVIEW
WITH THE POOR MAN WHICH HE PROMISED

BEVERLY HILLS, Cal., Jan. 3. — Hello, Mister, was you ever asked to make a New Year's prediction?

Say, I never even been asked to eat on New Year's.

Have you ever been appointed on a commission?

No, nor in jail, either.

Do you read prominent men's predictions?

No, I never read fiction.

Have you a job?

No, I am on a diet.

What does the New Year hold in store for you?

What New Year? Have they got another one?

Do you think the world leaders can get us out of this?

They might, ignorance got us in.

What do you think of technocracy?

Nothing you can't spell will ever work.

What about the debts?

Well, I hear England paid 90 million, but it's only hearsay as far as the unemployed is concerned.

Do you think we will get out of this depression just because we got out of all the others?

Lots of folks drown that's been in the water before.

What will give the unemployed employment?

If somebody will throw a monkey wrench into the machinery.

Won't light wines and beer be a big aid to the poor?

They will if they give 'em away.

Won't 1933 see a change for the better?

I don't think so. We haven't suffered enough, the Lord is repaying us for our foolishness during prosperous days. He is not quite ready to let us out of the dog house yet.

I will haul you down the road if you like.

What's down the road? I've been to both ends. One place is as good as another.

Well, good luck to you.

Yes, that's what my Congressman said.

Yours,
Will Rogers.

2003   MR. ROGERS GOES NATIVE TO SING
         PRAISES OF THE U. S. C. COACH

BEVERLY HILLS, Cal., Jan. 4. — Been stirring around the studio so fast since New Year's that I never did get a chance to talk to you about our New Year's football game at the Rose Bowl.

Andy Mellon's boys from Pittsburgh played U. S. C. The score was 35 to nothing. But I don't want you to think those Pennsylvania Republicans didn't do better than the score shows.

The highlight was a Pitt man had his pants tore off, the same as a Notre Dame man did a few weeks ago. These old grapefruit squirters out here in California beat you and then tear the breeches off you.

We got a man out here coaching, named Jones, that could take the Senate page boys and beat Harvard, Princeton and Yale with 'em.

Yours,
Will Rogers.

2004   WILL ROGERS PAYS TRIBUTE
        IN HIS OWN WAY TO COOLIDGE

BEVERLY HILLS, Cal., Jan. 5. — Mr. Coolidge, you didn't have to die for me to throw flowers on your grave. I have told a million jokes about you, but every one was based on some of your splendid qualities. You had a hold on the American people regardless of politics. They knew you were honest, economical and had a native common sense.

History generally records a place for a man that is ahead of his time. But we that lived with you will always remember you because you was WITH your time.

By golly, you little, red-headed New Englander, I like you. You put horse sense into statesmanship and Mrs. Coolidge's admiration for you is an American trait.

Yours,
Will Rogers.

2005   ROGERS DISCUSSES THE NEWS
        FROM IOWA AND COLORADO

BEVERLY HILLS, Cal., Jan. 6. — You got to hand it to Iowa for the best news today. Some "bird" tried to bid in a farm on a forced sale at less than the mortgage and come pretty near landing hanging under a giant oak. We hope the days of the old town skinflint sitting back with some ready money to buy in the widow's home is about over.

Did you read where some Senator from Colorado was giving up his seat to his successor right away. He figured that the folks elected the other fellow and he was the one they wanted in there. That's almost unheard of in political life. There is a "lame duck" that should have a statue.

Yours,
Will Rogers.

2006   WILL ROGERS PAYS A TRIBUTE
TO CALVIN COOLIDGE'S WIDOW

SANTA MONICA, Cal., Jan. 8. — To Mrs. Coolidge:

Mrs. Coolidge, your husband's head rests today not alone on his Vermont soil but pillowed on the sincere tributes of the millions he had served.

Every writer has written of the amazing hold he had on his countrymen and they attributed it to various causes. Now that he is beyond the receipt of more honor, what about the "amazing hold" you have on our people.

Naturally you aided your husband's career. All wives do that. But what made you so beloved by the people? Overnight you were swept into the highest position that can be held by an American woman. Other "first lady's" had had perhaps greater advantages, training, background and social distinction. But you showed that which teachers, travel, and social association can't compete with, something that was born in you, a native dignity, a serenity, a modest graciousness that endears you to all.

Calvin Coolidge left a great lesson to our government in "common sense." Yours is just as great a lesson to your sex, a homely loveliness, and, above all, a consideration for the feelings of others, which constitutes a "real" lady, be she pauper or queen.

Yours,
Will Rogers.

2007   MR. ROGERS JOINS THE HUDDLE OF EXPERTS
WITH A NEW PLAN FOR WORLD RECOVERY

BEVERLY HILLS, Cal., Jan. 9. — If ten men went on a hunting trip you would soon learn which was the best cook and which the surest hunter to bring in the meat. You would find that each excelled in something that was useful to all.

Now, nations are just so many men like these. Each can produce something better and cheaper than the rest. Maybe it's by nature, climate, talent or thrift.

The United States, Canada, Argentina and Russia could furnish the wheat, a set amount each, at a set price, which is profitable and livable to the producer. Cotton and meat producing countries the same way. In exchange for this, Germany could be allowed exclusiveness for the things she excels in, France for her luxuries, England, Japan and all of 'em the same.

Even every little nation has something they could make a good living on if given an exclusive world market at a reasonable price.

Why is it if I raise something and you make something, can't we made a trade? Why do I have to attempt making "at" what you make, and you have to try to raise what I raise on land that's not suitable.

Now don't write any letters telling me "your plan won't work." I know it won't, too. It will never be tried.

You ask, "What's the joke of it?" Well, here's the joke:

Among the commodities which we could prove we excelled in is officeholders and politicians. Along with a free market for our wheat, meat, cotton and automobiles, we could send 'em all the politicians they need. For instance, Russia some Senators for some vodka, little Nicaragua some Congressmen for some bananas.

I tell you, the whole fool scheme is worth trying, just for the sake of this last part. If we can furnish the world with our politicians, we can compete with 'em.

Yours,
Will Rogers.

2008   MR. ROGERS HAS A PLAN TO WIN
         KIND WORDS FROM G. B. SHAW

BEVERLY HILLS, Cal., Jan. 10. — Bernard Shaw stopped over just long enough to make one speech in Bombay, India, started a war and 100 Indians killed each other.

That's what I call good speech-making. The only enthusiasm any of our speakers can rouse is a demand to kill the speaker.

Shaw is headed for Hollywood. We will buy one of his scenarios and he will just love us.

They've got the beer thing so muddled up in this session of Congress that it looks like the people will get to vote on it again in the next campaign.

Yours,
Will Rogers.

2009   WILL ROGERS AGAIN FALLS BACK
ON THE PRESS FOR AMMUNITION

BEVERLY HILLS, Cal., Jan. 11. — Well, let's see what we can read in our daily paper and then agitate folks' breakfast with in the morning.

"Democrats in clash in Senate; Carter Glass and Huey Long fight over banks." Get your Senate gallery seats now for the next four years, for there is going to be fun and amusement for everybody. Bring the kiddies. Arguing over banks, I didn't know there was any left.

"Debt issue flares up again in Paris." It flares, but it didn't flare up enough to do us any financial good. Even at a French statesman's salary, it will cost France more than 20 million a year just to argue over it.

"Japan takes another hunk of China." That's a daily headline we don't pay any attention to any more. Japan's alibis are the most interesting and unique things about that war.

Yours,
Will Rogers.

2010   MR. ROGERS CANNOT FATHOM
THE MIND OF A LAME DUCK

BEVERLY HILLS, Cal., Jan. 12. — See where Arizona voted to do away with the "lame duck" Congress. If you don't know what a "lame duck" Congress is, it's the type of congress they are holding now, where nobody is going to try to do anything till another Congress is called.

Why this administration wants to stick in there till the last dog is hung and take this punishment is hard to understand.

It's like a troop of actors getting hissed off the stage but insisting on staying on because they had a two week's contract.

Yours,
Will Rogers.

2011   WILL ROGERS THINKS HUEY
               A MATCH FOR WHOLE SENATE

BEVERLY HILLS, Cal., Jan. 13. — Senate arguing over "who is to make refunds on income taxes, the Senate or the Treasury Department." Simplify the tax so that folks can tell what to pay and what not to pay and neither need make any refund.

    "Japan takes Je-whole of what? China?
    "Senate still in filibuster."

    Imagine just ninety-five Senators trying to out-talk Huey Long. That many can't get him warmed up, and Huey has got just enough of a sprinklin' of the truth of what has been going on in our high finance that Wall Street is just on the verge of calling him a "menace."
                              Yours,
                              Will Rogers.

2012   MR. ROGERS SEES THE KINGFISH
               AS OUR NATIONAL EMBLEM

SANTA MONICA, Cal., Jan. 15. — Well, the "Huey Long session" of Congress goes into its seventh week tomorrow.

    The Senate's principal claim to distinction has been that they have a rule where a man can talk as long as he wants to about anything he wants to. And they have worried the American taxpayer to death with that rule.

    Now to have somebody come in that can talk them ragged, like they been doing to the country, why Huey is our hero. If he was the means of making 'em change that rule, the kingfish would replace the American eagle as our national emblem.

    So, sic 'em, Huey! It's good to hear a new voice anyway.
                              Yours,
                              Will Rogers.

2013   MR. ROGERS, SINGING IN THE RAIN
               SOUNDS A WARNING TO FLORIDA

BEVERLY HILLS, Cal., Jan. 16. — California is happy today. It's raining! It's raining!

    That might mean just another mud hole to some places, but brother, when you haven't seen a drop of water that hasn't come through a faucet in ten months, why rain looks like a miracle from the Democrats. May it keep up as long as Huey Long. Long live the Democrats!

Give California two months of rain in the year, and nothing can stop us but lack of adjectives.

So, look out Florida. California is "all wet" and when she is "all wet" she is hard to compete with.

Yours,
Will Rogers.

2014   MR. ROGERS TRIES TO ANSWER A FEW QUERIES ON HUEY LONG

SANTA MONICA, Cal., Jan. 17. — Say, I got a good one on "Huey."

The very best female scenario writer at our studio said to me yesterday, "Who is this Chinaman, Huey Long, that you been writing about talking in the Senate? Do they let Chinamen in there, and how did they understand what he was saying?"

Now, that sounds funny, but try to answer it and it's not so funny.

First, of course, Huey is not a Chinaman.

"How did he get into the Senate?" Well, he got in over Carter Glass's veto.

"And did they understand what he was saying?" And that's the hard part to answer. "Did they understand him?" Well, it's always been a question whether it made any difference whether you did or didn't understand what any Senator was saying. Most people have just become reconciled to 'em.

Yours,
Will Rogers.

2015   MR. ROGERS SUMS UP THE TASK THAT CONFRONTS THE FILIPINOS

BEVERLY HILLS, Cal., Jan. 18. — Everything is different nowadays, even the way a country gets its freedom.

We give the Philippines twelve years. In two years they are to have a Constitution that is suitable to us. I hope they make it. Ours after 150 years is not suitable to us.

They owe us some money, so we bet their freedom against ten years that they can't pay us that. We can't pay our national debt in 100 years.

So, here is all they got to do to get their freedom. Get a Constitution that will suit Democrat and Republican, pay all their debts and keep out of the clutches of Japan.

That's what I call a sporting offer.

Yours,
Will Rogers.

2016   Mr. Rogers Sums Up Our Ills
And Sets Forth The Causes

BEVERLY HILLS, Cal., Jan. 19. — Here is how this two-headed President thing works out.

We have a President that's in, but has no authority; a President that's out, but has no authority; a Senate that's in, but has no leader; a House that's in, but has been voted out; a budget that both sides are afraid to try to balance; debts that are owed us that will never be paid, and debts that we owe which we keep adding to.

We are sore at Japan because they took Manchuria; sore at the world because they won't disarm. In fact, we are just sore at ourselves because we muddled everything up, and in the midst of it all we tell the Philippines "what constitutes liberty."

Yours,
Will Rogers.

2017   Rogers Doubts We Get Value
For That Increase In Taxes

BEVERLY HILLS, Cal., Jan. 20. — The No. 2 President went down to Washington to confer with Huey Long and Herbert Hoover. With Hoover about firewood in the White House basement and Long on international and national affairs.

Every U. S. citizen is taxed $77 a head. That's $10 more than last year. Every wage earner has been cut from 10 to 50 per cent, but the cost of being governed has taken a $12\frac{1}{2}$ per cent raise.

Then you hear birds say, "All you need to restore prosperity is confidence." Yeah? Well, you will help restore prosperity if you put taxes in proportion to the benefits you receive for them, the same as any other commodity. Did you receive $10.00 more protection this year than last?

Yours,
Will Rogers.

2018   Mr. Rogers Gets A New Slant At The Peaks Of The Sierras

OAKLAND, Cal., Jan. 22. — Fastest air trip I ever made in a commercial plane, Los Angeles to Sacramento, 411 miles, in two hours flat. That's two five an hour. It was on the Varney Line, Lockheed plane, Pilot Taft. Flying part of the Sierras, all snow-capped, at that speed was more of a kick than the Andes at about ninety miles.

Another big bank failure. Suppose the Fire Department was run like a bank. A fire examiner finds a small fire and goes back from time to time to see it getting bigger. Then, just as there is nothing left but the chimney he notifies the department, "we better see what we can save for those people?"

Yours,
Will Rogers.

2019   Mr. Rogers Slips Up In Front Of His Real Checker-Uppers

BEVERLY HILLS, Cal., Jan. 23. — Here's one on me for the book.

My wife and my sister from Oklahoma was reading and lamenting the "Scotty farewell," both agreeing it was too bad and that he was wonderful.

I lay down a Huey Long speech and say, "What do you mean farewell? I was up to his house two months ago."

"Why, you weren't, you didn't see him. You don't know him. You haven't been out of this canyon. He is going back to Italy. He has sung his last."

"Italy? Sing? He can't sing and don't know where Italy is, but he does know more about Death Valley than anybody living, and don't worry about old Death Valley Scotty. He will get along."

Yours,
Will Rogers.

2020   MR. ROGERS CALLS ON EVERY ONE
TO GIVE THE SENATE A BIG HAND

BEVERLY HILLS, Cal., Jan. 24. — Well, this is not only the lamest lame duck Congress, but it's our last lame duck Congress.

States stayed up all night in order to be able to ratify it, and here it was turned down by Congress six years in a row.

But, we got to give the old Senate credit. They passed it every year. So, quit knocking the Senate. They were six years ahead of the House. Give the Senate a great big hand.

If the House had followed out the people's wish like the Senate did, this session of Congress which is being held now just for amusements sake, would not have been held, and we would have been just three months nearer prosperity, or posterity, or whatever it is we are headed for.

Yours,
Will Rogers.

2021   MR. ROGERS DISCUSSES SILVER,
STRAYING KIN AND A NEW SONG

BEVERLY HILLS, Cal., Jan. 25. — On account of it being the only kind of money that 80 per cent of our people ever handle, they want to see silver given a real value. But Congress wants to keep it as it is, just to pound up and use as a wedding present.

See where the Roosevelts, even down unto the fifth cousins, are straying back into the fold. Nothing will bring back distant kin folks like the news spreading that you got a job.

The very popular wife of a very popular retiring Cabinet member has written a song, "My Homeland."

Yours,
Will Rogers.

2022   WILL ROGERS PUTS HIS FAITH
IN THE BANK BILL'S AUTHOR

SANTA MONICA, Cal., Jan. 26. — Glass banking bill passed the Senate. During the long argument over it so much was printed about what Huey said that the newspapers never did print what the bill said. We just trust to the good banking judgment of Carter Glass to have something worth while. Glass is an absolute authority on money, and it's astonishing that the Republicans were never able to win him over.

France wants to get in on the debt settlement. On account of them paying nothing as it is under the new settlement we are to start paying them.

Yours,
Will Rogers.

2023   ROGERS LINKS TECHNOCRACY
AND LAME-DUCK CONGRESS

SANTA MONICA, Cal., Jan. 27. — Saw today the first picture of the two men who manufacture technocracy.

My faith in the thing, which had started at nothing and grown less by leaps and bounds, took another nose dive. History will record as follows:

"Early in 1933 America sorely pressed economically and their sense of humor lost in a mad whirl of grappling at anything offering relief, took two events seriously, a thing called technocracy and a thing called a lame-duck Congress. Both tried to save the country by a confusion of words, words, words. With not an idea in a carload. Both of these afflictions passed out simultaneously."

Yours,
Will Rogers.

2024   MR. ROGERS TURNS HIS ATTENTION
TO THE DOINGS AT WASHINGTON

SANTA MONICA, Cal., Jan. 29. — The British Ambassador is a mighty popular man, guest of the Senate, guest of the President that's on deck waiting to go to bat. The poor French Ambassador, you can't help but feel kinder sorry for him, he is still in the dog house.

A Senator named Tydings the other day introduced a bill where the government couldn't appropriate more money than was coming in. That is, if you didn't have any money you could not dole out any.

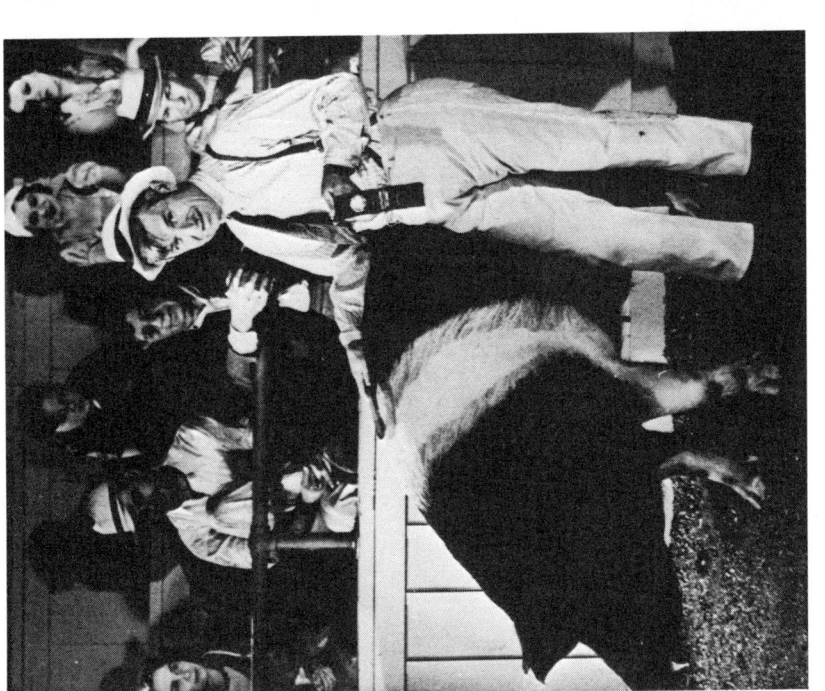

Will Rogers as "Abel Frake" in the motion picture State Fair, based on Phil Strong's novel (a Fox production, 1933).

Well the Senate like to mobbed him. They called the idea treason, sacreligious, inhuman and taking the last vestige of power for a politician, that is, the right to appropriate your money which you don't have.

Yours,
Will Rogers.

2025   MR. ROGERS SIZES UP THE NEWS
FROM AN ENTIRELY NEW ANGLE

BEVERLY HILLS, Cal., Jan. 30. — Well, let's see what we got in today's press that will stand up till tomorrow.

"Hundreds marooned by snow in Southern California mountains."

Well that will be melted by tomorrow.

"France throws overboard another government."

Well that won't stand up for another day, and neither will their new government.

"Roosevelt and Ambassador Lindsay of Great Britain reach understanding."

Well that won't stand up any longer than the Senate hears about it.

"Henry Ford licks the bankers again."

Well that's not news. He has always licked 'em. If more concerns were owned individually like his and not formed just to sell stock, we would be better off. If your business is any good, why do you want to let everybody in on it?

Yours,
Will Rogers.

2026   MR. ROGERS CITES THE GRAVITY
OF A CALIFORNIA SNOWSTORM

BEVERLY HILLS, Cal. Jan. 31. — My snow that was to melt yesterday didn't melt. It was unusual snow.

You see the Chamber of Commerce had led these folks to the mountains. (You can always trace all devilment to a Chamber of Commerce.) The chamber didn't figure it would snow, because they had passed no resolution demanding snow. But it did snow.

Well, you take a Southern Californian and put him in a snow drift, or anywhere else where he can't see a filling station or a cafeteria, and he is ready to write out his will. There wasn't a suit of long underwear in the bunch. Now we got to set 'em under these orange trees for three months to thaw 'em out.

We can and do live on climate but it takes a real Northerner to digest those snowballs.

Yours,
Will Rogers.

2027   WILL ROGERS REMARKS

BEVERLY HILLS, Cal., Feb. 1. — The Reconstruction Finance Corporation is made up of fine men, honest, and mean well and if it was water they were distributing it would help the people the plan was meant to help. For water goes down hill and moistens everything on its way, but gold or money goes uphill. The Reconstruction loaned the railroads money, medium and small banks money, and all they did with it was pay off what they owed to New York banks. So the money went uphill instead of down. You can drop a bag of gold in Death Valley, which is below sea level, and before Saturday it will be home to papa J. P.

Yours,
Will Rogers.

2028   MR. ROGERS IS TIRED OF FUSS
AND WORRY OVER THE DEBTS

BEVERLY HILLS, Cal., Feb. 2. — With a million and one home talent problems that ought to be worrying our lawmakers, why they are still excited about the debts. England is paid up till June, so why start worrying now about June.

Suppose the unemployed had work till June, the hungry food till June, they could rest mighty easy for awhile. But they haven't got it. But the debts are paid till June.

I bet if you diagnosed all our problems and listed 'em in the order of their importance to us right now, you would find debts awful near the bottom.

Any problem that is even temporarily settled up to four months ahead is no problem nowadays.

Yours,
Will Rogers.

2029 MR. ROGERS SEES LEAGUE
AND JAPAN BOTH DISGUSTED

SANTA MONICA, Cal., Feb. 3. — The League of Nations don't know whether to kick Japan out or Japan don't know whether to kick the League out. They are both equally disgusted with each other.

The League as conceived is a wonderful idea, and it works on small nations, but the minute a big one wants to "gobble up" something, then they say the League is interfering.

Japan wants a "Monroe Doctrine" now, with them playing the part of Monroe, doctoring on China. Not only "doctoring," but operating.

Yours,
Will Rogers.

2030 WILL ROGERS RECALLS OPINION
OF COOLIDGE REGARDING SENATE

BEVERLY HILLS, Cal., Feb. 5. — Funny thing, in the same paper Saturday that told about the Senate vs. Honesty, the Coolidge auto-biography in that very day's installment said: "If the Senate has weakness it's because the people send men lacking in ability and character, but that this is not the fault of the Senate, it can't choose its members. It has to work with what is sent to it. When I was elected Vice President I was going to learn the rules of the Senate, then I found that the Senate had but one rule and that was that the Senate would do anything it wanted to do whenever it wanted to do it."

Now there's the words of a man that listened to 'em for two years and argued with 'em for six.

Yours,
Will Rogers.

2031 WILL ROGERS REMARKS

BEVERLY HILLS, Cal., Feb. 6. — That was an impressive ceremony over the radio today held in the House of Representatives to pay a beautiful tribute to the memory of Calvin Coolidge. The lawmakers gathered in that body today can pay more homage to a President in death, and deal him more misery in life than happens in any civilized nation. After the Massachusetts jurist's fine oration on Mr.

Coolidge's achievements, we listened breathlessly for a moment for fear some Senator would get up, ((just out of force of habit) and denounce the oration as being, "partisan, misleading and made in the interest of the opposing party." And Mr. Hoover sitting there thinking "I have to die to get this."

Yours,
Will Rogers.

2032   MR. ROGERS JOINS THE ARMY
           OF DEPRESSION DIAGNOSTICIANS

BEVERLY HILLS, Cal., Feb. 7. — One of my broadminded papers wired me, "Didn't use your article today because you attacked credit and loans."

Well, credit means interest, and I will attack interest because interest attacks me and you. Not only attacks us, but has what you might call a constant attack.

There is not a man that's in the hole today but can look back and with the first guy had never loaned him anything. Any loan made was either to pay off another loan or to expand. It'd been better if we had let the first guy foreclose on us and shrunk instead of trying to expand.

Depression ain't nothing but old man interest just gnawing away at us.

Yours,
Will Rogers.

2033   MR. ROGERS REJOICES TO HEAR
           THAT THE SENATE IS NOT GUILTY

BEVERLY HILLS, Cal., Feb. 8. — Glad to see the old U. S. Senate come clear like it did.

We all felt that in a good fair trial with all the evidence brought out on both sides that she would clear her fair name. And sho' nuf she did it.

She just got right up and said, "I am not guilty," and said it so convincingly that she made her own members (which was the jury) believe it.

Mr. Barry takes up journalism exclusively now, and the next sergeant-at-arms engaged will be a blind man. Then there will be no writing about what he sees.

Yours,
Will Rogers.

2034 MR. ROGERS REVEALS NEW WOE WHICH PLAGUES HOLLYWOOD

BEVERLY HILLS, Cal., Feb. 9. — England had no idea they would kick up such a fuss just by suggesting that they settle in cash. The Senate howled, "How dare you offer us cash?" So I guess England will have to keep on owing us.

Here is one for the book. Hollywood is having its first divorce forced on it. That old rich Oklahoma Indian that lives out here, the government wants him to divorce his wife. Well, they are happy and don't want to be divorced. The government claims they could pick him out a cheaper wife. He says he don't want a cheap wife. I imagine the Indian agents would like to marry him themselves.

So poor old Hollywood they won't let you live happy if you want to.

Yours,
Will Rogers.

2035 WILL ROGERS SEES CHANCE NOW FOR REAL PRESIDENT

BEVERLY HILLS, Cal., Feb. 10. — See in all the papers today about making Mr. Roosevelt a President instead of just a man that sends plans up to Congress for the fun of having them vetoed. Now you will hear the wail go up, "We are not ready in this free country for a Mussolini."

Say, Mussolini could run this country with his eyes shut. In fact, that's the way our Congress has been running it. Mussolini, with no money, no natural resources, no nothing, has kept his country going; while us, with a surplus of everything under the sun, are mangy with Representatives and liberty. But we can't digest either one of 'em.

Yours,
Will Rogers.

2036 MR. ROGERS SIZES UP AGAIN
THE MUDDLE IN THE FAR EAST

BEVERLY HILLS, Cal., Feb. 12. — The League told Japan to get out of Manchuria and Japan says, "Yeah?"

The League suggested that wet nursing of it be turned over to America and Russia. Neither one belongs to the League.

That's like a policeman turning a desperate criminal over to a couple of civilians and telling 'em, "Here, you watch this fellow. I am busy."

Europe must sit up at night just thinking of ways to get us in worse than we are, if possible.

When Russia is ready, she will go down and look after Manchuria without our aid.

Yours,
Will Rogers.

2037 MR. ROGERS TURNS HIS ATTENTION
TO THE WORLD'S NAVAL NEWS

BEVERLY HILLS, Cal., Feb. 13. — Holland had a mutiny on one of her battleships. Now she is about to have one on their other one.

Our navy is out at sea in the Pacific trying to solve what they call Problem 14. They better see if they are going to be able to solve Problem 13 first. Problem 13 is to get the government to give 'em enough money to have a navy.

If Problem 13 ain't solved, they better just go to Japan and say, "We will give you California, but you got to take their Chamber of Commerce and Hollywood." That would start Japan to thinking.

Yours,
Will Rogers.

2038 MR. ROGERS SUFFERS A BLOW
IN THE PRESIDENT'S SPEECH

BEVERLY HILLS, Cal., Feb. 14. — Mr. Hoover who we looked to for a little encouragement in his radio talk gave us the worst news that's hit us yet. He said the Republicans are coming back.

And, by the way, here is one thing I want somebody to explain to me: Why is it, during a campaign, after a campaign, or at any other time, why can't our Presidents speak of each other by name and say, "Well, I wish Mr. So-and-so well. He is a fine man and will make you a good President."

Or, to have the victor say, "He had a hard time, and did the very best he could have under the circumstances."

Even small town Mayors have been known to speak of each other complimentary, but if Presidents ever did, I think we would drop dead.

Yours,
Will Rogers.

2039 Mr. Rogers Gives Some Advice
To The Members Of The Senate

SANTA MONICA, Cal., Feb. 15. — This depression must have finally hit the Senate. They are investigating it.

If they want to know what is holding back relief measures, all they got to do is look in the mirror.

Papers today stated that Mr. Hoover is going to issue a denunciation of Congress and the Senate. Denounce 'em? Everybody is surprised he hasn't shot 'em.

Yours,
Will Rogers.

2040 Will Rogers Remarks

BEVERLY HILLS, Cal., Feb. 16. — I never saw in any of our papers whether this Italian fellow was a citizen or not. If he wasn't it looks like they would have a way of deporting everybody that didn't belong here. All the good Italians in the country, (and there is many of them fine citizens) they would be tickled to death if all their renegade countrymen were out of here, for they have done nothing but bring disgrace on their whole race. And poor Tony Cermak, a fine fellow. I never went through Chicago that I didn't see him. And he was so proud of President Roosevelt. When he flew out there to accept the nomination Tony drove him all over Chicago to show him what a city he had, while thousands were waiting in the hall.

Yours,
Will Rogers.

2041   Mr. Rogers Thinks The Senate
            Has A Tough Job In Louisiana

BEVERLY HILLS, Cal., Feb. 17. — The United States Senate is holding some kind of investigation down in Louisiana.

From what we can gather from the evidence, the investigation is held to determine who is the biggest liar in Louisiana, and with the amount of competitors they are having a tough time finding out.

A repeal of prohibition was passed by the people last November. It finally reached the Senate yesterday. News travels fast in this country.

                           Yours,
                           Will Rogers.

2042   Will Rogers Pays Tribute
            To "Gentleman Jim" Corbett

BEVERLY HILLS, Cal., Feb. 19. — Jim Corbett, Gentleman Jim, truly a title earned and maintained through life.

My acquaintance with Corbett has been nearly twenty-five years, as he was a great friend of Fred Stone's, who is a great friend of mine. Fred was a great boxer. Corbett always said he would have been middleweight champion if he had taken up that line.

Corbett brought boxing out of the saloon into respectability. He would have been a credit to the ministry, to industry, to teaching, to anything, the same as he was to boxing, a great credit to the stage. He was a splendid actor, perhaps the best straight man that any comedian ever worked with.

He never spoke ill of any man. A career lived in good will and ended in glory.

                           Yours,
                           Will Rogers.

2043   Mr. Rogers Cites An Example
            Of Old-Time Common Sense

BEVERLY HILLS, Cal., Feb. 20. — Remember my old rich "Injun" that I was telling you about the government wanting him to get a divorce because he lived in Hollywood?

Well, they pulled one better than that the other day. They tried to prove that he wasn't in his right mind because one time when his car stalled and they couldn't get it going he traded it for an old pony, got on him and rode off. And they call that crazy.

If everybody did that, they would be out of debt in a couple of years. Just think, no gas, no tires, no roads to pay for.

Why, instead of prosecuting the old Indian they ought to erect a monument to him for being that far ahead of his time.

Yours,
Will Rogers.

2044   WILL ROGERS REMARKS

BEVERLY HILLS, Cal., Feb. 21. — Carter Glass when he told the Senate that the whole Reconstruction finance thing was bad, told them what every Senator knew in his heart, but didn't have the nerve to say. Every man, every industry in the United States was hit by depression. Before you start dealing out public funds to help, you should have first found out have we enough money to give aid to every one, every industry, if not, I am not going to give part of them a sandwich and leave the rest go hungry. But no, they didn't do that. They just started right in by helping the bankers, so every man, woman and child in the U. S. thinks, and rightfully so, that they have got as much right to get some sort of government aid as the bankers. Due to the lack of foresight of our lawmakers, the bankers, the railroads, and big business got the first U. S. dole, and it will never be finished till the last one hundred and twenty million reach in and get theirs, because they feel they got it coming. No wonder Glass was too smart to be Treasurer.

Yours,
Will Rogers.

2045   MR. ROGERS SEEMS TO APPROVE
OF THE EARLY CABINET CHOICES

BEVERLY HILLS, Cal., Feb. 22. — Well, for breakfast this morning we got three new Cabinet officers.

Cordell Hull is a mighty fine, able man. Ever since I been going to political conventions, no matter who the rest of the world nominated, Jefferson, Jackson, Wilson, Smith or Roosevelt, Tennessee went for Cordell Hull. Their loyalty has been rewarded. Secretary of State is quite a chore in these times.

This fellow Woodin that has inherited the deficit, I don't know him, but I, along with everybody, rush to offer him condolence. Accepting receivership of the U. S. is also no small chore.

Swanson for the navy post is ideal. He did inherit a navy if Congress don't kill it with no appropriations.

Yours,
Will Rogers.

2046   Mr. Rogers Decides To Give The Whole Cabinet His O. K.

BEVERLY HILLS, Cal., Feb. 23. — Say, that list of new Cabinet members sent everybody scurrying through Who's Who, World's Almanac and the United States finger print department trying to find out who they were.

The forgotten man has been found, and there was nine of 'em and a woman.

So we open March 4th with the "unknown Cabinet." The rogues gallery photographs show us that three of 'em escaped from the Senate. That's like going to the old man's home to get an athlete.

But I believe they are going to be all right. They all got their reputation to make, which is better than feeling that they have one already made.

Yours,
Will Rogers.

2047   Will Rogers Hails Douglas, Night Watchman Of Budget

BEVERLY HILLS, Cal., Feb. 24. — A lot of you are asking today, "Douglas, Douglas, who in the world is this Douglas that they have appointed night watchman of the budget?"

Well, there is one guy I can tell you about. I know him. He is the only Congressman from Arizona. Incidentally, every State ought to only have one. Arizona does better with one than N. Y. does with 45.

Douglas is a mighty able young man, a great grandson of Stephen A. Douglas. Douglas, Ariz., was named for him.

The budget is a mythical bean bag. Congress votes mythical beans into it, and then tries to reach in and pull real beans out.

Yours,
Will Rogers.

2048   WILL ROGERS GIVES HIS CURE
        FOR THE FAR EAST TROUBLE

SANTA MONICA, Cal., Feb. 26. — We never had a greater example of why there will always be war than we are having right now.

Twenty-one nations of the League denounce Japan's Chinese invasion, and the United States, while not a member, also agrees with them.

Now, all in the world they got to do to stop it instantly is to agree to not trade with an aggressor nation, meaning Japan, but they won't sacrifice their trade just to save bloodshed.

The League has got the weapon to stop war, but try and get the nations to give up that trade. What's a few thousand dead Chinamen compared to Japan as a cash customer?

Yours,
Will Rogers.

2049   WILL ROGERS SAYS WE THINK
        OF OURSELVES LATE IN THE DAY

BEVERLY HILLS, Cal., Feb. 27. — There wasn't a soul in America that when they picked up their paper today didn't utter the same expression "well, that's too bad," when they read that Mayor Cermak had pneumonia.

Lot of States and places are calling a moratorium on debts, taxes, banks, it takes us so long to think of anything for ourselves.

Funny we thought of it for Europe, but not for ourselves. Why pour all that reconstruction money into a bank when all you had to say was "We are going to pay you but as we are able to pay you out."

Yours,
Will Rogers.

2050   WILL ROGERS REMARKS

BEVERLY HILLS, Cal., Feb. 28. — England says "We won't sell war materials to Japan as she has been proven the aggressor nation." We say, "Well, that would be taking sides." We want to be in the position where we can sell to both sides. Then they wonder why

Europe thinks we are always out for the dough. Let's don't kid ourselves, we are out for it a lot of the time. England tries to stop war, we try to stop disarmament. One fellow tries to stop the actual fight, we try to regulate the number of bullets he shall have after the fight starts. Take your pick as to who is the humanitarian.

Yours,
Will Rogers.

2051   ROGERS COMMENTS ON BANKS,
HENRY FORD AND AL SMITH

BEVERLY HILLS, Cal., March 1. — I hear the inauguration is to be put off three weeks on account of the budget. Every time Detroit outgrows Henry Ford he has to go in and save 'em again. He is going to have a bank where you can leave your money and come back and find it before the banker does.

Al Smith told exactly what his ideas were on every important question. No wonder he can't be elected. Imagine a man in public office that everybody knew where he stood. We wouldn't call him a statesman, we would call him a curiosity.

Yours,
Will Rogers.

2052   WILL ROGERS SHOWS A FLASH
OF CALIFORNIA'S HOLIDAY SPIRIT

BEVERLY HILLS, Cal., March 2. — 'Twas a lovely morning sun shining bright. Arthur Brisbane and the fleet had just returned from somewhere, orange juice was in every glass, cameras were oiled and ready to crank on beautiful screen stars, the birds were singing in the eucalyptus trees.

The birds were singing, why? Because they couldn't read the papers. The papers said the bank clerks had worked so hard lately that they should have a holiday.

So, as we are all on a holiday, let's take it on the chin and grin. The Rogers having laid in no supplies against such an emergency will be living on horse meat as that's our sole product.

I love horses and I only ask, don't let me know which one we are eating today.

I hear they have called a moratorium on inaugurations.

Yours,
Will Rogers.

2053   Mr. Rogers Finds The People Carrying On In A Fine Spirit

BEVERLY HILLS, Cal., March 3. — Bankers, this moratorium you have asked for, everybody is joining in good faith, and with fine spirit.

The ones that had a little money have taken as their example the unemployed who have grinned and took it on the chin all this time. While being a victim of our country, the unemployed have been a credit.

Now the bankers say if we will bear with 'em they will work it out, and we are going to give 'em every change. BUT, (get that but in there with capital letters) if they are handing us the baloney, why then we will know for sure what this country needs. It will need new bankers.

Everybody is doing what you bankers ask, but remember we are watching you.

                          Yours,
                         Will Rogers.

NOTES

1440 *New York Times* (hereafter cited as *NYT*), Friday, March 6, 1931, 23:2. The editors throughout used *NYT* as the main source; however, variations appeared when other papers were checked. In that event, we relied upon the *Los Angeles Times* (hereafter cited as *LAT*) primarily and the *Tulsa Daily World* and *Kansas City Times* secondarily. Unless otherwise indicated, variants come from *LAT* but the *NYT* version is given in the footnotes. Also unless otherwise indicated, the heading of each DT is from *NYT*.

The Seventy-first Congress adjourned on March 4, 1931. In three sessions, it had set a record for peacetime appropriations—$10 billion.

Albert Einstein, German physicist whose theory of relativity earned for him a Nobel Prize in 1921. He served as a visiting professor at the California Institute of Technology in Pasadena during the winter of 1930-1931.

1441 *NYT*, Saturday, March 7, 1931, 19:7. Variant: *LAT* gives "of the split" in first sentence.

Prohibition of the sale, manufacture, and transportation of alcoholic beverages became law in the United States in 1920 after the ratification of the Eighteenth Amendment. The Volstead Act (1919) provided for the enforcement of prohibition, but control of the liquor traffic proved difficult to maintain.

A division in the Democratic National Committee between northern-urban "wets" and southern-rural "drys" was heightened in early March of 1931 by a suggestion that repeal of prohibition be made part of the Democratic platform for 1932.

1442 *NYT*, Monday, March 9, 1931, 21:7. Variants: *NYT* gives "relief there is a polo game between youth and some older boys." to end third sentence/ *NYT* gives "myself makes" in fifth sentence.

Arthur Brisbane, American newspaper editor and syndicated writer whose column "Today" appeared in more than 1,400 newspapers.

Max C. Fleischmann, chairman of the board of Fleischmann Company from 1925 to 1929. In 1930, after selling his interest in the Cincinnati-based yeast firm, Fleischmann moved to Santa Barbara, California, where he engaged in extensive philanthropy.

James A. Wigmore, Cleveland realtor and sportsman. An accomplished polo player, Wigmore was a member of the Cleveland side which won the National Twelve Goal Intercircuit championship in 1927.

Reginald L. Baker, Australian amateur boxer and fight promoter who was active for several years in athletic organizations in California.

1443 *NYT*, Tuesday, March 10, 1931, 25:7.

Jamaica ginger, popularly known as "jake," was a dangerous homemade liquor which had a crippling, paralyzing effect on the hands and lower legs of its victims.

1444 *NYT*, Wednesday, March 11, 1931, 25:7.

The Arkansas and Idaho legislatures passed laws in February of 1931 which allowed a petitioner to file for divorce after residing in the state for ninety days. Nevada lawmakers, fearful that the lucrative divorce business might be stolen from Reno, the "nation's divorce capital," hurriedly passed a measure which reduced the state residence requirement from ninety days to six weeks.

1445 *NYT*, Thursday, March 12, 1931, 25:7. Variant: *LAT* gives "caused naturally by" in first sentence.

James Eli Watson, Republican United States senator from Indiana from 1916 to 1933; majority leader from 1929 to 1933.

Progressives, claiming that the needs of the nation had been neglected by the major parties and President Hoover, met in Washington, D. C., on March 11-12 to formulate a program for the next session of Congress. Senator Watson, a conservative Republican, sent a list of fourteen questions to the leaders of the conference, requesting clarification of their positions on several issues.

1446 *NYT*, Friday, March 13, 1931, 23:7.

1447 *NYT*, Saturday, March 14, 1931, 19:7. Variant: *NYT* gives "can get" in third sentence.

Robert Marion La Follette, Jr., Republican United States senator from Wisconsin from 1925 to 1947. Son and namesake of "Fighting Bob" La Follette, he was one of the leaders at the conference of progressives (see Note 1445).

1448 *NYT*, Monday, March 16, 1931, 23:7. Variants: *LAT* gives "hero, you wonder if" in first sentence/*NYT* gives "there are no" in last sentence.

Mohandas Karamchand Gandhi, the extremely popular leader of the Indian struggle for independence from Great Britain; called Mahatma, or Great Soul.

Charles Spencer Chaplin, English comedian and motion picture star who won international acclaim for his film portrayal of the human condition as The Tramp. Chaplin was bestowed knighthood in 1975 at the age of eighty-five.

Herbert Clark Hoover, president of the United States from 1929 to 1933. A Republican, Hoover served as secretary of commerce from 1921 to 1928. He boarded the battleship *Arizona* on March 19 to begin an eleven-day vacation and business trip to Puerto Rico and the Virgin Islands.

1449 *NYT*, Tuesday, March 17, 1931, 31:7. Variants: *NYT* and *LAT* give "pay tax" in sixth sentence.

The withholding of federal income taxes from payrolls was introduced during World War II.

1450 *NYT*, Wednesday, March 18, 1931, 27:7. Variant: *LAT* gives "Ireland of all" in first and second sentences.

1451 *NYT*, Thursday, March 19, 1931, 25:7.

College students representing three generations of graduates of Harvard University and three generations of graduates of four eastern women's colleges were the subjects of a study in evolution by an anthropology student at Harvard.

1452 *NYT*, Friday, March 20, 1931, 27:7.

William Edgar Borah, Republican United States senator from Idaho from 1907 until his death in 1940. Chairman of the Senate Foreign Relations Committee and an outspoken critic of the Hoover administration, Borah met with Hoover at the White House on March 18 to discuss international affairs and domestic agrarian problems.

Benito Mussolini, Italian dictator and leader of the Fascist party from 1922 to 1943. Although Mussolini officially held only the position of premier, he in fact exerted total control of the Italian government.

1453 *NYT,* Saturday, March 21, 1931, 19:7.

In 1931 Nevada became the first state in modern history to legalize gambling. The action was taken to stimulate business and to generate revenue in the wake of the depression.

1454 *NYT,* Monday, March 23, 1931, 23:7. Variant: *LAT* gives "BEVERLY HILLS" as place of origin.

Theodore Dreiser, novelist whose *Sister Carrie* and *An American Tragedy* are classic examples of naturalism in American writing.

Sinclair Lewis, novelist whose satiric portrayals of middle-class American life in *Main Street* and *Babbitt* helped him gain prominence in American literature and allowed him to become, in 1930, the first American to win the Nobel Prize in literature.

Dreiser slapped Lewis repeatedly during an argument at the Metropolitan Club in New York City on March 19. The disagreement stemmed from Lewis's charge that Dreiser had plagiarized from a book written in 1928 by Mrs. Lewis, the former Dorothy Thompson.

George Bernard Shaw, Irish novelist, playwright, and literary critic noted for his satirical wit; winner of the Nobel Prize in literature in 1925.

The Agua Caliente Handicap, which was won by Mike Hall in an upset, attracted a crowd of 25,000 spectators.

1455 *NYT,* Tuesday, March 24, 1931, 29:7.

1456 *NYT,* Wednesday, March 25, 1931, 27:7. Variant: *LAT* gives "(Sealyham)" in fourth sentence.

Oscar Odd McIntyre, syndicated writer whose column "New York Day by Day" appeared in more than 550 newspapers from 1912 until his death in 1938. McIntyre's frequent stories about his dogs had a wide appeal.

Thomas Robert Dewar, British distiller and sportsman. When Rogers and his family were in Europe in 1926, Lord Dewar presented the Rogers children with a pedigreed Sealyham pup, which they named "Jock."

1457 *NYT,* Thursday, March 26, 1931, 29:7. Variant: *LAT* gives "wanted impart" in fifth sentence.

Hoover spoke at San Juan, Puerto Rico, on March 24. He cited the difficulties caused by an increase in population during a depression while praising the perseverence of the Puerto Ricans and offering general encouragement for the future.

Theodore Roosevelt, Jr., governor of Puerto Rico from 1929 to 1932; son and namesake of the former president of the United States.

Hoover spent five hours at St. Thomas, Virgin Islands, on March 25, before returning to the mainland.

1458 *NYT,* Friday, March 27, 1931, 27:7.

Gangster warfare raged in Los Angeles during March, with several brutal murders of members of rival criminal factions. The funerals of the slain gangsters featured the usual lavish displays of flowers and long motorcades of crime figures.

1459 *NYT*, Saturday, March 28, 1931, 15:2. Variants: *NYT* gives "Ghandi" in second sentence/*LAT* gives " 'Ye-ah? Ye-ah?' " and *NYT* gives " 'and then we . . . you?' " in fifth sentence/*LAT* gives "to, for their" in sixth sentence/ *NYT* omits sixth sentence.

Gandhi (see Note 1448) was attacked outside Karachi on March 25 by a member of an angry crowd of extremists opposed to his leadership and influence in the nationalist movement in India.

For Charles Spencer Chaplin see Note 1448.

Tammany Hall, a Democratic political organization in New York City that controlled party politics in the city and wielded much influence in municipal affairs. On March 24, the New York state legislature ordered an investigation of the administration of James John "Jimmy" Walker, the Tammany-backed mayor of New York City.

1460 *NYT*, Monday, March 30, 1931, 23:7.

Charles A. Otis, Cleveland investment banker and civic leader whose Otis & Co. ranked as one of the leading securities firms in the Middle West.

Hoover remarked on his return voyage that the United States had obtained "an effective poorhouse" by its "unfortunate" acquisition of the Virgin Islands. Hoover's statements provoked considerable protest by residents of the islands.

1461 *NYT*, Tuesday, March 31, 1931, 29:7. Variants: *LAT* gives "It gives" in third sentence/*NYT* gives "have to eat" in fifth sentence.

Massacre, written by American educator Robert Gessner, appeared in 1931 and depicted personal hardships as well as administrative difficulties on American Indian reservations. Reviewers noted that despite Gessner's bias his portrayal was well-founded in fact.

The Osage Indians of northern Oklahoma had acquired a reputation as the wealthiest tribe in the United States as a result of the discovery of oil on their land in the early 1900s.

The wretched condition of the Sioux Indians at the Pine Ridge reservation in South Dakota was the subject of a revealing article in the *New York Times* on March 15, 1931. The story described the pathetic life of a Sioux family who because of their extreme poverty were forced to subsist on horsemeat.

1462 *NYT*, Wednesday, April 1, 1931, 31:7. Variant: *LAT* gives "BEVERLY HILLS" as place of origin.

Knute Kenneth Rockne, football coach at Notre Dame University from 1918 to 1931. Personable and popular, Rockne compiled a record of 105 wins, 12 losses, and 5 ties as coach of the Fighting Irish. He and seven other persons perished in an airplane crash in southeastern Kansas on March 31.

1463 *NYT*, Thursday, April 2, 1931, 29:7. Variant: *LAT* gives "but was" in first sentence.

Robert C. Gillis, Los Angeles land developer and realtor.

Liberty Bonds were sold by public subscription, providing loans to help finance the Allied effort during World War I. One of the most effective sales techniques occurred when volunteer speakers delivered concise, brief speeches of about three minutes to groups such as movie audiences. These "three-minute" speakers exhorted their listeners to support the war effort through the purchase of Liberty Bonds.

John Calvin Coolidge, president of the United States from 1923 to 1929. A Republican, Coolidge was emphatically pro-business. His policies contributed to the speculative mood of the 1920s.

1464 *NYT*, Friday, April 3, 1931, 27:7.

Charles Augustus Lindbergh, American aviator who received international acclaim in May of 1927 for making the first solo, nonstop transatlantic flight.

Francis Monroe "Frank" Hawks, American aviator who established numerous transcontinental and point-to-point speed records in the 1920s and 1930s.

James Harold "Jimmy" Doolittle, American flier noted for his speed marks set in the 1920s and 1930s, his interest in commercial aviation, and his heroism during World War II.

Alford Joseph "Al" Williams, Jr., research pilot with the United States Navy from 1917 to 1930 and holder of several aviation records and awards.

David Sinton Ingalls, United States assistant secretary of the Navy for aeronautics from 1929 to 1932.

Federal aeronautical inspectors determined that the plane crash in which Rockne (see Note 1462) had died occurred when an accumulation of ice on a wing caused the wing to separate from the fuselage.

1465 *NYT*, Saturday, April 4, 1931, 19:7. Variant: *NYT* gives "Representative to Congress." to end first sentence.

California gained nine additional seats in Congress as a result of reapportionment based on the census of 1930. Controversy between the northern and southern sections of the state centered on whether to redistrict according to population figures, which would give the more populous south an advantage, or to divide the seats equally between the two sections.

1466 *NYT*, Monday, April 6, 1931, 23:7.

Harold J. Kelsey, American barnstormer and veteran commercial aviator who joined American Airways as a pilot in 1930.

Rogers was on his way to Managua, the capital of Nicaragua, where an earthquake on March 31 had devastated the city, leaving hundreds dead and thousands homeless (see DT and Note 1469).

1467 *NYT*, Tuesday, April 7, 1931, 29:7. Variant: *NYT* gives "This country" to begin sixth sentence.

Mexico was the scene of considerable political unrest and recurrent rebellions during the late 1920s.

Joshua Reuben Clark, Jr., United States ambassador to Mexico from 1930 to 1933.

Dwight Whitney Morrow, United States ambassador to Mexico from 1927 to 1930; Republican United States senator from New Jersey from 1930 until his death in 1931. Morrow retired as ambassador to seek election to the Senate.

1468 *NYT*, Wednesday, April 8, 1931, 25:7. Variants: *LAT* gives "ABOARD PLANE BOUND FOR SAN SALVADOR" as place of origin/*NYT* gives "run with big . . . pilots. Passed today" in first and second sentence/*LAT* gives "three-motored planes" in second sentence/*NYT* gives "New York and the whole" in ninth sentence, omitting ten words.

For Arthur Brisbane see Note 1442.

1469 *NYT*, Thursday, April 9, 1931, 18:2-3. Variants: *LAT* gives "Cross combined" in seventh sentence/*NYT* and *LAT* give "8,000. Now, we" in eighth and ninth sentences/*NYT* gives "Hanna, just appointed" in ninth sentence/*NYT* gives "He lost . . . he had . . . his back." in tenth sentence/*LAT* gives "backs—

he and . . . Cross. If through" in tenth and eleventh sentences/*LAT* gives "place. We are" in twenty-first sentence.

The earthquake that struck Managua, Nicaragua, on March 31, 1931, was a national disaster which cost 1,450 lives. Relief assistance flowed from many countries, including the United States. United States Army engineers stationed in Nicaragua rendered valuable service, and extensive medical supplies were flown in from American bases in the Canal Zone and Cuba. Rogers spent three days in Managua and personally contributed at least $5,000 to the relief cause.

Matthew Elting Hanna, United States minister to Nicaragua from 1929 to 1933. The Nicaraguan government awarded Hanna its Presidential Medal of Merit for his relief assistance in Managua.

President Hoover took immediate action upon hearing of the disaster; he ordered Army and Navy units in the area to assist in the relief operations.

United States Marines were sent to Nicaragua in 1912 to restore order during a rebellion against a pro-American ruler. A small detachment remained in the Central American republic until 1933, despite stubborn opposition from insurgent guerrillas.

A canal across Nicaragua had been desired for many years by American shippers and military strategists. Army engineers conducted surveys in 1930 and 1931 to determine possible routes and construction costs.

1470 *NYT*, Friday, April 10, 1931, 27:4-5. Variants: *NYT* gives "some news for" in fourth sentence/*LAT* gives "money and" in fourteenth sentence/*NYT* gives "Money is needed to help feed 'em and restore some sort of roof over their heads." for sixteenth sentence/*LAT* gives "Chic Sale" in sixteenth sentence.

José María Moncada, president of Nicaragua from 1929 to 1932.

For Mathew Elting Hanna see Note 1469.

Ralph Johnson Mitchell, American naval aviator stationed in Nicaragua with the Second Brigade, United States Marine Corps.

Charles Partlow "Chic" Sale, American character actor and comedian who first appeared in vaudeville in 1908 and later wrote syndicated newspaper articles.

1471 *NYT*, Saturday, April 11, 1931, 21:7. Variants: *NYT* gives "Gardner" in eighth sentence/*NYT* gives "by Democrats" in ninth sentence.

Costa Ricans celebrate April 11 as the anniversary of the defeat of William Walker, an American soldier of fortune who led an unsuccessful filibustering expedition against Costa Rica in 1856.

Nicholas Longworth, Republican United States representative from Ohio from 1903 to 1913 and from 1915 until his death in 1931. Longworth, who had served as Speaker of the House of Representatives since 1925, died of pneumonia on April 9 in Aiken, South Carolina.

John Nance Garner, Democratic United States representative from Texas from 1903 to 1933; Speaker of the House from 1931 to 1933. Although Garner was the minority leader in Congress at this time, he enjoyed a close personal friendship with Longworth.

1472 *NYT*, Monday, April 13, 1931, 21:7.

Smith Wildman Brookhart, Republican United States senator from Iowa from 1922 to 1925 and from 1927 to 1933. Brookhart had returned from a tour of the Canal Zone on April 16, incensed about the freedom allowed American servicemen in the zone area. He considered the habits of the troops as a disgrace to their uniforms.

The Panama Canal, built across a parcel of land leased by Panama, was completed by the United States in 1914. The Canal Zone, extending five miles on either side of the canal, was administered by the United States under terms of a treaty made with the Panamanian government in 1903 and revised in 1978.

1473 *NYT*, Tuesday, April 14, 1931, 28:7. Variants: *NYT* gives " 'us tomorrow,' Tuesday is" in fourth and fifth sentences/*NYT* gives "than the other" in seventh sentence.

The U. S. S. *Pennsylvania*, a 30,000-ton battleship, left Philadelphia on March 24 bound for San Diego.

Pan American Day—April 14—commemorates the spirit of cooperation and solidarity between the United States and other Western Hemispheric nations. The date marks the anniversary of the creation of the International Union of American Republics at the Pan-American Conference of 1890.

The American cruisers *Rochester* and *Sacramento* were among numerous ships and planes ordered to Nicaragua to assist in relief operations.

1474 *NYT*, Wednesday, April 15, 1931, 29:7.

Alfonso XIII, king of Spain from 1886 to 1931. Alfonso was forced to flee Spain in the face of a significant electoral victory by republicans on April 12. He died in exile in 1941.

For Benito Mussolini see Note 1452.

1475 *NYT*, Thursday, April 16, 1931, 27:7. Variant: *NYT* gives "then they get to" in fifth sentence.

Alfonso XIII and Rogers met during the Oklahoman's tour of Europe in 1926. For Rogers' impressions of the Spanish monarch, see *Letters of a Self-Made Diplomat to His President*.

1476 *NYT*, Friday, April 17, 25:7. Variants: *LAT* gives "not Sam—but" in first sentence/*LAT* gives "You can land and" to begin third sentence/*LAT* gives "dark, due to his foresight; they" in fourth and fifth sentences/*NYT* omits seventh sentence/*NYT* gives "I am nearing Venezuela. Will stop" in eighth sentence.

The San Blas Islands, near the northeastern coast of Panama, are inhabited by the Cuna Indians who have attempted to retain the culture and isolation of their ancestors. Until the 1950s few outsiders were allowed to visit the islands.

1477 *NYT*, Saturday, April 18, 1931, 21:7. Variant: *NYT* gives "ON PAN-AMERICAN AIRPLANE" as place of origin.

Juan Vicente Gómez, supreme dictator of Venezuela from 1908 to 1935, held absolute control over the country through harsh rule, strict censorship, and effective propaganda. Venezuela prospered economically, however, because Gómez welcomed and encouraged foreign investment.

William Henry "Alfalfa Bill" Murray, Democratic governor of Oklahoma from 1931 to 1935. Noted for his quick temper and eccentric behavior, Murray frequently summoned the Oklahoma National Guard to enforce his decisions.

For Theodore Roosevelt, Jr., see Note 1457.

1478 *NYT*, Monday, April 20, 1931, 21:7. Variants: *LAT* gives "MIAMI" as place of origin/*LAT* gives "Morrow: He had brought" in fifth and sixth sentences.

For Theodore Roosevelt, Jr., see Note 1457; for Dwight Whitney Morrow see Note 1467.

1479 *NYT,* Tuesday, April 21, 1931, 31:7. Variant: *NYT* gives "at Charleston, . . . (where Uncle . . .)" in third sentence.

Josephus Daniels, editor of the *Raleigh News and Observer* from 1894 to 1933 (see also Note 1911).

For the Managua earthquake see Note 1469.

1480 *NYT,* Wednesday, April 22, 1931, 27:7.

The Daughters of the American Revolution held their annual congress in Washington, D. C., from April 20 to 27. Rogers addressed the second session of the convention on April 21.

For William Edgar Borah see Note 1452.

Augusto César Sandino, Nicaraguan revolutionary leader who violently and stubbornly opposed the intervention of the United States in Nicaraguan affairs. At a press conference on April 21, Hoover condemned Sandino as a cold-blooded murderer and announced that the Nicaraguan government had committed more than 1,300 troops to a campaign to capture the rebel chief. Sandino was assassinated in 1934.

James John "Jimmy" Walker, Democratic mayor of New York City from 1925 until his resignation in 1932. The popular and debonair mayor was the subject of a state investigation of corruption in his administration (see Note 1459). On April 21 Walker responded to charges regarding his personal conduct by offering to match his private life with that of any of his accusers and by dismissing the charges as slanderous attempts to discredit his administration. The investigation, nevertheless, prompted his resignation the following year.

1481 *NYT,* Thursday, April 23, 1931, 27:7. Variants: *LAT* gives "Siamese—I am" in third and fourth sentences/*NYT* gives "somebody in New York" in ninth sentence.

Prajadhipok, king of Siam from 1925 to 1935. Accompanied by Queen Rambai Barni, Prajadhipok traveled to the United States in early 1931 to undergo eye surgery.

Siamese twins, conjoined twins who derived this name from the celebrated Chang and Eng Bunker, born at Maklong, Thailand (Siam), on May 11, 1811. They were joined by a cartilaginous band at the chest. They died within hours of each other on January 17, 1874.

Patrick Jay Hurley, United States secretary of war from 1929 to 1933. A native of Oklahoma, Hurley flew to Tulsa on April 21 for several business conferences.

References to the private life of Mayor Walker (see Note 1480) were eliminated from a report of the City Affairs Committee at a meeting of the National Republican Club on April 21. Club members voted to adopt the remainder of the seventy-page report and to send it to the governor and the legislative investigating committee (see Note 1459).

1482 *NYT,* Friday, April 24, 1931, 25:7. Variants: *LAT* gives "Newspaper publishers from" and *NYT* gives "last night was" in first sentence/*NYT* gives "I were" in second sentence/*NYT* gives "Charley made 'em . . . I brought 'em" in third sentence.

The American Newspaper Publishers Association held its forty-fifth annual meeting in New York City from April 23-24.

Charles Michael Schwab, founder and chairman of the board of Bethlehem Steel Corporation. A major spokesman for the American steel industry and big business, Schwab was noted also for his annual New Year's Day predictions of business prosperity.

King Alfonso XIII (see Note 1474), whose wife Victoria was a cousin of George V of Great Britain, left Spain in April to live in exile in France.

Hawks (see Note 1464) set a new record of five hours and twenty-four minutes for a London-to-Rome flight on April 23, breaking the previous mark by more than seven hours.

For Rambai Barni see Note 1481.

1483 *NYT*, Saturday, April 25, 1931, 21:7. Variants: *NYT* gives "here yesterday" in first sentence/*NYT* gives "folks. All over the country they" in third and fourth sentences.

Pynchon & Company, one of the oldest brokerage firms in the United States, was suspended from the New York Stock Exchange on April 24 because of a severe decline in the value of its securities.

1484 *NYT*, Monday, April 27, 1931, 23:7. Variant: *LAT* gives "horses; never . . . writes. He told" in fifth and sixth sentences.

For Arthur Brisbane see Note 1442.

William Joseph Donovan, assistant to the United States attorney general from 1925 to 1929. A New York City lawyer, Donovan was mentioned often in early 1929 as the leading candidate for attorney general in Hoover's cabinet.

Alfred Emanuel "Al" Smith, governor of New York from 1919 to 1921 and from 1923 to 1929. A candidate for the Democratic presidential nomination in 1920 and 1924, Smith finally won the nomination in 1928 only to lose the general election to Hoover. He again sought the nomination in 1932, but the honor fell that year to Franklin Delano Roosevelt.

1485 *NYT*, Tuesday, April 28, 1931, 29:7. Variants: *LAT* omits fifth and sixth sentences/*NYT* gives "plunder." to end sixth sentence, omitting last five words.

The Gridiron Club, an organization of newspaper correspondents in the national capital, held its annual spring banquet on April 27. Hoover and Rogers were among the more than 400 guests who watched a lighthearted performance of skits and songs parodying contemporary problems and personalities.

For Daughters of the American Revolution see Note 1480.

Amon Giles Carter, publisher of the *Fort Worth Star-Telegram* from 1923 until his death in 1955. A generous philanthropist and an energetic civic leader, Carter often lobbied for government projects and new industries for Fort Worth and west Texas.

Henry Lewis Stimson, United States secretary of state from 1929 to 1933. In 1927 while serving as special emissary to Nicaragua, Stimson helped to negotiate a temporary halt to the civil strife in that Central American country.

1486 *NYT*, Wednesday, April 29, 1931, 27:7.

Robert Tyre "Bobby" Jones, one of the best loved and most successful American golfers in the history of the sport. In 1930 he became the first player to win the so-called grand slam of golf—the United States and British amateur and open championships. Shortly thereafter, he announced his retirement from competitive golf. He returned to his law practice in Atlanta and also made a series of short instructional films on golf.

Stone Mountain Memorial near Atlanta commemorates Confederate leaders Robert Edward Lee, Thomas Jonathan "Stonewall" Jackson, and Jefferson Davis. The equestrian figures were commissioned in 1916, but disagreement about the sculptures, carved on the northern face of the granite mountain, delayed completion of the project until 1970.

John Sanford Cohen, publisher and editor of the *Atlanta Journal* from 1917 until his death in 1935.

Clark Howell, publisher and editor-in-chief of the *Atlanta Constitution* from 1897 until his death in 1936.

1487 *NYT*, Thursday, April 30, 1931, 25:7.

Herbert "Herb" Kindred, war veteran and barnstormer who flew for several years as a commercial pilot for Texas Air Transport.

John Davison Rockefeller, American industrialist and philanthropist. Born in 1839, Rockefeller had risen to dominate the American petroleum industry by 1882. Involved in other successful enterprises, the patriarch of the Rockefeller empire died in 1937 at the age of ninety-eight.

The East Texas oil field, discovered in late 1930, embraced more than 150 square miles and, by 1931, included more than 3,500 wells. Flush production of up to 1.000 barrels of crude oil daily caused the field to be closed in August of 1931 and reopened later under a restrictive production quota.

1488 *NYT*, Friday, May 1, 1931, 29:7. Variant: *LAT* gives "I don't want" in ninth sentence.

For Augusto César Sandino see Note 1480.

1489 *NYT*, Saturday, May 2, 1931, 21:7.

1490 *NYT*, Monday, May 4, 1931, 21:7.

1491 *NYT*, Tuesday, May 5, 1931, 29:7.

The League of Nations, an international organization for peace and security, was established in 1919 by the peace treaty which ended World War I. The League proved ineffective, however, in dealing with the aggressive actions of some member nations. It was superceded in 1946 by the United Nations.

The Child Welfare Committee of the League of Nations received a report on May 3 on moral and social dangers in the United States. The author of the study, Marie Chaptal of France, reported a noticeable disintegration of family life and a collapse of morals in the United States as a result of prohibition.

1492 *NYT*, Wednesday, May 6, 1931, 27:7.

Hoover addressed delegates from thirty-five nations at the International Chamber of Commerce Congress in Washington, D. C., on May 4. He stated that limitation of armaments would help alleviate the depression by freeing nations from the financial strain of maintaining huge standing armies and by relieving instability resulting from the constant threat of war.

1493 *NYT*, Thursday, May 7, 1931, 25:7.

Andrew William Mellon, United States secretary of the treasury from 1921 to 1931. An industrialist and financier, Mellon addressed foreign bankers at the International Chamber of Commerce Congress on May 5 (see Note 1492). He called for maintenance of a high standard of living and for individual effort in restoring financial stability in the wake of the worldwide depression.

The Panic of 1873, precipitated by the failure of several prominent eastern financial firms, led to a severe business depression in the United States in the 1870s.

The Department of the Treasury reported on May 6 a deficit of $903,320,757, which compared unfavorably with a deficit of only $152,950,984, recorded a year earlier.

[1494] *NYT*, Friday, May 8, 1931, 27:7. Variant: *LAT* gives "wife and I" in first sentence.

Betty Blake Rogers, a native of northwestern Arkansas, married Rogers on November 25, 1908.

Walker (see Note 1480) spent several days in March of 1931 vacationing at the desert resort of Palm Springs, California.

[1495] *NYT*, Saturday, May 9, 1931, 19:7.

The Maternity Center Association began a national drive in 1931 to educate the public about the importance of complete medical and hospital care for expectant mothers. The campaign was inaugurated at a special Mother's Day luncheon on May 6 in New York City.

Edith Kermit Carow Roosevelt, second wife of former president Theodore Roosevelt and one of the principal speakers at the Mother's Day banquet.

Lou Henry Hoover, wife of President Hoover, delivered a brief extemporaneous appeal in behalf of the work of the Maternity Center Association.

Anne Morrow Lindbergh, wife of aviator Charles Lindbergh and daughter of the Dwight W. Morrows.

Elsie Nicoll Sloane, president of the Maternity Center Association from 1929 to 1933 and a member of its board of directors from 1920 to 1947.

Belle Wyatt Willard Roosevelt, wife of Kermit Roosevelt, youngest son of former president Theodore Roosevelt.

[1496] *NYT*, Monday, May 11, 1931, 21:7. Variant: *LAT* gives "he had gone to" in sixth sentence.

Carlsbad Caverns, limestone caves in southeastern New Mexico whose stalactite and stalagmite formations are a major tourist attraction in the Southwest. Carlsbad Caverns National Park was established in 1930.

[1497] *NYT*, Tuesday, May 12, 1931, 27:7. Variants: *NYT* gives "off old accounts and" and *LAT* gives "off their losses and" in sixth sentence.

James Blake "Jimmy" Rogers, youngest son of Will Rogers. Jimmy, an expert polo player, attended New Mexico Military Institute at Roswell.

[1498] *NYT*, Wednesday, May 13, 1931, 27:7. Variants: *NYT* gives "New Mexico." to end first sentence, omitting last word.

The Petrified Forest in eastern Arizona includes the largest collection of petrified wood in the world. The area was made a national park in 1962.

Frederick Henry Harvey, founder in the 1870s of a chain of dining establishments along railroad routes in the West. Harvey Houses were noted for their cleanliness, decorum, good food, and efficient service.

[1499] *NYT*, Thursday, May 14, 1931, 25:7. Variant: *NYT* gives "Navy Adams is" in eighth sentence, omitting five words.

The provisional government of Spain, following the overthrow of Alfonso XIII (see Note 1474), continued to encounter severe difficulties in implementing social and political reforms.

Hawks (see Note 1464) made a record flight of two hours and fifty-seven minutes from London to Berlin on May 12, arriving in the German capital minutes before a telegram from London that announced his departure.

Edward Albert, the Prince of Wales, eldest son and heir apparent to the throne of George V of Great Britain. The prince, who recently had returned from South America, informed English businessmen on May 12 that British goods and selling methods were outdated and that the British should copy American methods of advertising to regain their share of the South American market.

Charles Francis Adams, United States secretary of the Navy from 1929 to 1933. A New England banker and philanthropist, Adams was descended from the famed Adams family of Massachusetts which included two American presidents among its members.

Thomas Adams, a pioneer in the chewing gum industry and founder of the American Chicle Company in New York City in 1899.

1500   *NYT*, Friday, May 15, 1931, 25:7.

George Fisher Baker, chairman of the board of the First National Bank of New York City from 1909 until his death on May 2, 1931. Baker's worth had been estimated by outsiders at from $200-$500 million, but his will, which was probated on May 13, revealed an estate valued at only $75 million. Transfers of stock and the decline of the market caused much of the difference.

For John Calvin Coolidge see Note 1463.

Alphonse "Scarface Al" Capone, Italian-born American gangster whose crime syndicate terrorized Chicago from 1920 until Capone's conviction for federal tax evasion in 1931.

1501   *NYT*, Saturday, May 16, 1931, 19:7.

Pius XI, chief prelate of the Roman Catholic Church from 1922 until his death in 1939. On May 15 in a worldwide broadcast from the Vatican, Pope Pius called for a return to Christian principles in the economic community and for a fairer distribution of wealth.

Takamatsu, younger brother of Japanese Emperor Hirohito, was enroute to Los Angeles on the last stage of a honeymoon around the world. He and his bride were accorded a festive reception by local civic officials and by members of the local Japanese community.

Aimee Semple McPherson, American evangelist, faith healer, and founder of the International Church of the Foursquare Gospel based in Los Angeles. The highly successful and controversial revivalist returned to the United States on May 12 from a four-month world tour.

1502   *NYT*, Monday, May 18, 1931, 19:7. Variants: *LAT* gives "home and all that, but do" in first and second sentences, omitting eleven words.

Clara Bow, American actress whose sex appeal and gay manner made her one of the most popular stars of the 1920s. As the "It" girl of the decade, Miss Bow personified playful feminine allure. A series of scandals in 1930 and 1931 destroyed her career, although she continued to appear in films for a time afterwards. A revealing biography written by columnist Louella Parsons appeared in newspapers beginning in May of 1931.

1503   *NYT*, Tuesday, May 19, 1931, 29:7. Variant: *NYT* gives "exhausted itself yesterday." to end second sentence.

The North Carolina legislature met in session for 123 days in 1931, compared to the customary 60 days.

James Rolph, Jr., Republican governor of California from 1931 until his death in 1934. The California legislature denied Rolph's request for $70,000 to buy an airplane which he intended to use during statewide promotional tours.

1504 *NYT,* Wednesday, May 20, 1931, 27:7.

For the League of Nations see Note 1491.

1505 *NYT,* Thursday, May 21, 1931, 29:7.

Sawtelle, located in western Los Angeles, was the site of the largest veterans' home in the United States. The American Legion sponsored an annual poppy drive to raise funds for disabled veterans in soldiers' institutions nationwide.

1506 *NYT,* Friday, May 22, 1931, 27:7.

1507 *NYT,* Saturday, May 23, 1931, 19:7.

Mayors of eighteen American cities visited France in May of 1931 as guests of the French government and the city of Paris.

John Clinton Porter, Republican mayor of Los Angeles from 1929 to 1933. On May 22 at the first official reception for the visiting mayors, Porter, in protest against the consumption of liquor, left the party with his wife when champagne toasts were offered

1508 *NYT,* Monday, May 25, 1931, 21:7.

Mayors from the South joined in a rendition of "Dixie" during ceremonies at Rouen, France, on May 23. Motion picture cameras recorded their performance.

For Charles Spencer Chaplin see Note 1448; for John Clinton Porter see Note 1507.

1509 *NYT,* Tuesday, May 26, 1931, 29:7. Variant: *NYT* gives " 'The Boss.' " in fourth sentence.

Hoover maintained a mountain retreat on the Rapidan River in Virginia to which he made frequent trips to fish and to relax.

For Andrew William Mellon see Note 1493.

Walter Folger Brown, United States postmaster general from 1929 to 1933. Brown and other high-level government officials conferred with Hoover at Rapidan Camp during the weekend of May 23-24.

1510 *NYT,* Wednesday, May 27, 1931, 29:7.

The World Grain Conference opened in London on May 18. Delegates from eleven wheat-exporting nations, including the United States and Russia, met to seek a solution to the worldwide wheat surplus which had glutted the grain market. The conference adjourned on May 23 with no agreement reached on marketing quotas.

1511 *NYT,* Thursday, May 28, 1931, 29:7. Variant: *NYT* omits third sentence.

Claremore, Oklahoma, which Rogers claimed as his hometown, had been a popular health spa since the discovery of radium water in the vicinity in 1903. In an effort to attract more health seekers, the city fathers proclaimed May 25-30 as Radium Water Bath Week in Claremore.

For William Henry Murray see Note 1477.

1512 *NYT*, Friday, May 24, 1931, 23:7.

Los Angeles politico Charles Crawford and local publishing executive Herbert Spencer were shot and killed in Crawford's real estate office on May 20. Five days later, authorities revealed that the two men had formulated plans to purchase a radio station in order to extend and strengthen their political influence. They had intended to hire a well-known minister to discuss state and national affairs. David H. Clark, a former deputy district attorney, initially was charged with the slayings; he was acquitted in October of 1931.

1513 *NYT*, Saturday, May 30, 1931, 17:7.

1514 *NYT*, Monday, June 1, 1931, 19:7.

Hoover addressed a Memorial Day crowd of 20,000 at Valley Forge, Pennsylvania. He urged Americans to persevere in the face of economic adversity in the same manner as the patriots at Valley Forge had endured the winter of 1777.

For Andrew William Mellon see Note 1493.

1515 *NYT*, Tuesday, June 2, 1931, 31:7.

Mary Louise Cecilia "Texas" Guinan, American actress and night club hostess noted for her frequent clashes with prohibition agents and for her brash greeting for patrons: "Hello, sucker!" Guinan and her troupe of thirty showgirls were detained in their Paris hotel on May 30 by French authorities. They later were deported from France for failure to obtain permission to enter the country as entertainers.

The American mayors touring France (see Note 1507) continued to excite concern about their conduct. Mayor George L. Baker of Portland, Oregon, violated the traditional silence at the Tomb of the Unknown Soldier in Paris on May 8 by delivering an extemporaneous speech.

1516 *NYT*, Wednesday, June 3, 1931, 27:7. Variant: *LAT* gives "BEVERLY HILLS" as place of origin.

Los Angeles voters rejected sewer bonds totaling $6 million in municipal elections on June 2.

National Cotton Week was endorsed by major cotton manufacturers, dry goods retailers, and the Department of Agriculture. American cotton producers, however, continually suffered from low prices caused in part by overproduction.

For Andrew William Mellon see Note 1493.

1517 *NYT*, Thursday, June 4, 1931, 29:7. Variants: *NYT* omits fourth sentence/*LAT* gives "had been accused of bumping off" in fourth sentence.

In elections in Los Angeles on June 2, attorney David Clark (see Note 1512) lost a race for a municipal judgeship while in jail awaiting trial for murder.

Rogers politely refused an offer on May 19 of an honorary doctorate from Oklahoma City University. He long had considered all such awards as "hooey" and "applesauce."

George Woodward Wickersham, former chairman of the National Commission on Law Observance and Enforcement, a Hoover-appointed body which in 1929 conducted an extensive investigation of the federal system of jurisprudence and administration of laws. Its final report, which called for the continuation of prohibition while providing evidence that it could not be enforced, generated much criticism and discussion. Wickersham received an honorary degree from Syracuse University on June 1, 1931.

1518 *NYT,* Friday, June 5, 1931, 25:7. Variant: *LAT* gives "BEVERLY HILLS" as place of origin.

"Normalcy," a term coined by presidential candidate Warren Gamaliel Harding in 1920, signified a shift from the Democratic policies of President Woodrow Wilson and a return to the Republican doctrines of free enterprise and governmental support of big business.

1519 *NYT,* Saturday, June 6, 1931, 19:7. Variants: *NYT* gives "there would be considerable political" to begin first sentence/*LAT* gives "and in saying . . . day he took" in third and fourth sentences.

Coolidge, who contributed several articles to magazines after his return to private life in 1929, also wrote a series of daily columns for the McClure Newspaper Syndicate, beginning in June of 1930. McClure, however, announced in early June of 1931 that the former president had decided to end his writing chores in July.

Presidential pensions were first authorized in 1958.

1520 *NYT,* Monday, June 8, 1931, 19:7. Variant: *LAT* gives "Every national and" in second sentence.

1521 *NYT,* Tuesday, June 9, 1931, 29:7. Variant: *LAT* gives "floated another" in first sentence.

The Treasury Department announced on June 7 that nearly $820 million in recently offered bonds had been purchased. The eighteen-year certificates were to provide funds to operate the government and to retire maturing treasury notes.

A bonus bill, which provided for adjusted compensation for World War I veterans, was passed in 1924. Payments averaging $1,000 were to be paid in 1945, but pressure by veterans led to passage of a bill in February of 1931 that authorized a loan of 50 percent of the anticipated payment.

For Alphonse "Scarface Al" Capone see Note 1500.

1522 *NYT,* Wednesday, June 10, 1931, 27:7.

Mellon (see Note 1493) and Stimson (see Note 1485) both announced in early June their plans to spend the summer in Europe. While on vacation, the two cabinet members were expected to meet with foreign officials and to discuss the payment of debts to the United States stemming from loans made during World War I.

The Conference for Limitation of the Manufacture of Narcotic Drugs, sponsored by the League of Nations, opened at Geneva, Switzerland, on May 27. Delegates from fifty nations, including the United States, discussed international cooperation to control illicit drugs.

1523 *NYT,* Thursday, June 11, 1931, 27:7. Variants: *LAT* gives "BEVERLY HILLS" as place of origin/*NYT* gives "forget, thinkers, that" in third sentence/*NYT* gives "So this is a reminder just" in fifth sentence.

The Los Angeles Parent Teacher Association announced on June 2 that funds for free school lunches for needy children in the city were exhausted. A plea for help was met by significant contributions from radio sponsors, movie studios, and dairy companies, as well as private citizens.

1524 *NYT,* Friday, June 12, 1931, 23:7. Variant: *NYT* gives "Mexicans, so" in second sentence.

Two Mexican college students, returning home from Kansas, were shot and killed by a deputy sheriff as they stood beside their parked car in Ardmore, Oklahoma, on June 8. The officer was tried and acquitted on the grounds that the students were carrying weapons at the time of the shooting. The incident nearly precipitated an international crisis when authorities discovered that one of the youths was a cousin of Mexican President Pascual Ortiz Rubio.

John Joseph "Black Jack" Pershing, general who led United States troops into Mexico in 1916 in an unsuccessful attempt to capture the Mexican bandit leader Francisco "Pancho" Villa. Pershing also commanded the American Expeditionary Force in Europe during World War I and served as Army Chief of Staff from 1921 to 1924.

1525   *NYT*, Saturday, June 13, 1931, 17:7.

Mary Amelia Rogers, only daughter of Will and Betty Rogers, graduated from Marlborough Preparatory School in Beverly Hills on June 11.

Douglas Fairbanks, American stage and screen actor famous for his agile acrobatics and flashy smile who starred in numerous silent spectaculars during a highly successful twenty-year film career.

Wallace Beery, American screen actor noted for his dynamic portrayals of hard-nosed villains and blustery tough guys. He won an Academy Award in 1931 for his performance in *The Champ*.

Frank Lloyd, Scottish-born American film director who began his career in England as an actor but worked in Hollywood from 1910 until his death in 1960. He won Academy Awards for best direction in 1929 and 1933.

1526   *NYT*, Monday, June 15, 1931, 21:7. Variants: *LAT* gives "their alumnis." in second sentence/*NYT* gives "number of these" in sixth sentence.

Brisbane (see Note 1442) noted in his daily newspaper column of June 16 that he admired Rogers' writings but that the Oklahoman's "early training at Eton and Oxford" made it difficult for him to maintain the "cowboy style." Brisbane's comments were prompted by Rogers' "surprise" that his daughter had received a degree in English (see DT 1525).

1527   *NYT*, Tuesday, June 16, 1931, 29:7.

1528   *NYT*, Wednesday, June 17, 1931, 27:7. Variants: *NYT* omits "finally (after years of delay)" in first sentence/*NYT* omits second, third, and fourth sentences.

Warren Gamaliel Harding, Republican president of the United States from 1921 until his death in 1923. Harding placed unquestioning faith in subordinates and cabinet officers. After his death, it was revealed that several of these men had used their positions for financial gain. Although Harding was unaware of the illicit activities, the resultant scandals obscured the positive achievements of his administration.

Coolidge served as vice president from 1921 to 1923, succeeding to the presidency upon Harding's death. He won election to a full term in 1924.

Hoover served as secretary of commerce from 1921 to 1929 in the cabinets of both Harding and Coolidge. Hoover and Coolidge addressed a crowd of 20,000 at Harding's hometown of Marion, Ohio, on June 16 during the dedication of their predecessor's tomb. The two men praised Harding's character and integrity and spoke of the accomplishments of his administration.

1529   *LAT*, Thursday, June 18, 1931, I:1:3. *NYT* did not print the DT.

Hoover addressed a crowd of 40,000 in Springfield, Illinois, on June 17 at the dedication of the reconstructed mausoleum of President Lincoln.

Franklin Delano Roosevelt, Democratic governor of New York from 1929 to 1933. Since his reelection as governor in 1930, the personable Roosevelt had been a leading candidate for the Democratic presidential nomination in 1932. H won the nomination and the election in 1932 and served as president from 1933 until his death in 1945.

1530 *NYT*, Friday, June 19, 1931, 25:7.

Capone (see Note 1500) pleaded guilty on June 16 to federal charges of income tax evasion and violation of the prohibition law. He entered a guilty plea on the assumption that he would receive a mild sentence in return. On June 30, when the possibility of a bargain with federal authorities was blocked by a judge, Capone withdrew his original plea; his trial was rescheduled for September.

Leavenworth Federal Penitentiary, located in northeastern Kansas, is a maximum security prison. Originally a military prison, it was taken over by the Department of Justice in 1895.

1531 *NYT*, Saturday, June 20, 1931, 19:7.

"Amos 'n Andy," a radio serial which began in 1928 and was aired five times weekly until 1943. The creators and stars were Freeman Fisher Gosden and Charles J. Correll, blackface comedians who played every male part and wrote every script. The escapades of two Harlem taxi drivers and their friends captivated an enormous and faithful listening audience.

For the Wickersham Commission report see Note 1517.

In Reno, Nevada, noted cartoonist Peter Arno reported to police that he had been threatened with a gun by Cornelius Vanderbilt, Jr., a journalist and socialite who blamed Arno for the breakup of his marriage. No arrests were made after Vanderbilt's attorney asserted that the gun was not loaded.

1532 *NYT*, Monday, June 22, 1931, 21:7.

Hoover, in a move to ease the financial situation in Europe, proposed on June 20 a one-year moratorium on both interallied debts and German reparations.

For Rogers' debt plan see DT 1520.

James Ramsay MacDonald, prime minister of Great Britain from 1929 to 1935. A member of the Labour party since 1894, MacDonald took an activist role in foreign affairs, constantly seeking international harmony, disarmament, and arbitration.

Paul Ludwig Hans Anton von Beneckendorff und von Hindenburg, president of Germany from 1925 to 1934. Born in 1847, von Hindenburg served as German Army Chief of Staff during World War I. He held the presidency during a time of extreme economic distress and political factionalism in Germany.

For Andrew William Mellon see Note 1493.

1533 *NYT*, Tuesday, June 23, 1931, 27:7. Variant: *NYT* gives "pass as" in fifth sentence.

1534 *NYT*, Wednesday, June 24, 1931, 25:7.

Morrow (see Note 1467) received an honorary doctorate from Syracuse University on June 22. Earlier in the month, he had received similar honors from Dartmouth and Bowdoin colleges.

1535 *NYT*, Thursday, June 25, 1931, 27:7. Variants: *NYT* gives "solution." to end first sentence, omitting last word/*NYT* gives "Young Vanderbilt" in P.S.

Cornelius Vanderbilt, Jr., and his wife, the former Mary Weir Logan, filed separate divorce actions in Reno in June. Vanderbilt's charge that his wife was romantically involved with cartoonist Peter Arno (see Note 1531) was denied on June 23 by Mrs. Vanderbilt, who in a cross-complaint asked for divorce on the grounds of mental cruelty. She won her suit on August 4, 1931.

1536 *NYT,* Friday, June 26, 1931, 25:7.

Hoover was suggested as a candidate for the Nobel Peace Prize of 1931 by the mayor of Berlin. The recommendation was made in recognition of Hoover's contribution to world peace by his debt moratorium proposal of June 20 (see Note 1532). Americans Jane Addams and Nicholas Murray Butler were the co-recipients of the award in 1931.

1537 *NYT,* Saturday, June 27, 1931, 19:7. Variants: *NYT* gives "has to explain" in first sentence, omitting four words/*NYT* gives " 'What you are . . . do is shorten . . . year?' " in sixth sentence.

Mellon (see Note 1493) arrived in Paris on June 25 to confer with French officials about Hoover's moratorium on debts (see Note 1532). The French were apprehensive about accepting the plan because of its possible effect on their payment of debts to the United States and on German reparations payments to France.

1538 *NYT,* Monday, June 29, 1931, 19:4-5. Variants: *LAT* gives "worst statement" in fifth sentence/*LAT* gives "d_____ foolishness" in seventh sentence/*NYT* gives "Presidential, Senator" in eighth sentence/*NYT* gives "years. Just go get" in eighteenth sentence.

Rogers "ran" for president in 1928 as the candidate of the Anti-Bunk party. His candidacy was suggested by Robert Sherwood, editor of *Life.* Rogers' articles in the weekly humor magazine set forth his platform and contained observations on the campaign and the issues, all of which he labeled "bunk."

George Creel, American journalist, government administrator, politician, and author who was a major contributor to *Collier's* magazine during the 1930s under the pseudonym of "The Gentleman at the Keyhole." In a recent issue, Creel had boosted Rogers for the presidency in 1932, asserting that the Oklahoman was more popular than any other candidate and would restore humor to American public life.

Charles Curtis, vice president of the United States from 1928 to 1933.

For Franklin Delano Roosevelt see Note 1529.

Owen D. Young, American lawyer and corporate officer who served on several government advisory boards for economic matters. In 1929 he assisted in the formation of the Young Plan, a proposal which scaled down German reparations payments.

Will Harrison Hays, former chairman of the Republican National Committee and postmaster general of the United States who became chairman of Motion Picture Producers and Distributors of America in 1922. During his twenty-three-year chairmanship, Hays became known as the "czar" of the motion picture industry.

1539 *NYT,* Tuesday, June 30, 1931, 27:7.

Wiley Hardeman Post, Oklahoma aviator who won the National Air Race for long-distance flight in 1930 and also set records for round-the-world and stratospheric flights. Post lost his left eye in an oil field mishap in 1926.

Harold Gatty, expert Australian navigator who began his study of flight navigation after his arrival in the United States in 1927. On June 23 Post and

Gatty left Roosevelt Field in New York City in the *Winnie Mae* on the first leg of a round-the-world flight. The fourteen-stage flight was completed on July 1, setting a record of eight days, fifteen hours, and fifty-one minutes.

1540   *NYT*, Wednesday, July 1, 1931, 25:7.

For the Post-Gatty world flight see Note 1539.

Methodist ministers in Southern California met in Long Beach in late June and overwhelmingly adopted a resolution to petition Congress for an exemption from military service for all church members who believed that war violated their religious principles.

For Andrew William Mellon see Notes 1493 and 1537.

1541   *NYT*, Thursday, July 2, 1931, 27:7. Variant: *NYT* gives "schools in Maine." to end third sentence, omitting last ten words.

Florence Hale, state supervisor of rural education in Maine from 1916 to 1932, was elected president of the National Education Association at its annual meeting in Los Angeles in July.

1542   *NYT*, Friday, July 3, 1931, 19:7. Variants: *LAT* gives "Robinson" in second sentence/*NYT* gives "loved the veterans and" in fourth sentence.

Alice Mary Robertson, Republican United States representative from Oklahoma from 1921 to 1923. Robertson was the first woman from Oklahoma and only the second in history to serve in Congress. She died of cancer in Muskogee, Oklahoma, on July 1.

For Nicholas Longworth see Note 1471; for the veterans' bonus bill see Note 1521.

1543   *NYT*, Saturday, July 4, 1931, 15:7.

Isaac Alfred Isaacs, governor-general of Australia from 1931 to 1936.

Florence C. Hall, Oklahoma oilman who provided the financing for the Post-Gatty flight (see Note 1539). Post was Hall's executive pilot during the late 1920s. On July 2, 1931, Post and Gatty were accorded the largest ticker tape parade in the history of New York City in recognition of their historic flight.

1544   *NYT*, Monday, July 6, 1931, 19:7.

For the Post-Gatty world flight see Note 1539; for Florence C. Hall see Note 1543.

1545   *NYT*, Tuesday, July 7, 1931, 23:7.

1546   *NYT*, Wednesday, July 8, 1931, 25:7.

Joe Crail, Republican United States representative from California from 1927 to 1933.

John Quillen Tilson, Republican United States representative from Connecticut from 1907 to 1913 and from 1915 to 1932. Tilson was House majority leader from 1925 to 1931 and a staunch supporter of the Hoover administration.

For Nicholas Longworth see Note 1471; for Hoover's debt moratorium see Note 1532.

1547   *NYT*, Thursday, July 9, 1931, 23:7. Variants: *LAT* gives "our Oklahoma" and *NYT* gives "world, outside of the Tempelhof Field in Berlin, just" in fourth sentence.

Citizens of Claremore responded to Rogers' jibes about the lack of air facilities in the Oklahoma community by buying an 80-acre oat field and constructing an airport in less than one week. The new installation was dubbed the Will Rogers Airport and was completed in time for the visit of world fliers Post and Gatty (see Note 1539).

Templehof Airport in Berlin, Germany, was one of the busiest airfields in Europe, handling more than 750,000 passengers in 1929, the first year of its operation.

For Francis M. "Frank" Hawks see Note 1464.

1548   *NYT*, Friday, July 10, 1931, 19:7. Variant: *LAT* gives "received" in second sentence.

Hesitation by France to accept Hoover's debt moratorium (see Note 1532) was based on the French contention that payment of debts to the United States depended on the payment of German reparations to France. Hoover refused to recognize the connection, however.

Vanilla was one of more than 100 characters on the popular radio show "Amos 'n Andy" (see Note 1531).

1549   *NYT*, Saturday, July 11, 1931, 15:7. Variant: *NYT* gives "Every man" to begin fifth sentence, omitting first three words.

1550   *NYT*, Monday, July 13, 1931, 19:7.

The German economy in the post-World War I era was marked by mass unemployment and rampant currency inflation, brought about in part by huge reparations payments. German officials attempted to obtain short term credit from international sources in July of 1931 in an effort to avoid economic ruin.

The Federal Farm Board was established in 1929 to buy agricultural surpluses in order to stabilize farm prices. In March of 1931, the board announced that it had exhausted its funds. Hoover, afraid that the board would disrupt prices by placing surplus crops on the market, asked for and received assurances that it would not pursue unlimited sale of the surpluses.

Doles, payments to unemployed individuals by the British government, created much controversy because of abuses of the system by recipients and administrators.

The Crusaders, an antiprohibition organization, won the top award for floats in a Fourth of July parade in Santa Barbara, California. Local members of the Women's Christian Temperance Union asked the city council to bar such "unpatriotic" exhibits from future parades.

For Charles Curtis see Note 1538.

1551   *LAT*, Tuesday, July 14, 1931, I:1:6. Variants: *LAT* gives "EN ROUTE TO TULSA" as place of origin/*LAT* gives "passengers" in tenth sentence/*NYT* did not print the DT.

Rogers returned to Claremore to dedicate the new Will Rogers Airport (see Note 1547) and to honor world fliers Post and Gatty (see Note 1539).

Hamilton Lee, veteran airmail pilot for Bowen Airlines of Fort Worth, Texas.

1552   *NYT*, Wednesday, July 15, 1931, 21:7.

For the Post-Gatty world flight and the *Winnie Mae* see Note 1539.

1553   *NYT*, Thursday, July 16, 1931, 21:7.

A severe drought in 1931 cut crop production in the spring wheat states of the Upper Northwest by more than one half of the annual average.

1554 *NYT*, Friday, July 17, 1931, 19:7. Variants: *LAT* gives "LOS ANGELES," as place of origin/*NYT* gives "and we will" and *LAT* gives "and here at" in third sentence.

Shady Oak Farm, a lakeshore resort and retreat near Fort Worth, Texas, was owned by publisher Amon G. Carter (see Note 1485).

1555 *NYT*, Saturday, July 18, 1931, 15:7.

Pedro Leon, veteran Mexican-born stuntman and motion picture performer.

1556 *NYT*, Monday, July 20, 1931, 19:7.

Mate won the Arlington Classic on July 18 in an upset over Twenty Grand. It was Mate's second victory over Twenty Grand in three meetings in 1931, with Mate winning the Preakness on May 9 and Twenty Grand taking the Kentucky Derby a week later.

For the overseas trips of cabinet members see Note 1522.

Clarence Hungerford MacKay, chairman of the board of Postal Telegraph and Cable Corporation, married American opera star Anna Case on July 18.

1557 *NYT*, Tuesday, July 21, 1931, 21:7.

Minnie Pearce "Ma" Kennedy, mother of evangelist Aimee Semple McPherson (see Note 1501), was examined in Los Angeles on July 18 by two psychiatrists in response to a complaint filed by an officer at her daughter's Angelus Temple. Also an evangelist, Kennedy had worked closely with McPherson until July of 1927, at which time the two disagreed about control of the temple and ended their association. The doctors dismissed the complaint against Kennedy.

Albert Bacon Fall, United States secretary of the interior from 1921 to 1923. While serving as secretary, Fall secretly leased naval oil reserves to Edward Laurence Doheny, an American oil producer who previously had loaned Fall $100,000 to buy a ranch in New Mexico. Fall was convicted of bribery and received a sentence of one year and a fine of $100,000. His prison term began on July 20, 1931. Doheny purchased Fall's ranch at a sheriff's sale in May of 1929 for $168,250.

1558 *NYT*, Wednesday, July 22, 1931, 21:7. Variant: *LAT* gives "it, even, and Andy" in fourth and fifth sentences.

MacDonald (see Note 1532) delivered the opening address on July 20 at an international conference in London, held to discuss the financial problems of Germany. Secretaries Mellon and Stimson (see Notes 1492 and 1485) represented the United States.

1559 *NYT*, Thursday, July 23, 1931, 19:7.

Hoover believed that Germany needed long-term loans in order to have time to solve immediate financial problems.

1560 *NYT*, Friday, July 24, 1931, 19:7. Variant: *NYT* gives "fine German" in last paragraph.

For the Post-Gatty world flight see Note 1539.

Nancy Langhorne Astor, American-born English viscountess who was the first woman to sit in the House of Commons, serving from 1919 to 1945. Noted for her caustic and irreverent comments on virtually any subject, Lady Astor accompanied Shaw (see Note 1454) on a well-publicized tour of Russia in July of 1931.

The Apple Cart, a play by Shaw first produced in 1929, concerns the humorous struggle for power between a crafty prime minister and an equally crafty monarch.

Germany received assurances of short-term credits on July 21 from the countries attending the economic conference in London (see Note 1558). The loans helped to steady German finances.

1561 *NYT,* Saturday, July 25, 1931, 15:7.

For Andrew William Mellon see Notes 1493 and 1522; for Henry Lewis Stimson see Notes 1485 and 1522.

McIntyre (see Note 1456) left New York City on July 12 for a trip to Paris and London.

1562 *NYT,* Monday, July 27, 1931, 17:7.

Plutarco Elías Calles, president of Mexico from 1924 to 1928 and the dominant force in Mexican politics during the early 1930s. As president of the Bank of Mexico, Calles helped to develop a plan under which Mexico was placed on a silver monetary standard in an effort to stem the rapid decline in value of the precious metal.

1563 *NYT,* Tuesday, July 28, 1931, 21:7.

Carlos Ibáñez del Campo, president of Chile from 1927 until mobs protesting his dictatorial rule forced his resignation on July 26, 1931. The deposed dictator fled to Argentina. He later returned to Chile and regained the presidency in 1952.

Harry Carr, reporter and columnist for the *Los Angeles Times* from 1897 until his death in 1936. Three American women tourists, two of whom were Carr's sisters, were robbed by bandits near Peking, China, on July 25.

1564 *NYT,* Wednesday, July 29, 1931, 19:7. Variant: *NYT* gives "We ought to take . . . practice, then Arkansas and then" in third sentence.

Murray (see Note 1477) called out the Oklahoma National Guard in mid-July after Texas authorities had blocked access to the Texas end of a free bridge across the Red River. In further retaliation, Murray ordered the Oklahoma end of a toll bridge blocked. The trouble stemmed from a suit by owners of the latter facility who had sued the state of Texas for losses incurred because of the operation of the free bridge. The incident ended when the toll bridge proprietors received compensation for their losses.

Murray named Rogers a colonel on his staff in February of 1931. Rogers took command of the "nut brigade."

1565 *NYT,* Thursday, July 30, 1931, 19:7. Variant: *NYT* gives "dig one there. It will cost" in fifth and sixth sentences.

Daniel Isom Sultan, lieutenant colonel in the United States Army Corps of Engineers. Sultan conducted a survey from 1929 to 1931 of the feasibility of an inter-oceanic canal across Nicaragua. He found that the canal was constructible but unnecessary and, at $700 million, prohibitively expensive. Sultan played a major role in relief operations in earthquake-devastated Managua, Nicaragua, in March of 1931 (see Note 1466).

1566 *NYT,* Friday, July 31, 1931, 19:7.

For the Federal Farm Board see Note 1550.

1567 *NYT*, Saturday, August 1, 1931, 15:7.

Capone (see Notes 1500 and 1530) appeared in United States District Court on July 30 to face charges of income tax evasion and liquor conspiracy. Judge James Herbert Wilkerson warned Capone that the court would not necessarily honor a plea bargain made between prosecuting attorneys and Capone. The judge's firm stand prompted Capone to change his plea from guilty to not guilty. His case went to trial in September of 1931.

Two aviators from Boston, Russell N. Boardman and John Polando, set a world distance record for a nonstop flight on July 30. Their 5,014-mile flight from New York City, New York, to Istanbul, Turkey, took forty-nine hours.

1568 *NYT*, Monday, August 3, 1931, 19:7.

1569 *NYT*, Tuesday, August 4, 1941, 21:7.

1570 *NYT*, Wednesday, August 5, 1931, 21:7.

For Dwight Whitney Morrow see Note 1467.

1571 *NYT*, Thursday, August 6, 1931, 21:7.

Murray (see Note 1477) invoked martial law on August 4 in an attempt to shut-down all oil wells in Oklahoma to stem overproduction and to raise prices. Murray's action marked the second time in less than a month that he had called out the National Guard to enforce his orders (see Note 1564).

1572 *NYT*, Friday, August 7, 1931, 19:7. Variant: *LAT* gives "again." to end seventh sentence, omitting last seven words and eighth sentence.

The Yangtze River in China flooded in late July, leaving thousands of persons dead or homeless. In August, in the worst flood disaster in history, 3,700,000 Chinese perished when the Yellow River burst from its banks.

Mae Murray, American screen actress who reigned as one of the top film stars of the 1920s. On August 5 Murray announced that she had abandoned her much discussed divorce suit against her husband, Prince David Mdivani.

For George Bernard Shaw see Notes 1454 and 1560; for the Wickersham Commission report see Note 1517.

William Harrison "Jack" Dempsey, American boxer who held the world heavyweight title from 1919 to 1926. On August 4 the popular ex-champion announced that he would end a four-year retirement and would tour the United States in a series of exhibition matches. He fought fifty-six bouts in six months and then retired permanently in 1932.

Grace Goodhue Coolidge, wife of former president Calvin Coolidge.

Lindbergh (see Note 1464) and his wife began an aerial journey from Washington, D.C., to the Orient on July 28. During their flight across Canada, atmospheric conditions disrupted radio communications, making contact with many ground stations impossible.

1573 *NYT*, Saturday, August 8, 1931, 15:7. Variant: *NYT* gives "The treasury ought to get" to begin fifth sentence, omitting eight words.

For Betty Blake Rogers see Note 1494; for Mary Amelia Rogers see Note 1525.

James Alexander Reed, Democratic United States senator from Missouri from 1911 to 1929. An antiprohibitionist, Reed charged in the September issue of *Cosmopolitan* magazine that the federal government operated speakeasies, condoned rum-running, and financed the manufacture of illicit liquor by loaning money to grape growers.

Governor Rolph (see Note 1503) created a furor when he called for a six-day general holiday in California to begin on September 4. Businessmen and bankers flooded the governor's office with a deluge of protests, prompting Rolph to cancel the planned "fiesta."

1574 *NYT,* Monday, August 10, 1931, 17:7. Variants: *NYT* gives "back to where it belonged." to end third sentence/*NYT* gives "Well, there you go Hoover," in sixth sentence.

Helen Wills Moody, American amateur tennis star of the 1920s and 1930s. As Helen Wills she won numerous national and foreign titles before her marriage in 1929 to stockbroker Fred Moody. In 1931 she continued her domination of women's tennis, winning several prestigious tournaments, including the United States Open championship at Forest Hills in August.

American fliers Hugh Herndon, Jr., and Clyde Pangborn left New York City on July 28 in an attempt to break the record for a round-the-world flight. They were detained in Tokyo on August 6, however, on charges that they had violated Japanese espionage laws when they flew over fortified areas. The fliers claimed innocence but were forced to pay $2,050 in fines before they were allowed to leave the country on September 29, too late to break any records.

1575 *NYT,* Tuesday, August 11, 1931, 23:7. Variant: *LAT* gives "out of the picnic" in fifth and sixth sentences.

1576 *NYT,* Wednesday, August 12, 1931, 21:7. Variant: *NYT* gives "fine, Mabel, and" in third sentence.

Mabel Walker Willebrandt, lawyer who served as United States assistant attorney general from 1921 to 1929 in charge of cases involving tax laws, prohibition, and federal prisons. In 1931, as counsel for a firm which manufactured grape concentrates known as wine bricks, Willebrandt sought a federal loan to offset losses by her client from heat and drought. The sale of wine bricks had caused consternation among anti-liquor forces who charged that the concentrates were being processed into homemade wine.

1577 *NYT,* Thursday, August 13, 1931, 21:7.

The Wickersham Commission (see Note 1517) turned in the last of fourteen reports on August 23. The study criticized the deportation practices of the Bureau of Immigration and exonerated the foreign-born from the widely-held theory that they were responsible for most of the crime in the country. The report also condemned the methods of police when interrogating prisoners.

1578 *NYT,* Friday, August 14, 1931, 19:7. Variants: *NYT* gives "then think of her being simp" in second sentence/*NYT* gives "to block these malsharpers" in fifth sentence.

1579 *NYT,* Saturday, August 15, 1931, 15:7.

England, Arkansas, was the scene of a nationally-publicized demonstration by more than 500 hungry and drought-stricken farmers and their families on January 3, 1931. The protesters demanded food and threatened to take it by force from local merchants. A riot was thwarted when the Red Cross authorized the distribution of relief supplies. In August of 1931, the citizens of England, having improved their condition with government assistance and greater crop production, sent a caravan of food and supplies to unemployed residents of Henryetta, Oklahoma.

1580 *NYT*, Monday, August 17, 1931, 17:7. Variant: *NYT* gives "Silence one-third" in sixth sentence.

The Federal Farm Board (see Note 1550) wired the governors of fourteen southern states on August 12 to seek their support for a plan to plow under every third row of cotton in order to avoid overproduction.

1581 *NYT*, Tuesday, August 18, 1931, 23:7. Variants: *NYT* gives "made news by" in second sentence/*NYT* omits fourth sentence.

Earth tremors caused slight damage in communities in Texas, New Mexico, and northern Mexico on August 16.

Winston Leonard Spencer Churchill, British statesman who served as chancellor of the exchequer from 1924 to 1929 and as prime minister from 1940 to 1945 and from 1951 to 1955. An ardent anticommunist, Churchill criticized Shaw (see Note 1454) and Astor (see Note 1560) for having expressed pro-Soviet views during their trip to Russia.

For William Edgar Borah see Note 1452.

1582 *NYT*, Wednesday, August 19, 1931, 23:7.

1583 *NYT*, Thursday, August 20, 1931, 21:7.

Russia implemented a five-year plan in 1928 that called for complete governmental planning of the economy.

Samuel Roy McKelvie, former governor of Nebraska and a member of the Federal Farm Board, serving from 1929 to 1931. On August 18 McKelvie recommended that the surplus of wheat held by the government be used to feed the unemployed.

Huey Pierce "Kingfish" Long, Democratic governor of Louisiana from 1928 to 1932; United States senator from 1932 until his death in 1935. Long proposed on August 16 that officials of cotton-producing states ban the production of all cotton in 1932. This action, Long predicted, would restore prosperity to cotton farmers and still provide enough of the staple to meet world demand.

1584 *NYT*, Friday, August 21, 1931, 19:7.

Walter Sherman Gifford, president of American Telephone & Telegraph Company from 1925 to 1948. On August 19 Hoover appointed Gifford to head the Organization on Unemployment Relief, a federal agency which would help local and state officials meet the unemployment crisis.

1585 *NYT*, Saturday, August 22, 1931, 15:7.

Hoover asked sixty leaders from the business, finance, social, and industrial sectors to serve as an advisory committee to the newly-formed Organization on Unemployment Relief (see Note 1584).

1586 *NYT*, Monday, August 24, 1931, 17:7.

James Couzens, Republican United States senator from Michigan from 1922 until his death in 1936. Couzens offered on August 22 to donate $1,000,000 to the city of Detroit for unemployment relief if local citizens would raise an additional $9,000,000. The local campaign collapsed in November, however, and Couzens replaced his original offer of $1,000,000 with a gift of $200,000.

Samuel Insull II, English-born American utilities and transportation magnate. Insull contributed $300,000-$400,000 in 1931 to cover the deficit of the Chicago Civic Opera.

For the Organization on Unemployment Relief see Note 1584; for Andrew William Mellon see Notes 1493 and 1537.

1587 *NYT,* Tuesday, August 25, 1931, 23:7.

For Alphonse "Scarface Al" Capone see Note 1567.

MacDonald (see Note 1532) and other members of the Labour ministry resigned on August 24 because of its inability to meet a budgetary crisis. Several Labourites then joined in a coalition government with MacDonald at its head. The Labour party denounced the action and moved to oust coalitionists from party membership.

For Andrew William Mellon and the federal deficit see Note 1493.

Charles and Anne Lindbergh (see Notes 1464 and 1572) landed in Nemuro, Japan, on August 24. Citizens of Nemuro had waited for the couple for almost a week, but fog and mechanical difficulties caused the Lindberghs to delay their arrival. Despite the setback, local residents accorded the famous fliers a hospitable reception.

1588 *NYT,* Wednesday, August 26, 1931, 21:7.

Japanese authorities denied widespread rumors that the Lindberghs (see Notes 1572 and 1587) had breached national security by flying over fortified areas of the country. Japan earlier had detained two other American fliers for photographing restricted sectors (see Note 1574).

For the Labour party in Great Britain see Note 1587.

1589 *NYT,* Thursday, August 27, 1931, 19:7.

Violent debate in the Mexican Chamber of Deputies on August 25 led to an exchange of gunfire in which one representative was slain and two others and a spectator were wounded.

Estelle Taylor, American stage and screen actress. After a tonsilectomy in 1931, Taylor underwent such a successful regimen of voice exercises that she aspired to a singing career. Married to Jack Dempsey (see Note 1572) in 1925, she was divorced by the boxer in 1931.

1590 *NYT,* Friday, August 28, 1931, 17:7.

Rogers wrote this column while on the set of *Ambassador Bill,* a film released in 1931 in which Rogers portrayed an Oklahoman serving as ambassador to a small European nation.

1591 *NYT,* Saturday, August 29, 1931, 15:7.

The coalition government of Great Britain (see Note 1587) received assurances of substantial banking credit and other financial support from major New York City banking firms on August 27.

1592 *NYT,* Monday, August 31, 1931, 17:7. Variant: *LAT* gives "their family" in first sentence/*NYT* and *LAT* give "in the kind" in seventh sentence.

For Wiley Hardeman Post and Harold Gatty see Note 1539.

In the National Air Races of 1931, Doolittle (see Note 1464) used a secretly-built Laird biplane to outdistance eight other competitors and win the

Bendix Trophy for long-distance flight. Post did not participate in the air races at Cleveland.

1593 *NYT,* Tuesday, September 1, 1931, 25:7.

For floods in China see Note 1572.

The Treasury Department offered $1.1 billion in government securities on August 30 to offset dwindling revenues resulting from the general business depression. The public offering included $800 million in long-term bonds at 3 percent interest and $300 million in short-term certificates at 1.5 percent interest.

1594 *NYT,* Wednesday, September 2, 1931, 23:7.

The United States Golf Association adopted a new, slightly larger and lighter golf ball in 1931. The rule change generated considerable debate and numerous alibis.

Jones (see Note 1486) joined a large gallery at the Beverly Country Club in Chicago to watch the first qualifying round of the United States Amateur Golf championship on August 31.

1595 *NYT,* Thursday, September 3, 1931, 23:7.

Young was appointed on September 1 to chair a special committee within the Organization on Unemployment Relief (see Notes 1584 and 1585). His group was responsible for the coordination and administration of local fund raising campaigns.

1596 *NYT,* Friday, September 4, 1931, 21:7.

1597 *NYT,* Saturday, September 5, 1931, 15:7.

The Bureau of the Census announced on September 3 that illiteracy in the United States had decreased from 6 to 4.3 percent during the period from 1920 to 1930.

Sale (see Note 1470) wrote *The Specialist* in 1929 and followed it the next year with another bestseller, *I'll Tell You Why.*

1598 *NYT,* Monday, September 7, 1931, 15:7. Variant: *NYT* gives "a golfer was" in fifth sentence.

George Hubert Wilkins, Australian soldier, aviator, and polar explorer who was knighted in 1928 for having made the first flight over a polar region. In early September of 1931, Wilkins attempted to cross under the North Pole in an old American submarine, the *Nautilus.* He abandoned the effort after losing radio contact and sustaining minor damage to the craft.

Francis de Sales Ouimet, American golfer who became the first amateur to win the United States Open championship (1913). He won his first United States Amateur title in 1914 and his second seventeen years later on September 5, 1931.

Fred Andrew Stone, American vaudeville and musical comedy star and close personal friend of Rogers.

1599 *NYT,* Tuesday, September 8, 1931, 27:7. Variant: *NYT* omits seventh sentence.

1600 *NYT,* Wednesday, September 9, 1931, 29:7. Variant: *NYT* gives "something. This time he says that" in third sentence.

George V, king of Great Britain and Ireland from 1910 until his death in 1936. George V and his son, the Prince of Wales (see Note 1499), indicated on September 7 that they would donate to the national treasury a significant portion of their personal income to ease the financial crisis in the British government.

Murray (see Note 1477) addressed several thousand labor union leaders and members at a Labor Day celebration in Chicago on September 7. The colorful governor of Oklahoma called for a change in the national administration and urged laborers to vote for those principles that would benefit the ordinary citizen.

Borah (see Note 1452), in a speech in Idaho on September 7, condemned extravagant government spending and warned that, if the wealthy did not help feed the poor and unemployed, taxes would be increased to enable the government to provide assistance.

1601   *NYT,* Thursday, September 10, 1931, 27:7.

Mexico received and accepted an invitation to join the League of Nations (see Note 1491) on September 8. Although over the years the United States participated in many League affairs, it never formally joined the international organization.

For the cotton reduction plan see Note 1583.

Wilkins (see Note 1598) returned the *Nautilus* to its home port in Norway on September 8.

1602   *NYT,* Friday, September 11, 1931, 23:7.

Garfield A. "Gar" Wood, American motorboat champion of the 1920s and 1930s. Wood's chief rival, British racer Kaye Don, was disqualified from the Harmsworth Trophy championship in Detroit on September 7 when he crossed the starting line too early. Wood also was disqualified for the same reason, leaving the only competitor in the race, an associate of Wood's, as the automatic winner. Don accused Wood of intentionally having lured him across the starting line, causing the disqualifications.

1603   *NYT,* Saturday, September 12, 1931, 19:7.

Income taxes in Great Britain were raised to 25 percent and numerous other taxes were increased as the result of emergency action taken by the House of Commons on September 10. British lawmakers also drastically pared government expenditures in a move to reduce the budget deficit.

For Alfred Emanuel "Al" Smith see Note 1484.

1604   *NYT,* Monday, September 14, 1931, 19:7. Variant: *LAT* gives "one continent" in third sentence.

Walker (see Note 1480) was accorded the prestigious rank of Commander of the Legion of Honor by the French government on September 4 during a visit to Paris.

For American mayors in France see Notes 1507 and 1515; for Paul Ludwig Hans Anton von Beneckendorff und von Hindenburg see Note 1532; for James Ramsay MacDonald see Note 1532; for Benito Mussolini see Note 1452.

1605   *NYT,* Tuesday, September 15, 1931, 27:7.

McPherson (see Note 1501) married David Hutton, a singer and a member of her Angelus Temple, in Arizona on September 13. She recently had written a sacred opera, *The Iron Furnace,* that depicted the flight of Moses and the Israelites from Egypt.

For Minnie Pearce "Ma" Kennedy see Note 1557.

La Fiesta de Los Angeles, held from September 4 to 13, celebrated the sesquincentennial anniversary of the founding of the city by Spanish colonizers.

1606 *NYT,* Wednesday, September 16, 1931, 25:7. Variant: *NYT* gives "old she-goat goes" in fourth sentence.

Gandhi (see Note 1448) arrived in London on September 12 to confer with British officials about the constitutional status of India.

1607 *NYT,* Thursday, September 17, 1931, 27:7. Variant: *NYT* omits sixth sentence.

Walker (see Note 1480), in Europe on vacation, had accepted Gandhi's invitation to visit him at a settlement project in London on September 15. When the moment came, however, the New York City mayor elected to tour London night spots rather than meet the Indian leader.

Hoover announced on September 15 that a conference of representatives from every state would meet in Washington, D. C., in December to discuss and study all aspects of homeowning, including finance, design, construction, and availability.

Aimee Semple McPherson's new husband, David Hutton (see Note 1605), was sued two days after his marriage by a woman who claimed that he had broken his promise to marry her. McPherson's mother, Minnie Kennedy (see Note 1557), had married G. Edward "Whataman" Hudson on June 28, 1931, but had the marriage annulled the next month because of bigamy charges against Hudson.

1608 *NYT,* Friday, September 18, 1931, 25:7. Variant: *NYT* gives "Huey Long" in fourth sentence.

For the Texas-Oklahoma bridge dispute see Note 1564.

Long (see Note 1583), angered by opposition in the Texas legislature to his cotton reduction plan, charged on September 15 that the legislators had been bribed to obstruct the proposal. The indignant solons responded by passing a resolution condemning Long as a liar.

1609 *NYT,* Saturday, September 19, 1931, 19:7. Variant: *NYT* gives "Washington had" in fourth sentence.

For Mohandas Karamchand Ghandhi see Notes 1448 and 1606.

Harry Bartow Hawes, Democratic United States senator from Missouri from 1927 to 1933. Hawes, long an advocate of independence for the American-owned Philippine Islands, coauthored the Hawes-Cutting bill in 1930 which called for independence five years after acceptance of a Philippine constitution. Hawes visited the islands in July of 1931 and assured the inhabitants that he would continue to work for independence. The United States granted independence in 1946.

Hurley (see Note 1481) toured the Philippines from September 1-26 to investigate popular support and conditions for independence. Upon his return to the United States, he stated that the people were unprepared for freedom.

1610 *NYT,* Monday, September 21, 1931, 19:7.

Japan and Russia both maintained commercial interests in northern China. Japanese military activity in the region in the 1920s and 1930s caused considerable apprehension among the Russians, especially after Japanese troops seized the important Manchurian city of Mukden on September 19, 1931. Japanese and Chinese troops clashed repeatedly during the next several months in a bitter struggle for control. The Japanese army completed the occupation of Manchuria in February of 1932 and, soon thereafter, proclaimed the puppet state of Manchukuo.

For the League of Nations see Note 1491.

Manual Andrada, Argentine polo player of the 1920s and 1930s who was considered one of the best of his day at "back." Although injured, team captain Andrada led the national team of Argentina to the United States Open polo title on September 19 by defeating an American team, 11 to 8.

1611 *NYT,* Tuesday, September 22, 1931, 29:7. Variant: *NYT* gives "time for" in seventh sentence.

The British government suspended the gold standard on September 21 in an attempt to stabilize the monetary system. The Bank of England, the central depository and issuing facility of the government, had experienced heavy withdrawals of gold by foreign investors who feared the economic collapse of the nation.

For Mohandas Karamchand Gandhi see Note 1448.

1612 *NYT,* Wednesday, September 23, 1931, 25:7.

Hoover addressed the opening session of the annual convention of the American Legion in Detroit on September 21. He told the legionnaires that the federal treasury could not afford additional expenses such as the veterans' bonuses (see Note 1521). The delegates, who were concerned with another issue, interrupted Hoover's speech with chants of "We want beer!"

For war in China see Note 1610; for the English dole see Note 1550; for G. Edward "Whataman" Hudson see Note 1607.

"It," a slang word denoting sex appeal, was popularized in the late 1920s by American movie idol Clara Bow who was billed as the "It Girl."

1613 *NYT,* Thursday, September 24, 1931, 27:7.

Hal E. Roach, American producer of comedy films, including the profitable serials *Lonesome Luke, Our Gang,* and *Laurel and Hardy.*

James B. Dickson, veteran military and private pilot who served in the United States Army Air Service during the 1920s.

Rogers was visiting his youngest son Jimmy (see Note 1497), a student at New Mexico Military Institute in Roswell, while on his way to Oklahoma.

1614 *NYT,* Friday, September 25, 1931, 27:7. Variant: *NYT* gives "that. Here . . . section are bins" in second and third sentences.

Oil wells in Oklahoma had been shut down by Governor Murray in August (see Note 1571).

Venezuela was the major exporter of oil to the United States. Leaders of the American petroleum industry had called for a reduction of such imported oil in light of a surplus domestic production.

1615 *NYT,* Saturday, September 26, 1931, 21:7.

Murray (see Note 1477) was in St. Louis in late September to head a conference on unemployment relief in the Mississippi Valley region. The Oklahoma governor was in Little Rock on September 26 on the last leg of a four-state speaking tour to stimulate support for his candidacy for the Democratic presidential nomination in 1932.

For James John "Jimmy" Walker see Notes 1480 and 1604.

1616 *NYT,* Monday, September 28, 1931, 21:9.

The citizens of Claremore hosted a sports festival in honor of Rogers on September 26. Activities included an air circus, a polo match, a football game, and dances.

1617 *NYT,* Tuesday, September 29, 1931, 27:7. Variant: *LAT* gives "BEVERLY HILLS" as place of origin.

The decision by Great Britain to abandon the gold standard (see Note 1611) led several other countries with close financial ties to England to follow suit.

John Jacob Astor, German-born American capitalist who accumulated a vast fortune from the fur trade in the United States during the early nineteenth century.

William Jennings Bryan, American statesman and orator who ran unsuccessfully as the Democratic nominee for president in 1896, 1900, and 1908. Bryan campaigned on a platform of free and unlimited coinage of silver in 1896. He lost decisively in the election to William McKinley, a staunch supporter of the gold standard.

1618 *NYT,* Wednesday, September 30, 1931, 27:7.

Republican party leaders had sought the assistance of the administration to cut expenses in government in order to forestall a threat by some congressmen to enact higher taxes. In late September of 1931, Treasury Department officials were studying several such expense-cutting plans.

Taxes on incomes, excess profits, corporations, and luxury items were increased dramatically in the United States during World War I to provide revenue for the war effort.

1619 *NYT,* Thursday, October 1, 1931, 27:7. Variants: *NYT* gives "In addition to . . . now yesterday's" and *LAT* gives "In addition to . . . W.C.T.U.'s) yesterday's" in second and third sentences.

The Women's Christian Temperance Union, an international organization which was founded in the United States in 1874 and which sought through education and legislation to prevent the use of alcohol and other dangerous and harmful drugs.

1620 *NYT,* Friday, October 2, 1931, 25:7.

1621 *NYT,* Saturday, October 3, 1931, 19:7. Variant: *NYT* gives "entirely in that way. It" in third and fourth sentences.

For Hoover's moratorium on debts see Note 1532.

1622 *NYT,* Monday, October 5, 1931, 21:7. Variant: *LAT* gives "Say it all too, why us and France will have to take our gold and fill our teeth with it." for the first sentence.

For Plutarco Elías Calles see Note 1562.

1623 *NYT,* Tuesday, October 6, 1931, 27:7.

William Randolph Hearst, American journalist, publisher, and political figure who during a turbulent sixty-year career in journalism fashioned a nationwide newspaper empire based in California. The Hearst-owned Babicora Ranch, headquartered 160 miles south of El Paso, embraced more than 900,000 acres of northern Mexico.

Coolidge, in an article in the October 3 issue of *Saturday Evening Post*, denied rumors that he was a candidate for the presidential nomination in 1932.

1624 *NYT*, Wednesday, October 7, 1931, 25:7. Variant: *NYT* gives "came in" in first sentence.

Morrow (see Note 1467) died from a cerebral hemorrhage at his home in Englewood, New Jersey, on October 5.

The Mexico Northwestern Railway Company was incorporated in 1909 to provide commercial rail transportation in the northern Mexican province of Chihuahua. Civil disturbances in the area frequently caused damage to company facilities, leading to severe financial losses for the railroad.

1625 *NYT*, Thursday, October 8, 1931, 25:7.

The World Series of 1931 began on October 1 and matched the Philadelphia Athletics of the American League against the St. Louis Cardinals of the National League. The Cardinals won the fall baseball classic, four games to three.

For Alphonse "Scarface Al" Capone see Note 1500.

The average price of securities on the New York Stock Exchange rose sharply on October 6 following reports that Hoover and leading bankers were working together to effect an economic recovery.

Hoover was unable to attend Morrow's funeral (see Note 1624) because of several important conferences that could not be postponed. From such meetings came plans for the National Credit Association (see Note 1627).

1626 *NYT*, Friday, October 9, 1931, 23:7.

Johnny Leonard Roosevelt "Pepper" Martin, Oklahoman who played center field for the St. Louis Cardinals from 1928 to 1944. Martin's aggressive play helped the Cardinals defeat the favored Philadelphia Athletics in the World Series of 1931 (see Note 1625). Martin had twelve hits in twenty-four times at bat and stole five bases in the first five games.

For William Edgar Borah see Note 1452; for Aimee Semple McPherson see Note 1501; for Alphonse "Scarface Al" Capone see Note 1500; for Mohandas Karamchand Gandhi see Note 1448; for William Henry "Alfalfa Bill" Murray see Note 1477.

1627 *NYT*, Saturday, October 10, 1931, 19:7.

Martin (see Note 1626) failed to hit safely in four times at bat in the sixth game of the World Series on October 9. The Philadelphia Athletics defeated Martin's St. Louis Cardinals, 8 to 1, and tied the series at three games apiece.

Hoover proposed on October 7 the formation of the National Credit Association, a corporation of private bankers that would establish a $500 million reservoir to stimulate the flow of money in the United States.

1628 *NYT*, Monday, October 12, 1931, 21:7.

For the National Credit Association see Note 1627.

1629 *NYT*, Tuesday, October 13, 1931, 21:7.

Several United States senators suggested on October 10 that disarmament should be a prerequisite for extending the moratorium on intergovernmental debts (see Note 1532). Because some European nations had sought to scale down wartime debts owed to the United States, the senators maintained that there should be a corresponding reduction of armament budgets in those countries.

For the English dole see Note 1550.

1630 *NYT,* Wednesday, October 14, 1931, 23:7.

For war in China see Note 1610; for the League of Nations see Note 1491.

1631 *NYT,* Thursday, October 15, 1931, 23:7. Variant: *NYT* gives "We got just as used" in fourth sentence.

Silk underwear, diamond belt buckles, and expensive automobiles were among items mentioned by prosecution witnesses on October 12 during Capone's trial for income tax evasion (see Notes 1530 and 1567). The unusual testimony was part of an attempt by the government to show the ostentatious and lavish lifestyle of the Chicago gangster.

1632 *NYT,* Friday, October 16, 1931, 23:7.

Elizabeth Cutter Morrow, educator, author, and widow of Dwight Whitney Morrow (see Notes 1467 and 1624). Although Mrs. Morrow was mentioned frequently as a possible successor to her husband in the Senate, she denied all such rumors.

1633 *NYT,* Saturday, October 17, 1931, 17:7. Variants: *NYT* omits first sentence.

The entire cabinet of President Pascual Ortiz Rubio resigned on October 15 during a major shake-up in the Mexican government. A new cabinet was named six days later.

Four convicted murderers died in the electric chair at the Cook County jail in Chicago on October 16.

Harvard University administrators pressured a group of students to withdraw their invitation to McPherson to speak at the school. The students, however, met with the California evangelist at a hotel in Boston.

The League of Nations Council (see Note 1491) voted thirteen to one on October 15 to invite the United States to participate in deliberations concerning the Japanese takeover of Manchuria. The Japanese representative cast the lone dissenting ballot.

1634 *NYT,* Monday, October 19, 1931, 3:3. Variant: *LAT* gives "counts: silk" in first sentence.

Capone was found guilty on October 17 on five counts of evasion of federal income taxes. He was sentenced to eleven years in prison and fined $70,000. He served eight years and then retired to his Florida estate where he died in 1947.

For Andrew William Mellon see Note 1493.

1635 *LAT,* Tuesday, October 20, 1931, I:1:6. *NYT* did not print the DT.

Thomas Alva Edison, productive American inventor who was responsible for practical applications of electricity, including the first commercially successful incandescent lamp and the phonograph. Edison, who had grown increasingly deaf since childhood, died on October 18 at the age of eighty-five.

Florenz "Flo" Ziegfeld, Jr., American theatrical producer best known for the elaborately-staged *Ziegfeld Follies*. First produced in 1907, these musical revues featured a troupe of beautiful chorus girls and many of the leading stage performers of the day. Rogers performed in the *Follies* from 1916 to 1925.

For Owen D. Young see Note 1538.

Henry Ford, American automobile innovator and manufacturer. An admirer and friend of Edison, Ford held a celebration at Dearborn, Michigan, on October 21, 1929, to commemorate the fiftieth anniversary of Edison's incandescent lamp and the formal dedication of the Edison School of Technology, founded by Ford. The auto pioneer also transplanted to Dearborn Edison's laboratory at Menlo Park, New Jersey, in which much of the inventor's work had taken place.

1636 *NYT*, Wednesday, October 21, 1931, 21:7.

Charles Cornwallis, British statesman and general who was forced to surrender his troops to a combined American and French army at Yorktown, Virginia, in 1781, effectively ending the American Revolutionary War. On October 19, 1931, representatives of the thirteen original colonies joined other dignitaries to celebrate the sesquicentennial anniversary of the battle.

For Andrew William Mellon see Note 1493; for the Philippines see Note 1609.

1637 *NYT*, Thursday, October 22, 1931, 23:7. Variants: *LAT* gives "BEVERLY HILLS" as place of origin/*NYT* omits third sentence/*NYT* gives "wires, among them Mr. Gifford," in fourth and fifth sentences/*NYT* gives "father." to end seventh sentence, omitting last four words.

Rogers participated in a nationwide radio broadcast on October 18 as part of a national drive for unemployment relief.

For Walter Sherman Gifford see Note 1584; for Owen D. Young see Note 1538.

Edsel Bryant Ford, son of automobile pioneer Henry Ford (see Note 1635) and president of Ford Motor Company from 1919 until his death in 1943.

Hurley (see Notes 1481 and 1609) visited at the Rogers home on October 21 upon his return from the Philippine Islands.

1638 *NYT*, Friday, October 23, 1931, 23:7.

For the Philippine Islands see Note 1609; for war in China see Note 1610; for the Russian five-year-plan see Note 1583.

1639 *NYT*, Saturday, October 24, 1931, 19:7.

Shaw (see Note 1454), in an address to the World Prohibition Federation in London on October 22, asserted that prohibition had succeeded in the United States. He also stated that the growth of criminal elements in America since the advent of prohibition only revealed the necessity for more effective laws and enforcement procedures.

For Nancy Langhorne Astor see Note 1560; for Thomas Alva Edison see Note 1635; for Arthur Brisbane see Note 1442.

1640 *NYT*, Monday, October 26, 1931, 19:7. Variant: *LAT* gives "BEVERLY HILLS" as place of origin.

Pierre Laval, premier and minister of foreign affairs of France from 1931 to 1932. Laval arrived in Washington, D. C., on October 22 to discuss with

Hoover war debts, national security, and the flow of gold. The talks ended on October 25, and Laval departed for France two days later.

Borah, chairman of the Senate Committee on Foreign Affairs (see Note 1452), talked with Laval on October 24 about the two men's differing views on international issues, including reparations and war debts.

1641   *NYT*, Tuesday, October 27, 1931, 25:7.

Smith (see Note 1484) vigorously opposed as unnecessary a proposed constitutional amendment in New York which called for state financing of reforestation. The amendment, supported by Governor Roosevelt (see Note 1529), was approved by voters on November 3, 1931.

For Pierre Laval see Note 1640.

1642   *NYT*, Wednesday, October 28, 1931, 26:7. Variant: *LAT* gives "build battleships," in third sentence.

Navy Day, first celebrated in 1922, commemorated the anniversary (1775) of the first naval bill to be introduced in the Continental Congress.

For the financial crisis in Great Britain see Notes 1587 and 1611.

1643   *NYT*, Thursday, October 29, 1931, 23:7.

Charles Leo O'Donnell, American priest and educator who served as president of Notre Dame University from 1928 until his death in 1934.

Heartley W. "Hunk" Anderson, football coach at Notre Dame University from 1931 to 1933. A former player and assistant coach under Rockne (see Note 1462), Anderson succeeded Rockne as coach in April of 1931 and went on to compile a three-season record of sixteen wins, nine losses, and two ties.

Elections in Great Britain on October 28 gave the Conservative party an overwhelming majority in Parliament and crushed the power of the Labour party opposition to the coalition government.

1644   *NYT*, Friday, October 30, 1931, 23:7.

William Vann "Bill" Rogers, Will's eldest son, graduated from Stanford University in Palo Alto, California, in 1935.

For James Blake "Jimmy" Rogers see Notes 1497 and 1631.

1645   *NYT*, Saturday, October 31, 1931, 19:7. Variant: *NYT* gives "Few changes" in fourth sentence.

For Hal E. Roach see Note 1613.

Eric Pedley, California stock broker and internationally-acclaimed polo player of the 1920s and 1930s. Rogers and Pedley often played polo together.

For James B. Dickson see Note 1613.

Rogers and the others flew to Mexico City to make arrangements for a Mexican polo team to tour California in December of 1931.

For Plutarco Elías Calles see Note 1562; for Dwight Whitney Morrow see Note 1467.

1646   *NYT*, Monday, November 2, 1931, 19:7.

1647 *NYT,* Tuesday, November 3, 1931, 25:7. Variants: *NYT* gives "Tulsa football Saturday," in fourth sentence/*NYT* gives "Mexican studios . . . movies, too." in fifth sentence.

For Dwight Whitney Morrow see Note 1467; for Joshua Reuben Clark, Jr., see Note 1467.

The National University of Mexico football team was defeated, 89 to 0, by the University of Tulsa in an international game in Mexico City on November 7.

The Mexico City Aztecas baseball team and a minor league team from Memphis, Tennessee, competed in a nine-game series in Mexico City in late October and early November of 1931. The Aztecas took the series, five games to four.

A polo team from the Mexican army played three matches in Los Angeles in December against local teams led by Eric Pedley (see Note 1645). The Mexicans won the series, two matches to one.

A Mexican government decree in July which placed high duties on imported motion pictures caused the cost of foreign-made films to rise to prohibitive levels.

1648 *NYT,* Wednesday, November 4, 1931, 21:7.

Hoover appointed a five-man committee on November 2 to examine complaints that his naval policies had stifled naval development. The commission issued a report five days later which upheld the president's actions and rejected critics' charges.

1649 *NYT,* Thursday, November 5, 1931, 25:7.

Democrats won three of five special congressional elections held on November 3, insuring the party that it would hold 217 of 435 seats in the next Congress. The Democratic plurality enabled Garner (see Note 1471) to be elected Speaker of the House.

For Nicholas Longworth see Note 1471.

1650 *NYT,* Friday, November 6, 1931, 23:7. Variant: *NYT* gives "branding fire" in second sentence.

The King Ranch in southern Texas was founded in 1852 by cattleman Richard King. Embracing more than 1,000,000 acres spread over five counties, the ranch raised enormous quantities of livestock and originated the Santa Gertrudis breed of cattle.

Robert Justus Kleberg, manager and controller of the King Ranch from 1885 to 1927. He married Richard King's daughter, Alice Gertrudis King, in 1886. The couple had three girls and two boys.

Jack H. Lapham, wealthy Texas rancher, oil executive, sportsman, and private pilot. Lapham was married to the former Lucy Jane Thomas; they had four children—David, John, Julie, and Jean.

For Francis Monroe "Frank" Hawks see Note 1464.

1651 *NYT,* Saturday, November 7, 1931, 19:7. Variant: *NYT* gives "any other man" in second sentence.

For the King Ranch see Note 1650; for John Nance Garner see Notes 1471 and 1649; for Nicholas Longworth see Note 1471.

1652 *NYT,* Monday, November 9, 1931, 19:7. Variant: *NYT* gives "of humor" in eighth sentence.

For Hoover's naval commission see Note 1648.

William Howard Gardiner, president of the Navy League of the United States from 1928 to 1933 and a life-long advocate of a strong American navy. Although Gardiner and the Navy League had criticized Hoover's naval policies (see Note 1648), the executive council of the league voted seven to one to endorse the report of the naval commission.

Thaddeus Horatius Caraway, Democratic United States senator from Arkansas from 1921 until his death from a heart ailment on November 6, 1931. He was noted as one of the most outspoken and partisan members of the Senate.

"Felix the Cat," cartoon character which first appeared about 1921 and became one of the earliest cinematic cartoon animal stars. Felix was noted especially for strolling casually through danger with his "hands" behind his back.

1653 *NYT*, Tuesday, November 10, 1931, 25:7. Variant: *LAT* gives "BEVERLY HILLS" as place of origin.

1654 *NYT*, Wednesday, November 11, 1931, 23:7.

For war in China see Note 1610.

1655 McNaught Syndicate; heading from *Tulsa Daily World,* Thursday, November 12, 1931, I:1:5. *NYT* and *LAT* did not print the DT.

The American Newspaper Publishers' Association began its seventh annual fall meeting in Los Angeles on November 11.

1656 *NYT*, Friday, November 13, 1931, 23:7.

Bernard Mannes Baruch, American multi-millionaire financier and an advisor to the federal government on economic matters. A Democrat, Baruch served as chairman of the War Industries Board which coordinated industrial production during World War I. In a speech to a reunion of members of the board on November 11, Baruch predicted that the United States was emerging from economic depression and offered several suggestions to speed recovery.

1657 *NYT*, Saturday, November 14, 1931, 19:7. Variant: *LAT* gives "Somebody invited" in first sentence.

Curtis (see Note 1538) was a guest speaker at the convention of the American Newspaper Publishers' Association (see Note 1655). While in California the vice president visited with many local government officials and with leaders of the motion picture industry.

1658 *NYT*, Monday, November 16, 1931, 21:7. Variant: *LAT* gives "in tomorrow." to end third sentence.

Tsang Hsih-yi, a former general in the Chinese army, was released from detention in November and then given the governorship of Mukden province of Manchuria on December 15 as part of a Japanese effort to provide a stable Chinese government in Japanese-controlled areas.

For Alphonse "Scarface Al" Capone see Note 1500.

Dino Grandi, foreign minister of Italy from 1929 to 1932. Grandi arrived in New York City on November 16 to begin talks with Hoover and Secretary of State Stimson about intergovernmental debts and disarmament and with American bankers about economic problems. Grandi left the United States to return to Italy on November 27.

For Mohandas Karamchand Gandhi see Note 1448.

1659 *NYT*, Tuesday, November 17, 1931, 27:7.

Movie theaters throughout the United States sponsored benefits during National Motion Picture Week, November 18-25, to raise funds for unemployment relief.

Hoover announced on November 13 a plan to establish under government control a series of discount banks for home mortgages that would help revive the stagnant construction industry in the United States. Hoover recommended the legislation to Congress on December 8, 1931, and it was enacted into law as the Federal Home Loan Bank Act on July 22, 1932.

1660 *NYT*, Wednesday, November 18, 1931, 25:7. Variant: *NYT* gives "out for this fellow Grandi. I" in third and fourth sentences.

Grandi (see Note 1658) and Laval (see Note 1640) represented their respective countries at the London Five Power Naval Conference in early 1930. Italy and France, however, refused to agree about limitations on major warships and left the conference without reconciling their differences. Rogers spent two weeks at the international meeting as an interested observer.

1661 *NYT*, Thursday, November 19, 1931, 25:7.

For war in China see Note 1610; for Dino Grandi see Note 1658.

The Prince of Wales (see Note 1499), in a radio speech on November 15, urged his fellow countrymen to purchase only products manufactured in Great Britain or in one of its colonies rather than goods produced in foreign countries. His speech was part of a "Buy British" campaign designed to reduce unemployment by boosting home production.

United States congressmen visited Canada in mid-November to study the Canadian sales tax system and to determine if a similar plan could be implemented at home.

A man hospitalized in Ohio with incessant hiccupping received numerous suggested cures from doctors and sympathizers throughout the nation. The proposed remedies included standing on his head, eating a quart of ice cream, and putting a coin between his toes.

For the League of Nations see Note 1491; for James John "Jimmy" Walker see Note 1480.

1662 *NYT*, Friday, November 20, 1931, 25:7. Variants: *LAT* omits second sentence/*LAT* gives "airplane pilot" in sixth sentence.

Richard Mifflin Kleberg, son of Robert Justus Kleberg (see Note 1650), was elected as a Democrat on November 24 to represent the Fourteenth Congressional District of Texas, filling a vacancy created by the death of Republican Representative Harry McLeary Wurzbach. The victory clinched a majority for the Democratic party in the House of Representatives and insured the election of Garner (see Note 1471) as Speaker. Kleberg served in Congress from 1931 to 1945.

1663 *NYT*, Saturday, November 21, 1931, 19:7.

League of Nations officials announced on November 20 that Japan and China apparently had agreed to a cessation of hostilities and to an international inquiry in Manchuria. Both belligerents, however, rejected the peace proposal shortly after it was announced. The League continued plans for a committee of inquiry to settle the dispute.

Rogers was enroute to the Orient to observe and to report on the situation in Manchuria.

1664 *NYT*, Monday, November 23, 1931, 21:7.

Vladimir Ilych Ulyanov (Lenin), Russian revolutionary who led a Bolshevik uprising in 1917 which overthrew the government in Russia and established Communist rule. He remained in control of the Soviet government until his death in 1924.

Raphael Floyd Phillips Gibbons, American journalist, author, and radio commentator who as an internationally known roving reporter was recognized as the "premier war correspondent of his generation."

Joseph Pilsudski, Polish general and politician who led the fight for Polish independence in the early twentieth century. He established himself as dictator in 1926 and remained in control of the Polish government until his death in 1935.

1665 *NYT*, Tuesday, November 24, 1931, 27:7. Variants: *NYT* gives "man, don't get around much." to end first sentence/*NYT* gives "ones on board." to end second sentence/*NYT* gives "I found" to begin third sentence, omitting first seven words.

For Raphael Floyd Phillips Gibbons see Note 1664.

Notre Dame University suffered its first loss of the football season on November 21. The University of Southern California defeated the Fighting Irish, 16 to 14.

1666 *NYT*, Wednesday, November 25, 1931, 23:7. Variant: *NYT* omits sixth sentence.

Fan-tan, a Chinese gambling game in which a number of objects are placed under a bowl and wagers are made as to what the remainder will be after the objects are divided by fours.

Clara Bow (see Note 1502) had received recent publicity about her fondness for gambling.

Henri Le Baily de la Falaise de la Coudraye, French marquis and sometime actor, married American motion picture actress Constance Bennett on November 27. Coudraye had been divorced recently from Bennett's chief rival in Hollywood, Gloria Swanson.

Tilson (see Note 1546) was considered the leading Republican candidate for the Speakership of the House if the Republican party retained a majority after several special congressional elections (see Note 1649). For the election in Texas see Note 1662; for John Nance Garner see Note 1471.

1667 *NYT*, Thursday, November 26, 1931, 29:7. Variant: *LAT* gives "Saturday. Maybe we come" in seventh and eighth sentences.

For George Woodward Wickersham see Note 1517.

LAT printed the following for Friday, November 27, 1931:

"Will Rogers 'A.W.O.L.' Owing, apparently, to failure to make contact in midocean with the ship bearing Will Rogers to China, Mr. Rogers's daily remarks are omitted from The Times this morning. It is hoped that the Sage of Santa Monica will be able to re-establish relations with Times readers promptly."

1668 *NYT*, Saturday, November 28, 1931, 19:7. Variant: *NYT* omits sixth sentence.

For Raphael Floyd Phillips Gibbons see Note 1664.

1669 *NYT*, Monday, November 29, 1931, 21:7.

Thomas Joseph Mooney, American labor agitator who was convicted as a participant in the bomb killings of nine persons during a San Francisco parade in 1916 and sentenced to death. His case aroused international interest because of the widely held belief that he was innocent. In 1918 his sentence was commuted to life imprisonment. Twenty-one years later he was granted an unconditional pardon and was released.

Walker (see Note 1480)) left New York City on November 20 for California where he intended to plead with Governor James Rolph, Jr., for Mooney's release. Walker visited Mooney at San Quentin Prison and then presented his case to Rolph, stressing alleged perjury in the original trial. The governor, however, refused to grant Mooney a pardon.

1670 *NYT,* Tuesday, December 1, 1931, 27:7. *LAT* did not print the DT but printed the following: "WILL ROGERS REMARKS: Will Rogers's daily wireless message from aboard the steamship Empress of Russia failed to reach The Times last night."

For Raphael Floyd Phillips Gibbons see Note 1664.

1671 *NYT,* Wednesday, December 2, 1931, 25:7. Variants: *NYT* gives "an Esquimox, . . . the Esquimox" in third sentence/*NYT* gives "Tom Mix" in fourth sentence/*NYT* gives "change my trip into" in seventh sentence.

Thomas Edwin "Tom" Mix, American cowboy motion picture star who was one of the greatest box-office attractions in the history of the screen. Mix was hospitalized in late 1931 for treatment of inflammation resulting from a ruptured appendix.

Zachary Mulhall, Oklahoma rancher and showman whose Mulhall Wild West Show debuted in 1904 at the Louisiana Purchase Exposition in St. Louis. On April 23, 1905, Rogers made his New York City premiere with the Mulhall performers, a troupe of ropers and riders that included Tom Mix.

Charles Gates Dawes, United States ambassador to Great Britain from 1929 to 1932. Dawes, who served as vice president under Coolidge, conferred with the Council of the League of Nations in November regarding the Sino-Japanese conflict in Manchuria.

1672 *NYT,* Thursday, December 3, 1931, 27:7.

1673 *NYT,* Friday, December 4, 1931, 23:7.

1674 *NYT,* Saturday, December 5, 1931, 19:7.

For Raphael Floyd Phillips Gibbons see Note 1664; for the *Ziegfeld Follies* see Note 1635.

The Washington Conference of 1921-1922 produced several treaties limiting tonnage of major war vessels, outlawing the use of poison gas, and establishing rules for naval warfare. Conferees included representatives from the United States, Great Britain, France, Japan, and Italy.

1675 *NYT,* Monday, December 7, 1932, 19:7. Variant: *LAT* gives "the deck away" in second sentence.

1676 *NYT,* Tuesday, December 8, 1931, 29:7.

1677 *NYT,* Wednesday, December 9, 1931, 25:7.

For Raphael Floyd Phillips Gibbons see Note 1664.

Chinchow, in southwestern Manchuria, served as the temporary headquarters of Chinese troops in Manchuria. In early December of 1931, the Japanese army was preparing to push from Mukden to Chinchow in an effort to eliminate opposition in the area. The defenders of Chinchow evacuated the city to the Japanese on December 30.

1678 *NYT,* Thursday, December 10, 1931, 23:7. Variants: *LAT* gives "KEIJO" and *NYT* gives "KAIJO (Seoul)," as place of origin.

Eugenia Maria de Montijo de Guzman, Spanish-born empress of France from 1853 to 1870 and wife of Emperor Louis Napoleon. Her selections of dress dictated fashion to those who followed the lead of French design in feminine wear.

1679 *NYT,* Friday, December 11, 1931, 27:7. Variant: *LAT* gives "Japanese are flying" in second sentence.

For Raphael Floyd Phillips Gibbons see Note 1664.

The Russo-Japanese War of 1904-1905 grew out of the rival imperialistic designs of Russia and Japan on Korea and Manchuria. In February of 1904, the Japanese launched a surprise attack on Russian-held Port Arthur. After several Japanese victories, the war ended in September of 1905 with the signing of the Treaty of Portsmouth. The surprising success of Japan brought that country recognition as a world power and was one of the causes of unrest in Russia that led to the Revolution of 1905.

1680 *NYT,* Saturday, December 12, 1931, 19:7.

For Mukden, China, see Note 1610.

Garner (see Notes 1471 and 1649) was elected Speaker of the House on December 7. This marked the first time since 1919 that a Democrat had held the Speakership.

1681 *NYT,* Monday, December 14, 1931, 19:7. Variant: *NYT* gives "MUKDEN, Japan." as place of origin.

Harbin, Manchuria, provided a refuge for thousands of White Russians who had opposed the Bolsheviks in the Russian Revolution of 1917. Most of the Russians left the city following the rise to power of the Chinese Communists in the 1940s.

1682 *NYT,* Tuesday, December 15, 1931, 27:7.

Kolenskies are buff-colored Asian minks.

Daniel Boone, American frontiersman and Indian fighter who led the westward movement into Kentucky during the late eighteenth century.

Abie's Irish Rose, a sentimental American comedy which concerned the romance between a Jewish youth and an Irish lass. Written by Ann Nichols and first produced in 1922, the play ran in New York City for a record 2,327 performances.

1683 *NYT,* Wednesday, December 16, 1931, 25:7.

The League of Nations announced the appointment of an international commission on December 10 to study the crisis in Manchuria. The commissioners spent six weeks in the Far East and later issued the Lytton Report which provided an historical background of the conflict and which offered recommendations for a peaceful settlement.

Ma Chan-shan, Chinese general who led military opposition to the Japanese presence in Manchuria and who served as governor of Hejlungkiang province in northern Manchuria.

1684   *NYT,* Thursday, December 17, 1931, 23:7.

1685   *NYT,* Friday, December 18, 1931, 23:7. Variants: *NYT* gives "railroad, then I found that's" in second sentence/*NYT* gives "am going on a boat." to end third sentence.

Eighty thousand Chinese students, disenchanted with the uncertain policies of the government toward Manchuria, rioted in Nanking on December 10, demanding the removal of top government officials.

For Chinchow, China, see Note 1677.

1686   *NYT,* Saturday, December 19, 1931, 19:7. Variant: *LAT* gives "same anywhere." to end fourth sentence.

In China, Chiang Kai-shek, leader of the Nationalist government at Nanking, had come under public pressure to terminate the war against the Communists in China and to establish a united front against the encroaching Japanese. Chiang refused to cooperate with the Communists and resigned from the government on December 15. His full cabinet resigned a week later.

The entire Japanese cabinet resigned on December 11 as a result of internal political discord and pressure from militarists seeking a more aggressive policy in Manchuria.

1687   *NYT,* Monday, December 21, 1931, 21:7. Variant: *LAT* gives "to see if you are wrong" in eighth sentence.

European editorial criticism of the United States centered on the unwillingness of many American congressmen to reduce or to scale down the intergovernmental debts or to extend the moratorium on payment of debts (see Note 1532).

1688   *NYT,* Tuesday, December 22, 1931, 23:7. Variants: *LAT* gives "PEIPING" as place of origin/*LAT* did not print the first paragraph.

The *Japan Advertiser,* a pro-government, English-language newspaper published in Tokyo.

1689   *NYT,* Wednesday, December 23, 1931, 19:7. Variant: *NYT* gives "all of" in third sentence.

Thomas Riley Marshall, vice president of the United States from 1913 to 1921. Once while presiding over a tiresome debate in the Senate, Marshall coined one of his most famous remarks: "What this country needs is a really good five-cent cigar!"

1690   *NYT,* Thursday, December 24, 1931, 19:7.

1691   *NYT,* Friday, December 25, 1931, 2:2.

For Great Britain and the gold standard see Note 1611.

1692   *NYT,* Saturday, December 26, 1931, 13:7. Variants: *LAT* gives "Chang Hsueh-liang." in first sentence/*NYT* gives "Manchuria and all Manchuria spoke" in second sentence.

Chang Hsueh-liang, Chinese war lord of Manchuria from 1928 until his ouster by the Japanese in 1931.

Mongols, an Asiatic people who in the thirteenth century conquered most of China and eastern Asia and thereafter spread into Russia and Europe. With the decline of their empire in the fourteenth century, the Mongols eventually located along the northern border of China.

1693 *NYT*, Monday, December 28, 1931, 19:7.

1694 *NYT*, Tuesday, December 29, 1931, 21:7.

For Chincow, China, see Note 1677.

1695 *NYT*, Wednesday, December 30, 1931, 19:7. Variant: *NYT* gives "have gobbled it up and" in fifth sentence.

1696 *NYT*, Thursday, December 31, 1931, 4:2.

1697 *NYT*, Friday, January 1, 1932, 19:2.

For Chinchow, China, see Note 1677.

1698 *NYT*, Saturday, January 2, 1932, 13:7. Variant: *NYT* gives "suey that" in sixth and seventh sentence.

Andrew John Volstead, Republican United States representative from Minnesota from 1903 to 1923. Volstead authored the Volstead Act of 1919 which provided for enforcement of prohibition (see Note 1441).

1699 *NYT*, Monday, January 4, 1932, 23:7.

The Chinese government was reconstituted and reorganized in early January of 1932 following the departure of Chiang Kai-shek (see Note 1686). The new cabinet included representatives of several factions of the Kuomintang, or Nationalist party.

1700 *NYT*, Tuesday, January 5, 1932, 27:7.

For the Philippines see Note 1609; for Patrick Jay Hurley see Note 1609.

1701 *NYT*, Wednesday, January 6, 1932, 23:7. Variant: *LAT* gives "here. ... ..." to end DT.

1702 *NYT*, Thursday, January 7, 1932, 25:7.

1703 *NYT*, Friday, January 8, 1932, 23:7. Variant: *NYT* gives "of looking in Liberia" in second sentence.

Ford (see Note 1635) developed a rubber plantation in Brazil during the late 1920s to reduce the dependence of his firm on foreign suppliers of the raw material.

Harvey Samuel Firestone, founder of Firestone Tire and Rubber Company in 1900, serving with company until his death in 1938. When British suppliers restricted rubber production in 1922 in an effort to raise prices, Firestone established rubber plantations in Liberia to provide an American source of rubber for American industry.

1704 *NYT*, Saturday, January 9, 1932, 19:7.

For the gold standard see Notes 1611 and 1617.

1705 *NYT*, Monday, January 11, 1932, 23:7.

Democrats met in Washington, D. C., on January 8 for the annual Jackson Day Dinner, a partisan celebration commemorating Andrew Jackson. Discussion centered on the shortcomings of the Hoover administration and on speculation about possible Democratic candidates in 1932, including Smith (see Note 1484) and Roosevelt (see Note 1529).

1706 *NYT*, Wednesday, January 13, 1932, 25:7. Variant: *NYT* gives "the Stimson" in third sentence.

British officials in India jailed Gandhi and several hundred other nationalists following civil disobedience demonstrations in early January.

Stimson (see Note 1485) had sought a formal apology from Japan for an incident in Harbin, Manchuria, on January 3 in which three Japanese men assaulted the United States consul. Japan issued an apology on January 11 and assured the United States that the offenders would be punished.

1707 *NYT*, Thursday, January 14, 1932, 23:7. Variant: *NYT* gives "Made a 1,200-mile flight" in first sentence.

Riza Shah Pahlavi, shah of Iran from 1926 until his abdication in 1941.

1708 *NYT*, Friday, January 15, 1932, 23:7. Variant: *LAT* gives "who is Rubber?" to end fifth sentence.

For James John "Jimmy" Walker see Notes 1480 and 1669; for Thomas Joseph Mooney see Note 1669.

In the Rose Bowl game at Pasadena, California, on January 1, the University of Southern California defeated Tulane University, 21 to 12.

Ely Culbertson, American author, lecturer, and bridge expert. Culbertson defeated fellow games authority Sidney Lenz at contract bridge on January 8 after a marathon 150-rubber match. Culbertson won with a margin of 8,980 points.

1709 *NYT*, Saturday, January 16, 1932, 17:7. Variant: *LAT* gives "Book first. These" in second and third sentences.

1710 *NYT*, Monday, January 18, 1932, 17:7. Variants: *LAT* gives "Jan. 17." in dateline/*NYT* gives "telegraph office here." to end first sentence/*NYT* gives "Flying to Cairo over . . . Land from Bagdad." in seventh sentence/*NYT* adds the following "Editor's Note" to explain the appearance of two DTs with a dateline of January 15: "Mr. Rogers appears to have been unduly optimistic over the telegraph office he finally found in Bagdad. His dispatch filed there Friday, reached New York last night. He arrived in Cairo Friday night and his dispatch from that city was printed in THE TIMES Saturday morning."

1711 *NYT*, Tuesday, January 19, 1932, 21:7. Variants: *NYT* gives "Will take the Holland" and *LAT* gives "Tomorrow from" in third sentence.

Eleutherios Venizelos, statesman who served as premier of Greece six times, including from 1928 to 1932.

1712 *NYT*, Wednesday, January 20, 1932, 19:7.

For Benito Mussolini see Note 1452.

1713 *NYT*, Thursday, January 21, 1932, 21:7.

Napoleon I, emperor of France from 1804 to 1814 and in 1815. Napoleon was born on the Mediterranean island of Corsica in 1769.

1714 *NYT*, Friday, January 22, 1932, 19:7. Variant: *NYT* gives "off entirely" in sixth sentence.

Dawes (see Note 1671) announced on January 8 that he would resign as ambassador to Great Britain and would resume his banking activities in Chicago.

At the Lausanne Conference of 1932 more than 90 percent of the reparations required to be paid under previous plans were canceled.

1715 *NYT*, Saturday, January 23, 1932, 17:7. Variant: *LAT* gives "has absolutely" in second sentence.

Congress passed and Hoover signed on January 22 a bill establishing the Reconstruction Finance Corporation (RFC), a $2 billion government agency organized to lend money to industrial, financial, and agricultural concerns in order to stimulate the economy and to alleviate the depression. The RFC made loans totalling approximately $50 billion during its thirty-five-year existence.

1716 *LAT*, Monday, January 25, 1932, I:1:5. *NYT* did not print the DT.

For William Edgar Borah see Note 1452.

1717 *NYT*, Tuesday, January 26, 1932, 23:7. Variant: *NYT* omits P.S.

A bill which increased the capitalization of Farm Land Banks by $125 million was passed by Congress on January 21. The land banks, established by the Federal Farm Loan Act of 1916, provided loans to farmers for payment of mortgages and other debts, for the purchase of machinery and livestock, and for improvements on farms.

For the Reconstruction Finance Corporation see Note 1715.

J. P. Morgan & Company, international banking house established in 1895 by American financier John Pierpont Morgan. Morgan developed a financial and industrial empire which wielded tremendous influence on American and world economies. His son, John Pierpont Morgan, Jr., assumed control of the firm upon the death of his father in 1913. During World War I, the Morgan firm raised huge sums for the allied nations and during the postwar period floated foreign and domestic securities of more than $6 billion.

1718 *NYT*, Wednesday, January 27, 1932, 21:7. Variant: *LAT* gives "troupe." in fifth sentence.

Members of the American delegation to the Geneva World Disarmament Conference left New York City on January 20 bound for Switzerland. The conference, which met from 1932 to 1937, failed because of disagreements over definitions of categories of war materials, the reluctance of France to agree to any form of military limitation, and the desire of Germany to achieve military equality.

1719 *NYT*, Thursday, January 28, 1932, 21:7.

For Betty Blake Rogers see Note 1494; for Francis Monroe "Frank" Hawks see Note 1464; for the Geneva World Disarmament Conference see Note 1718.

Jesse Holman Jones, Houston financier, builder, and newspaper publisher.

Harvey Crowley Couch, president of Arkansas Power and Light Company from 1913 until his death in 1941. On January 25 Hoover announced the appointment of Jones and Couch, both Democrats, as directors of the newly-created Reconstruction Finance Corporation (see Note 1715). Jones later served as chairman of the RFC (1933 to 1945). Couch served as a director from 1932 to 1934.

1720 *NYT*, Friday, January 29, 1932, 19:7.

Japanese military activity in Manchuria led to a successful boycott throughout China of Japanese-made products. In retaliation, Japan concentrated troops and warships at Shanghai and demanded an end to the anti-Japanese economic campaign. On January 28 Japanese soldiers entered several sections of Shanghai and Japanese planes strafed and bombed the city.

In India British officials arrested more than 600 followers of Gandhi (see Note 1448) on January 26 and dispersed thousands of other nationalists who were demonstrating in support of Gandhi's declaration of India independence.

For the "Buy British" campaign see Note 1661.

1721 *NYT*, Saturday, January 30, 1932, 19:7.

For the Geneva World Disarmament Conference see Note 1718.

Gold worth more than $140 million was shipped to France in early 1932 from a reserve held in the United States by the Bank of France. Other transfers were made to Holland, Belgium, and Switzerland.

1722 *NYT*, Monday, February 1, 1932, 19:7.

Formal notes of protest from the League of Nations and major powers failed to halt the Sino-Japanese conflict. Japanese forces occupied additional areas of Shanghai in late January (see Note 1720).

1723 *NYT*, Tuesday, February 2, 1932, 25:7. Variants: *NYT* gives "mind." to end tenth sentence, omitting last eleven words/*NYT* omits twelfth sentence.

Mary Emma Woolley, president of Mount Holyoke College in Massachusetts from 1901 to 1937. Long active in promoting international peace, Woolley was appointed by Hoover as a delegate to the Geneva World Disarmament Conference (see Note 1718) in response to pressure from women's organizations.

1724 *NYT*, Wednesday, February 3, 1932, 19:7. Variant: *NYT* gives "Some are here" to begin sixth sentence.

For Mary Emma Woolley see Note 1723.

Appropriations for the expenses of the American delegates to the Geneva World Disarmament Conference were decreased from an unlimited amount suggested by Hoover to a figure of $450,000 set by the House of Representatives. A further slash by Congress on January 29 reduced the budget of the delegation by another $150,000.

1725 *NYT*, Thursday, February 4, 1932, 21:7.

The opening on February 2 of the Geneva World Disarmament Conference was delayed one hour when Great Britain convoked the Council of the League of Nations to ask Japan and China to cease hostilities and to submit their dispute to arbitration. Laughter erupted when a Japanese delegate expressed his satisfaction with the firm action of the League in dealing with the Chinese aggressor.

Great Britain and the United States ordered their Asiatic fleets to Shanghai on January 31 to provide protection for British and American citizens and property in the beseiged Chinese city.

1726 *NYT*, Friday, February 5, 1932, 21:7.

For the Geneva World Disarmament Conference see Note 1718; for Mary Emma Woolley see Note 1723.

1727 *NYT*, Saturday, February 6, 1932, 19:7.

Mellon (see Note 1493) was appointed by Hoover on February 3 to succeed Charles Gates Dawes as ambassador to Great Britain (see Note 1714). Mellon served as ambassador from 1932 to 1933.

1728 *NYT*, Monday, February 8, 1932, 19:7.

For gold shipments to France see Note 1721.

Walter Evans Edge, United States ambassador to France from 1929 to 1933. Edge served as United States senator from New Jersey from 1919 until his appointment as ambassador in 1929.

For the League of Nations' Commission on Manchuria see Note 1683.

1729 *NYT*, Tuesday, February 9, 1932, 25:7.

Smith (see Note 1484) announced on February 7 that he would not campaign actively for the presidency in 1932 but would accept the nomination of the Democratic party if it was offered. Smith's announcement ended several months of speculation about his electoral intentions.

Japan rejected significant parts of a peace plan submitted by several major powers on February 2 and continued to demand withdrawal of Chinese troops from Shanghai. At the same time, Japanese troops launched new attacks on Chinese-held sectors of Shanghai.

1730 *NYT*, Wednesday, February 10, 1932, 23:7.

1731 *NYT*, Thursday, February 11, 1932, 23:7.

Borah (see Note 1452) addressed the Senate on February 10 in support of a bill for direct federal aid to the unemployed. Opponents of the measure argued that relief should be the responsibility of state and local governments. In his speech, Borah reminded these critics that while they oppose federal aid to the unemployed they support such federal agencies as the Reconstruction Finance Corporation which loaned public funds to banks and businesses.

For John Nance Garner see Note 1471.

Alice Roosevelt Longworth, daughter of President Theodore Roosevelt, widow of Speaker of the House Nicholas Longworth, and prominent Washington hostess.

Ogden Livingston Mills, undersecretary of the United States Department of the Treasury from 1927 to 1932. On February 10 the Senate confirmed Mills' nomination to replace Andrew W. Mellon as secretary of the treasury. Mills served in that post until March of 1933.

1732 *NYT*, Friday, February 12, 1932, 21:7.

Hoover issued a national plea on February 3 for Americans to stop hoarding money and, instead, to stimulate the economy by returning the money to circulation. He claimed that more than $1 billion had been removed from circulation and that for each $1 hoarded, $10 worth of credit was lost.

1733 *NYT*, Saturday, February 13, 1932, 15:7. Variant: *LAT* gives "November 8, 1932," in third sentence.

1734 *NYT*, Monday, February 15, 1932, 19:7.

For Dwight Whitney and Elizabeth Cutter Morrow see Notes 1467, 1624, and 1632.

Charles Augustus Lindbergh, Jr., son of Charles Augustus and Anne Morrow Lindbergh (see Notes 1464 and 1495), was born on June 22, 1930. The Lindbergh child was the victim of a sensational kidnap-murder crime in 1932 (see Note 1749).

For Betty Blake Rogers see Note 1494.

Ringgold Wilmer "Ring" Lardner, American satirist, journalist, author, and playwright. A former sportswriter and long-time baseball fan, Lardner contributed a series of short stories to the *Saturday Evening Post* in which he portrayed the life of a simple, gullible major league ballplayer as seen through the player's correspondence to his sweetheart. The stories were published in book form in 1933 as *Lose With a Smile*.

Chu Chin Chow, a musical play which was based loosely on the tale of "Ali Baba and the Forty Thieves" and which proved popular in London and New York City during World War I. For Chinchow, China, see Note 1677.

Smith (see Note 1484) was cobuilder and coowner of the Empire State Building in New York City. The 102-story structure, which was opened in 1931, was for many years the tallest building in the world.

1735 *NYT*, Tuesday, February 16, 1932, 21:7. Variant: *NYT* gives "latest and greatest" in first sentence.

Hot-Cha!, a two-act musical comedy produced by Ziegfeld (see Note 1635), which featured his usual lavish display of sets, showgirls, and exotic dances.

For Henry Lewis Stimson see Note 1485; for Shanghai, China, see Note 1720.

Dawes (see Note 1671) served as chairman of the Reconstruction Finance Corporation from 1932 to 1933.

For John Pierpont Morgan, Jr., see Note 1717.

1736 *NYT*, Wednesday, February 17, 1932, 23:7.

For David Sinton Ingalls see Note 1464.

Newton Diehl Baker, American attorney and statesman who served as United States secretary of war from 1916 to 1921.

For John Nance Garner see Note 1471.

1737 *NYT*, Thursday, February 18, 1932, 23:7.

For Henry Ford see Note 1635.

1738 *NYT*, Friday, February 19, 1932, 19:7. Variant: *NYT* gives "I'm surprised . . . hear." in seventh sentence.

The mayor of Chicago threatened to halt city services on February 17 after the Illinois state legislature adjourned without appropriating sufficient funds for the city. Thousands of public employees went unpaid, and the city hall and schools faced closing until the legislature provided the necessary financial relief.

Dempsey (see Note 1572) dropped an unofficial four-round bout to an unheralded heavyweight, King Levinsky, on February 18 in Chicago. A record crowd of more than 23,000 watched the former champion in his first heavyweight fight since his championship title challenge in 1927.

The United States and other major world powers increasingly grew concerned during February about Japanese military aggression in Shanghai (see Note 1720). Foreign diplomats sent sharp notes of protest to the Japanese government, warning of severe international repercussions and hinting that the conflict might involve other nations if the hostilities continued.

1739   *NYT,* Saturday, February 20, 1932, 17:7. Variant: *NYT* gives "full that I'm going to stay here . . . at Claremore." in second sentence.

Pilots for Century Airlines in Chicago found themselves locked out of company hangars when they reported for work on February 9. Company officials refused to arbitrate a wage dispute in which the pilots were asked to accept a 40 percent cut in monthly salary. Twenty-two pilots were handed their "resignations."

For William Henry "Alfalfa Bill" Murray see Note 1477.

1740   *NYT,* Monday, February 22, 1932, 19:7. Variant: *NYT* gives "for my" in second sentence/*NYT* gives "and whack" in fifth sentence/*NYT* gives "A farmer . . . named Haas" in seventh sentence/*NYT* omits eighth sentence.

For the anti-hoarding campaign see Note 1732; for George Woodward Wickersham see Note 1517.

Herbert Thomas McSpadden, second son of Will's sister, Sallie, and John Thomas McSpadden. McSpadden worked at and later managed the Rogers ranch at Oolagah, Oklahoma.

Morris Haas, Claremore dry goods merchant and civic leader.

1741   *NYT,* Tuesday, February 23, 1932, 19:7.

Herbert Prior "Rudy" Vallee, American bandleader, composer, singer, and screen actor; an early crooner who influenced musical trends in the late 1920s and early 1930s.

For William Henry "Alfalfa Bill" Murray see Note 1477.

1742   *NYT,* Wednesday, February 24, 1932, 23:6.

For Shanghai, China, see Note 1720.

1743   *NYT,* Thursday, February 25, 1932, 23:7. Variant: *NYT* gives "asked several" in third sentence.

For Charles Gates Dawes see Notes 1671 and 1735; for Henry Ford see Note 1635: for John Nance Garner see Note 1471; for Newton Diehl Baker see Note 1736; for William Edgar Borah see Note 1452; for Charles Curtis see Note 1538; for Bernard Mannes Baruch see Note 1656.

1744   *NYT,* Friday, February 26, 1932, 21:7. Variants: *NYT* gives "charge of the New" in first sentence, omitting seven words/*LAT* gives "scarce" in first sentence/*NYT* omits "terrible" in second sentence.

Richard Whitney, American stockbroker and financier who served as president of the New York Stock Exchange from 1930 to 1935. Whitney told a House subcommittee on February 24 that proposed federal regulation of short selling of securities would be ineffective and would be detrimental to the securities market and the economy.

1745   *NYT,* Saturday, February 27, 1932, 17:7.

San Simeon, the 230,000-acre Southern California estate of William Randolph Hearst (see Note 1623), featured an imported Spanish castle with lavish furnishings, a private zoo, and extensive recreational facilities.

For Hal E. Roach see Note 1613; for Charles Gates Dawes see Notes 1671 and 1735.

¹⁷⁴⁶ *NYT,* Monday, February 29, 1932, 19:7. Variant: *NYT* gives "Hearst has" in fourth sentence.

For San Simeon see Note 1745; for William Randolph Hearst see Note 1623; for Leavenworth Federal Prison see Note 1530.

Pauline Theresa "Polly" Moran, American vaudeville comedienne and screen actress.

Thornwell Jacobs, American author, minister, and educator. Jacobs founded Oglethorpe University in Atlanta, Georgia, in 1915 and served as its president from 1915 to 1943. Hearst was a major contributor to the school.

Paul Block, American newspaper publisher and advertising executive.

¹⁷⁴⁷ *NYT,* Tuesday, March 1, 1932, 25:7. Variant: *NYT* gives "direct session" in second sentence.

¹⁷⁴⁸ *NYT,* Wednesday, March 2, 1932, 21:7. Variant: *NYT* gives "papers out here" in first sentence.

The refusal of China and Japan to agree to terms of an armistice continued to hamper efforts of foreign powers to end hostilities in Shanghai (see Note 1735). China maintained that Japan had started the conflict and should withdraw its troops. Japan insisted that Chinese forces should destroy their fortifications in Shanghai and should abandon the city. The Japanese began a new offensive against Shanghai on the morning of March 1.

¹⁷⁴⁹ *NYT,* Thursday, March 3, 1932, 8:5-6. Variants: *LAT* gives "nineteen months" in eighteenth sentence/*LAT* gives "him with" in twentieth sentence.

For Dwight Whitney Morrow see Notes 1467 and 1624.

Charles Augustus Lindbergh, Jr., the twenty-month-old son of Charles and Ann Lindbergh (see Notes 1464 and 1495), was kidnapped from his parents' home at Hopewell, New Jersey, on the night of March 1. Young Lindbergh's body was found on May 12, 1932, after a $50,000 ransom had been paid. Outraged public opinion of this and other abductions forced the adoption of the death penalty in federal kidnapping cases.

For Betty Blake Rogers see Note 1494.

¹⁷⁵⁰ *NYT,* Friday, March 4, 1932, 21:7.

For the Lindbergh kidnapping see Note 1749.

¹⁷⁵¹ *NYT,* Saturday, March 5, 1932, 17:7. Variants: *NYT* gives "Met Mrs. Rogers here. She came out" in escond sentence/*NYT* gives "we did today." to end third sentence/*NYT* gives "We asked . . . never heard . . . and he said" in sixth sentence/*NYT* omits "and 'tripe' " in eighth sentence.

For James B. Dickson see Note 1613; for Hal E. Roach see Note 1613; for Betty Blake Rogers see Note 1494; for the Lindbergh kidnapping see Note 1749; for James Blake "Jimmy" Rogers see Note 1613.

¹⁷⁵² *NYT,* Monday, March 7, 1932, 19:7.

Pearl Sydenstricker Buck, American author who lived and taught in China during the 1920s. Her novel, *The Good Earth,* which described peasant life in China, won a Pulitzer Prize in 1931.

¹⁷⁵³ *NYT,* Tuesday, March 8, 1932, 25:7. Variant: *NYT* gives "It Lindbergh" to begin first sentence, omitting first four words.

Lindbergh issued a statement on March 4 in which he promised not to prosecute his son's kidnappers if the baby was returned safely.

1754 *NYT*, Wednesday, March 9, 1932, 23:7. Variant: *NYT* gives "stature, very modest" in first and second sentences.

John Philip Sousa, American musician, composer, and conductor known as the "March King" for his compositions of more than 100 marches. Sousa led the Marine Band at the White House from 1880 to 1892. He formed his own band in 1892 and led it until his death on March 6, 1932.

1755 *NYT*, Thursday, March 10, 1932, 23:7.

For the Geneva World Disarmament Conference see Note 1723; for Charles Gates Dawes see Notes 1671 and 1714.

1756 *LAT*, Friday, March 11, 1932, I:1:2. *NYT* did not print this DT on this date but combined it with that of March 12, 1932, and printed both as one column.

For Rogers' remarks about bankers see DT 1743.

1757 *LAT*, Saturday, March 12, 1932, I:1:2. Variants: *LAT* gives "me, showing" in first and second sentences/*NYT* omits "(that raises Arthur one hour)" in third sentence/*NYT* omits fourth sentence/*NYT* gives "write what he told me and" in fifth sentence/*NYT* omits ninth sentence/*NYT* combined the DTs of March 11 and 12 and printed them as one column on March 12.

Brisbane (see Note 1442) talked with gangster chief Capone (see Note 1634) in jail in Chicago on March 10. Capone told the columnist that he would use his connections in the underworld to help locate the kidnapped Lindbergh child (see Note 1749). He offered to post bond and to conduct the hunt accompanied by a federal agent.

1758 *NYT*, Monday, March 14, 1932, 19:7. Variants: *LAT* gives "BEVERLY HILLS" as place of origin/*NYT* gives "ex-Secretary" and *LAT* gives "former Senator" and *NYT* gives "fine men" in first sentence.

Frank Billings Kellogg, United States secretary of state from 1925 to 1929. Kellogg coauthored the Kellogg-Briand Pact of 1928, an international agreement which renounced war as national policy and called for arbitration of multinational disputes.

Frederick Huntington Gillett, Republican United States senator from Massachusetts from 1925 to 1931.

1759 *NYT*, Tuesday, March 15, 1932, 23:7.

Hindenburg (see Note 1532) appeared certain of reelection to the presidency of Germany when he polled almost one-half of the votes cast in elections on March 13.

Adolph Hitler, German dictator and founder and leader of the National Socialist (Nazi) party in Germany. Hitler's organization steadily gained support after its birth in 1921, basing its appeal on hatred, anti-Semitism, and German world power. The economic depression added to the nationalistic appeal of the Nazis. Hitler garnered the second highest total of votes in the elections of March 13 but lost to Hindenburg in a runoff election on April 10.

1760 *NYT*, Wednesday, March 16, 1932, 23:7.

Prohibitionists in Congress defeated a proposal by wets on March 14 that called for a constitutional amendment to permit state control of liquor traffic.

This marked the first time since passage of the Volstead Act in 1919 that Congress had conducted a vote on the prohibition question.

1761 *NYT,* Thursday, March 17, 1932, 23:7. Variant: *NYT* omits seventh sentence.

John Hays Hammond, American mining engineer who engaged in several successful mining ventures in the United States and abroad from 1879 until his death in 1936. He worked in South Africa from 1893 to 1900.

Frederick Russell Burnham, American explorer and adventurer who traveled extensively in South Africa, South America, and North America. He went to South Africa in 1893 as a mining inspector and, while there, served in the British Army. His *Scouting on Two Continents* was published in 1926.

Rogers worked in South Africa in 1902 and 1903 at various jobs, including performing as a roper and rider in a wild west show.

1762 *NYT,* Friday, March 18, 1932, 23:7.

A group of Democrats in the House met on March 16 to organize opposition to a proposed national sales tax which was part of a tax bill pending in Congress. Advocates of the levy considered it essential in order to balance the federal budget.

1763 *NYT,* Saturday, March 19, 1932, 17:7.

The Geneva World Disarmament Conference (see Note 1723) was scheduled to reconvene on April 11 after a three-week Easter vacation.

Japanese troops began to withdraw from Shanghai on March 17 after Chinese forces, at the insistence of Japan, had moved twelve and one-half miles outside the city. Japanese control of Shanghai was established sufficiently to allow the planned withdrawal of almost one-half of its army.

1764 *NYT,* Monday, March 21, 1932, 17:7.

The House adopted on March 18 an amendment to a revenue bill which would provide a surtax of up to 65 percent on annual incomes of more than $5,000,000. House members also voted to raise to 7 percent the rate on annual incomes of more than $8,000.

1765 *NYT,* Tuesday, March 22, 1932, 23:7. Variant: *LAT* gives "Australia now has the fastest auto and aeroplane, and" in third sentence.

Phar Lap, an Australian thoroughbred, set a new track record in the Agua Caliente Handicap on March 20. It was the first appearance on a North American track for the six-year-old chestnut gelding, and the victory placed him second among money-winning horses in the world.

Percy Williams, an unheralded high school runner from Vancouver, British Columbia, who won both the 100- and 200-yard sprint events at the Olympic Games of 1928.

1766 *NYT,* Wednesday, March 23, 1932, 23:7.

"Block-aid," a welfare plan originated by the Block Community Organization of New York City, was initiated to collect money from residents of each of the 16,000 blocks in the city. Block chairmen requested pledges of between ten cents and one dollar per week for twenty weeks. The money was to be distributed to destitute unemployed persons who could not get financial assistance from regular welfare agencies.

¹⁷⁶⁷ *NYT,* Thursday, March 24, 1932, 23:7.

The House voted on March 22 to increase inheritance tax rates on estates to a maximum of 45 percent. This measure applied only to estates valued at more than $10 million and was part of an effort in Congress to raise revenue to balance the federal budget by conscripting wealth rather than taxing consumers.

For the tax on high incomes see Note 1764.

¹⁷⁶⁸ *NYT,* Friday, March 25, 1932, 19:7.

John Joseph McGraw, manager of the New York Giants baseball team from 1902 to 1932. McGraw led the Giants to ten league and three world championships.

James J. Jeffries, American prizefighter who held the world heavyweight championship from 1899 until his retirement in 1905.

James Forman "Tod" Sloan, American jockey who popularized the forward crouch riding style in the 1890s. Sloan rode in England from 1897 to 1900.

Berna Eli "Barney" Oldfield, pioneer American automobile racer who is credited with being the first person to drive a mile a minute.

John Tortes "Chief" Meyers, full-blood American Indian who starred at catcher for the New York Giants from 1909 to 1915. Meyers hit fourteen home runs during his major league career.

Michael Joseph Donlin, personable major league outfielder who played for several teams from 1899 to 1914, including a usually successful on-again, off-again stint with the New York Giants from 1904 to 1911.

Mabel Hite, American vaudeville singer and comedienne who married Donlin in 1909. After his marriage, Donlin left professional baseball temporarily to appear with his new wife on the stage and in films. They performed together until her death in October of 1912.

¹⁷⁶⁹ *NYT,* Saturday, March 26, 1932, 15:7.

The Democratic leadership in the House pressed for passage of a national sales tax proposal, but the measure was defeated on March 24 by a vote of 233 to 153. Only 45 Democrats voted for the bill.

¹⁷⁷⁰ *NYT,* Monday, March 28, 1932, 17:7.

Coolidge wrote in the March 26 issue of the *Saturday Evening Post* that excessive government spending and high taxation had caused the economic depression. He called for a significant reduction of each as a means to recovery.

¹⁷⁷¹ *NYT,* Tuesday, March 29, 1932, 21:7. Variant: *NYT* gives "something, but I think we . . . doing. Look" in second and third sentences.

Three leading citizens of Norfolk, Virginia, claimed on March 24 that they were in contact with the kidnappers of the Lindbergh baby (see Note 1749). They offered to act as intermediaries between the Lindbergh family and the kidnappers to bring about the safe return of the child. The whole affair later proved to be a hoax (see Note 1815).

¹⁷⁷² *NYT,* Wednesday, March 30, 1932, 21:7.

The Reconstruction Finance Corporation (see Note 1715) loaned several million dollars to railroad companies in late March. The money borrowed by these firms was used to pay off financial obligations, and a significant portion went to repay loans from major banks.

¹⁷⁷³ *NYT*, Thursday, March 31, 1932, 23:7.

For John Nance Garner see Note 1471; for the income tax see Note 1764; for the inheritance tax see Note 1767; for the national sales tax see Notes 1762 and 1769.

Manufacturers' excise taxes on numerous items were included in the tax bill under consideration in Congress. Final form of the bill provided levies of three cents per pound on liquid or extract malt, two cents per 1,000 matches, 2 percent of the selling price on candy, and 2 percent of the retail price on chewing gum.

¹⁷⁷⁴ *NYT*, Friday, April 1, 1932, 21:7.

For the national sales tax see Note 1769; for manufacturers' excise taxes see Note 1773.

¹⁷⁷⁵ *NYT*, Saturday, April 2, 1932, 17:7.

Three-year-old Gerald Collins, who had been trapped in a small drill-hole in a zinc mine near Picher, Oklahoma, was rescued on the evening of March 31 after an all-day effort by more than 100 miners and lawmen.

For the Lindbergh kidnapping see Note 1749.

¹⁷⁷⁶ *NYT*, Monday, April 4, 1932, 19:7. Variants: *NYT* gives "Polo and horse" to begin eighth sentence/*NYT* gives "We ought to legalize" to begin ninth sentence/*LAT* gives "certainly can see" in tenth sentence.

Harry Dwight Chamberlain, major in the United States Army and an internationally known horseman. Chamberlain was a member of the American riding team at the Olympics of 1920 and 1928 and captain of the team at the Los Angeles Olympics of 1932. Chamberlain's Olympic team of 1932 stayed at Rogers' ranch near Santa Monica for a few days prior to the opening on August 11 of the equestrian events.

¹⁷⁷⁷ *NYT*, Tuesday, April 5, 1932, 23:7. Variant: *NYT* gives "pleasant and as nice a soul" in sixth sentence.

Stimson (see Note 1485) left the United States on April 8 to attend the Geneva World Disarmament Conference (see Note 1718). During his two-month stay in Europe, Stimson made a great show of American cooperation with the League of Nations and sought, unsuccessfully, the support of European statesmen for a united front against Japanese aggression in China.

For Mary Emma Woolley see Note 1723.

Coolidge was named in a $100,000 libel suit filed in late 1931 by Lewis B. Tebbetts, a St. Louis insurance executive. The legal action stemmed from a radio broadcast by Coolidge on insurance in October of 1931. Tebbetts dropped the suit on April 7, 1932, after Coolidge had issued an apology and had reimbursed Tebbetts $2,500 for legal expenses.

For John Davison Rockefeller, Sr., see Note 1487.

¹⁷⁷⁸ *NYT*, Wednesday, April 6, 1932, 21:7. Variant: *LAT* gives "rare never" in fifth sentence.

The House voted on April 4 after a forty-minute debate to grant independence to the Philippine Islands, effective in 1940. The independence bill then went to the Senate where it was passed in December of 1932 with modifications. The resulting Hares-Hawes-Cutting Act provided for complete independence for the Philippines in 1945. The Philippine legislature, however, rejected the measure, primarily because of provisions leaving naval bases in American hands. The Tydings-McDuffie Independence Act of 1934, without the provisions for American bases, later was ratified by the Philippine legislature, and a constitution was soon promulgated.

1779 *NYT,* Thursday, April 7, 1932, 23:7.

Phar Lap (see Note 1765) died suddenly on April 5 at a ranch near Palo Alto, California. Although poison was suspected initially, experts later attributed the death to natural causes.

Herbert Austin Wolfe, racing editor for the *Sidney Daily Telegraph* and *Sunday Sun* from 1931 to 1933. Wolfe accompanied Phar Lap to the United States as a representative of the Australian press.

1780 *NYT,* Friday, April 8, 1932, 21:7. Variant: *NYT* gives "but what are" in fourth sentence.

Mills (see Note 1730), testifying at a Senate hearing on April 6, advocated that proposed taxes on stock and bond transfers and on inheritance, stock dividend, and corporate incomes be reduced or stricken from legislation pending in Congress.

Alexander Hamilton, the first United States secretary of the treasury, serving from 1789 to 1795.

For John Nance Garner see Note 1471.

Hawks (see Note 1464) sustained serious facial injuries when he crashed on takeoff from a rain-soaked airfield at Worcester, Massachusetts, on April 7. He underwent extensive plastic surgery during the next several months but eventually recovered and resumed his flying career.

1781 *NYT,* Saturday, April 9, 1932, 15:7.

Mrs. Hoover (see Note 1495) was the special guest at a luncheon attended by 700 Republican women in Washington, D. C., on April 7. With Mrs. Hoover's assistance, Ida Harris Mondell, wife of Congressman Franklin Wheeler Mondell, read a letter from President Hoover in which he expressed his appreciation for the women's support of the Republican party.

1782 *NYT,* Monday, April 11, 1932, 17:7.

The Soviet government may have intended to divert heavy winter snow from Moscow and through electrical ionization cause it to fall on nearby farms. The results of the project are unknown.

A major economy bill designed to reduce salaries of federal employees and to effect other cost-saving measures in government was proposed by Hoover and the House Economy Committee on April 9. Congress passed the bill on June 28, 1932, and Hoover signed it the next day.

1783 *LAT,* Tuesday, April 12, 1932, I:1:2. *NYT* did not print the DT.

The Senate, at the insistence of Hoover, began an investigation of the New York Stock Exchange in the spring of 1932. Top New York City bankers and stockbrokers were called to testify and to explain their financial dealings on the stock market. The inquiry, which revealed large-scale manipulation, price-fixing, and thievery, led to passage of the Securities Exchange Act of 1934.

1784 *LAT,* Wednesday, April 13, 1932, I:1:6. *NYT* did not print the DT.

Whitney, head of the New York Stock Exchange (see Note 1744), was the first witness to testify in the Senate investigation of the securities market (see Note 1783). His testimony lasted several hours but produced only denials of wrongdoings.

1785 *NYT*, Thursday, April 14, 1932, 23:7. Variant: *NYT* gives "Sassoon" in fourth and sixth sentences.

For Raphael Phillips Floyd Gibbons see Note 1664.

Victor Sassoon, British baronet who headed a vast financial empire in the Far East during the 1920s, including large banking interests and real estate investments in China.

For John Pierpont Morgan, Jr., see Note 1717.

1786 *NYT*, Friday, April 15, 1932, 19:7.

Democrats gathered in Washington, D. C., on April 13 for the annual dinner to commemorate former president Thomas Jefferson. Al Smith created a sensation when he made a veiled threat at the banquet to oppose the presidential candidacy of Franklin Roosevelt. Despite the apparent rift in the party, Democratic leaders forecasted an electoral victory in 1932.

1787 *NYT*, Saturday, April 16, 1932, 17:7.

Willie M. "Bill" Pickett, Oklahoma Negro cowboy and champion rodeo performer. Pickett died on April 2 at the age of seventy-two from injuries received while roping a bronc.

1788 *NYT*, Monday, April 18, 1932, 17:7.

Hoover's economy bill (see Note 1782) included a one-year trial proposal to reduce by staggered furloughs the number of work days for federal employees in order to avoid an across-the-board salary reduction.

1789 *NYT*, Tuesday, April 19, 1932, 23:7.

Coxey's Army, a band of jobless men who marched to Washington, D. C., following the Panic of 1893, to demonstrate for relief of unemployment and public distress. Largely unsuccessful, the demonstrators were led by Jacob Seckler Coxey, an Ohio manufacturer and political figure.

Automobile makers were among many manufacturers, importers, and growers who appeared before Congress in the spring of 1932 to protest a proposed tax bill that would place heavy levies on their products. Despite their opposition, the $1,118,500,000 revenue measure was enacted by Congress on June 6, 1932.

1790 *NYT*, Wednesday, April 20, 1932, 25:7. Variant: *NYT* gives "items, 'Monte' " in first sentence.

The Monte Carlo casino usually reaped such huge profits from its gambling operations that it annually declared dividends of from 100 to 200 percent. The worldwide depression and competition from other Riviera resorts, however, resulted in a diminishing number of tourists in Monte Carlo and a corresponding loss of revenue. The casino announced on April 18 that it would pass a dividend for the first time in its history.

For the stock exchange investigation see Note 1783.

1791 *NYT*, Thursday, April 21, 1932, 23:7. Variant: *LAT* gives "One of this" to begin second sentence.

1792 *NYT*, Friday, April 22, 1932, 21:7.

Schwab (see Note 1482) declared in a speech before the Pennsylvania Society of New York City on April 20 that because of the stock market crash and the economic depression there were no longer any rich men in the United States. He reasserted his optimism, however, to predict that the country would regain its former prosperity.

1793   *NYT,* Saturday, April 23, 1932, 17:7. Variant: *NYT* omits last paragraph.

William A. Gray, chief counsel for the Senate Banking and Currency Committee, the congressional body which conducted the stock exchange inquiry (see Note 1783). Gray's examination of Richard Whitney (see Notes 1744 and 1784) provided some tense moments at the committee hearing on April 21. On the same day, Senate investigators released a list of 350 alleged short-sellers, including three Frenchmen.

The Morgan syndicate (see Note 1717) purchased a large number of German bonds on the open market in 1930 and then resold them in units at $90 each. Soon after the syndicate ceased to purchase the bonds, their per unit price began to fluctuate and then to drop, dipping to $35.50 by April of 1932.

1794   *NYT,* Monday, April 25, 1932, 17:7.

For William A. Gray see Note 1793.

Dawes (see Note 1671) testified before the House Ways and Means Committee on April 21 about the policies of the Reconstruction Finance Corporation. In his usual colorful style, Dawes lashed out ot the operations of the stock exchange: "The whole country, it seems, is watching the quotations of a little group of speculators in Wall Street—a peanut-stand affair magnified out of its proper relation in comparison to its importance."

For Andrew William Mellon see Notes 1493 and 1727.

1795   *NYT,* Tuesday, April 26, 1932, 23:7.

Wilhelm II, emperor of Germany and king of Prussia from 1888 until his abdication in 1919 following the defeat of Germany in World War I. Kaiser Wilhelm spent the remainder of his life in retirement in the village of Doorn, Holland.

For William A. Gray see Note 1793.

Alienist, an obsolete term to denote a psychiatrist who offers expert opinion about a person's mental health or sanity. Four alienists testified in Honolulu at a widely-publicized trial of four whites accused of the murder of a native Hawaiian. The defendants were found guilty of manslaughter. Their sentences later were commuted after they had served but one hour in jail.

1796   *LAT,* Wednesday, April 27, 1932, I:1:2. *NYT* did not print the DT.

Fiorello Henry La Guardia, Republican United States representative from New York from 1923 to 1933 and, later, mayor of New York City. La Guardia presented evidence at the Senate Wall Street inquiry (see Note 1783) on April 26 that certain investors had manipulated publicity about the stock market by making regular payments to financial writers and reporters.

1797   *NYT,* Thursday, April 28, 1932, 23:7.

Smith (see Note 1484) won a decisive victory over Roosevelt (see Note 1529) in the Massachusetts presidential primary on April 26. Despite the setback, Roosevelt went on to win the Democratic nomination on the fourth ballot at the national convention in June.

Smedley Darlington Butler, major general in the United States Marine Corps, veteran of fifteen military operations, and former director of the Department of Public Safety in Philadelphia. Butler, a prohibition candidate, was defeated by incumbent James John Davis, a wet, in a race for the Republican nomination for United States senator from Pennsylvania. Davis won with a plurality of almost 400,000 votes.

1798 *NYT*, Friday, April 29, 1932, 19:7. Variants: *LAT* gives "it's one you" in fifth sentence/*LAT* gives "land and property . . . pay 35 per cent" in ninth sentence.

The Senate Finance Committee revised a pending revenue bill on April 27 by raising the surtax maximum to 45 percent on incomes of $1 million or more. The final draft of the measure, which was passed on June 6, called for a maximum tax of 55 percent.

1799 NYT, Saturday, April 30, 1932, 17:7.

Ford (see Note 1635) told Hoover during a visit to Washington, D. C., on April 26 that he had devised a plan whereby industrial workers could save $500 a year by growing their own foodstuffs. Complete details of the scheme were never revealed.

1800 *NYT*, Monday, May 2, 1932, 19:7.

Hawaii was the scene of racial conflict in 1932 involving native Hawaiians and United States naval personnel stationed on the islands. Part of the trouble stemmed from a sensational, racially-tinged murder trial that aroused a storm of protest on the islands and on the mainland (see Note 1795). As a result, a number of bills were introduced to restrict the autonomy of Hawaii, but the measures failed to attract legislative support.

1801 *NYT*, Tuesday, May 3, 1932, 23:7.

In the California Democratic presidential primary on May 3, Garner (see Note 1471) won a surprisingly easy victory over runner-up Roosevelt (see Note 1529) and third-place finisher Smith (see Note 1484). Garner's strength in California came from a huge "Texas-California" association in the state and influential editorial support.

William Gibbs McAdoo, United States secretary of the treasury from 1913 to 1918. McAdoo entered the Democratic National Convention of 1924 as the leading contender, but the conventiion deadlocked between McAdoo and Al Smith. John William Davis, a compromise candidate, won the nomination on the 103rd ballot.

James Beauchamp "Champ" Clark, Democratic United States representative from Missouri from 1893 to 1895 and from 1897 to 1921; Speaker of the House of Representatives from 1911 to 1919. Clark had a clear majority on twenty-seven ballots for the Democratic presidential nomination in 1912 but nevertheless lost the contest to Woodrow Wilson on the forty-sixth ballot.

1802 *NYT*, Wednesday, May 4, 1932, 21:7.

For James Rolph, Jr., see Note 1503.

Frederick Bennett Balzar, Republican governor of Nevada from 1927 until his death in 1934. Known as "the Flying Governors," Balzar and Rolph flew from Washington, D. C., to Los Angeles, California, in twenty-three hours, becoming the first state chief executives to fly coast-to-coast in less than one day.

Dr. J. D. Cockroft and Dr. E. T. S. Walton, two young British scientists at Cambridge University, succeeded in 1932 in forming a helium atom electrically.

1803 *NYT*, Thursday, May 5, 1932, 21:7.

The Senate Finance Committee removed from the revenue bill (see Note 1798) on May 3 a tax on stock sales and, in its place, substituted a new levy at the flat rate of four cents per share. The revision reduced the bill by $42 million.

1804 *NYT*, Friday, May 6, 1932, 19:7.

Coolidge, who took frequent fishing vacations while president, was the subject of a nationally-distributed photograph on May 5 in which he was shown attired in suit and hat clutching a string of prize trout.

1805 *NYT*, Saturday, May 7, 1932, 17:7. Variant: *LAT* gives "told the country" in third sentence.

Hoover sent a sharply-worded message to Congress on May 5 in which he criticized Congress for upsetting the economy by delaying passage of important legislation. The president's note evoked spirited debate in both the Senate and the House.

1806 *NYT*, Monday, May 9, 1932, 17:7.

1807 *NYT*, Tuesday, May 10, 1932, 23:7.

Thomas H. Massie, United States naval lieutenant stationed in Hawaii who was one of four persons accused of killing native Hawaiian, Joseph Kahahawai, the alleged assailant of Massie's wife. All four were convicted of manslaughter. Their sentences, however, were commuted on May 4 after they had served only one hour in jail (see Notes 1795 and 1800). Four days later, Massie and his wife, the former Thalia Fortescue, left Hawaii for the mainland.

Clarence Seward Darrow, prominent American defense attorney and civil libertarian whose court cases were almost invariably headline material. Darrow defended Massie and the others accused of the murder of Kahahawai.

Bryan (see Note 1617) opposed Darrow in the famous Scopes "Monkey Trial" in 1925.

1808 *NYT*, Wednesday, May 11, 1932, 21:7.

For Andrew William Mellon see Notes 1493 and 1727; for Charles Gates Dawes see Note 1671.

1809 *NYT*, Thursday, May 12, 1932, 21:7.

Beer enthusiasts in New York City staged an all-day "Beer Parade" on May 14 in support of legislation to legalize the beverage. Several thousand New Yorkers participated in the massive demonstration.

Ingalls, ace pilot for the United States naval reserves in World War I (see Note 1464), won the Republican gubernatorial nomination in Ohio on May 10. Ingalls, who ran on a repeal ticket, lost the general election in November to the incumbent, George White.

The permanent chairmanship of the Democratic National Convention in 1932 was held by Senator Thomas James Walsh, a Roosevelt supporter who won the post after a bitter struggle between Smith and Roosevelt forces.

1810 *NYT*, Friday, May 13, 1932, 21:7. Variants: *NYT* gives "like he hung to" in fourth sentence/*NYT* gives "the crow flies" in fifth sentence.

Three ground crewmen attempting to moor the United States naval dirigible *Akron* at Camp Kearney, California, on May 11, were dragged aloft when a trailing line broke. Two of the sailors lost their grip on the rope and plunged to their deaths. The third, Bud Cowart of Sand Springs, Oklahoma, managed to cling to the line until his rescue two hours later.

1811 *NYT*, Saturday, May 14, 1932, 17:7.

The body of the Lindbergh child was discovered on May 12 less than five miles from the Lindbergh home near Hopewell, New Jersey (see Note 1749).

1812 *NYT*, Monday, May 16, 1932, 17:7. Variant: *NYT* gives "beer there is" in tenth sentence.

For the New York City "Beer Parade" see Note 1809.

1813 *NYT*, Tuesday, May 17, 1932, 23:7.

For the revenue bill see Notes 1789 and 1798.

1814 *NYT*, Wednesday, May 18, 1932, 23:7. Variant: *NYT* gives "time Governor" in first sentence.

Murray (see Note 1477) decided to keep oil production in Oklahoma under martial law (see Note 1571) despite a decision of the United States Supreme Court in May of 1932 that held valid a state oil proration act. The governor feared that inferior federal courts would ignore the upper court action and would proceed to issue injunctions affecting proration.

Will Keith Kellogg, breakfast cereal manufacturer and founder in 1906 of the Kellogg Company at Battle Creek, Michigan. Kellogg donated his 800-acre Arabian horse ranch at Pomona, California, and an endowment of $600,000 to California State Polytechnic College as a stimulus for teaching and research in animal husbandry.

For James Rolph, Jr., see Note 1503.

1815 *NYT*, Thursday, May 19, 1932, 23:7. Variants: *NYT* gives "that some preachers" in fifth sentence.

Since March of 1932, three prominent citizens of Norfolk, Virginia—businessman John Hughes Curtis, Father Harold Dobson-Peacock, and Admiral Guy Hamilton Burrage—had claimed that they were in contact with the Lindbergh kidnappers (see Note 1771). Under constant questioning, Curtis finally admitted on May 17 that the story was a hoax. He was convicted of the crime and sentenced to one year in jail. The priest and the admiral escaped prosecution.

William Allan Pinkerton, head of Pinkerton's National Detective Agency from 1884 until his death in 1923.

1816 *NYT*, Friday, May 20, 1932, 21:7.

Helen Dinsmore Huntington Astor, first wife of American philanthropist William Vincent Astor.

1817 *NYT*, Saturday, May 21, 1932, 17:7.

1818 *NYT*, Monday, May 23, 1932, 17:7.

For Rogers' comments on prohibition repeal see DT 1816.

1819 *NYT*, Tuesday, May 24, 1932, 21:7.

Amelia Mary Earhart Putnam, American aviator who on May 21-22, 1932, became the first woman to fly the Atlantic Ocean alone. She married American book publisher George Palmer Putnam in 1930.

¹⁸²⁰ *NYT*, Wednesday, May 25, 1932, 21:7.

Nicholas Murray Butler, president of Columbia University from 1902 to 1945; corecipient of the Nobel Peace Prize of 1931.

For Alphonse "Scarface Al" Capone see Notes 1500 and 1634.

¹⁸²¹ *NYT*, Thursday, May 26, 1932, 27:7.

¹⁸²² *NYT*, Friday, May 27, 1932, 23:7.

For James John "Jimmy" Walker see Note 1480; for Tammany Hall see Note 1459.

¹⁸²³ *NYT*, Saturday, May 28, 1932, 17:7. Variants: *NYT* gives "hospitals, given . . . over. War" in third and fourth sentences/*LAT* gives "boys' regular customers are" in fifth sentence.

For Liberty Bonds see Note 1463; for the sale of poppies see Note 1505.

¹⁸²⁴ *NYT*, Monday, May 30, 1932, 15:7.

Block (see Note 1746), in testimony during the state investigation of Mayor Walker of New York City, claimed that stock payments totaling $246,000 from himself to Walker originated from an idea of his ten-year-old son, Billy Block, who was worried about Walker's ability to support himself on a mayor's salary of only $25,000. The boy's concern stirred the elder Block to "try to make a little money for Jimmy."

Rogers, one of the first residents of Beverly Hills, California, served as honorary mayor of that city from December of 1926 to August of 1927.

¹⁸²⁵ *NYT*, Tuesday, May 31, 1932, 19:7.

For the revenue bill see Note 1798.

Hoover firmly opposed a national sales tax but, nevertheless, insisted that the budget must be balanced and that this "must in the main be accomplished by an increase in taxation."

¹⁸²⁶ *NYT*, Wednesday, June 1, 1932, 25:7. Variants: *LAT* gives "November 8" in first sentence/*NYT* omits second paragraph.

Hoover condemned a $3 billion relief bill proposed by Speaker Garner (see Note 1471) on May 19 as "pork barrel" legislation that would require excessive taxation and that would make a balanced budget unattainable. Congress passed the measure in July of 1932, but Hoover immediately vetoed it. A revised version was then offered which the president accepted.

For the Reconstruction Finance Corporation see Note 1715.

¹⁸²⁷ *NYT*, Thursday, June 2, 1932, 23:7.

Greta Garbo, Swedish film actress whose sultry sexuality and beautiful features made her one of the greatest star personalities ever to appear on the screen. She arrived in Hollywood in 1926 where she soon became one of the highest paid performers in films; she retired suddenly in 1941 at the age of thirty-six.

For William Vann Rogers see Note 1644.

Hoover was born in West Branch, Iowa, but claimed Palo Alto, California as his permanent place of residence.

Hoover took what was for him the unusual step of addressing the Senate in person on May 31. He demanded an end to an impass that had delayed passage of the revenue and economy bills (see Notes 1798 and 1782). The Senate, momentarily sobered, stayed in session until midnight and passed the tax measure. Hoover signed it on June 6.

1828 *NYT*, Friday, June 3, 1932, 21:7. Variant: *NYT* gives "Fleischaker," in third sentence.

Herbert Fleishhacker, San Francisco financier, park commissioner, and utilities magnate; served as president of Anglo California National Bank from 1911 to 1938.

For John Pierpont Morgan, Jr., see Note 1717; for Owen D. Young see Note 1538.

Carter Glass, Democratic United States senator from Virginia from 1920 until his death in 1946. Recognized as a financial expert, Glass served as United States secretary of the treasury from 1918 to 1920.

For Andrew William Mellon see Note 1493.

1829 *NYT*, Saturday, June 4, 1932, 17:7.

A general sales levy was not included in the revenue legislation enacted by Congress on June 1 (see Note 1827).

James Hamilton Lewis, Democratic United States senator from Illinois from 1913 to 1919 and from 1931 until his death in 1939.

1830 *NYT*, Monday, June 6, 1932, 17:7.

The Senate voted on June 4 to reduce all federal government salaries, except those under $1,000, by 10 percent. The pay cut, estimated to produce a savings of $117,150,000, was included in an amendment to the economy bill (see Note 1782).

Chilean president Juan Esteban Montero was overthrown on June 4 in a relatively bloodless coup. Power passed into the hands of a revolutionary junta, consisting of Carlos Guillermo Dávila Espinoza, Arturo Puga, and Eugenio Matte. Dávila assumed the title of provisional president.

Friedrich Wilhelm Viktor August Ernst, German crown prince and eldest son of Kaiser Wilhelm II. Friedrich Wilhelm fled Germany after his father's abdication in 1918. He returned to his homeland five years later and remained there until his death in 1951.

1831 *NYT*, Tuesday, June 7, 1932, 21:7.

For the Democratic plan, the Garner-Wagner emergency relief bill, see Note 1826. Congressional Republicans introduced a relief measure on June 4 that authorized the Reconstruction Finance Corporation to lend an additional $1 billion for self-liquidating projects. The bill died in committee.

1832 *NYT*, Wednesday, June 8, 1932, 21:7.

John Davison Rockefeller, Jr., American philanthropist and eldest son and namesake of the petroleum tycoon (see Note 1487). A Baptist Sunday School teacher and one of the largest contributors to prohibition causes, Rockefeller declared himself on June 6 in favor of repeal of the Eighteenth Amendment, claiming that the evils of the dry law outweighed the benefits.

1833 *NYT*, Thursday, June 9, 1932, 23:7.

The American Institute of Banking, the educational arm of the American Bankers' Association, opened its thirteenth annual meeting in Los Angeles on June 7.

1834 *NYT*, Friday, June 10, 1932, 21:7. Variant: *NYT* gives "Morocco." to end DT, omitting fourteen words.

Henry Field, a radio station operator and seed merchant, defeated incumbent Smith Brookhart to win the Iowa Republican senatorial nomination on June 6. Field lost the general election in November to his Democratic opponent.

McAdoo (see Note 1801) suggested on June 8 that a national referendum be held to settle the issue of prohibition. In that manner, he claimed, the question could be dealt with quickly and decisively. No such referendum was ever conducted.

Dawes had averaged a change in jobs once every year since 1929 (see Notes 1671 and 1714).

For Aimee Semple McPherson see Note 1501.

1835 *NYT*, Saturday, June 11, 1932, 17:7. Variants: *LAT* gives "Hays" in second sentence.

Hays (see Note 1538) announced on June 9 that he favored the earliest possible resubmission to Congress of the prohibition question. His change-of-heart statement came only a few days after that of fellow dry, John D. Rockefeller, Jr. (see Note 1832).

James Cannon, Jr., prominent American prohibitionist, reformer, and bishop in the Methodist Episcopal Church, South. Cannon dismissed Rockefeller's wet pronouncement of June 6 as a "city-warped" point of view. Even after the repeal of prohibition in 1933, the bishop continued to fight against liquor traffic.

1836 *NYT*, Monday, June 13, 1932, 17:7.

No DT's are available for June 14-17, 1932, during which time Rogers attended the Republican National Convention in Chicago. The articles he wrote while at the convention appear in *Convention Articles of Will Rogers*.

1837 *NYT*, Saturday, June 18, 1932, 15:7.

For Alive Roosevelt Longworth see Note 1730.

Hurley (see Note 1481) was one of several administration officials who attended the Republican National Convention and who helped to engineer Hoover's renomination.

The prohibition plank of the Republican platform called for an amendment that would allow states to deal with the question as their citizens would determine and that would protect those states where prohibition was retained. The Democratic platform favored the outright repeal of the Eighteenth Amendment and encouraged, instead, state control of liquor traffic.

1838 *NYT*, Monday, June 20, 1932, 17:7.

Hoover originally intended to stay in Washington, D. C., throughout the campaign, but an unexpected Democratic victory in Maine in September, coupled with signs of increased Democratic support in the West, led him to make two speaking tours in October and early November.

1839 *NYT*, Tuesday, June 21, 1932, 23:7.

For John Nance Garner see Note 1471.

Albert Cabell Ritchie, Democratic governor of Maryland from 1920 to 1935. Ritchie, an active foe of prohibition, received twenty-one votes for the Democratic presidential nomination in 1932.

Most local postmasters owed their jobs to a Republican administration.

1840 *NYT,* Wednesday, June 22, 1932, 23:7.

The House passed the economy bill (see Note 1782) on June 20 and returned it to the Senate for recognition of House amendments. Among its features, the bill provided that congressmen's salaries be reduced by 10 percent.

For the revenue bill see Note 1798.

1841 *NYT,* Thursday, June 23, 1932, 23:7.

For Liberty Bonds see Note 1463.

1842 *NYT,* Friday, June 24, 1932, 21:7.

Hoover proposed on June 22 that, for the sake of peace and economy, all nations should reduce their arms, armies, navies, and air forces by one-third. Of the major powers, only Italy endorsed the plan.

Maximilian Siegfried "Max" Schmeling, German professional boxer who held the world heavyweight title from 1930 until his fifteen-round, split-decision loss to American Joseph Paul "Jack" Sharkey on June 21, 1932. Sharkey's victory was one of the most bitterly disputed in boxing history.

For William Harrison "Jack" Dempsey see Note 1572.

Robert L. "Bob" Fitzsimmons, English-born prizefighter who held the world heavyweight title from 1879 to 1899 and the world light heavyweight title from 1903 to 1905.

1843 *NYT,* Saturday, June 25, 1932, 15:7.

For the Hoover disarmament plan see Note 1842.

No DTs are available for June 27-July 2, 1932, during which time Rogers attended the Democratic National Convention in Chicago. The articles he wrote while at the convention appear in *Convention Articles of Will Rogers.*

1844 *NYT,* Monday, July 4, 1932, 13:7.

Roosevelt (see Note 1529) won the Democratic presidential nomination on the fourth ballot and flew with his family from Albany, New York, to Chicago, Illinois, to make his acceptance speech on the final day, thus breaking the precedent of waiting for a formal notification.

A deadlock between Roosevelt and Al Smith was broken when the California delegation switched its vote at the fourth ballot, on the evening of July 1, from Jack Garner to Roosevelt. Garner at the same time released the delegates of his home state, Texas.

1845 *NYT,* Tuesday, July 5, 1932, 17:7. Variant: *LAT* gives "gigolos" in fifth sentence.

For Tammany Hall see Note 1459; for Alfred Emanuel "Al" Smith see Note 1484.

1846 *NYT,* Wednesday, July 6, 1932, 21:7.

1847 *NYT,* Thursday, July 7, 1932, 19:7. Variants: *NYT* gives "Ranches . . . gone? Yeah?" and *LAT* gives "Yes, ranches . . . gone? Yeah;" to begin DT.

William Thomas Waggoner, Texas cattle baron and oilman whose W. T. Waggoner Ranch sprawled over six counties of northwestern Texas.

Garner (see Note 1471) received the Democratic vice presidential nomination in 1932. He served as vice president of the United States from 1933 to 1941.

1848   *NYT,* Friday, July 8, 1932, 19:7.

1849   *NYT,* Saturday, July 9, 1932, 13:7. Variant: *NYT* gives "at the Halsell" in first sentence, omitting six words.

Mashed O, a 120,000-acre hereford ranch in Lamb and Bailey counties, Texas, is owned by the Halsell Cattle Company of Texas and Oklahoma. The ranch was started in 1889 by Glenn and William Electious Halsell.

David Hutton (see Note 1605) was sued shortly after his marriage to Aimee Semple McPherson (see Note 1501) for breaking a promise to marry a nurse from California. The case went to trial in June of 1932, and on July 9 of that year a jury awarded the plaintiff a verdict of $5,000 damages.

Al Smith (see Note 1484), who was known as the "Happy Warrior," had just lost the Democratic presidential nomination to Roosevelt. On July 7 he announced his continued support of the party but failed to mention the new nominee.

1850   *NYT,* Monday, July 11, 1932, 15:7. Variant: *NYT* omits "an amateur" in third sentence.

The Democratic platform included a plank that, pending repeal, favored immediate legalization of the manufacture and sale of a mild beer.

1851   *NYT,* Tuesday, July 12, 1932, 19:7.

Willie "Will" Rogers, an Oklahoma school teacher and administrator, capitalized on his famous name to run a strong second in the Democratic primary on July 6 for congressman at large. Rogers went on to win the runoff contest on July 26 and the general election in November. He served in Congress from 1933 to 1943.

1852   *NYT,* Wednesday, July 13, 1932, 19:7.

Hoover vetoed the Garner-Wagner emergency relief bill (see Note 1826) on July 11. He opposed extending authority to the Reconstruction Finance Corporation to make loans to individuals and businesses for what he termed "any conceivable purpose, on any conceivable security." Congress removed the objectionable features and repassed the bill. The president signed it on July 21.

The Two Black Crows, a vaudeville and motion picture comedy team popular during the 1920s and early 1930s. The blackface act featured the duo of George Moran and Charles E. Mack.

1853   *NYT,* Thursday, July 14, 1932, 21:7.

1854   *NYT,* Friday, July 15, 1932, 17:7.

Paavo Nurmi Finnish long-distance runner who was a gold medal winner in the Olympics of 1920, 1924, and 1928. Nurmi wanted to end his career with a gold medal at the Los Angeles Olympics of 1932 but was suspended from amateur ranks because of alleged professionalism.

Roosevelt took a cruise along the New England coast in mid-July, prior to the commencement of his presidential campaign.

1855 *NYT*, Saturday, July 16, 1932, 13:7.

Legalization of beer was offered in the Senate on July 1 as an amendment to a home loan bank bill. Prohibitionists in Congress sidetracked and scuttled the beer measure later in the month.

1856 *NYT*, Monday, July 18, 1932, 15:7. Variant: *LAT* gives "complexion and show up as competitor." in third sentence.

Black Americans excelled at the Los Angeles Olympics of 1932, winning two gold and two silver medals, including the first gold won by an American black in Olympic competition.

Booker Taliaferro Washington, black American scientist and educator who organized and headed Tuskegee Institute in Alabama from 1884 until his death in 1915.

1857 *NYT*, Tuesday, July 19, 1932, 19:7. Variant: *LAT* gives "Americans used" in seventh sentence.

The Seventy-second Congress adjourned late Saturday night, July 16, after passing a number of important appropriation bills, including the Garner-Wagner emergency relief measure (see Notes 1826 and 1852) and the home loan bank bill (see Note 1659). Both bills later received Hoover's signature.

For the national sales tax see Note 1769.

1858 *NYT*, Wednesday, July 20, 1932, 17:7.

Matthew Chauncey Brush, president of American International Corporation, investment bankers, from 1923 to 1935. He appeared in April before the Senate Banking and Currency Committee investigating short selling on the stock market (see Note 1783). An entertaining man, Brush remarked during testimony that "no one is in Wall Street for his health."

1859 *NYT*, Thursday, July 21, 1932, 2:6.

Mellon (see Note 1493) sailed to the United States in July to confer briefly with administration officials and to tend to private business matters. He returned to his ambassadorial post in London in September of 1932.

For the Lausanne Conference of 1932 see Note 1714.

1860 *NYT*, Friday, July 22, 1932, 17:7. Variants: *NYT* gives "idea when . . . he resigns. He" in first and second sentences.

Mussolini (see Note 1452) dismissed from the Italian government on July 20 the foreign minister, four other ministers, and eleven undersecretaries of state. He then assumed two of the vacated ministries, bringing to four the number of cabinet portfolios that he held concurrently.

The Bonus Army, a group of more than 15,000 mostly unemployed veterans who, in the spring of 1932, marched to Washington, D. C., to demand immediate payment of their World War I bonus. They conducted themselves peaceably, but when the Senate defeated bonus legislation on June 17, the marchers refused to return home. In the first week of July, Hoover asked Congress to appropriate money for the removal of the veterans to their homes. A measure was passed providing for transportation, plus subsistence at seventy-five cents a day. The money was to be deducted ultimately from the payments on their bonus certificates. See also Notes 1521 and 1867.

1861 *NYT*, Saturday, July 23, 1932, 13:7. Variant: *NYT* omits fourth sentence.

For William Vann Rogers see Note 1644; for Mary Amelia Rogers see Note 1525.

1862   *NYT*, Monday, July 25, 1932, 17:7. Variant: *NYT* gives "proud; "I worked" in tenth sentence, omitting fourteen words.

Ziegfeld (see Note 1635) died in Hollywood on July 22 following a long illness. Rogers, one of Ziegfeld's closest friends and a man the producer guided to stardom, took charge of the arrangements for his funeral and burial.

1863   *NYT*, Tuesday, July 26, 1932, 17:7.

Borah (see Note 1452), in a radio speech at Minneapolis on July 23, called for a world economic conference to consider cancellation of all war debts, restoration of world trade, reorganization of the monetary system, and revision of the Versailles Treaty of 1919.

1864   *NYT*, Wednesday, July 27, 1932, 19:7.

For Liberty Bonds see Note 1463.

The Reconstruction Finance Corporation was flooded with loan applications soon after passage of the Garner-Wagner Act (see Note 1826) which provided an additional $2 billion for loans. Early loan applicants included representatives of thirty states.

1865   *NYT*, Thursday, July 28, 1932, 19:7. Variant: *NYT* gives "along and service" in sixth sentence.

The National Editorial Association, a 6,800-member organization of editors and publishers of newspapers in small towns, met in annual convention in San Francisco and Los Angeles from July 19-26.

1866   *NYT*, Friday, July 29, 1932, 17:7. Variant: *NYT* omits "In figuring these statistics" in fifth sentence.

For the Bonus Army see Note 1862.

The cost of living in the United States, according to the Bureau of Labor Statistics, was 6.9 percent lower in June of 1932 than in the preceding December.

1867   *NYT*, Saturday, July 30, 1932, 15:7. Variant: *NYT* gives "that body" in sixth sentence.

Members of the Bonus Army refused to leave Washington, D. C., after the Senate failed to enact bonus legislation (see Note 1862). On July 28 Hoover ordered the army to evict the marchers forcibly. The army set the veterans' camps on fire and drove them from the city. Hoover was rebuked by the press and the general public for the severity of his actions. See also Note 1521.

1868   *NYT*, Monday, August 1, 1932, 17:7.

In Olympic weight lifting competition, the lightweight event was won by René Duverger of France with a lift of 715 pounds. Another Frenchman, Louis Hostin, won the light heavyweight division with a lift of 803 pounds.

1869   *NYT*, Tuesday, August 2, 1932, 19:7.

Everett Sanders, chairman of the Republican National Committee from 1932 to 1934. Sanders, who was presidential secretary during the Coolidge administration, announced on August 8 that the former president had decided to campaign actively for Hoover. Coolidge addressed a campaign rally in New York City in October and broadcast a reelection plea in November.

For the Bonus Army see Notes 1862 and 1867.

1870 *NYT,* Wednesday, August 3, 1932, 17:7. Variants: *NYT* gives "Twenty-five" in second sentence/*NYT* gives "solid. If a" in second and third sentences.

In Olympic competition the United States equestrian team won a gold medal in the three-day event and a bronze for dressage.

For Arthur Brisbane see Note 1442.

1871 *NYT,* Thursday, August 4, 1932, 21:7. Variant: *LAT* gives "November 8" in sixth sentence.

Eddie Tolan, American sprint champion who, in 1932, became the first black in Olympic history to win the 100-meter dash. On August 1 Tolan just edged Ralph Metcalfe to win the fabled event in 10.3 seconds. Two days later Tolan became the first double winner of the Olympics when he won the 200-meter event in an Olympic record time of 21.2 seconds.

Ralph Metcalfe, American sprinter who established several collegiate track records while at Marquette University in the early 1930s. Metcalfe won an Olympic gold medal as a member of the world record 400-meter relay team in 1936.

Mildred "Babe" Didrikson Zaharias, American track and golf star and one of the most accomplished female athletes of all time. In the Olympics of 1932, she set world records in the javelin (143' 4") and 80-meter hurdles (11.7 seconds).

1872 *NYT,* Friday, August 5, 1932, 15:7.

Roy Dikeman Chapin, president of Hudson Motor Car Company from 1910 to 1923 and from 1933 until his death in 1936. Chapin was named on August 4 to replace Robert Patterson Lamont as United States secretary of commerce. He served in that post from 1932 to 1933. The Economy Act which was passed in June (see Note 1782) included a salary cut for cabinet officers.

The American team finished last in the Olympic 100-kilometer bicycle race on August 4. A squad from Italy, paced by Attilio Pavesi, won the team trophy.

1873 *NYT,* Saturday, August 6, 1932, 13:7.

1874 *NYT,* Monday, August 8, 1932, 17:7. Variant: *LAT* gives "power that shows" in third sentence.

Stock prices, after experiencing record lows in early 1932, rose two to twelve points on the New York Stock Exchange on August 6 following unusually heavy trading. The market continued its general upward swing through the remainder of 1932.

1875 *NYT,* Tuesday, August 9, 1932, 19:7.

Japanese men and American women dominated the swimming events at the Olympics. The Japanese men won every race except one.

Juan Carlos Zabala, a youthful Argentine long-distance runner, won the marathon on August 7 with an Olympic record time of two hours, thirty-one minutes, and thirty-six seconds.

1876 *NYT*, Wednesday, August 10, 1932, 17:7.

Coolidge surprised and dismayed many fellow Republicans when he announced on August 8 that a chronic case of hay fever precluded his attendance at Hoover's notification ceremonies scheduled for August 11.

Lester Jesse Dickinson, Republican United States senator from Iowa from 1931 to 1937. Well-known as an orator, Dickinson delivered the keynote address at the Republican National Convention of 1932.

Roosevelt summoned Mayor Walker (see Note 1480) to the state capital on August 11 to answer charges of corruption in Walker's administration. The governor's hearings began on the same day as Hoover's notification of his nomination.

1877 *NYT*, Thursday, August 11, 1932, 17:7. Variant: *NYT* gives "to be notified." to end second sentence, omitting last four words.

Hoover was notified officially on August 11 of his nomination for reelection. The ceremonies took place in Constitution Hall in Washington, D. C.

For James John "Jimmy" Walker and the Roosevelt hearings see Note 1876.

Stimson (see Note 1485), in an address on August 9, appeared to refer to Japan as an aggresor nation in the Far East. Although the Japanese complained that the inference would tend to aggravate the situation in Manchuria, they did not lodge a formal protest.

For Japanese swimmers at the Olympics see Note 1875.

1878 *NYT*, Friday, August 12, 1932, 17:7.

The stock market registered a substantial advance (see Note 1874) on August 11 in a new wave of buying. Farm implement manufacturers were among the strongest gainers as they benefited from reports that the United States would recognize the Soviet Union and that the Soviet government would make large-scale purchases of American goods.

Samuel Seabury, American jurist and attorney who became nationally prominent when he headed (1930-1931) the state investigation of the municipal government of New York City and the administration of Mayor Walker (see Note 1480).

1879 *NYT*, Saturday, August 13, 1932, 15:7.

Hoover, in a radical departure from an earlier stance, proclaimed during the notification ceremonies on August 11 that the Eighteenth Amendment was a failure. He declared that national prohibition, which four years earlier he had labeled the "noble experiment," should be replaced by state control.

Roosevelt, in a radio speech in April of 1932, called for new economic plans that would uplift "the forgotten man at the bottom of the economic pyramid." The Forgotten Man thus became one of Roosevelt's most remembered phrases.

1880 *NYT*, Monday, August 15, 1932, 15:7.

1881 *NYT*, Tuesday, August 16, 1932, 19:7. Variant: *NYT* gives "particular Olympia competition." in second sentence.

The Tenth Cavalry, an all-black regiment that served with distinction in the Indian wars in the American West and in the Spanish-American War of 1898.

1882 *NYT*, Wednesday, August 17, 1932, 19:7.

For the Walker investigation see Note 1876; for Mildred "Babe" Didrikson Zaharias see Note 1871.

A farm strike erupted in the late summer of 1932 in the usually conservative Middle West in an effort to bring higher prices for agricultural products. The strike featured a "farmers' holiday" during which growers withheld their produce from the market.

1883 *NYT*, Thursday, August 18, 1932, 21:7.

1884 *NYT*, Friday, August 19, 1932, 19:7.

Santa Barbara, California, annually hosted thousands at its presentation of Old Spanish Days, a three-day fiesta with a colorful pageant parade that emphasized events in the history of the city.

For Arthur Brisbane see Note 1442; for the Walker investigation see Note 1876.

1885 *NYT*, Saturday, August 20, 1932, 15:7.

Curtis (see Note 1538) formally received notification of his renomination for the vice presidency on August 18 in his home town of Topeka, Kansas. In his acceptance speech, he declared that he was opposed to repeal of the Eighteenth Amendment, thus taking a stand in opposition to his runningmate, Hoover (see Note 1879).

1886 *NYT*, Monday, August 22, 1932, 17:7.

Evangeline Cory Booth, commander of the Salvation Army in the United States from 1904 to 1934 and leader of the international organization from 1934 to 1939.

1887 *NYT*, Tuesday, August 23, 1932, 21:7. Variant: *NYT* gives "nine points . . . nine points . . . nine point" in third sentence.

Roosevelt addressed a campaign rally in Columbus, Ohio, on August 20, during which he outlined a nine-point program to curb abuses in the financial system of the country. Many of the points of his program later formed the basis of the Securities Exchange Act of 1934.

For the stock market see Notes 1874 and 1878.

1888 *NYT*, Wednesday, August 24, 1932, 19:7. Variants: *LAT* gives "why, they" in fourth sentence.

For Arthur Brisbane see Note 1442; for Will Harrison Hays see Note 1538.

1889 *NYT*, Thursday, August 25, 1932, 21:7.

For Hoover on prohibition see Note 1879; for the Walker investigation see Note 1876.

1890 *NYT*, Friday, August 26, 1932, 19:7.

1891 *NYT*, Saturday, August 27, 1932, 15:7. Variant: *NYT* gives "two people in worse with" in first sentence.

1892 *NYT*, Monday, August 29, 1932, 15:7. Variants: *NYT* gives "100,000 Democrats" in second sentence / *LAT* gives "Charlie's actors" in eighth sentence / *NYT* omits tenth and eleventh sentences.

Roosevelt told a partisan crowd of 100,000 at Sea Girt, New Jersey, on August 27 that Hoover had used "meaningless" and "pussy-cat" words in his acceptance speech (see Note 1879) in an effort to please both sides of the prohibition issue. Roosevelt also called the Republican prohibition plank "ambiguous and insincere."

Theodore Roosevelt, president of the United States from 1901 to 1909. Vigorous and enthusiastic, Roosevelt was noted for his ability to coin vivid phrases. The two Roosevelts were fifth cousins.

Chaplin (see Note 1448) moved to nullify a contract made by his former wife that would have put his two sons in films. Chaplin argued that he was interested only in his children's happiness and well-being. The court agreed with the comedian and nullified the contract. His sons, Charley and Sidney Earl, entered films in 1952.

1893 *NYT*, Tuesday, August 30, 1932, 19:7.

Rogers was in Bishop, California, in August to film his ninth talking picture, *Too Busy To Work*, which was released in late 1932.

Ross Shaw Sterling, Democratic governor of Texas from 1931 to 1933.

Miriam Amanda Wallace "Ma" Ferguson, Democratic governor of Texas from 1925 to 1927 and from 1933 to 1935. Sterling defeated Ferguson for the governorship in 1930 but was defeated by her in the election of 1932.

For the Two Black Crows see Note 1852.

1894 *NYT*, Wednesday, August 31, 1932, 19:7.

1895 *NYT*, Thursday, September 1, 1932, 21:7.

The Los Angeles bank robbery gang was led by Robert York, a noted California crime figure who earlier in the year had been tried and acquitted of murder.

1896 *NYT*, Friday, September 2, 1932, 17:7. Variant: *NYT* gives "Rock business." in tenth sentence.

Montagu Collet Norman, governor of the Bank of England from 1920 to 1944. A powerful figure in international finance, Norman bewildered American government officials when he unexpectedly visited the United States in the late summer of 1932, mysteriously traveling under an assumed name. He spent most of the time visiting friends.

For Andrew William Mellon see Note 1493.

In California primary elections on August 30, the Republican vote was larger than the Democratic tally by more than 350,000 ballots. Moreover, a greater percentage of registered Republicans went to the polls than did Democrats in the state.

1897 *NYT*, Saturday, September 3, 1932, 15:7. Variant: *NYT* gives "poor fellow" in tenth sentence.

Walker (see Note 1480) suddenly resigned as mayor of New York City on September 1 in the midst of an investigation of alleged corruption in his administration (see Note 1876). Soon after his resignation, Walker went to Europe where he lived for many years. Later he returned to the United States where he died in 1946.

For Miriam Amanda Wallace "Ma" Ferguson see Note 1893; for Amon Giles Carter see Note 1485.

James Edward "Pa" Ferguson, Democratic governor of Texas from 1915 until his impeachment and removal from office in 1917 for various reasons, including misappropriation of state funds. He attempted to run again in 1924, but a court ruled that he could not be a candidate. His wife, Miriam Ferguson, promptly entered the race and won with the open support of her husband.

For Greta Garbo see Note 1827.

1898   *NYT*, Monday, September 5, 1932, 13:7.

Luther Burbank, American horticulturist who first took up market gardening in 1868 and who developed the Burbank potato and new and improved variaties of other cultivated plants.

For Will Harrison Hays see Note 1538.

1899   *NYT*, Tuesday, September 6, 1932, 21:7. Variant: *NYT* gives "ago Battling" in fourth sentence.

Tonopah, located in western Nevada, was the site in 1902 of one of the greatest silver bonanzas in the history of the state.

Goldfield, also located in western Nevada, was the scene of an immensely rich gold strike in 1902-1903.

George Lewis "Tex" Rickard, American prizefighter promoter who started in the business in 1906 by staging the Nelson-Gans lightweight championship bout in Goldfield, Nevada.

Oscar "Battling" Nelson, hard-punching Danish-born boxer who held the world light-weight championship from 1908 to 1910.

Joseph "Joe" Gans, American prizefighter known as the "Old Master," held the world lightweight crown from 1902 to 1908. Gans and Nelson met on September 3, 1906, in a scheduled forty-five round championship bout in Goldfield, Nevada. Gans won the epic battle in the forty-second round when Nelson was disqualified for striking a low blow.

Walter Scott, "Death Valley Scotty," self-styled prospector and miner who left his native Kentucky in the 1890s to travel through the West. Scott eventually settled in Death Valley, California, where his publicity stunts and money-making schemes earned him a small fortune and a legendary reputation. In the 1920s he built a huge, lavish castle on his desert estate.

Rhyolite, located near the north end of Death Valley in Nevada, was a mining boom town of 1906. The mining district, also known as Bullfrog, was named for rhyolite, the predominant rock in the area.

Boulder Dam, formally renamed Hoover Dam in 1947, is the highest concrete arch dam in the United States. Construction of the dam, located on the Arizona-Nevada border, began in 1931 and was completed in 1936. It provides flood control, water, and electrical power for Arizona, Nevada, and California.

1900   *NYT,* Wednesday, September 7, 1932, 21:7.

A Senate investigation was threatened in August of 1932 concerning charges of unfair labor practices by the builders of Boulder Dam (see Note 1899). The allegations were dismissed.

1901   *NYT,* Thursday, September 8, 1932, 23:7.

George Horace Lorimer, American magazine publisher and editor. In an article in Lorimer's *Saturday Evening Post* of September 10, Coolidge presented "The Republican Case" in which he strongly recommended the reelection of Hoover.

For "Amos 'n Andy" see Note 1531.

1902 *NYT,* Friday, September 9, 1932, 21:7. Variant: *NYT* omits fourth and fifth sentences.

France rejected a German proposal in September that the two countries discuss armament equality. The French claimed that German armaments were fixed by the Versailles Treaty and that neither nation could modify the document.

Smith (see Note 1484), writing as editor-in-chief of *New Outlook* magazine in the September issue, predicted an easy victory for Democratic candidates in the national elections. The name of Franklin Roosevelt, the Democratic presidential nominee and Smith's chief political rival, did not appear in the article.

Vallee (see Note 1741) and his wife of fourteen months, actress Fay Webb, decided in early September to abandon their highly-publicized divorce plans and to reconcile their differences.

For the farm strike see Note 1882.

1903 *NYT,* Saturday, September 10, 1932, 17:7.

Mexico ceded California to the United States in 1848 as a result of the Mexican War. Gold was discovered in California on the South Fork of the American River on January 24, 1848, less than ten days before the signing of the treaty that ended the Mexican war. A great migration immediately followed, increasing the population of the territory from 15,000 to 250,000. In 1849 California applied for statehood, and on September 9, 1850, it entered the union.

1904 *NYT,* Monday, September 12, 1932, 17:7.

Walker (see Notes 1480 and 1897) sailed for Italy on September 11 for a twenty-day vacation. He returned to the United States in October, and then in November he again sailed for Europe. He remained there for several years.

Joseph Vincent McKee, New York City politician who served as acting mayor of the city for four months following the resignation of Walker. McKee taught Latin and Greek at his alma mater, Fordham University, from 1913 to 1916.

For Tammany Hall see Note 1459.

1905 *LAT,* Tuesday, September 13, 1932, I:1:7. *NYT* did not print the DT.

1906 *NYT,* Wednesday, September 14, 1932, 23:7.

The "Flying Family," a family of four from Richmond, Virginia, were feared lost on September 12 in the North Atlantic during the early stages of a transatlantic flight. Two days later, British rescuers found the fliers—George Hutchinson, his wife, two daughters, and four crewmen—safe on Greenland.

A student nurse from Pennsylvania, Edna Newcomer, and two men, pilot William Ulbrich and Dr. Leon M. Pisculli, left New York City on September 13 in the monoplane the *American Nurse* bound for Rome. Two days later, they were reported lost at sea. No trace of them was ever found.

Hurley (see Note 1481) spoke at the opening session of the annual convention of the American Legion on September 12. Despite considerable opposition from legionnaires, the secretary of war used the occasion to defend the methods of the administration in ousting the Bonus Army from the capital in July (see Note 1867).

Kingfish was one of the recurring characters on the radio serial "Amos 'n Andy" (see Note 1531).

1907   *NYT,* Thursday, September 15, 1932, 23:7.

In the Maine state election on September 13, Democrats scored impressive, unexpected victories in the traditionally Republican state, winning the governorship and two of three congressional seats.

Prices on the stock market dropped three points on September 12 and 13, partially because of news of the Maine election.

Hoover telegraphed Sanders (see Note 1869) on September 13 to urge a new and stronger effort by the Republican party in the wake of its defeat in the Maine election. The upset in Maine also prompted the president to embark on a speaking tour in early October.

1908   *NYT,* Friday, September 16, 1932, 23:7.

Roosevelt, speaking at a campaign rally in Topeka, Kansas, on September 14, proposed in general terms his plan for restoring farm prosperity. He favored the "planned use of land," lower taxes for farmers through tax reform, federal credit for refinancing farm mortgages, and lower tariffs.

1909   *NYT,* Saturday, September 17, 1932, 17:7.

Smith (see Note 1484) discussed the issue of veterans' pensions and bonuses in relation to the taxpayer in an article in the *Saturday Evening Post* of September 17.

Roosevelt embarked on a three-week, 8,900-mile campaign speaking tour of the West and Middle West on September 12. More than a dozen addresses were delivered, including two speeches in Los Angeles on September 25.

Hoover made a speaking trip early in October as far west as Iowa.

1910   *NYT,* Monday, September 19, 1932, 19:7. Variant: *LAT* omits second paragraph.

Fire blackened more than 120,000 acres of the Santa Barbara National Forest watershed area in Southern California in September.

Germany declared on September 16 that it would withdraw from the Geneva World Disarmament Conference (see Note 1718) because France had rejected German demands for equality of arms. German delegates nevertheless returned to the conference when it reconvened on September 20. The equality issue remained unsettled.

Railways in the United States suffered from a dire loss of credit, loss of earning power, and loss of buying power in 1932 because of decreased income and the deterioration of physical properties. In a campaign speech in Salt Lake City on September 17, Roosevelt outlined a six-point program for reform of national railroad policy. Some of the reforms were incorporated in legislation enacted in 1933.

1911   *NYT,* Tuesday, September 20, 1932, 23:7. Variants: *NYT* gives "Roosevelt, who worked" in third sentence / *NYT* gives "again—forest fires," in tenth sentence.

Daniels (see Note 1479) served as United States secretary of the navy in World War I, during which time Roosevelt served as his assistant secretary. Daniels campaigned actively for Roosevelt in 1932. When he became president, Roosevelt reappointed the North Carolinian as secretary of the navy. He served in that post from 1933 to 1941.

James Michael Curley, Democratic mayor of Boston from 1914 to 1918, 1922 to 1926, 1930 to 1934, and 1946 to 1950. One of the last of the big city political bosses, Curley served a part of one term in jail for mail fraud (1947).

For Amon Giles Carter see Note 1485.

Vitamin A, which in its primary form was so rare that it sold for more than $11,000 a pound, was lowered in cost considerably in 1932 when two Cleveland scientists discovered an improved process of extracting the vitamin from carrots and other vegetable sources.

1912 *NYT*, Wednesday, September 21, 1932, 23:7.

Hoover met with campaign aides on September 18 to plan his October speaking tour (see Note 1907).

1913 *NYT*, Thursday, September 22, 1932, 23:7. Variant: *NYT* gives "old trait." in first sentence.

Hoover urged Germany on September 20 to withdraw its threat to leave the negotiations at the Geneva World Disarmament Conference. The president avoided the equality issue, however, saying that it was "solely a European question."

1914 *NYT*, Friday, September 23, 1932, 21:7.

In the Wisconsin primary on September 20, former governor Walter Jodok Kohler, a regular Republican, defeated the incumbent, Philip Fox La Follette, a member of a prominent family of progressive politicians in Wisconsin, for the gubernatorial nomination. Regular Republicans hailed La Follette's defeat as a trend to Hoover. Kohler lost the general election.

The stock market made a partial recovery on September 20 from its decline of a week earlier (see Note 1907).

McKee (see Note 1904) was certified by the state supreme court on September 22 as acting mayor of New York City until January 1, 1934, the date of the next scheduled inauguration. Tammany had sought a special election in the fall of 1932 to fill the post vacated by Jimmy Walker (see Note 1897).

1915 *NYT*, Saturday, September 24, 1932, 17:7.

For Roosevelt in the West see Note 1909.

1916 *NYT*, Monday, September 26, 1932, 17:7.

1917 *NYT*, Tuesday, September 27, 1932, 23:7.

1918 *NYT*, Wednesday, September 28, 1932, 21:7.

The federal government, acting as legal guardian, attempted in late 1932 to restore to Jackson Barnett, a ninety-year-old Creek Indian who had made millions from oil in Oklahoma, $500,000 which he had given to his wife. Officials contended that Barnett had been coerced into his marriage and that he was incompetent at the time and unable legally to make the gift.

For Betty Blake Rogers see Note 1494.

Rogers was 9/32 Cherokee Indian.

1919 *NYT*, Thursday, September 29, 1932, 23:7.

William De Wolf Hopper, American musical comedian and actor who first appeared on the professional stage in 1879 and who was celebrated for reciting "Casey at the Bat" as a curtain speech. Hopper recited the classic baseball ballad during the radio broadcast of the opening game of the World Series on September 28.

Graham McNamee, sports and general announcer for National Broadcasting Company and one of the best known broadcasters in the country. McNamee was the chief commentator for NBC broadcasts of the World Series.

Edward Britt "Ted" Husing, resonant-voiced sports announcer for Columbia Broadcasting System from 1927 to 1954. Considered one of the best in the business, Husing provided the play-by-play report of the World Series for CBS.

George Herman "Babe" Ruth, popular American baseball star and renowned home run slugger. Ruth played for the New York Yankees from 1920 to 1934.

Gandhi (see Note 1448) ended a six-day hunger strike on September 26 when British authorities acceded to his demands for the abolition of separate electorates for the depressed classes in India.

1920 *NYT*, Friday, September 30, 1932, 21:7.

Henry Louis "Lou" Gehrig, hard-hitting first baseman for the New York Yankees from 1925 to 1939. Known to admirers as the "Iron Horse," Gehrig established a record of playing in 2,130 consecutive games.

Ruth scored three runs and Gehrig contributed a homer, as the New York Yankees defeated the Chicago Cubs, 12 to 6, in the opening game of the World Series on September 28. The Yankees swept the series from the Cubs in four games.

The House post office subcommittee recommended on September 28 a return to a two-cent rate for first class mail to provide more revenue and work opportunities. Since the imposition of a three-cent rate earlier in the year the volume of first class mail had decreased significantly. In May of 1933, Congress reduced local first class postage to two cents.

1921 *NYT*, Saturday, October 1, 1932, 17:7.

For Japanese swimmers at the Olympics see Note 1875.

1922 *NYT*, Monday, October 3, 1932, 19:7. Variant: *LAT* gives "November eighth." in eighth sentence.

The Prince of Wales (see Note 1499) and a brother, Prince George, visited the Swedish royal family in Stockholm in October. Newspapers speculated that the visit would be followed by an announcement of the engagement of George and Princess Ingrid of Sweden; however, the rumors proved false.

Garbo (see Note 1827) left the United States for Sweden in July of 1932. She returned to Hollywood in 1933 to begin work on a new motion picture. The Prince of Wales and Garbo did not meet while the two were in Sweden.

In the World Series of 1932, the Yankees and Cubs committed fourteen errors, the most miscues in a four-game series.

1923 *NYT*, Tuesday, October 4, 1932, 23:7.

Japan had gained military control of South Manchuria by January 4, 1932 (see Note 1677). On September 15, 1932, Japan formally recognized the new puppet state of Manchukuo. Japanese forces were not driven from the region until the end of World War I.

For Raphael Floyd Phillips Gibbons see Note 1664; for Rogers in Manchuria and China see DTs 1680-1696.

League of Nations experts issued the Lytton Report on October 2 which found Japan completely at fault in Manchuria. League officials recommended a peace parley be held to settle the Manchurian problem and, hopefully, to force Japan to return to China the three provinces it had seized.

For the Kellogg-Briand Pact see Note 1758.

Nine-Power Treaty, an international pact that guaranteed the independence and territorial integrity of China and reiterated the "Open Door" principle. The treaty was one of several that were signed at the Washington Armament Conference of 1921-1922.

World Court, the popular name of the Permanent Court of International Justice which was established in 1921 as part of the League of Nations.

1924 *NYT*, Wednesday, October 5, 1932, 23:7. Variant: *NYT* gives "convention? The bankers!" in first and second sentences, omitting ten words.

The American Bankers' Association held its annual convention in Los Angeles in early October.

For the Reconstruction Finance Corporation see Note 1715.

1925 *NYT*, Thursday, October 6, 1932, 25:7. Variants: *NYT* gives "stand a" in seventh sentence / *NYT* gives "They are going . . . hatchet, and have decided" in ninth and tenth sentences.

Hoover delivered a major campaign address at Des Moines, Iowa, on October 4 in which he defended Republican economic policies and offered a twelve-point farm plan.

Smith and Roosevelt, meeting on the speakers' platform at the New York Democratic Convention on October 4, shook hands for the first time since the Democratic National Convention in July.

1926 *NYT*, Friday, October 7, 1932, 23:7.

Alsace-Lorraine, provinces of northeastern France, linked in name after annexation by Germany in 1871. The territories were restored to France by the Treaty of Versailles (1919).

For James Edward "Pa" Ferguson see Note 1897; for Miriam Amanda Wallace "Ma" Ferguson see Note 1893.

1927 *NYT*, Saturday, October 8, 1932, 19:7.

President Pascual Ortiz Rubio of Mexico resigned his office on September 3 because of ill health and political difficulties. A day later, General Abelardo L. Rodríguez was named provisional president. He remained in that post until 1934.

For Joshua Reuben Clark, Jr., see Note 1467; for Dwight Whitney Morrow see Note 1467; for Plutarco Elías Calles see Note 1562.

For Texas politics see Note 1893.

1928 *NYT*, Monday, October 10, 1932, 17:7. Variants: *NYT* gives "is Salvador." in first sentence / *NYT* gives "and Alfalfa Bill" in fourth sentence.

When General Maximiliano Hernández Martínez seized the presidency of El Salvador in 1931, the United States refused to continue diplomatic relations with the El Salvadoran government. The United States finally relented in 1934, following similar action by other Central American republics.

For Huey Pierce Long see Note 1583; for James Edward "Pa" Ferguson see Note 1897; for William Henry "Alfalfa Bill" Murray see Note 1477.

1929 *NYT*, Tuesday, October 11, 1932, 23:7.

1930 *NYT*, Wednesday, October 12, 1932, 25:7. Variant: *NYT* gives "passenger plan breezed . . . country yesterday—Salvador," in first sentence.

Gerald Dempsey, California sportsman and member of the Santa Barbara Polo Club.

For the Managuan earthquake see Note 1469; for Matthew Elting Hanna see Note 1469.

All American marines were evacuated from Nicaragua by February of 1933, ending a commitment the United States had assumed there in 1927.

1931 *NYT*, Thursday, October 13, 1932, 21:7.

For Raphael Floyd Phillips Gibbons see Note 1664.

1932 *NYT*, Friday, October 14, 1932, 21:7. Variant: *NYT* gives "Peru yesterday." in first sentence.

Lima was founded in 1535. Santo Domingo, the capital of the Dominican Republic and the oldest permanent settlement in the Western Hemisphere, was founded in 1496.

Coolidge, in a rare public appearance, addressed a Republican campaign rally in New York City on October 11.

1933 *NYT*, Saturday, October 15, 1932, 17:7. Variant: *NYT* gives "country— Red Inca." in seventeenth sentence.

Tacna-Arica, border provinces of Chile and Peru, had been the object of a bitter dispute between the two countries since the occupation of the territories by Chile in 1883. The controversy was settled finally in 1929 when Peru and Chile accepted an American proposal that Chile retain Arica and that Peru receive Tacna.

William David Upshaw, Democratic United States representative from Georgia from 1919 to 1927. An extreme prohibitionist, Upshaw left the Democratic party over the liquor issue in 1932 and ran for the presidency on the Prohibition ticket.

1934 *NYT*, Monday, October 17, 1932, 17:7.

Robert LeRoy Ripley, American cartoonist who in 1918 created the newspaper series "Believe It or Not," a popular illustrated feature which highlighted unusual facts and feats.

Peru and Colombia both claimed ownership of the Leticia Corridor, a sparsely inhabited area in the upper Amazon valley. There were minor armed clashes in the region in 1932 and 1933. The League of Nations attempted to mediate the dispute, but Peru who had the weaker claim to the area refused to accede. The assassination of the Peruvian dictator in April of 1933 made settlement possible. A year later an international commission returned the Leticia to Colombia.

Chile experienced much disorder in 1932, under many short-lived administrations. On September 13 President Carlos Guillermo Davilá Espinoza was ousted in a bloodless coup by General Bartolomé Blanché, who in turn was followed in office on October 2 by Abraham Oyanedel. A regular election was held on October 30; and on December 24, 1932, the winner, former president Arturo Alessandri Palma, commenced a six-year administration.

1935 *NYT*, Tuesday, October 18, 1932, 21:7.

1936 *NYT*, Wednesday, October 19, 1932, 21:7. Variants: *NYT* gives "The Presidents down here are just" in second sentence / *NYT* gives "it's just as bad to" in fifth sentence.

Although Brazil was troubled by many localized disputes in the 1930s and 1940s, the fifteen-year strong-arm rule of President Getulio Dornelles Vargas brought considerable political and economic stability to the country.

1937 *NYT*, Thursday, October 20, 1932, 23:7.

For William Edgar Borah see Note 1452.

The Irish Free State sought the settlement of a long-standing land annuities dispute with Great Britain. In October of 1932 negotiations were opened in London between Irish and British officials, but the parleys ended in failure, the British insisting on observance of previous agreements and the Irish denying their validity.

1938 *NYT*, Friday, October 21, 1932, 23:7.

Gaucho, a native cowboy of the Argentinian and Uruguayan plains, usually of mixed Spanish and Indian ancestry.

Bolas, or *boleadoras*, a lasso made from two or three united thongs with weights at the end of each. Originally used by the Indians of Argentina, they were later adopted by the *gauchos*.

1939 *NYT*, Saturday, October 22, 1932, 17:7.

The Uruguayan peso ($1.0147 at par in 1929) declined to an average of $0.8586 in 1930, $0.5536 in 1931, and about $0.474 in 1932.

Uruguayan soccer teams took gold medals at the Olympics of 1924 and 1928 and won the World Cup in 1930. Uruguay hosted the latter tournament at its newly constructed stadium, the Centenario, in Montevideo.

1940 *NYT*, Monday, October 24, 1932, 17:7. Variant: *NYT* gives "Oct. 21 (Delayed)." in dateline.

1941 *NYT*, Tuesday, October 25, 1932, 21:7.

The Rockefeller Foundation, an American philanthropic institution established in 1913 by John D. Rockefeller, Sr. (see Note 1487), and administered by John D. Rockefeller, Jr. (see Note 1832), contributed significantly in the early 1930s to the eradication of disease-bearing mosquitoes in South America.

Henry Ford (see Note 1635) established a 3,906-square-mile rubber plantation in the Brazilian jungle in 1927. Trouble over tree culture developed early, however. It was not until 1934 that a suitable tree stock could be found that would root and produce. The development problems and the excessive costs forced Ford Company to sell its holdings to the Brazilian government in 1945.

1942 *NYT*, Wednesday, October 26, 1932, 19:7.

Alfred Dreyfus, French army officer of Jewish ancestry who was convicted in 1894 of treason and imprisoned on Devil's Island. An investigation later proved that the papers used to prove his guilt were forged. In 1906 his original conviction was set aside, and he was restored to rank in the army and given the decoration of the Legion of Honor.

Lewis Edward Lawes, warden of Sing Sing Prison in New York from 1920 to 1941.

¹⁹⁴³ *NYT,* Thursday, October 27, 1932, 21:7. Variants: *LAT* gives "let me race" in seventh sentence / *NYT* gives "it right." and *LAT* gives "Roosevelt's" in ninth sentence / *NYT* gives "Over San . . . Rico now, looking" in tenth and eleventh sentences.

Roosevelt was criticized widely for remarking in a speech in Baltimore on October 26 that the United States Supreme Court was controlled by the Republican party.

A disastrous hurricane struck northern Puerto Rico on September 26, killing 245 persons, injuring 3,329, leaving 18,957 families homeless, and inflicting $30 million property damage.

¹⁹⁴⁴ *NYT,* Friday, October 28, 1932, 21:7. Variants: *NYT* gives "place to play." in first sentence / *NYT* gives "the great Garbo." in twenty-first sentence.

Janet Gaynor, American film star of the 1920s and 1930s who gained immense popularity in sentimental roles. Gaynor won an Academy Award in 1927 for her performance in *Seventh Heaven.*

Sally Eilers, American leading lady who achieved screen stardom in the late 1920s and early 1930s.

For Clara Bow see Note 1502; for Greta Garbo see Note 1827.

¹⁹⁴⁵ *NYT,* Saturday, October 29, 1932, 17:7.

Hoover embarked on a campaign tour of Indiana, Ohio, and West Virginia on October 27.

For Charles Curtis see Note 1538.

¹⁹⁴⁶ *NYT,* Monday, October 31, 1932, 17:7.

For Betty Blake Rogers see Note 1494.

¹⁹⁴⁷ *NYT,* Tuesday, November 1, 1932, 23:7.

Hoover, having returned from his Midwestern tour (see Note 1945), addressed a campaign gathering in New York City on October 31.

For John Quillen Tilson see Note 1546.

Mason and Dixon Line, the southern boundary of Pennsylvania, is best known historically as the dividing line between slavery and free soil in the period before the American Civil War.

Cary Travers Grayson, former medical director of the United States Navy. Rear Admiral Grayson, the personal physician to President Wilson, retired from the service in 1928.

¹⁹⁴⁸ *NYT,* Wednesday, November 2, 1932, 21:4-5.

Hoover made the remarks at a campaign rally in New York City on October 31.

¹⁹⁴⁹ *NYT,* Thursday, November 3, 1932, 23:7.

¹⁹⁵⁰ *NYT,* Friday, November 4, 1932, 21:7.

For Charles Francis Adams see Note 1499.

Ingalls (see Notes 1464 and 1809) lost his bid for governor of Ohio to the incumbent, George White.

1951 *NYT*, Saturday, November 5, 1932, 17:7.

1952 *NYT*, Monday, November 7, 1932, 19:7.

1953 *NYT*, Tuesday, November 8, 1932, 21:7.

1954 *NYT*, Wednesday, November 9, 1932, 21:7.

For Benito Mussolini see Note 1452.

1955 *NYT*, Thursday, November 10, 1932, 23:7.

Roosevelt won the election with a plurality of more than 7,000,000 votes and the electoral votes of all but six states. The total of electoral votes for Roosevelt in 1932 was greater numerically than that of any previous presidential candidate in American history and the greatest proportionately since 1864.

1956 *NYT*, Friday, November 11, 1932, 19:7.

Hoover polled 5,170 votes in Mississippi to Roosevelt's 140,168. In Louisiana Hoover received 18,853 votes to Roosevelt's 249,418.

By state law Kentucky could not start its vote tabulation until 10:00 the morning after the election.

Prohibition referenda were held in eleven states on November 7. Nine of them, including California, voted to repeal state constitutional dry laws and state enforcement acts.

1957 *NYT*, Saturday, November 12, 1932, 17:7.

For John Nance Garner see Notes 1471 and 1847. Schuyler Colfax was the first person in American history to be elevated from Speaker of the House to the vice presidency. He served as Speaker from 1863 to 1869 and as vice president from 1869 to 1873.

1958 *NYT*, Monday, November 14, 1932, 19:7. Variant: *LAT* gives " 'Miss Robertson room.' " in eleventh sentence.

For Rogers' trip to South America see DTs 1927-1943; for Nicholas Murray Butler see Note 1820.

1959 *NYT*, Tuesday, November 15, 1932, 23:7.

Roosevelt visited the White House, at Hoover's invitation, on November 22. The president sought to convince him that decisions on matters such as war debts would be worthless without assurance that they would be honored after March 4. Roosevelt, however, decided to make no commitments before his inauguration. He told reporters unofficially that "it was not his baby."

1960 *NYT*, Wednesday, November 16, 1932, 19:7.

Germany announced on September 3, 1932, that it would be unable to pay $7,800,000 due the United States at the end of the month toward payment of mixed claims and costs of the American army of occupation. In accordance with provisions of the debt agreement, payment was postponed for two years to September 30, 1934.

Total funded debt owed by fifteen European nations as of November 14, 1932, was $11,229,968,706, to which later was added $184,000,000 in interest postponed because of the Hoover moratorium for the fiscal year 1932. Only one country, Finland, paid its debt in full.

1961 *NYT*, Thursday, November 17, 1932, 21:7.

Both France and Great Britain asked for the postponement of war debt installments due on December 15, 1932. The United States replied that it had no authority to grant extensions and that payment of the sum due in December would help to improve relations among the countries.

1962 *NYT*, Friday, November 18, 1932, 21:7. Variant: *NYT* gives "your last cent" in eighth sentence.

1963 *NYT*, Saturday, November 19, 1932, 17:7.

For Roosevelt's visit with Hoover see Note 1959.

Roosevelt purchased a $500,000 life insurance policy in 1930 with the Georgia Warm Springs Foundation named as beneficiary.

Roosevelt had suffered from the crippling effects of poliomyelitis since August of 1921. In early 1927 he formed the Georgia Warm Springs Foundation, a nonprofit institution which operated a hydrotherapeutic center at Warm Springs, Georgia, for the treatment of polio.

A nationwide "straw ballot" taken by *Literary Digest* magazine was 98.85 percent accurate in its prediction of the percentage of vote for Roosevelt in 1932. Four years later, the *Digest* poll was discredited when it produced a staggeringly inaccurate forecast of the presidential election of 1936.

1964 *NYT*, Monday, November 21, 1932, 19:7.

For Roosevelt's visit with Hoover see Note 1959; for Henry Lewis Stimson see Note 1485.

1965 *NYT*, Tuesday, November 22, 1932, 23:7.

For Roosevelt's visit with Hoover see Note 1959.

Raymond Robins, American social economist, lecturer, and writer. A militant dry leader and a personal friend of Hoover, Robins mysteriously disappeared while en route to a visit with the president. He was found alive on November 18 near Asheville, North Carolina, apparently a victim of amnesia.

1966 *NYT*, Wednesday, November 23, 1932, 21:7. Variant: *LAT* gives "Mrs. Ned McLean" in eighth sentence.

Walter Lippmann, American editor, columnist, and author who served on the editorial staff of the *New York World* from 1921 to 1931 and later contributed columns to the *New York Herald-Tribune* and the *Washington Post*. In his column of November 22, Lippmann questioned the accuracy of Rogers' statements in DT 1964. Lippmann contended that neither Hoover nor Roosevelt had promised "no postponements and no cancellation."

For Arthur Brisbane see Note 1442.

Evalyn Walsh McLean, American gold mining heiress and society hostess, was the wife of Edward Beale "Ned" McLean, owner and publisher of the *Washington Post*.

1967 *NYT*, Thursday, November 24, 1932, 27:7. Variant: *LAT* gives "BEVERLY HILLS," as place of origin.

The *Los Angeles Times* made the statement in its editorial column of November 19.

1968 *NYT*, Friday, November 25, 1932, 17:7.

For Roosevelt's visit with Hoover see Note 1959.

1969 *NYT*, Saturday, November 26, 1932, 17:7.

McAdoo (see Note 1801) chaired the California delegation at the Democratic National Convention. California broke a deadlock at the convention when it switched its forty-four votes on the fourth ballot from Garner to Roosevelt (see Note 1844). McAdoo was elected in 1932 as United States senator from California. He served in that position from 1933 to 1939.

Ruth Bryan Owen, Democratic United States representative from Florida from 1929 to 1933. The daughter of William Jennings Bryan (see Note 1617), Owen was an unsuccessful candidate for renomination in 1932.

1970 *NYT*, Monday, November 28, 1932, 17:7.

For Arthur Brisbane see Note 1442; for William Randolph Hearst see Note 1623.

1971 *NYT*, Tuesday, November 29, 1932, 21:7. Variants: *LAT* gives "says read" in fourth sentence / *NYT* omits tenth sentence.

For Robert LeRoy Ripley of "Believe It or Not" fame see Note 1934; for the *Literary Digest* poll see Note 1963; for Charles Spencer Chaplin see Note 1448.

Stan Laurel and Oliver Hardy, American comedians who first teamed in 1927 to initiate a brilliant series of short and feature films. Laurel, British-born, played a child-like character who was the antithesis of Hardy's pompous father-figure.

Joe E. Brown, American comedian noted for his extraordinarily wide mouth. Brown reached the height of his screen popularity in the 1930s and early 1940s.

1972 *NYT*, Wednesday, November 30, 1932, 21:7. Variant: *NYT* gives "Thanksgiving and an airplane ride cured her?" in first sentence.

1973 *NYT*, Thursday, December 1, 1932, 23:7.

1974 *NYT*, Friday, December 2, 1932, 23:7.

The American Federation of Labor endorsed in mid-November a national trend to a five-day work week and a six-hour day. Hearings on legislation to enact such a plan began in the Senate on January 5, 1933. Although no such law was ever passed, many companies voluntarily adopted such measures.

For the national sales tax see Note 1769.

The second session of the Seventy-second Congress convened on December 5, 1933, with 158 defeated members sitting in the Senate and House. The Twentieth Amendment to the Constitution abolished the "lame-duck" session of Congress—so-called because it included members who had failed of reelection a month before the "short" session opened in December of even-numbered years. The amendment, ratified in 1933, moved back the day on which terms of congressmen begin from March 4 to January 3 and required Congress to convene each year on January 3.

1975 *NYT*, Saturday, December 3, 1932, 19:7.

1976 *NYT*, Monday, December 5, 1932, 19:7.

For lame duck Congress see Note 1974.

¹⁹⁷⁷ *NYT,* Tuesday, December 6, 1932, 23:7. Variant: *LAT* omits third sentence.

Congress Dances (Kongress Tanzt), a commercially a successful motion picture which was produced in Germany in 1931 and which characterized the Congress of Vienna of 1815 in operatic style.

The House on December 5, the first day of the lame-duck session of Congress (see Note 1974), failed to pass a resolution for repeal of prohibition. The measure fell six votes short of the necessary two-thirds majority to send it to the Senate. Eighty-one lame-duck congressmen voted no.

¹⁹⁷⁸ *NYT,* Wednesday, December 7, 1932, 23:7.

Samuel George Blythe, American writer, editor, and columnist. A long-time contributor to the *Saturday Evening Post,* Blythe wrote in a feature article in the December 3 issue of the magazine that Americans could improve the economic state of the country by buying American-made products.

¹⁹⁷⁹ *NYT,* Thursday, December 8, 1932, 23:7. Variant: *LAT* gives "readers of The Times" in first sentence.

Rogers responded to an editorial in the *New York Times* on December 1 which disavowed responsibility for Rogers' columns in November regarding war debts.

¹⁹⁸⁰ *NYT,* Friday, December 9, 1932, 23:7.

For lame-duck Congress see Note 1974.

Owen (see Note 1969) was one of 168 Democrats who voted on December 5 for a resolution for repeal of prohibition (see Note 1977).

¹⁹⁸¹ *NYT,* Saturday, December 10, 1932, 17:7.

The Notre Dame University football team lost to the University of Southern California, 13 to 0, in Los Angeles on December 10.

For Knute Kenneth Rockne see Note 1462.

¹⁹⁸² *NYT,* Monday, December 12, 1932, 17:7.

The University of Pittsburgh was defeated by the University of Southern California, 35 to 0, in the Rose Bowl game on January 1, 1933. U. S. C. shut out eight of its ten opponents in 1932. Only thirteen points were scored against the undefeated Trojans during the season.

Although the Colgate University football team went undefeated, untied, and unscored upon in 1932, it did not receive an invitation to the Rose Bowl.

¹⁹⁸³ *NYT,* Tuesday, December 13, 1932, 21:7.

¹⁹⁸⁴ *NYT,* Wednesday, December 14, 1932, 23:7.

Air express service between the east and west coasts on a daily schedule of less than eighteen hours began on December 13. The rate for first class air mail postage had increased in July of 1932 from five to eight cents an ounce.

¹⁹⁸⁵ *NYT,* Thursday, December 15, 1932, 21:7. Variant: *LAT* omits "(my mother paper)" in first sentence.

Charlton Ogburn, Jr., honors graduate of Harvard University in 1932 who later achieved success as a writer and specialist in Far Eastern affairs. Ogburn, whose father, a prominent labor lawyer, had worked in Europe for American bankers seeking payment of European war debts, roundly criticized Rogers for his "dirty foreigner" views, specifically the Oklahoma's insistence that foreign debtors "pay or default" (see DTs 1960-1962 and 1964). His letter appeared on the editorial page of the *New York Times* on November 28. The managing editor of the *Times* wired Rogers a copy of Ogburn's letter, and Rogers answered Ogburn two days later with a lengthy, but humorous rebuttal. On the same day, ten other letters-to-the-editor appeared in the *Times,* in praise or rebuke of Rogers.

1986 *NYT,* Friday, December 16, 1932, 21:7. Variants: *NYT* omits first and second sentences / *NYT* gives "A fellow came" to begin third sentence.

A House spectator, twenty-five-year-old Marlin R. M. Kemmerer, a store clerk from Pennsylvania, quickly emptied the House chambers on December 13 when he suddenly leaned over the gallery rail, displayed a pistol, and demanded time to address Congress. Kemmerer was charged with assault and battery.

Great Britain and five other nations paid their December 15 installments of war debts in full. The British payment totaled $95,550,000.

1987 *LAT,* Saturday, December 17, 1932, I:1:6. *NYT* did not print the DT.

The French government was ousted on December 13 when the Chamber of Deputies rejected a government request for authority to make the debt payment, causing France to default on its debt obligation of $19,261,432. Four other nations also failed to make their December 15 installment.

1988 *NYT,* Monday, December 19, 1932, 17:7.

For Philippine independence see Note 1778.

1989 *NYT,* Tuesday, December 20, 1932, 19:7. Variant: *LAT* gives "BEVERLY HILLS," as place to origin.

Joseph Paul-Boncour, premier of France from 1932 to 1933. Known especially for his advocacy of international cooperation, Paul-Boncour headed the French delegation at the Geneva Preliminary Disarmament Conference of 1926.

For France and the war debts see Note 1987.

The House passed the Collier bill on December 21 legalizing the manufacture and sale of beer. The Senate did not act on the measure in 1932, but early the next year it passed the Blaine resolution for repeal of the Eighteenth Amendment; the House soon followed suit. The Twenty-first Amendment, repealing prohibition, was ratified by the necessary two-thirds of the states by December 5, 1933. Beer was legalized in March of 1933.

1990 *NYT,* Wednesday, December 21, 1932, 21:7.

The technocracy movement was a short-lived (1932-1933) effort to arouse popular support for a political-industrial organization of American society based on advanced technology. First used in 1919, the term technocracy was revived during the Great Depression when an audience was assured for almost any proposal to revive the economy.

1991 *NYT,* Thursday, December 22, 1932, 19:7.

For war debts see Notes 1986 and 1987.

¹⁹⁹² *NYT,* Friday, December 23, 1932, 19:7.

Eskimo pies were invented by Christian Nelson of Waukon, Iowa, in the early 1920s. Their appearance on the market helped to stimulate the growing demand for ice cream during the decade.

Miniature golf produced a brief craze in the United States in the late 1920s and early 1930s. The first American course appeared in 1927 on Lookout Mountain near Chattanooga, Tennessee. The popularity of the game spread through the southern resorts, took fire in California, and by 1931 had resulted in the establishment of 25,000 of the Lilliputian links throughout the country. The coming of the depression, however, lessened the popular appeal of the pastime.

¹⁹⁹³ *NYT,* Saturday, December 24, 1932, 15:7.

Didrikson (see Note 1871) was accused of professionalism and suspended by the Amateur Athletic Union in early December because her picture had appeared with an automobile advertisement. Didrikson attempted to prove her innocence, but the AAU would not relent. Finally, on December 21 she turned professional. A day later, the AAU cleared her of all charges.

Hoover revealed on December 22 that negotiations for payment of war debts had failed and that he would leave the question of debts for Roosevelt's incoming administration.

¹⁹⁹⁴ *NYT,* Monday, December 26, 1932, 25:7.

For technocracy see Note 1992; for legislation of beer see Note 1989.

¹⁹⁹⁵ *NYT,* Tuesday, December 27, 1932, 15:7.

¹⁹⁹⁶ *NYT,* Wednesday, December 28, 1932, 19:7.

For technocracy see Note 1992.

¹⁹⁹⁷ *NYT,* Thursday, December 29, 1932, 21:7. Variant: *LAT* gives "Congress; 'where can we lay the blame on Congress?' " in fifteenth sentence.

The Twentieth Amendment, or the Lame-Duck Amendment (see Note 1974), provided that the terms of the president and vice president commence on January 20 in the year after the general election.

Thomas Woodrow Wilson, president of the United States from 1913 to 1921. In November of 1920, William Jennings Bryan sought the resignation of Wilson in order to permit Vice President Marshall to assume the presidency on the condition that Marshall would appoint President-elect Harding secretary of state.

¹⁹⁹⁸ *NYT,* Friday, December 30, 1932, 19:7. Variant: *NYT* omits "late" in P.S.

Income tax refunds totaling $80,583,504 were made in 1932. The names of many wealthy individuals prominent in the political, social, and business life of the country appeared on the refund list.

For Charlton Ogburn, Jr., see Note 1985.

¹⁹⁹⁹ *NYT,* Saturday, December 31, 1932, 17:7.

Insull (see Note 1686) went to Europe in April of 1932, soon after his utility companies went into receivership. On learning in October of 1932 that he was to be indicted in a United States federal court for mail fraud, he fled from Paris to Greece to avoid extradition. A spectacular international legal fiasco ensued with the United States bending all efforts to obtain Insull's return. In 1934 he finally was seized, returned to America, and tried on mail-fraud charges. He was acquitted.

The French government, which had refused two weeks earlier to pay $19 million to the United States, approved a $14 million loan to Austria on December 30. The Austrian loan was the French share of a new financial advance provided by a five-power protocol of July of 1932.

2000 *NYT*, Monday, January 2, 1933, 25:7.

2001 *NYT*, Tuesday, January 3, 1933, 3:5. Variant: *LAT* gives "Everyone have enough" in third sentence.

2002 *NYT*, Wednesday, January 4, 1933, 21:6-7.

For technocracy see Note 1992; for British war debts see Note 1986.

2003 *NYT*, Thursday, January 5, 1933, 23:7.

For the Rose Bowl game of 1933 see Note 1981; for Andrew William Mellon see Note 1493.

Howard Harding Jones, football coach at the University of Southern California from 1925 until his death in 1941. A leading figure in collegiate football, Jones directed U.S.C. to two national titles and five Rose Bowl triumphs.

2004 *NYT*, Friday, January 6, 1933, 21:7. Variant: *NYT* gives "statesmanship." to end eighth sentence, omitting next ten words.

Coolidge died of a heart attack on January 5 at the age of sixty.

For Grace Goodhue Coolidge see Note 1572.

2005 *NYT*, Saturday, January 7, 1933, 17:7.

Farmers' inability to meet mortgages greatly impaired the fiscal and commercial conditions in the country during the 1930s. Efforts in many localities to effect public sales under foreclosure were defeated by threatening or violent mobs. In one such incident in Lemars, Iowa, on January 4, 800 farmers forcibly prevented the sale of a foreclosed farm after threatening to lynch an agent of the mortgage holder.

Karl Cortlandt Schuyler of Colorado was elected to the Senate on November 8, 1932, to fill a vacancy. At the same election he was an unsuccessful candidate for a full term to begin on March 4, 1933. Although Schuyler announced in January that he would resign in favor of his successor, he remained in the Senate until the inauguration of the new Congress.

2006 *NYT*, Monday, January 9, 1933, 21:7.

For Grace Goodhue Coolidge see Note 1572.

2007 *NYT*, Tuesday, January 10, 1933, 23:6-7. Variant: *NYT* gives "way, in . . . this. Germany" in seventh and eighth sentences.

2008 *NYT*, Wednesday, January 11, 1933, 21:7.

Shaw (see Note 1454) arrived in Bombay on January 8 and immediately expressed his admiration for Mahatma Gandhi. A day later in an unrelated incident, 1,000 Indian troops were rushed to Alwar City to quell a revolt by 80,000 Moslem tribesmen.

Shaw, who was in the midst of the world tour, vistited the Metro-Goldwyn-Mayer motion picture studios near Hollywood on March 28.

For legalization of beer see Note 1989.

2009 *NYT,* Thursday, January 12, 1933, 19:7. Variant: *NYT* gives "paper." to end first sentence, omitting next nine words.

Glass (see Note 1828) and Long (see Note 1583) clashed repeatedly in early 1933 over the Glass banking bill which came up for debate in the Senate on January 5. Long and a small group of senators championed the local banker against the provisions of the measure for wider latitude in branch banking. The Louisiana Democrat led a filibuster that delayed the bill until the twenty-first. After a compromise was reached, the measure passed the Senate on January 25. It died in the House Finance Committee.

The future of American banking stirred great anxiety among experts in early 1933. Bank failures occurred continuously, and general conditions suggested the probability of a widespread breakdown. The situation was eased somewhat when Roosevelt, after taking office, declared a national bank holiday, allowing banks to suspend specie payments. The passage in June of the Glass-Steagall Banking Act of 1933, a revised version of the earlier Glass bill (see above), provided basic reform of the banking system.

The French government, hard pressed to balance the budget and to eliminate a $40 million treasury deficit, remained firm in January of 1933 in its decision to defer payment of its war debt. It also failed to make the June 15 installment on its $3.9 billion obligation to the United States.

Japanese forces opened an offensive against the Chinese province of Jehol on January 10. They captured Chengteh, the capital, on March 4 and swept south of the Great Wall to within a few miles of Peiking and Tientsin. Facing the loss of these important cities, the Chinese on May 31, 1933, concluded a formal truce with the Japanese which provided for the demilitarization of a large section of China. By signing the truce, China tacitly abandoned Manchuria and Jehol to Japan.

2010 *NYT,* Friday, January 13, 1933, 17:7. Variant: *NYT* gives "last minute and" in third sentence.

Arizona on January 13 became the twenty-fourth state to ratify the Twentieth Amendment (see Note 1974). Final ratification of the so-called Lame-Duck Amendment came on January 23.

2011 *NYT,* Saturday, January 14, 1933, 15:7.

The Senate voted on January 12 that all income tax rebates in excess of $5,000 must be approved by Congress. Previously, Congress had controlled only rebates of $75,000 or more, and all others had been subject to the approval of the Bureau of Internal Revenue (later known as the Internal Revenue Service).

2012 *NYT,* Monday, January 16, 1933, 17:7.

For Huey Pierce "Kingfish" Long see Notes 1583 and 2009.

2013 *NYT,* Tuesday, January 17, 1933, 21:7.

Rain drenched parched California on January 16, dispelling worries of an unusually dry season in the state. Although the storm doubled the rainfall total for the year in California, much of the state remained 50 percent drier than during the same period a year earlier.

For Huey Pierce "Kingfish" Long see Notes 1583 and 2009.

²⁰¹⁴ *NYT*, Wednesday, January, 18, 1933, 27:7.

For Huey Pierce "Kingfish" Long see Notes 1583 and 2009; for Carter Glass see Notes 1485 and 2009.

²⁰¹⁵ *NYT*, Thursday, January 19, 1933, 17:7.

The Philippine independence bill (see Note 1778) became law on January 17 and included a provision that a constitution was to be drafted and submitted within two years to the president of the United States for his approval. When approved, it was then to be submitted to a direct vote of the Philippine people.

²⁰¹⁶ *NYT*, Friday, January 20, 1933, 19:7.

²⁰¹⁷ *NYT,* Saturday, January 21, 1933, 17:7.

Roosevelt, noted for his successful campaign tactic of intimate fireside chats, met with Hoover on January 20 to discuss foreign affairs. A day earlier, the president-elect and Long (see Note 1583) conferred about the Glass banking bill and international war debts.

²⁰¹⁸ *NYT*, Monday, January 23, 1933, 15:7.

Jeff Taff, veteran commercial pilot for Varney Air Service, Ltd., of California.

Rogers was a guest speaker at the annual meeting of the California Newspaper Publishers' Association in Marysville, near Sacramento, on January 23.

Five California banks, including the large California National Bank of Sacramento, closed their doors on January 23 because of heavy withdrawals. For the banking crisis in the United States see Note 2009.

²⁰¹⁹ *NYT*, Tuesday, January 24, 1933, 21:7.

For Betty Blake Rogers see Note 1494.

Sallie Clementine Rogers McSpadden, sister of Will Rogers and a resident of Chelsea, Oklahoma.

Antonio Scotti, opera star who was the principal baritone of the Metropolitan Opera in New York City for thirty-five years. His last appearance at the Metropolitan took place on January 20, 1933, as Chim-fen in *L'Oracolo*. He then retired to his native Italy, where he died in 1936.

For Huey Pierce "Kingfish" Long see Note 1583 and 2009; for Walter Scott, "Death Valley Scotty," see Note 1899.

²⁰²⁰ *NYT,* Wednesday, January 25, 1933, 19:7.

For the Lame-Duck Amendment see Notes 1974 and 2010.

²⁰²¹ *NYT,* Thursday, January 26, 1933, 19:7.

An amendment to remonetize silver was added to the Glass banking bill on January 23, precipitating a serious debate in the Senate on the question of currency inflation. Denouncing the measure as class legislation, opponents of the silver amendment were able to defeat it on January 24 by a vote of fifty-six to eighteen.

A rift that had existed since 1920 between the two branches of the Roosevelt family appeared to have been healed on January 24 when Kermit Roosevelt, the second son of former president Theodore Roosevelt, joined President-elect Franklin D. Roosevelt on a yacht cruise off the Florida coast.

Ruth Wilson Hurley, wife of Secretary of War Patrick J. Hurley (see Note 1481), dedicated the new composition to her adopted homeland, the southwestern United States.

2022   *NYT*, Friday, January 27, 1933, 21:7.

For the Glass banking bill see Note 2009; for Carter Glass see Note 1828; for Huey Pierce "Kingfish" Long see Note 1583.

2023   *NYT*, Saturday, January 28, 1933, 15:7.

Howard Scott, a well-trained American construction engineer, and M. King Hubbert, a professor of geophysics at Columbia University, were the two major proponents of technocracy in the United States (see Note 1992). Their pictures appeared in newspapers nationally on January 27.

2024   *NYT*, Monday, January 30, 1933, 15:7. Variants: *LAT* gives "liked to move him" in fifth sentence / *NYT* gives "appropriate money" in sixth sentence.

Ronald Charles Lindsay, British ambassador to the United States from 1930 to 1939.

Paul Louis Charles Claudel, French ambassador to the United States from 1927 to 1933.

Millard Evelyn Tydings, Democratic United States senator from Maryland from 1927 to 1951. Tydings' bill to force drastic cuts in appropriation bills was blocked by the Democratic caucus in the Senate which then convinced Tydings to substitute a simple declaration of policy in place of his bill.

2025   *NYT*, Tuesday, January 31, 1933, 19:7.

In France a new Radical-Socialist ministry was formed on January 31 by Édouard Daladier. It remained in power for only a few months.

Roosevelt met with British Ambassador Lindsay, (see Note 2024) in late January at Warm Springs, Georgia, concerning arrangements for negotiation of the British war debts. The formal negotiations took place in Washington, D. C., in March.

Ford (see Note 1637) accused certain American bankers of having strikes instigated in a number of his plants. He alleged that the guilty bankers held interlocking directorates on the boards of his competitors. The auto maker, however, vowed on January 28 to break the strikes and to resume full production.

2026   *NYT*, Wednesday, February 1, 1933, 19:7. Variant: *NYT* omits sixth sentence.

Between 2,000-3,000 persons were stranded at a resort in the snow-swept Sierra Nevada mountains on January 29 (see also D⁻ 2025). The weekend crowd had gone to the resort to participate in a winter sports carnival sponsored by the California Junior Chamber of Commerce. The group was rescued two days later.

2027   *LAT*, Thursday, February 2, 1933, I:1:5. *NYT* did not print the DT.

For the Reconstruction Finance Corporation see Note 1715; for John Pierpont Morgan see Note 1717.

2028   *NYT*, Friday, February 3, 1933, 19:7.

Some congressmen feared that Great Britain would attempt to negotiate a reduction of its debt obligation to the United States. Discussions between American and British officials began in Washington, D. C., in March. No agreement on reduction was reached at that time, but Great Britain notified the United States on June 13, two days before the next installment came due, that it would make only a partial payment of $10 million.

2029 *NYT,* Saturday, February 4, 1933, 17:7.

A committee of the League of Nations submitted draft resolutions early in 1933 for a settlement of the Manchurian question favorable to China. Despite a Japanese rejection of the proposal, the League assembly adopted the draft report of the committee on February 24, thus passing unprecedented censure upon Japan and prompting Japanese delegates to walk out of the assembly hall. On March 27, 1933, Japan announced that it had withdrawn from the League.

James Monroe, president of the United States from 1817 to 1825. In December of 1823, Monroe announced a far-reaching principle of American foreign policy which became known as the Monroe Doctrine. The two-part doctrine held that the American continents were no longer to be considered as a field for European colonization and that the United States would not interfere in European affairs.

The so-called Japanese Monroe Doctrine was set forth by the Japanese foreign minister on January 20 and asserted that Japan would not permit the intervention of the League or of individual powers in its controversy with China.

2030 *NYT,* Monday, February 6, 1933, 17:7.

The Senate voted on February 3 to suspend David Sheldon Barry, the Senate sergeant-at-arms, for authoring a magazine article in which he wrote that "there are not many Senators or Representatives who sell their vote for money, and it is pretty well known who those few are." The Senate Judiciary Committee briefly considered bringing a libel suit against Barry but later decided to drop the matter.

Coolidge's *Autobiography* was published in serial form in Cosmopolitan magazine during the spring and summer of 1929 and in book form later in the year.

2031 *LAT,* Tuesday, February 7, 1933, I:1:5. *NYT* did not print the DT.

Arthur Prentice Rugg, chief justice of the Massachusetts Supreme Court from 1911 to 1938. Rugg, a life-long friend of Coolidge, delivered the eulogy at the memorial service in the capitol on February 6.

2032 *NYT,* Wednesday, February 8, 1933, 21:7. Variants: *NYT* gives " 'attacked character and loans' " in first sentence/*LAT* gives "made was better" in fifth and sixth sentences.

2033 *NYT,* Thursday, February 9, 1933, 19:7.

Barry (see Note 2030) was tried openly in the chambers of the Senate on February 3 and then dismissed from his job four days later.

2034 *NYT,* Friday, February 10, 1933, 19:7. Variant: *NYT* omits tenth sentence.

Speculation that Great Britain would pay its entire war debt in one "lump sum" provoked criticism from some members of Congress who opposed the arrangement unless it was accompanied by the settlement of the currency problem and by the restoration of markets abroad.

For Jackson Barnett, the millionaire Creek Indian, see Note 1918.

2035 *NYT*, Saturday, February 11, 1933, 17:7.
Democratic leaders in Congress attempted in early February to grant Roosevelt absolute control of government spending during the first two years of his administration in order to insure economy in federal expenditures. The action was blocked by Republicans and conservative Democrats.

For Benito Mussolini see Note 1452.

2036 *NYT*, Monday, February 13, 1933, 17:7.

Japan rejected a League proposal that it abandon its claims in Manchuria (see Note 2029). The League, however, stiffened its demands and then invited the United States and Russia to serve on a committee to draft a final settlement. Neither country participated.

2037 *NYT*, Tuesday, February 14, 1933, 17:7.

The Dutch battleship *De Zeven Procincien* was seized by 400 native marines in the Dutch East Indies on February 5. The ship was recaptured five days later after an airplane bomb was dropped on the deck, killing twenty-two of the crew. In Holland there was fear that the mutiny was the forerunner of communist-instigated disorders; accordingly, the navy meted out severe punishment to the mutineers.

The United States Navy performed maneuvers in the Pacific during much of February to determine whether an enemy fleet with aircraft could conduct a successful raid on the West Coast. The maneuvers were code-named Problem 14.

2038 *NYT*, Wednesday, February 15, 1933, 23:7.

Hoover was the main speaker at the Lincoln Day Dinner of the National Republican Club in New York City on February 13. The speech, which was broadcast nationally, was Hoover's final address before leaving office.

2039 *NYT*, Thursday, February 16, 1933, 21:7.

Hoover intimated on February 14 that he would issue a rebuke of Congress if that body followed through with its promise to grant President-elect Roosevelt dictatorial economic powers (see Note 2035). Hoover had asked for such powers earlier but had failed to obtain them.

2040 *LAT*, Friday, February 17, 1933, I:1:5. *NYT* did not print the DT.

Anton Joseph Cermak, Democratic mayor of Chicago from 1931 to 1933. Cermak was vacationing in Miami when Roosevelt arrived there on February 15. In an attempt to assassinate the president-elect, Giuseppe Zangara, an Italian-born naturalized citizen of the United States, wounded Cermak and a number of bystanders. Cermak died nineteen days later.

2041 *NYT*, Saturday, February 18, 1933, 17:7.

A committee of the Senate convened in New Orleans in February to investigate charges against the election of John Holmes Overton to the Senate in 1932. In January of 1934 the committee reported that the elections in Louisiana were questionable but upheld the right of Overton to be seated.

The Senate passed on February 16 the so-called Blaine resolution for the repeal of prohibition (see Note 1989).

2042 *NYT*, Monday, February 20, 1933, 17:7.

James John "Gentleman Jim" Corbett, American prizefighter who held the world heavyweight title from 1892 to 1897. After his retirement from the ring in

1903, Corbett appeared on the stage, in motion pictures, and on radio. He died on February 18 in New York City.

2043 *NYT*, Tuesday, February 21, 1933, 21:7.

For Jackson Barnett, the millionaire Creek Indian, see Note 1918.

2044 *LAT*, Wednesday, February 22, 1933, I:1:4-5. *NYT* did not print the DT.

Glass (see Note 1828) made the remarks during a debate in the Senate on February 20 over a bill to provide an expansion of the federal unemployment relief program. Glass, who earlier had declined Roosevelt's offer of a position in his cabinet, denounced the proposed relief bill and called for the abolition of the Reconstruction Finance Corporation.

2045 *NYT*, Thursday, February 23, 1933, 19:7.

Cordell Hull, Democratic United States senator from Tennessee from 1931 to 1933. Hull served as secretary of state under Roosevelt from 1933 to 1944. He was awarded the Nobel Peace Prize in 1945.

William Hartman Woodin, American industrialist and financial expert. Woodin, a conservative, served as secretary of the treasury from 1933 to 1934.

Claude Augustus Swanson, Democratic United States senator from Virginia from 1910 to 1933. Swanson served as secretary of the navy from 1933 to 1939.

2046 *NYT*, Friday, February 24, 1933, 19:7.

Roosevelt's cabinet, in addition to Hull, Woodin, and Swanson (see Note 2045), included Senator Thomas James Walsh of Montana as attorney general, former governor George Henry Dern of Utah as secretary of war, James Aloysius Farley of New York City as postmaster general, Harold LeClare Ickes of Chicago as secretary of the interior, Henry Agard Wallace of Iowa as secretary of agriculture. Daniel Calhoun Roper of Washington, D.C., as secretary of commerce, and Francis Perkins of New York as secretary of labor. Perkins was the first woman cabinet member in history.

For the "Forgotten Man" see Note 1879.

2047 *NYT*, Saturday, February 25, 1933, 17:7.

Lewis Williams Douglas, Democratic United States representative from Arizona from 1927 to 1933. Douglas served as director of the budget from 1933 to 1934.

Stephen Arnold Douglas, Democratic United States senator from Illinois from 1847 until his death in 1861. Known as the "Little Giant," Douglas was a leading statesman of the pre-Civil War era. Stephen A. and Lewis W. Douglas were not related.

Douglas, Arizona, was named for James Douglas, a Canadian-born physician who achieved fame as a pioneer in Arizona mining. Lewis W. Douglas was a grandson of James Douglas.

2048 *NYT*, Monday, February 27, 1933, 17:7.

2049 *NYT*, Tuesday, February 28, 1933, 21:7. Variants: *NYT* omits third sentences / *NYT* gives " 'you out when we are' " in fourth sentence.

For Anton Joseph Cermak see Note 2040.

For the Hoover debt moratorium see Note 1532.

Bank holidays of various lengths had been proclaimed in most states by March 4, Inauguration Day. The action was prompted by the serious condition of the banking system in the United States in early 1933 (see Note 2009).

2050 *LAT,* Wednesday, March 1, 1933, I:1:2. *NYT* did not print the DT.

Great Britain announced on February 27 that it had imposed a temporary arms embargo against both China and Japan. The United States opposed the trade restriction because of fears that it would prove more harmful to China than to Japan.

2051 *NYT,* Thursday, March 2, 1933, 19:7.

Ford (see Note 1635) was asked in January to lend several million dollars to two financially troubled banks in Detroit. He refused to make the loan, but in late February he proposed the takeover of the two banks and "the creation of two new banks." Although the public applauded the offer, owners of the banks blocked Ford's move. General Motors later underwrote the capitalization of an entirely new bank, and in August of 1933 Ford also established a new bank. The two ailing institutions eventually folded, and the two new ones prospered.

Smith, appearing at a hearing of the Senate Committee on Economics on February 28, advocated recognition of Russia, a national highway construction program, and a war debt moratorium and announced his opposition to inflation as a remedy to the depression.

2052 *NYT,* Friday, March 3, 1933, 19:7.

For Arthur Brisbane see Note 1442.

A three-day bank holiday was declared in California on March 1; it later was extended. Banks began to reopen on March 12.

2053 *NYT,* Saturday, March 4, 1933, 15:7.

For the bank holiday in California see Note 2052.

INDEX

"Abie's Irish Rose" (song): 108
Abilene, Tex.: 54
Abyssinia: see Ethiopia
Actors and acting: 98, 189, 203, 256, 262
Adams, Charles Francis: 30, 232
Advertising: 29, 207
AFL: 245
Africa: 28, 96
Air mail: 249
Akron (dirigible): 164
Alaska: 78
Albany, N. Y.: 199
Alfonso XIII: 18, 19, 22
Alienists: 157
Alimony: 25
Allegheny Mountains: 233
Alsace-Lorraine: 219
Amarillo, Tex.: 53, 134
Amazon River: 226, 227
Ambassadors: see Diplomats
American Athletic Union: 253
American Federation of Labor: see AFL
American Indians: 10; see also under names of tribes
American Institute of Banking: 175
American Legion: 78-79, 210
American Red Cross: 14, 16, 228
American Revolutionary War: 88
"Amos 'n Andy" (radio show): 43, 52, 207; "Kingfish" character from, 210
Amsterdam, Holland: 119
Anderson, Heartley W. (Hunk): 91
Andes Mountains: 224, 229, 237, 266
Andrada, Manual: 78
Antiques: 189
Argentina: 57, 78, 192, 195, 220, 224, 261; national anthem of, 195; gauchos of, 225
Arizona: 29, 207, 262, 279
Arkansas: 3, 95
Armistice Day: 135
Asia: 106
Astor, John J.: 81
Astor, Helen D. H. (Mrs. W. Vincent): 168
Astor, Nancy L. (Mrs. Waldorf): 56, 66, 89
Athens, Greece: 120
Athletes: 193, 198
Atlanta, Ga.: 24
Atlantic Ocean: 159, 169, 180
Atoms: "splitting" of, 160
Australia: 49, 145, 151, 256
Autographs: 194
Automobiles: 7, 39, 50, 131, 159, 187, 200, 261; accidents, 71; speed records set by, 75, 145; industry, 194; deaths involving, 254
Aviation: 29, 31, 47-48, 49, 50, 51, 53, 56, 60, 63, 71, 75, 79, 139, 151, 156, 160, 164, 166, 169, 180, 193, 209, 234, 244, 249, 254, 266; accidents, 7; commercial, 11-12, 12-13, 14, 20, 21, 24, 25, 53, 54, 98-99, 120, 132, 176, 178, 233, 234; in Nicaragua, 16; military, 21; airfields, 50, 51, 53, 54, 106; air races, 71; in Japan, 106; in Korea, 106; in Middle East, 118, 119; in Europe, 119-120, 122; speed records in, 145; in South America, 222, 223, 234; in Argentina, 225
Aviators: 132; salaries of, 158-159
Azore Islands: 159

Babicora Ranch: 83, 128, 135, 136
Baghdad, Iraq: 119
Baker, George F.: 30
Baker, Newton D.: 131, 135
Baker, Reginald L.: 2
Baldness: 3
Baltimore, Md.: 160
Balzar, Frederick B.: 160
Bank of England: 205
Bankers: 82, 85, 121, 128, 130, 135, 136, 140-141, 144, 148, 173, 175, 192, 217-218, 245, 270, 278, 282; international, 46, 145, 202
Banks and banking: 66, 70, 72, 207, 271; bill to regulate, 262; insolvency, 245, 266; moratoriums on, 280; in Detroit, 281; holiday in Calif., 281-282
Banquets: 53, 62
Baptists: 29
Barnett, Jackson: 215, 274, 277-278
Barry, David S.: 274
Baruch, Bernard M.: 96, 135
Baseball: 93, 130, 146, 177, 215
Battle Creek, Mich.: 167
Beatty, Nev.: 206
Beer: 60, 79, 116, 164, 183, 184, 251, 253, 258, 262; parades held for, 164, 166
Beery, Wallace: 41
"Believe It or Not": 243
Berengaria, S. S.: 127
Berlin, Germany: 123, 124; airport at, 51
Bethlehem, Palestine: 119
Beverly Hills (Calif.) *Citizen:* editor of, 243
Beverly Hills, Calif.: 18, 98, 224, 243, 250

377

Bible: 119
Bicycles and bicycling: 31, 194
Big business: 64, 85
Big Springs, Tex.: 54
Black Crows, The: 184, 203
Blacks: 198; as athletes, 186-187, 193
Block, Paul: 136, 171; son of, 171
Blythe, Samuel G.: article by, 246
Boll weevils: 74
Bombay, India: 261
Bonus Army: 191-192, 193
Boone, Daniel: 108
Booth, Evangeline C.: 200
Bootleggers and bootlegging: 63, 81, 83, 87
Borah, William E.: 6, 21, 66, 74, 84, 90, 121, 128, 135, 190, 225
Boston, Mass.: 212
Boulder Dam: 206, 207
Bow, Clara: 100, 228; biography of, 31
Boxing: 50, 55, 132, 146, 179, 206, 277
Brazil: 117, 220, 226
Breakfast food: 167
Bridge (card game): 118-119, 169, 194
Brisbane, Arthur: 2, 13, 23, 41, 89, 141, 193, 199, 201, 241, 243, 281
British Guiana: 227
Brookhart, Smith W.: 17
Brooklyn, N. Y.: 115
Brown, Joe E.: 243
Brownsville, Tex.: 93, 225, 234
Brush, Matthew C.: 187
Bryan, William Jennings: 81, 163, 242
Buck, Pearl S.: book by, 139
Buckingham Palace: 76
Buenos Aires, Argentina: 224, 237
Buffalo: 29
Bulldogging: 154
Bullfights: 13, 62, 92
Bullfrog, Nev.: 206
Burbank, Luther: 206
Burnham, Frederick R.: 143
Businessmen: integrity of, 167
Butler, Nicholas Murray: 169, 237
Butler, Smedley D.: 158
"Buy American": 246-247, 250-251
"Buy British": 123, 247

Caesar: 120
Cairo, Egypt: 199
California: 1, 11, 12, 20, 65, 72, 93, 98, 160, 167, 180, 181, 194, 204, 205, 207, 208, 211, 212, 219, 223, 228, 236, 243, 248-249, 259, 263, 264, 275; legislature of, 31; newspapers in, 57, 66; primary election in, 159
"California, Here I Come" (song): 33
Calles, Plutarco E.: 57, 82, 92, 219

Campaign contributions: 163
Canada: 52, 99, 145, 175, 180, 192, 261; sales tax in, 143
Canals: 16; in Nicaragua, 58-59; *see also* Panama Canal
Cannon, James, Jr.: 176
Cape Horn: 220
Capone, Alphonse (Scarface Al): 30, 39, 43, 69, 84, 97, 141, 170; trial of, 59, 86, 87
Caraway, Thaddeus H.: 95
Carlsbad Caverns, N. M.: 28
Carr, Harry: relatives of, 58
Cartagena, Colombia: 19
Carter, Amon G.: 23, 205, 212; Shady Oak Farm of, 54
Cartoonists: 43
"Casey at the Bat" (poem): 215
Catalina Island, Calif.: 228
Cattle: 139, 181, 182, 224, 243
Cedar Rapids, Iowa: 17
Censorship: 134
Centralia (Wash.) *Daily Chronicle:* 99
Cermak, Anton J.: 276, 280
Chamberlain, Harry D.: 149
Chambers of commerce: 26, 35, 36, 80, 93, 202, 205, 248, 270, 275
Chang Si Liang: 111-112
Chapin, Roy D.: 194
Chaplin, Charles S.: 4-5, 9, 34, 203, 243
Charity: 145, 254
Charleston, S. C.: 20
Chautauqua lecture circuit: 229
Chicago, Ill.: 14, 32, 59, 68, 87, 131, 132, 155, 163, 166, 176, 177, 178, 181, 183, 224, 276; crime in, 9, 33
Chile: 58, 174, 220, 223, 224
China: 58, 70, 78, 89, 95, 97, 98, 99, 100, 102, 103, 105, 108, 109, 110, 111, 112, 113, 114, 115, 120, 123, 124, 125, 126, 131, 134, 137, 139, 144, 153, 262, 263, 272, 280; flood in, 62, 71; war in, 78, 86; army of, 107; government of, 109; *see also* Manchuria
Chinchow, China: 106, 109, 112, 113, 130
Chop-suey: 115
Christmas: 99, 111, 112, 113, 197, 252, 253, 254
Chu Chin Chow (musical): 130
Churchill, Winston: 66
Civilization: 82
Claremore, Okla.: 35, 50, 51, 53, 80, 106, 109, 128, 132, 134, 181, 182, 224
Clark, J. Reuben, Jr.: 13, 92, 219
Clark, James B. (Champ): 160
Claudel, Paul L. C.: 268
Clergymen: 167, 192, 216-217
Cleveland, Ohio: 164; air races at, 71

Coal mining: 65
Coalition governments: 69
Coffee: cultivation of, 226
Cohen, John S.: 24
Colgate University: football team from, 248
Colleges and universities: women at, 6; graduates of, 41; professors at, 244
Collier's (magazine): 46-47
Colombia: 19, 222, 223
Colonization: by U. S., 10
Columbus, Christopher: 50
Comedians: 46, 241
Commissions and committees: 66, 68, 72, 93, 129, 257, 258
Communists: 25
Concord, N. C.: 236, 237
Conferences: 84, 140, 188; at London, 34, 39, 55-56, 76, 77; on agriculture, 34; international, 35, 104; on narcotics, 40; on home-building, 77; on disarmament, 179; *see also* Lausaunne Conference *and other related topics*
Confidence: 27
Confucius: 113
Congress Dances (film): 246
Conscientious objectors: 48
Coolidge, Calvin: 11, 30, 38, 42, 46, 63, 64, 83, 84, 96, 119, 136, 142, 147, 150, 162, 176, 192, 193, 196, 207, 223, 233, 234, 242; speech by, 222, 223; death of, 259, 260; autobiography of, 272; congressional tribute for, 272-273
Coolidge, Grace G.: 63, 259, 260
Corbett, James J. (Gentleman Jim): death of, 277
Corn: 54, 67, 79
Cornwallis, Charles: 88
Corsica Island: 120
Cosmetics: 3-4
Cost of living: 191
Costa Rica: 17, 220
Cotton: 24, 37, 60, 67, 74, 77, 80, 109, 261
Couch, Harvey C.: 123
Coudraye, Henri de la: 100
Couzens, James: 68
Cowboys: 52, 54, 94, 139, 154, 182, 219
Coxey's Army: 155
Crail, Joe: 50
Credit: 197, 273; buying on, 82, 241
Creel, George: 46
Crime: 7, 31, 33, 35, 42, 71, 87, 204; in Chicago, 9, 33; in Los Angeles, 9, 32-33
Criminals: pardoning of, 204
Cuba: 20
Culbertson, Ely: 118-119
Curley, James M.: 212

Currency and exchange: in Uruguay, 225-226
Curtis, Charles: 47, 52, 96, 135, 200, 229

Dairen, Japan: 107
Daniels, Josephus: 20, 212
Darrow, Clarence S.: 163
Daughters of the American Revolution: convention of, 21, 23
Dawes, Charles G.: 102, 121, 130, 135, 140, 157, 163, 164, 175
Dead Sea: 119
Dearborn, Mich.: 87-88
Death Valley, Calif.: 223, 271
Death Valley Scotty: *see* Scott, Walter
Debts: 31, 44, 46, 166, 190; personal, 39; international, 57; borrowing and, 133; and loans, 273; moratoriums on, 280; *see also* War debts and reparations
Democracy: 234
Democratic National Convention of 1932: 160, 164, 170, 172, 174, 177, 178, 180-181, 183
Democratic party and Democrats: 1, 4, 17, 19, 23, 36, 43, 45, 47, 50, 59, 72, 75, 93, 96, 99, 105, 107, 115, 117, 118, 119, 123, 131, 146, 150, 153-154, 159-160, 172, 173, 174, 176, 177-178, 184, 189, 191, 192, 193, 194, 195, 196, 201, 202, 203, 205, 209, 210, 212, 214, 215, 217, 223, 226, 228, 230, 232, 233, 235, 236, 240, 242, 248, 249, 254, 255, 262, 264, 265; platform of, 175, 177, 194
Dempsey, Gerald: 220
Dempsey, William H. (Jack): 63, 70, 132, 179
Department of Indian Affairs: 10
Department of the Treasury: 263
Depression: *see* Economic depression
Des Moines, Iowa: 250
Desert: 29, 201-202, 249
Detroit, Mich.: 131, 281; unemployment relief in, 68
Devil's Island, French Guiana: 227
Dewar, Thomas R.: 8
Dickinson, Lester J.: 196
Dickson, James B.: 79, 92, 138
Dictators: 20, 120, 174, 253; in Chile, 58
Didrikson, Mildred (Babe): *see* Zaharias, Mildred (Babe) Didrikson
Diplomacy: 20, 76, 96, 124
Diplomats: 62, 78, 96, 97, 98, 164, 198; from Japan, 104; from China, 111
Disarmament: 26, 90, 98, 122, 123, 124, 125, 178-179, 180, 208, 211, 213, 243, 249, 281; *see also* Geneva

World Disarmament Conference
and other related topics
Divorce: 1, 3, 25-26, 70, 274, 277
"Dixie" (song): 33
Dogs: 8
Doheny: Edward L.: 55
"Dole": 135, 278; in England, 52, 69, 78, 85
Donlin, Michael J.: 146
Donovan, William J.: 23
Doolittle, James H. (Jimmy): 11, 71
Douglas, Ariz.: 54, 279
Douglas, Lewis W.: 279
Douglas, Stephen A.: 279
Dreiser, Theodore: 7
Dreyfus, Alfred: 227
Drought: 48, 54, 57, 60, 65, 69, 81, 84; in California, 263-264
Dutch Guiana: 227
"Dutch wife": 116

Earhart, Amelia: 169
Earthquakes: 14, 16, 17, 21, 196; in Nicaragua, 59, 222; in Texas, 66
East (as a region of U.S.): 48, 54, 138, 159
Eclipse: of the sun, 205
Economic depression: 5, 6, 25, 26, 35, 38, 39, 57, 58, 60, 64, 68, 72, 95, 97, 104, 122, 127, 135, 156, 162, 164, 187, 189, 194, 208, 218, 227, 233, 258, 273, 276, 278; in England, 29, 78; in Germany, 142; worldwide, 225, 256
Economists: 198
Economy: condition of, 9, 13, 23, 25, 26, 28, 51, 64, 70, 72, 74, 127, 128, 194, 229, 245; in government, 12, 34, 51, 147, 162, 178, 181, 186, 191-192, 246, 252
Ecuador: 222
Edge, Walter E.: 127
Edison, Thomas Alva: 87-88; funeral of, 89
Education: 41, 72
Edward Albert: 29, 74, 98, 216
Eighteenth Amendment: repeal of, 244; *see also* Prohibition
Einstein, Albert: 1
"El Capitan" (tune): 140
El Paso, Tex.: 13, 24, 54
Election of 1932: 23, 34, 36, 43, 52, 60, 62, 71, 72, 75, 84, 89, 103, 129, 131, 132, 144, 146-147, 153-154, 158, 159, 160, 162, 171-172, 174, 175, 177, 181, 183, 186, 187, 190, 192, 193, 194, 195, 196, 203, 205, 207, 209, 210, 211, 212, 213, 214, 217, 220, 223, 225, 229, 230, 232, 233, 234, 235, 236, 239, 240, 243, 246, 252, 277
Elections: in Los Angeles, 37

Elks Clubs: 218
Empire State Building: 130
Empress of Russia, S. S.: 99
England: 22, 51, 52, 66, 69, 70, 75, 78, 80, 85, 88, 90, 91, 97, 111, 117, 123, 125, 126, 145, 163, 204, 219, 225, 239, 261, 280-281; economic depression in, 29, 56, 78; "dole" in, 52, 69, 78, 85; Labour party in, 69, 70; navy of, 111; king of, 204; and war debts, 250, 258, 271, 274
England, Ark.: 65-66
English language: 41, 91, 209
Equator: 222, 229
Escalante Desert, Calif.: 254
Eskimo Indians: 102
Eskimo pies: 252
Ethiopia: 125
Eton College: 41
Eugenia: 106
Euphrates River: 119
Europa, S. S.: 127
Europe: 33, 55, 56, 109, 120, 121, 122, 142, 178, 179, 219, 234, 238, 240, 275, 280, 281; motion picture produced in, 246

Fairbanks, Douglas: 41
Fall, Albert B.: 55
Far East: 107, 153
Farm machinery: 196-197
Farm products: prices of, 80
Farmers: 59, 135, 150, 182, 192, 241; in U. S., 14, 24; relief for, 14, 53-54, 103, 210-211; in Spain, 18; condition of, 107, 183, 197; strike by, 198, 208
Farms: foreclosure sales on, 259-260
Federal Farm Board: 52, 59, 66
Federal Home Loan Bank Act (1932): 97
Federal Reserve System: 85
"Felix the Cat" (cartoon character): 95
Ferguson, James E. (Pa): 205, 219, 220
Ferguson, Miriam A. (Ma): 203, 205, 219
Financiers: 54, 251
Finland: 186, 187
Firestone, Harvey S.: 117
Fireworks: danger of, 50
Fishing: 162, 186, 199, 204, 206, 228, 230, 236, 253-254, 255
Fitzsimmons, Robert L. (Bob): 179
Fleischacker, Herbert: 173
Fleischmann, Max C.: 2
Floods: in China, 62, 71
Florence, S. C.: 20
Florida: 20, 228, 243, 264
Football: 11, 28, 91, 118, 248; bowl

380

games, 248, 258-259; collegiate coaches of, 248
Ford, Edsel B.: 88
Ford, Henry: 87-88, 117, 131, 135, 159, 270, 281; rubber plantation of, 227
Foreign languages: 20, 30
"Forgotten man": 197, 279
Fort Worth, Tex.: 23, 24, 54, 178, 205, 234
Forts: 69
Fourth of July: 17, 33, 50
France: 36, 46, 48, 51, 56, 66, 67, 75, 83, 85, 87, 89, 98, 127, 156, 192, 211, 219, 238, 239, 261; and war debts, 250-251, 252, 254, 256, 262, 268; government of, 251, 270
Freedom: 77, 251
French Guiana: 227
Friedrich Wilhelm: 174
Friendship: 42
"Frozen assets": 84-85, 148
Fujiyama, Mount: 106

Gamblers and gambling: 6, 100, 135
Gandhi, Mohandas K. (Mahatma): 4-5, 9, 76, 77, 78, 84, 97, 123, 215
Gangsters: 13, 66, 71, 87, 141
Gans, Joseph (Joe): 206
Garbo, Greta: 172, 205, 216, 228
Gardiner, William H.: 95
Garner, John Nance: 17, 93, 94, 99, 100, 107, 128, 131, 135, 148, 151, 159, 160, 178, 182, 236; relief plan of, 172
Gatty, Harold: 47-48, 49, 50, 51, 53, 56, 71
Gaynor, Janet: 228
Gehrig, Henry L. (Lou): 215
Geneva Preliminary Disarmament Conference: 251
Geneva World Disarmament Conference: 124, 125, 126, 140, 144, 150, 211
Geneva, Switzerland: 32; conference on narcotics at, 40
George V: 74, 78
Georgia: 201, 228
Georgia Warm Springs Foundation: 239
Germans: 187
Germany: 1, 46, 52, 56, 57, 60, 121; elections in, 142, 174, 211, 213, 237-238, 261; economic conditions in, 53; government bonds of, 156
Gibbons, Floyd: 99-100, 101, 102, 104, 106-107, 153, 217, 222
Gifford, Walter S.: 67-68, 88
Gillett, Frederick H.: 141-142
Gillis, Robert C.: 11
Glass, Carter: 173, 262, 264, 267-268, 278; banking bill sponsored by, 267

Gold: 57, 78, 80, 82, 83, 111, 123, 206, 208, 238, 271
Goldfield, Nev.: 206
Gold standard: 117
Golf: 24, 66, 71, 73, 104, 169, 176, 194
Gomez, Juan V.: 19-20
Good Earth: 139
Grand Canyon: 28, 207
Grandi, Dino: 97, 98
Grasshoppers: plague of, 59, 60, 84; "ranch" of, 206
Gray, William A.: 156, 157
Grayson, Cary T.: 230
Great Britain: *see* England
Greece: 120
Greek language: 209
Guatemala City, Guatemala: 13
Guinan, Mary L. (Texas): 36-37

Haas, Morris: 134
Haiti: 20
Hale, Florence: 48
Hall, Florence C.: 49, 50
Halsell, Ewing: ranch of, 182
Hamilton, Alexander: 151
Hammond, John Hays: 143
Hanna, Matthew E.: 14, 16, 222
Harbin, China: 107, 108
Harding, Warren G.: memorial for, 42
Hardy, Oliver: 243
Harvard University: 87, 248, 256, 259; graduates of, 249-250
Harvey, Frederick H. (Fred): 29
Hawaii: 159
Hawes, Harry B.: 77
Hawks, Francis M. (Frank): 11, 22, 29, 51, 122, 151
Hays, Will H.: 47, 176, 201, 206
Hearst, William Randolph: 83; Babicora Ranch, 83, 135, 136; San Simeon, 135; cattle of, 243
Henryetta, Okla.: 65
Heroes: 9, 45, 166
Hindenburg, Paul von: 44, 75, 142
History: 243, 259; of U. S., 164
Hitchhikers: 130, 240
Hite, Mabel: 146
Hitler, Adolph: 142
Holding companies: 36
Holland: 275
Hollywood, Calif.: 5, 24, 25, 55, 76, 96, 128, 261, 274, 275, 277
Holy Land: 119
Honduras: 220
Hong Kong, China: 115
Honolulu, Ha.: 63, 159, 163
Honorary degrees: 37, 44-45
Hoover, Herbert C.: 5, 6, 7, 8, 9-10, 16, 18, 21, 23, 26, 30, 34, 36, 42, 43, 44, 45, 46, 47, 50, 52, 55, 56, 60, 63, 67, 68, 72, 77, 78-79, 82,

381

84, 85, 89, 93, 95, 97, 98, 118, 121, 128-129, 135, 152, 153, 154, 156, 159, 162, 172, 177, 179, 183, 188, 191, 192, 194, 196, 197, 199, 201, 205, 206, 210, 211, 212, 214, 220, 229, 230-232, 233, 235, 237, 239-240, 241, 242, 252, 253-254, 255, 265, 273, 275, 276; cabinet of, 55, 191, 194, 229; birthday of, 64; and "frozen assets," 84-85, 148; handwriting of, 151-152; Palo Alto home of, 172, 173; speech by, 218
Hoover, Lou H.: 28, 151
Hopper, William De Wolf; 215
Horsemanship: 149, 193
Horseracing: 7, 55, 145, 150, 151; at Agua Caliente, 7
Horses: 23, 149-150, 199, 227, 241, 281; Phar Lap, 145, 151
Horseshoe pitching: 228
Horse shows: 150
Hot Cha! (musical): 130
House of Commons: 251
Houston, Tex.: 178
Howell, Clark: 24
Hudson, G. Edward (Whataman): 78
Hull, Cordell: 278
Hunger: 6, 40, 45, 65-66, 67, 145, 191, 245, 246, 258, 271
Hunting: 260-261
Hurley, Patrick J.: 21, 77, 88, 89, 115, 128, 177, 210
Hurley, Ruth W. (Mrs. Patrick J.): 267
Hurricane: at Puerto Rico, 228
Husing, Edward B. (Ted): 215

Idaho: 225
Illinois: 173
Illiteracy: in U. S., 72
Immigration: 41, 150
Inca Indians: 223
India: 9, 28, 120, 123, 153, 169; and independence, 97; unrest in, 118, 261
Indiana: 229
Infants: 149; mortality rates of, 28; birth rates of, 122
Ingalls, David S.: 11, 130, 164, 233
Insull, Samuel, II: 68, 256
Interest rates: 39, 60, 245, 273
International dateline: 101, 102
Investigations: 26, 27, 65, 67, 75, 95, 197, 209, 212; senatorial, 86, 152, 153, 155, 156, 157, 160, 188, 207, 277; of stock exchanges, 277; *see also* Walker, James J. (Jimmy): investigation of
Investments: 11, 30
Iowa: 175, 198, 199, 224, 259; farmers in, 198, 208
Iran: 118, 119; sultan of, 118

Ireland: 5, 225
Irish: in New York City, 144
Isaacs, Isaac A.: 49
Isolationism: 159
Italy: 85, 192, 209, 235, 266; government of, 188

Jackson, Andrew: 278
Jacksonville, Fla.: 20
Jacobs, Thornwell: 136
Jamaica ginger: 2
Japan: 63, 69, 78, 86, 87, 89, 95, 97, 98, 99, 100, 101, 102, 103, 104, 105, 107, 109, 112, 114, 123, 124, 125, 127, 130, 137, 144, 150, 153, 187, 195, 196, 216, 217, 261, 262, 263, 265, 272, 275, 280; Sea of, 106; army of, 127
Java: 119
Jealousy: 98
Jefferson, Thomas: 153, 278
Jeffries, James J.: 146
Jerusalem: 119
Jews: in New York City, 144
Jones, Howard H.: 259
Jones, Jesse H.: 123
Jones, Robert T. (Bobby): 24, 71
Juarez, Mexico: 13

Kamchatka: 103
Kansas: 40, 58, 59, 117, 224, 229
Kansas City, Mo.: 176
Kellogg-Briand Pact (1928): 217
Kellogg, Frank B.: 141-142
Kellogg, W. K.: 167
Kelsey, Harold J.: 12
Kennedy, Minnie P. (Ma): 55, 76
Kentucky: 235-236
Kidnappings: 137, 139
Kindred, Herbert (Herb): 24
King Ranch: 94
Kiwanis Clubs: 35
K¹eberg, Richard M.: 99
Kleberg, Robert J.: 94; family of, 94
Kobe, Japan: 106
Korea: 106

Labor: 23, 135, 244-245
Labor Day: 206
La Follette, Robert M., Jr.: 4
La Guardia, Fiorello H.: 157
Lakewood, N. J.: 23
Lapham, Jack H.: and family, 94
"Lame ducks": 245-246, 247, 255, 260, 262, 265, 267, 268
Lardner, Ringgold W. (Ring): 130
Las Vegas, Nev.: 206
Latin language: 209

Laurel, Stanley: 243
Lausanne Conference of 1932: 121, 188
Laval, Pierre: 89-90, 98
Lawes, Lewis E.: 227
Law schools: graduates of, 42
Lawyers: 42
League of Nations: 26, 32, 74, 78, 86, 87, 98, 105, 107, 108, 110, 111, 112, 114, 125, 127, 217, 272, 275, 280; American membership in, 108
Leavenworth Federal Prison: 43, 136
Lee, Hamilton: 53
Lee, Robert E.: 24
Lenin, Vladimir I.: 99
Leon, Pedro: 54
Letter writing: 216
Lewis, J. Hamilton: 173
Lewis, Sinclair: 7
Liberia: 117
Liberty loans: 11, 171, 178, 190
Life (magazine): 46
Lima, Peru: 222, 237
Lincoln, Abraham: 233; tomb of, 42; Gettysburg Address of, 140
Lindbergh, Anne Morrow (Mrs. Charles A.): 28, 137, 138, 166
Lindbergh, Charles A.: 11, 63, 69, 137, 138, 139, 166, 168
Lindbergh, Charles A., Jr. (son): 129; abduction and murder of, 137-138, 139, 147, 149, 166, 167-168
Lindsay, Ronald C.: 268, 270
Lions Clubs: 35
Lippmann, Walter: 240-241
Liquor: 58, 60
Literary Digest (magazine): 239; polls by, 243
Little Rock, Ark.: 80
Lloyd, Frank: 41
Lobbyists: 23, 77, 136, 155, 191
London Five Power Naval Conference: 39, 76, 77, 98
London, England: international conference at, 34, 39, 55-56, 76, 122, 169
Long, Huey P. (Kingfish): 67, 77, 220, 262, 263, 264, 265, 267; speech by, 266
Longworth, Alice Roosevelt (Mrs. Nicholas): 128, 177
Longworth, Nicholas: 17, 49, 50, 93, 94
Lorimer, George H.: 207
Los Angeles, Calif.: 12, 14, 31, 40, 48, 54, 65, 69, 92, 135, 172, 195, 200, 202, 213, 234, 254, 266; crime in, 9, 32-33; mayor of, 33, 34; elections in, 37; murder trial in, 37; newspapers in, 48, 241; "fiesta" at, 76; airports of, 156; bank robbery in, 204
Los Angeles County, Calif.: 222

Louisiana: 236, 277
Lynching: 137

McAdoo, William G.: 160, 175, 242
McDonald, J. Ramsey: 44, 56, 69, 75
McGraw, John J.: 146
Ma Chan-shan: 108
Machinery: 254
McIntyre, Oscar O.: 8, 57
MacKay, Clarence H.: 55
McKee, Joseph V.: 209, 213
McKelvie, Samuel R.: 67
McLean, Evalyn W. (Mrs. Edward B.): 241
McNamee, Graham: 215
McPherson, Aimee S.: 31, 55, 76, 77, 84, 87, 158, 175, 182-183
McSpadden, Herbert T. (Herb): 132
McSpadden, Sallie Rogers: 266
Madrid, Spain: 92
Magazines: 208
Maine: 33, 48, 210
Managua, Nicaragua: 14, 16, 17, 21, 222
Manchuria: 108, 110, 111, 113, 265, 275; war in, 78, 99, 102, 103, 109, 112, 113, 114, 118, 123, 124, 125, 126, 127, 128, 130, 131, 134, 137, 153, 217; *see also* China *and related topics*
Maracaibo, Venezuela: 19
Marriage: 1, 3, 63, 76
Marshall, Thomas R.: 110
Martin, Johnny L. (Pepper): 84
Maryland: 228
Mashed O Ranch: 182
Mason-Dixon Line: 230
Massachusetts: 158; judge from, 272
Massacre (book): 10
Massie, Thomas H.: 163
May Day: 25
Mayors: 33-34, 36, 171
Medford, Ore.: 99
Mellon, Andrew W.: 27, 34, 36, 37, 39, 44, 46, 47, 48, 56, 57, 68, 69, 71, 87, 88, 126, 157, 164, 173, 188, 205, 259, 263
Memphis, Tenn.: baseball team from, 93
Mesopotamia: 120
Metcalfe, Ralph: 194
Mexico: 7, 13, 27, 40-41, 57, 58, 62, 70, 74, 82, 83, 84, 86, 92, 180, 208, 219; revolutions in, 13; government of, 87; army of, 93
Mexico City, Mexico: 13, 91, 92, 93
Mexico, University of: 93
Meyers, John T. (Chief): 146
Miami, Fla.: 20, 234
"Mickey Mouse": 164
Middle West (as a region of the U. S.): 80

383

Millionaires: 66, 228
Mills, Ogden L.: 128, 151
Miniature golf: 252
Mining: 208
Mining camps: 206
Missionaries: 100, 111, 115, 145
Mississippi (state): 187, 236
Missouri (state): 63
Mitchell, Ralph J.: 16
Mix, Thomas E. (Tom): 102
Moncada, Jose M.: 16
Money: hoarding of, 129, 132-133, 144
Mongolians: 112
Monroe Doctrine: 272
Monroe, James: 272
Monte Carlo, Monaco: 155
Montevideo, Uruguay: 225
Moody, Helen Wills: 63
Mooney, Thomas J.: 101-102, 118
Moral leadership: 44
Morality: 186
Morals: 197
Moran, Pauline T. (Polly): 136
Morgan, J. P., Jr.: 130, 153, 156, 173, 271
Morgan, J. P., Sr.: banking firm of, 122
Morocco: sultan of, 175
Morrow, Dwight W.: 13, 20, 44-45, 62, 86, 92, 219; death of, 83, 84; family of, 129, 137-138
Morrow, Elizabeth (Mrs. Dwight W.): 86-87
Mortgages: 22, 31, 51, 77, 127, 168, 259
Moscow, Russia: 152
Moses: 68, 76
Mothers: 163-164
Mother's Day: 28
Motion pictures: 1, 33, 47, 54, 70, 91, 100, 122, 208, 281; in Mexico, 93; in Europe, 246
Mukden, China: 107, 109, 113, 217
Mulhall, Zachary: 102; wild west show of, 102
Murder: trials for, 157
Murray, Mae: 62
Murray, William H. (Alfalfa Bill): 19, 35, 58, 62, 74, 77, 79, 80, 84, 132, 134, 167, 220
Mussolini, Benito: 6, 18, 75, 120, 188, 235, 274

Nagasaki, Japan: 106
Nanking, China: 115
Napoleon Bonaparte: 120
Narcotics: conference on, 40
National debt: *see* United States: budgetary deficit of
National Educational Association: 48, 190-191

Nautilus: 74
Navy Day: 90
Negroes: *see* Blacks
Nelson, Oscar (Battling): 206
Nevada: 3, 6, 115, 160, 207
New England: 205
New Jersey: 88, 129, 203, 228, 251
New Mexico: 29, 91
New Mexico Military Academy: 28
New Orleans, La.: 93
Newspaper Publishers' Association: 22
Newspapers: 191, 209, 267; Republican oriented, 1; in Los Angeles, 48; columnists for, 38, 66; in Calif., 57, 66; correspondents for, 96, 107, 113, 134, 190-191, 217
New Year's Day: 197, 248, 257, 258
New York (state): 90, 227, 279
New York City, N. Y.: 3, 18, 20, 21, 22, 25, 28, 32, 49, 51, 70, 71, 75, 102, 144, 145, 155, 157, 164, 166, 168, 171, 179, 181, 186, 189, 213, 220; relief in, 145; society women of, 152
New York Stock Exchange: 135; *see also* Stock Market *and related topics*
New York Times: 247, 249
Niagara Falls: 188
Nicaragua: 14, 16-17, 23, 25, 111, 220, 261; U. S. intervention in, 18; canal in, 58-59
Nine-Power Treaty (1922): 217
Nitrate mining: 223
Noah: 29, 207
Nobel Peace Prize: 45
"Noble Experiment": 197
"Normalcy": 38, 64, 174
Norman, Montague C.: 205
North (as a region of U. S.): 67
Northampton, Mass.: 192
North Carolina: 228, 240; legislature of, 31
Northwest (as a region of U. S.): 52, 59, 244
Notre Dame, University of: 11, 91, 100; football team of, 248, 259
Nurmi, Paavo: 186

O'Donnell, Charles L.: 91
Ogburn, Charlton, Jr.: 249-250, 256
Oglethorpe University: 136
Ohio (state): 42, 201, 233
Ohio River: 230
Oil: 10, 19, 24, 28, 55, 62, 66, 79, 181
Oklahoma: 21, 47, 49, 50, 51, 58, 62, 65, 80, 84, 101, 107, 112, 154, 164, 183, 241, 250, 266; lawmen in, 40
Oklahoma City, Okla.: 134
Oldfield, Berna E. (Barney): 146
Olympics of 1928: 145

384

Olympics of 1932: 149, 179, 186, 187, 188, 192, 193-194, 195, 197-198, 216
Oolagah, Okla.: 132
Optimism: 22, 54, 60, 66, 173
Orators: 171, 212; in California, 208
Orient: 110
Osage Indians: 10
Ostriches: 225
Otis, Charles A.: 9
Ouimet, Francis de Sales: 73
Outlook (magazine): 208
Overproduction: 8, 110
Owen, Ruth Bryan: 242, 247
Oxford University: 41, 47, 109

Pacific Ocean: 2, 127, 159, 180, 275
Pacifists: 153
Palm Springs, Calif.: 27
Palo Alto, Calif.: 172
Panama: 17-18, 220
Panama Canal: 17-18
Pan-American Day: 18
Para, Brazil: 226
Parachutes: 11-12, 50
Parades: 52, 76, 199
Paris, France: 46, 70, 120, 138, 224, 262
Paris, S. S.: 127
Pasadena, Calif.: 118
Patriotism: 146, 247
Paul-Boncour, Joseph: 251
Pecans: 94
Pedestrians: 143
Pedley, Eric: 92
Peiking, China: 109, 110
Pennsylvania: 56, 88, 128-129, 158
Pennsylvania, U. S. S.: 18
Persia: *see* Iran
Pershing, John J. (Black Jack): 41
Peru: 222, 223
Philippines: 67, 88, 159; and independence, 77, 89, 115-116, 150, 251, 264-265
Phoenix, Ariz.: 54
Pickett, Willie M. (Bill): 154
Pilsudski, Joseph: 99
Pinkerton, William A.: 167
Pipesmoking: by women, 152
Pittsburgh, Pa.: 46
Pittsburgh, University of: football team of, 248, 259
Pius XI: 30
Plato: 120
Plymouth Notch, Vt.: 196
Plymouth Rock.: 205
Poison gas: 193
Poland: revolution in, 99
Political candidates: 46-47
Political conventions: delegates to, 176, 180, 182
Politicians: 17, 35, 55, 59, 78, 80, 158, 159, 170, 173, 196, 198, 201, 203, 207, 211, 215, 216, 230, 234, 241, 248, 252, 261, 270, 281; promises made by, 174, 177, 210, 211, 214, 216, 239-240, 248; as speakers, 66, 156
Politics: 38, 46, 47, 49, 55, 73, 74, 163, 181, 183, 184, 186, 197-198, 199, 200, 202, 205, 212, 214, 230, 232, 242, 259; in Latin America, 19; in England, 75; and patronage, 202, 233, 236, 242, 243; in Texas, 219
Polo: 2, 27, 28, 57, 78, 92, 93, 150, 225, 227
Poppy Day: 32
Port Arthur, Japan: 107, 110
Population: of Virgin Islands, 8
Postal rates: 216
Post Office Department: 34, 216
Post, Wiley H.: 47-48, 49, 50, 51, 53, 56, 71
Potomac River: 211, 255
Prajadhipok: 21
Prayers: 192
Predictions: on New Year's Day, 257-258
Prince of Wales: *see* Edward Albert
Princeton University: 259
Progressives: 3, 4
Prohibition: 1, 2, 4, 7, 13, 16, 33, 34, 52, 64, 79, 80, 81, 89, 115, 142-143, 157, 158, 160, 164, 169, 174, 175, 176, 177, 178, 186, 200, 201, 218, 223, 240, 246, 247, 249; enforcement director of, 64; enforcement of, 97, 236; repeal of, 168, 184, 247, 254, 277; as a "noble experiment," 197
Promoters: 49, 50, 206
Prosperity: 26, 66, 67, 99, 144, 183, 258, 265-266; predictions of, 200
Pyramids: in Egypt, 119; in Mexico, 119
Public opinion: 191
Publicity: 45, 147, 149, 168, 253
Puerto Rico: 5, 6, 7, 8, 9-10, 20
Putnam, Amelia Earhart: *see* Earhart, Amelia
Pyorrhea: 144

Racketeers and racketeering: 9, 32, 153, 186
Radio: 1, 30, 43, 147, 213, 215, 216, 232, 233, 248, 254; announcers on, 156, 175, 179, 215; in Peru, 222
Railroads: 211, 224, 271, 278; regulation of, 79; in Mexico, 83
Raleigh, N. C.: 20
Rambai Barni: 21
Ranchers and ranches: 63, 83, 150, 181, 182, 183; dude, 52; in California, 204; in Texas, 219; in Argentina, 225

385

Rapidan River: presidential retreat on, 34, 52
Reconstruction Finance Corporation: see RFC
Reed, James A.: 63
Reforestation: 90
Reno, Nev.: 3, 25-26, 43, 127
Republican National Convention of 1932: 155-156, 170, 172, 174, 176, 177, 181, 183
Republican party and Republicans: 3, 4, 9, 35, 42-43, 47, 49, 51, 59, 70, 75, 81, 85, 91, 93, 95, 96, 99, 102, 121, 128, 130, 152, 153, 157, 159, 160, 164, 170, 174, 181, 183, 184, 192, 193, 194, 195, 196, 201, 202, 203, 205, 207, 209, 210, 212, 214, 217, 219, 220, 223, 226, 230, 233, 235, 236, 238, 240, 241, 243, 255, 265, 268, 275; platform of, 156, 194; from Pennsylvania, 259

Revolutions: 5, 21, 58, 108, 220; in Mexico, 13; in Poland, 99; in San Salvador, 219; in South America, 222; in Brazil, 226; in Uruguay, 226
RFC: 121-122, 129, 135, 148, 172, 217, 271, 278, 280
Rhyolite, Nev.: 206
Richmond, Va.: 20
Rickard, George L. (Tex): 206
Rickshas: 104, 115
Rio de Janeiro, Brazil: 226, 237
Ripley, Robert L.: 223, 243
Ritchie, Albert C.: 178
Roach, Hal E.: 79, 92; airplane of, 135-136
Robertson, Alice M.: 49
Robins, Raymond: 240
Rockefeller family: 226
Rockefeller Foundation: 226
Rockefeller, John D., Jr. (son): 174-175
Rockefeller, John D., Sr.: 24, 150
Rockne, Knute K.: 10-11, 12, 91, 248
Rodriguez, Abelardo L.: 219
Rogers County, Okla.: 181
Rogers Ranch: at Oolagah, Okla., 132
Rogers, Betty Blake (wife): 27, 28, 63, 91, 122, 129, 137-138, 215, 229, 266
Rogers, James Blake (son): 138
Rogers, Mary Amelia (daughter): 41, 63, 189
Rogers, William Vann (son): 172, 189
Rogers, Willie (congressman): 183
Rogers, Will Penn Adair: 215, 241; as a polo player, 2; in other countries, 13-20, 83-84, 91-93, 99-127, 143, 153, 217, 219-228, 229, 236-237; as banquet speaker, 22; education of, 41; as presidential candidate, 46-47, 180, 183; as air traveler, 53, 79, 98-99, 106-107, 118, 119, 124, 130, 134, 135-136, 138, 176, 178, 217, 220, 222, 223, 224, 225, 226, 227, 228, 229, 233, 234, 237, 254, 266; as Oklahoma "colonel", 58, 62; in vaudeville, 73; as writer, 73, 141, 240-241, 243; family of, 80, 281; speech by, 88; sons of, 91, 95; as actor, 94, 141, 203; motion pictures by, 97, 208; as sea traveler, 100, 101, 102, 103, 110, 119, 127; as wild west performer, 102; at disarmament conferences, 125-126, 150, 179, 251; anti-hoarding campaign of, 132-133; criticism of, 140-141, 241-242; Santa Monica ranch of, 141, 149, 198; Oklahoma home of, 164; as mayor of Beverly Hills, 171; at Republican National Convention, 176, 177; at Democratic National Convention, 180, 181; his banker, 227; and New York Times, 247, 250; and Coolidge, 259
Rolph, James, Jr.: 31, 63, 160, 167
Rome, Italy: 120, 199, 209
Roosevelt family: 236, 267
Roosevelt, Belle W. W. (Mrs. Kermit): 28
Roosevelt, Edith K. (Mrs. Theodore, Jr.): 28
Roosevelt, Franklin D.: 43, 47, 90, 117-118, 158, 159, 180, 181, 182, 186, 194, 196, 201, 203, 210, 211, 212, 214, 218, 219, 220, 227, 230-232, 233, 236, 237, 239-240, 241, 242, 248, 252, 257, 265, 268, 270, 274, 278; and the "forgotten man", 197; cabinet of, 249, 278-279; attempted assassination of, 276
Roosevelt, Theodore: 219
Roosevelt, Theodore, Jr.: 8, 20
Roswell, N. M.: 28, 79
Rotary Clubs: 35
Royalty: 22
Rubber: 117, 227
Russia: 23, 32, 34, 56, 62, 70, 78, 89, 99, 107, 108, 144, 152, 153, 217, 261, 275; five-year plan of, 67; czarists of, 107
Russo-Japanese War (1904-1905): 107
Ruth, George H. (Babe): 215

Sacramento, Calif.: 62, 266
Saint Louis, Mo.: 79, 139
Salaries: of government employees, 173; of senators, 173; of congressmen, 178
Sale, Charles P. (Chic): 17, 73
Salt Lake City, Utah: 127, 254
Salvation Army: 200
San Antonio, Tex.: 93, 99

San Blas Indians: 19
Sanders, Everett: 192, 210
San Diego, Calif.: 149
Sandino, Augusto C.: 21, 25
San Francisco, Calif.: 76, 93, 172
San Juan, P. R.: 20, 228
San Salvador: 13, 219-220
San Simeon, Calif.: 136
Santa Barbara, Calif.: 2, 52, 199, 220
Santa Monica, Calif.: 53
Santiago, Chile: 237
Santa Domingo, Dominican Republic: 20
Sassoon, Victor: 153
Saturday Evening Post (magazine): 83, 147, 211, 246
Savannah, Ga.: 20
Sawtelle, Calif.: 32
Schmeling, Maximilian S. (Max): 179
Schuyler, Karl C.: 260
Schwab, Charles M.: 22, 156
Scientists: 252; in England, 160
Scott, Walter (Death Valley Scotty): 206, 266
Scotti, Antonio: 266
Scouting on Two Continents (book): 143
Seabury, Samuel: 197
Seattle, Wash.: 98
Self-determination: and nationalism, 251
"Self-made men": 89
Shakespeare, William: 170, 254
Shanghai, China: 100, 112, 115, 128, 130, 134, 137, 144
Sharkey, Joseph P. (Jack): 179
Shaw, George Bernard: 7, 56, 62, 66, 89, 261
Siam: *see* Thailand
Siamese twins: 21
Siberia: 103, 107, 150
Sierra Nevada Mountains: 206, 266
Silver: 57, 81, 82, 111, 206, 267
Sing Sing Prison: 227
Singapore: 116
Sioux Indians: 10
Sloan, James F. (Tod): 146
Sloane, Elsie N. (Mrs. John): 28
Slogans: 38
Smith, Alfred E. (Al): 23, 75, 90, 117-118, 127, 130, 158, 159, 181, 208, 211, 218, 278, 281; "Happy Warrior," 183
Snow: in Southern California, 152, 270-271
"Soaking the Rich": 163
Soccer: in Uruguay, 226
Sousa, John Philip: death of, 140
South (as a region of U. S.): 37, 67, 74, 242, 253, 255
South Africa: 143
South America: 220, 222, 226, 234, 236

South Carolina: 228
Southern California: 7, 270, 271
Southern California, University of: football team of, 248, 259
Southern Methodist Conference: 48
Southwest (as a region of U. S.): 94
Soviet Union: *see* Russia
Spain: 18, 19, 22, 29; Republicans in, 18
Speculators: 135; of grain, 63
Speeches: 80, 261; political, 156, 180, 197-198, 199, 200, 201, 209, 211, 213, 229, 230, 232, 250
Speed boat racing: 74-75
Sphinx: 119
"Staggering of hours": 154
Stanford University: 172, 186
"Stars and Stripes Forever": 140
"Star-Spangled Banner, The": 33
States' rights: 167
Statesmanship: 259
Statesmen: 171, 281
"Stein Song": 33
Sterling, Ross S.: 203
Stimson, Henry L.: 23, 39, 57, 118, 130, 150, 196, 240
Stockbrokers: 66, 68, 157
Stock market: 200, 201; crash of 1929, 28, 30, 188, 196; *see also* Wall Street
Stocks and bonds: buying and selling of, 11, 36, 38, 135, 150, 156, 182, 188, 190, 192, 196, 210, 213; buying of on margin, 11
Stone Mountain, Ga.: 24
Stone, Fred A.: 73, 277
Stuntmen: 54
Submarines: 73
Suez, Egypt: 112
Sugar: 150
Suicide: 209
Sultan, Daniel I.: 58-59
Supply and demand: 210
Surf boarding: 63, 159
Swanson, Claude A.: 279
Swindles: 65
Sweden: 216
Swedes: 187
Swimming and diving: 195, 196, 216
Switzerland: lakes of, 219
Syracuse, University of: 37

Tacna-Arica: 223
Taff, Jeff: 266
Takamatsu: 31
Tammany Hall: 9, 170, 181, 201-202, 209
Taxes: 6-7, 44, 60, 71, 73, 75, 81, 103, 126, 129, 136, 155, 166-167, 172, 178, 186, 197, 210-211, 265-266; on gasoline, 5, 73, 116, 143; on incomes, 5, 87, 96, 144, 146,

387

148, 158, 255; on beer, 60; on inheritance, 73, 146; on sales, 73, 96, 116, 143, 146-147, 148-149. 171-172, 173, 187, 245, 255; in England, 75; in Canada, 98; in Chicago, 131; on chewing gum, 148; on malt, 148; on matches, 148, 149; on candy, 149; on crude oil, 149; on property, 158; on stock transfers, 160, 163; refunds, 255, 263; moratoriums on, 280
Taxpayers: 12, 25, 38, 79, 122, 159, 168, 172, 181, 263
Taylor, Estelle: 70
Teapot Dome Affair: 55
"Technocracy": 252, 253, 254, 258, 268
Tennessee: 278
Tennis: 63, 228
Texas: 24, 54, 58, 62, 77, 93, 99, 110, 159, 178, 180, 182, 183, 203, 212, 218-219; earthquake in, 66; election in, 99, 100
Thailand: 21, 22
Thanksgiving holiday: 99, 101, 242, 244
Tilson, John Q.: 50-51, 100, 230
Tigris River: 119
Time: buying on, 30
Tokyo Advertiser: 109
Tokyo, Japan: 134
Tolan, Eddie: 194
Tonopah, Nev.: 206
Tourists: 202, 228; Americans abroad, 57
Track and field: 193-194, 197; marathon competition, 195, 198
Trade: 280
Travelers: 29
Treaties: 217; Nine-Power (1922), 217; Kellogg-Briand (1928), 217
Trinidad: 20, 227
Truth: 77
Tsang Hsih-Yi: 97
Tucson, Ariz.: 27, 54
Tulsa, Okla.: 53, 93
Turkey, Republic of: 60, 125
Tydings, Mildred E.: 268-270
Typhoons: 101

Ulyanov, Vladimir I. (Lenin): *see* Lenin, Vladimir I.
Upshaw, William D.: platform of, 223
Unemployment and the unemployed: 10, 12, 26, 41, 45, 67-68, 93, 103, 147, 214, 224, 243, 257, 258, 271, 282; relief for, 67, 128-129, 173, 174, 184, 276
Union of Soviet Socialist Republics: *see* Russia
United States: 225; intervention by, 14, 16, 18, 20, 222; foreign relations of, 18, 219, 280-281; federal budget of, 27, 34, 36, 144, 151, 158, 172, 265, 279, 281; budgetary deficit of, 36, 63, 69, 87, 103, 144, 147, 151, 168, 264, 279; government bonds, 39, 71; federal employees of, 152, 194; security of, 159; peace commission of, 223; and League of Nations, 275
United States Army: 12, 21, 26, 193; equestrians, 149; horses of, 193
United States Congress and congressmen: 1, 12, 17, 34, 45, 48, 49, 50, 51, 66, 67, 83, 93, 98, 99, 103, 116, 118, 121, 125, 128, 135, 136, 142, 144, 146, 148, 149, 150, 151, 152, 156, 157, 158, 162, 166, 168, 170, 173, 174, 178, 182, 183, 187, 188, 190, 232, 245-246, 247, 250, 251, 255, 256, 258, 261, 262, 263, 267, 268, 274, 276, 279; franking privileges of, 34; appropriations by, 128, 129, 156, 162-163, 187, 268-270, 279; wives of, 151-152; salaries of, 178; adjournment of, 256
United States Constitution: 174, 264
United States House of Representatives: 12, 94, 116, 146, 230, 236, 265, 267, 272, 274; *see also* United States Congress
United States Marines: 14, 16, 17, 20, 59, 78, 158, 222
United States Navy: 12, 21, 26, 30, 93, 95, 159, 275, 279; fleet of, 281
United States presidents: 43, 276; retirement of, 38; terms of office, 232
United States Senate and senators: 3, 5, 8, 46, 66, 68, 86, 87, 95, 116, 125, 127, 128, 146, 155, 162, 166-167, 169-170, 172, 173, 175, 186, 192, 202, 203, 236, 242, 251, 261, 262, 263, 264, 265, 267, 268, 270, 272, 273, 274, 276, 277, 278, 279; investigations by, 152, 153, 155, 156, 157, 160, 188, 207, 276, 277; salaries of, 173; pages in, 259; filibuster in, 263
United States Tenth Cavalry: 198
Uruguay: 225-226
Uvalde, Tex.: 93
Vallee, Herbert P. (Rudy): 134, 208
Valley Forge, Pa.: 36
Vanderbilt, Cornelius, Jr.: 45
Vaudeville: 73
Vegetarians: 89
Venezuela: 19-20, 79; oil from, 149
Venizelos, Eleutherios: 120
Vernon, Tex.: 182
Vesuvius, Mount: 120
Veterans: 32; disabled, 171
Veterans' Bonus: 39, 49, 79, 192
Virgin Islands: 8, 10, 20, 201, 227
Virginia: 88, 147, 228-

388

Vitamin A: 212
Volstead, Andrew J.: 115
Voters: 63, 72, 158, 171, 177, 201, 211, 214, 216, 243, 248
Waggoner, William T.: ranch of, 181
Wagoner (pilot): 224
Walker, James J. (Jimmy): 21-22, 27, 75, 76, 80, 101-102, 118, 170, 171, 201, 205, 209, 213; opponents of, 21-22; investigation of, 98, 102, 196, 197, 198, 199
Wall Street: 6, 22, 36, 45, 52, 64, 79, 84, 92, 103, 139, 163, 187, 202, 210, 230, 263; senatorial investigation, 152, 153, 155, 156, 157, 160, 188; *see also* Stock Market *and related topics*
Wall Street Journal: 140-141
War: 33, 48, 62, 95, 96, 97, 104, 110, 132, 142, 171, 193, 196, 217, 243, 281; between Peru and Colombia, 223; in Tacna-Arica, 223; in Europe, 256; in India, 261; in China, 262, 263, 280; *see also* Manchuria
War debts and reparations: 39, 56, 57, 85, 109-110, 122, 237-238, 240, 241, 242, 243, 248, 250, 252, 253, 258, 262, 265, 271; moratorium on, 44, 46, 50, 60, 82; cancellation of, 96, 120, 121, 123, 157, 178-179, 190, 239, 246; default on, 238-239
Warsaw, Poland: 99
Washington Disarmament Conference (1922-1924): 104
Washington Post: 140
Washington, D. C.: 3, 4, 17, 21, 23, 24, 50, 67, 71, 90, 94, 98, 107, 129, 130, 135, 155, 162, 166, 182, 188, 191, 193, 196, 229, 236, 239, 265, 267
Washington, George: 36, 77, 219, 233
Water: 206, 207, 271
Watson, James E.: 3
WCTU: 81
Weight lifting: 192
West (as a region of U. S.): 29, 43, 52, 79, 172, 181, 206, 211
Wheat: 54, 60, 62, 63, 67, 79, 109, 117, 135, 210, 261
White House: 196, 199, 265

Whitney, Richard: 135, 153, 156
Who's Who in America: 279
Wickersham Commission: report of, 43, 62, 64-65
Wickersham, George W.: 37, 101, 132
Widows: 65
Wigmore, James A.: 2
Wilhelm II: 157
Wilkins, George H.: 73, 74
Willebrandt, Mabel W.: 64
Williams, Alford J. (Al): 11
Williams, Percy: 145
Wilson, Woodrow: 255
Winnie Mae: 53
Wisconsin: 213
Wives: 260; in India, 169; in U. S., 169
Wolfe, Herbert A.: 151
Women: 124, 168, 243; as holders of speed records, 75; smoking pipes, 152; antiprohibitionists, 184; as voters, 235
Women's Christian Temperance Union: *see* WCTU
Wood, Garfield A. (Gar): 74
Woodin, William H.: 279
Woolley, Mary E.: 124, 125, 126, 150
World Almanac: 279
World Court: 217
World Series: of 1931, 84; of 1932, 215, 216, 217
World War I: 66, 81, 109-110, 124, 138, 157, 164, 188, 190; armistice, 238
Worms: ranches, 204, 206
Wrestling: 55
Wyoming: 52

Yale University: 259
Yokohama, Japan: 104
Yorktown, Va.: 88
Young, Owen D.: 47, 72, 87-88, 173

Zaharias, Mildred (Babe) Didrikson: 194, 198, 253
Ziegfeld, Florenz "Flo" Jr.: 130, 189
Ziegfeld Follies: 87, 104